Charles Eugene Knox

David the King

With a Study on the Location of the Psalms in the Order of David's Life

Charles Eugene Knox

David the King

With a Study on the Location of the Psalms in the Order of David's Life

ISBN/EAN: 9783744783613

Printed in Europe, USA, Canada, Australia, Japan

Cover: Foto ©Lupo / pixelio.de

More available books at **www.hansebooks.com**

DAVID THE KING;

WITH A STUDY

ON

THE LOCATION OF THE PSALMS

IN THE

ORDER OF DAVID'S LIFE.

By the Rev. CHARLES E. KNOX,
AUTHOR OF "A YEAR WITH ST. PAUL."

NEW YORK.
ANSON D. F. RANDOLPH & CO.,
770 BROADWAY.

INTRODUCTION.

It is my conviction that the best method of studying or of teaching the Bible is by biographical centres. The doctrinal and abstract books should live and move in the very life of their author. They were so connected in the minds of the original readers. The epistles of St. Paul are new letters to one who has read them as a part of the active magnetic career of the great apostle. The dry chapters of Leviticus and Numbers will be instinct with vitality, when they move in the person of Moses and in the Hebrew and Egyptian society which surrounded him. The greater part of the whole Scriptures really revolves around the few lives of Abraham, Moses, David, Isaiah, St. Paul, St. John, and our Lord. Whoever can infuse into these more abstract doctrines the real spirit which they had to living men when they were written, by making them flow along the thought, feeling and action of the life which produced them, does a valuable service. I have tried to do this in respect to David and his Psalms, in pursuance of a plan which includes the leading biographical centres of the Scriptures and the doctrinal, legal, devotional or prophetical books which surround these centres.

It is remarkable that no modern exploration of the land and of the history of Palestine has been made consecutively along the line of David's life. It is of course impossible to give an exact location to every Psalm, but enough may be suggested to show how full of fresh power the Psalms were when first written. Any probable arrangement will make these wonderful songs of the Sweet Hebrew Singer, start into livelier action and into stronger command of our spiritual feeling. I have freely taken many suggestions from other writers than those whom I have quoted.

This life of the King was principally written in the midst of the busy cares of a pastor's work, and doubtless will appear in many places hasty and defective, to the more critical student. It is designed, however, for the people, and especially for the young—in Bible-classes, colleges, schools, and families, and I hope may help them to a clearer conception of the great Psalmist, Warrior, Priest, and Ruler.

BLOOMFIELD, N. J., *November*, 1875.

CONTENTS.

I.—THE KING'S BIRTH-PLACE	1
II.—BROTHERS AND SISTERS OF DAVID	9
III.—THE TRIBE OF JUDAH	15
IV.—THE FAMILY IN THE TRIBE	23
V.—RELIGION AND EDUCATION IN BETHLEHEM	30
VI.—FROM THE OLD GOVERNMENT TO THE NEW	37
VII.—THE KING	44
VIII.—THE KING'S SON	50
IX.—THE RISE AND THE FALL	56
X.—THE SEER AT BETHLEHEM	62
XI.—THE KING SENDS FOR DAVID	68
XII.—THE PUBLIC INTRODUCTION	73
XIII.—AN EVIL EYE	81
XIV.—DAVID'S FIRST PSALMS	86
XV.—DECEPTION AND FALSEHOOD	95
XVI.—OUTLAWS AND CAVES	101
XVII.—THE HIGH-PRIEST TRANSFERRED TO DAVID	107
XVIII.—RESCUE FROM GOD	113
XIX.—A SOFT ANSWER	120
XX.—NABAL AND ABIGAIL	127
XXI.—COALS OF FIRE	136
XXII.—"GONE OVER TO THE PHILISTINES"	142
XXIII.—TAKEN AWAY IN WRATH	151
XXIV.—THE CROWN AND THE BRACELET	158
XXV.—DAVID, KING OF JUDAH	167
XXVI.—KING ISH-BOSHETH	175
XXVII.—ABNER AND DAVID TRANSFER THE KINGDOM	183

XXVIII.—Psalms in Hebron	. . . .	192
XXIX.—The Coronation	. . . .	200
XXX.—The Capture of Jebus	. . .	206
XXXI.—David's Growing Fame	. . .	216
XXXII.—The New Tabernacle for the Ark		224
XXXIII.—Michal and David	. . .	233
XXXIV.—Psalms for the Tabernacle	. .	241
XXXV.—A Holy House of Cedar	. .	251
XXXVI.—Full Conquest	. . . .	259
XXXVII.—The Conquest Complete	. .	269
XXXVIII.—East of Jordan	. . . .	278
XXXIX.—Order, Renown, and Power	.	288
XL.—The Royal Court and Family	.	297
XLI.—A Generous and Adoring Heart	.	305
XLII.—The Heathen and their Insult	.	314
XLIII.—Psalms of Victory and Praise	. .	321
XLIV.—Crime in the King	. . .	327
XLV.—The Curse of Sins at Home	. .	338
XLVI.—Conspiracy by Absalom	. .	346
XLVII.—The King's Escape	. . .	355
XLVIII.—The Rebellion and the Rebels	.	366
XLIX.—Tumult and Restoration	. . .	376
L.—The Rebellion of Sheba	. .	382
LI.—Songs of Faith in Trouble	. .	389
LII.—Three Years' Famine	. . .	398
LIII.—Songs in Old Age	. . . .	405
LIV.—The Census and the Pestilence	.	411
LV.—Preparations for the Future Temple	. . . . . .	420
LVI.—Adonijah's Conspiracy	. . .	430
LVII.—Jehovah's Choice	. . .	439
LVIII.—Jehovah's House and Jehovah's Builder	. . . . .	446
LIX.—The Last Days	. . . . .	454

DAVID THE KING.

First Sunday.

THE KING'S BIRTH-PLACE.

LESSON.
1 Samuel xvii. 12 ; xvi. 1, 11-13 ; 2 Samuel xxiii. 15, 16 ; Luke ii. 4 ; John vii. 42.

KING DAVID must have gone often to visit the place where he was born. He was such a warm-hearted man that persons and places became greatly endeared to him. And Bethlehem was about half-way between his two royal capitals. Hebron and Bethlehem and Jerusalem were the three most elevated towns along the ragged water ridge between the Salt Sea and the great sea westward. They were in a straight line. Seven and a-half years king in Hebron, thirty-two and a-half king in Jerusalem, we may be sure that he often drank of the well at the gate of Bethlehem, as, alone with Joab, or with a troop of warriors, he threaded the ups and downs of that rocky road.

But when David was born, there was no such city as Jerusalem. There was a city, Jebus, six miles north of Bethlehem. And there those strong mountaineers still defended themselves, of whom the twelve spies brought back word to Moses that the Jebusites dwell in the mountains. Even after Joshua was dead, a Levite traveling past Jebus, although permitted, would not lodge in that "city of a stranger" over night.*

Bethlehem itself—Ephratah, or Ephrath it used to be called, from the time of Jacob downwards—must have been a well-fortified place in Jesse's day, with those resolute and insolent enemies only six miles away. Jesse's grandfather, Boaz, called the elders together at the *gate* of the city, which shows that the city had walls then. The action of the judges at the gate, the conference of the people, the elders called in accordance with law, the dignity and influence of Boaz in connection with judges and people and elders—all these show that it was the same little center of the same little district as it was when, more than a thousand years later, Cyrenius, Governor of Syria, appointed his publicans there to gather the Emperor Augustus's tax. It *was* a *little* city—little among the thousands of Judah†—one of about a hundred conquered towns that fell to the lot of Judah at the first distribution of Joshua, when "the children of Judah" could not drive out the inhabitants of Jebus. The two cities, therefore, looked askance at each other in rude oriental defiance and challenge at every outbreak between the new-comers and the old inhabitants of the land; for, throughout David's life, as in modern times, Bethlehem has been noted for good fighters, fierce and ready. It is altogether likely that Bethlehem was only a strong fortification—a natural height, "fenced" with limestone walls, which here and there had been broken through in turbulent times, and patched with masonry again. Its little cluster of houses, Jesse and Obed and Boaz and Salmon, had helped to defend, by arts of peace and war, from the days of the conquest.

Beautiful as the name now is to us, Bethlehem never

---

* Judges xix. 10-12.   † Micah v. 2.

had the attractions of our American or English village. No spires of churches glistened in the sunlight through all the centuries. And no large windows looked out like eyes from intelligent houses along the streets. The little half or quarter-windows with their lattice, the blank house-walls, one principal narrow street, the low flat roofs—these certainly, were the features of the town even at that early time.

But, if the little city was not beautiful itself, it was beautifully situated for a town of Judæa, and perhaps that was all the beauty which any city of the land possessed. From whatever direction you approached, the appearance of Bethlehem was striking. The whole rocky crest, stretching from Jebus to "the South," was then, no doubt, as now, gnawed by the tooth of torrents which plunged into the Salt Sea. Gaps, chasms, channels, ravines, of the most fantastic and mixed forms, abounded in a wilderness of limestone and chalk-rocks, and opened and yawned towards a sea that seemed to lie in the crater of an extinct volcano.* Towards the west this crest widens into a high rocky table, the western edge of which was cut by less steep ravines, which, at first sloping rapidly, at length swept out to the smiling plain of the Philistines. From Hebron to Jebus the rocky mule and camel path, rough and mountainous, runs straight along nearly the centre of this table, dipping into little valleys, cutting obliquely over ridges, making its way along the side of rocky hills, around rocky points, but crossing always the heads of torrent-beds which take their way to the Salt Sea, till, just at Jebus, the waters run east and west to both seas. Only half-a-mile west of Bethlehem, over the hill from the town, a little valley bears the rains off to the great sea towards the sun-

---

* The strata are sometimes level, and formed into rough terraces, but are violently disarranged. From Jerusalem to Jericho the contortions are twisted into every shape.

set. Taking this hill as the head, a long, narrow rocky height, lying *across* the north and south crest, stretches off,

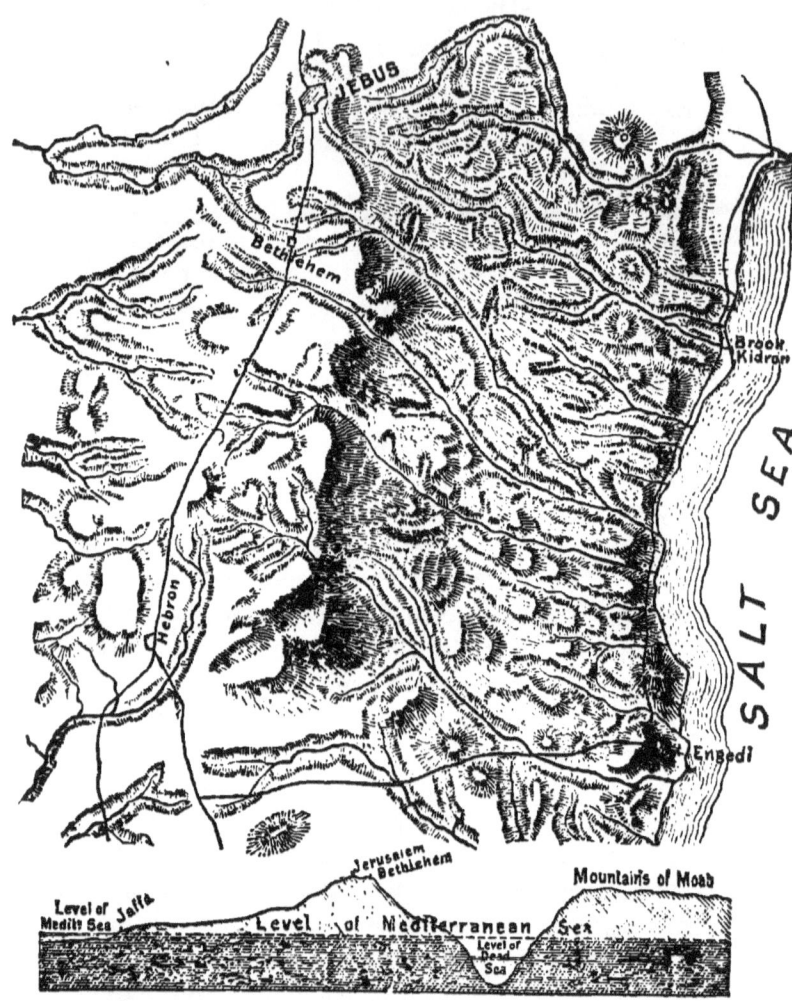

from west to east, towards the Salt Sea. There is a deep valley on the north and a deep valley on the south. Just near the head of this long *east and west* mountain-hill sat the city, a maiden then of only six or seven centuries old,* looking off into the valleys north and east and south, and upon the hills across the valleys, where her eyes fell upon gardens and olive-orchards and fig-orchards, and vineyards, and grain on stony fields, and flocks of sheep and goats. From the gate at the western end of the town—even if the western end were differently located from what it now is—Jesse or Obed could see "the long, solid purple wall of the Moab and Gilead mountains," far across the deep, mysterious gulf of the Salt Sea and Jordan. We may suppose, from the present size and surface of the place, that the principal street rapidly descended from this western gate, and then ran nearly level to the eastern gate, about half-a-mile away. Round, grey hills of barren limestone now fill up the view from every height around, with but scanty vegetation, and fields of grass here and there; but in that early day their sides, at least, and the valleys between, were covered with verdure, diversified with forests, and terraced, as they still are, for gardens, orchards, and vineyards. The numerous palms on the shore of the Salt Sea, washed up in modern times, where the living tree has not been seen for many centuries;† the forests mentioned in the books of Samuel and Kings, in places where there are now no forests; the thickly-strewn ruins of all this region, which show that a far denser population was once supported here; the waste, in forests especially, of centuries of war; the increased dryness and heat when forests are removed, and the consequent rapid decrease of vegetation and soil—all go to show a higher vegetation in ancient days than now. We suppose, then, that,

---

* The first notice of Ephrath, or Bethlehem, is in Jacob's time. See Genesis xxxv. 16–19.

† "The whole shore of the Salt Sea," says Mr. Poole, in the English *Geographical Society's Journal*, "is strewn with palms." See, too, Stanley's "Sinai and Palestine," p. 26.

on the sides of these present naked grey hills, and in these half-fertile valleys, Boaz and Jesse saw woods of oak, the small and the large species; widespread orchards of the dusky-green olive, with its twisted stem and luxuriant foliage; everywhere through the land groves of the stately palm, with its feathery branches set like a fan in the top of the trunk, and supported by clustering dates; the carob-tree, here and there, dense with leaves and hanging pods; abundant vineyards, only less fruitful and less celebrated than those of Eshcol, just north of Hebron; the plane-tree, the poplar, the tamarisk, wherever there were streams; the beautiful oleander, filled with bright flowers and dark-green leaves; the large sycamore on the plains; orchards of broad-leaved figs, with their two or three crops a year; the bright-green thorn-bushes; the wild olive and hawthorn shrubs; the pomegranate bush, a tender green in leaf, scarlet in blossom, red in fruit; gardens of balsam and of roses next the villages; rows of quince, apple, almond, walnut, apricot, and peach; white daisies and crimson anemones, tulips and poppies in the Spring, with a great variety of beautiful and brilliant flowers; and that, when they went down a thousand feet into the hot Jordan chasm, all about them were other and different classes of tropical plants and flowers, and beneath their feet, even at the Salt Sea, an abundant saline vegetation. Far and wide, as Boaz or Jesse climbed a commanding height, his eye could penetrate through the transparent air to objects great and small, made distinct by the exceeding brightness of the light. From heights about Hebron he could see the land of Moab and "the South;" from hills three or four miles west from Bethlehem the ocean of barley and golden wheat and green millet along the Philistine plain, with villages and walled towns, with herds of cattle and sheep and goats on their way, in various directions, to pasture; with reapers, and wells, and threshing-floors, and dunes along the sea-shore. A sharp-nosed fox or two, darting out of cover, remind him of Samson's firebrands in yonder grain-fields; or dripping honey and a buzzing swarm suggest Samson's riddle. An eagle wheeling in the air, a vulture or a hawk, meets his eye as he turns homewards, or an owl under the deep shadow in a rock-crevice, or a flock of partridges on the quick run across the path, or pigeons and turtle-doves alighting at their cotes. Next morning, taking his way down the eastern ravines, he hears, long before sunrise, the Jordan nightingale, the finest songster of the land, pouring upwards its sweet notes from the thick jungles of that tumbling stream, and, later in the day, the glossy starling, from low down the Kedron gorge, "the roll of whose music makes the rocks resound."

We must notice one feature more of the country around the infant at Ephratah, and then we are prepared to begin with that little life which, even in this distant land, has become to us so precious and so great. We must look into the caverns of that rocky district. No description of the Judæa of the Judges and the Kings would be complete without them. All limestone districts abound in caverns. They abound, therefore, throughout Judæa; but from Jebus along the tooth-gnawed crest to the lower end of the Salt Sea, and down the second steep to the very shores of the sea, they are innumerable. "Every hill and ravine is pierced with them." There are rents and cavities, and holes and caves, some large, some small, some hollowed out and enlarged by man's device, and some mere grottoes. Here were some of the "dens," and "caves," and "pits," and "holes," and "rocks," in which the Hebrews hid, when the Midianites and the Philistines pressed them too hard. Sometimes these caverns were inhabited by shepherds and herdsmen to be near their flocks, as a cool retreat from the scorching heat of summer, and by robbers, who enlarged them into connected chambers, secret and unseen. Some were made use of as cisterns and sepulchres. And some were the lairs of wild beasts,—the lion, the panther, the bear, the hyena and the wolf, the jackal and the fox—not all at once, perhaps, but as they crept in through the jungles of Jordan or the southern wilderness.

Here, in this wild region, then, we suppose far more beautiful than its barren rocks now—here, in this little city, the King was born. Who can tell the year? Who can point out Jesse's house? Was the house on the principal street? Yes. Boaz was a mighty man in station, and his family has not lost place on the way towards royalty. It is enough to know that in the inner court of a house on this street, and in the women's apartments, carried out now and then on the shoulder or the hip, according to the oriental custom, the child's first three or four or five years were passed, until at length, his hand in his father's, little David is able to walk even out of the city gate.

Second Sunday.

BROTHERS AND SISTERS OF DAVID.

LESSON.

1 Chronicles ii. 13–17; 1 Samuel xvi. 1, 6–12; xvii. 12–14, 28, 42; xx. 29; 2 Samuel ii. 18; iii. 39; viii. 16; xvi. 9; 1 Chronicles xxvii. 18.

DAVID himself was the youngest of the eight sons—probably of all the children—in the house of Bethlehem. As the child begins now to walk and speak, he is the attraction of the house. His eyes were sharp and bright; his complexion ruddy, or his hair auburn, for we cannot tell to which the description, "he was ruddy," applies, and it may have included both complexion and hair;* the expression of his face attractive, as the twice-repeated phrase, "fair of eyes," indicates;† and his form handsome and graceful.‡ The gifts of speech in the man show what the prattling child was; just as the loveliness and affectionateness of his childhood are reflected to us in the natural facility with which he inspired love afterwards.

---

* The word rendered "ruddy" means red, or reddish. Both the Greek word of the Septuagint and the Hebrew word seem to signify all shades of red, and they are sometimes applied to *hair*. "The reddish color of the hair was regarded as a mark of beauty in southern lands, where the hair is generally black." *Keil and Delitzsch.*

† "Fair of eyes" is the Hebrew in 1 Samuel xvi. 12 (see margin), and xvii. 42.

‡ "A comely person." 1 Samuel xvi. 18. "A man of figure" is the Hebrew.

We see him as the youngest, "the Beloved" or "the Darling" of the house, as the name which his parents gave him means.* And names in that family evidently had been given for personal qualities; for the great-great-grandmother was Naomi, *pleasant*, and the great-grandmother, Ruth, *a friend*, and the great-grandfather was Boaz, *fleetness*, and swiftness of foot was still characteristic of the family, as we shall see; and the grandfather was Obed, *servant (of God)*, and the name of Jesse probably means *the firm*, or *the upright*. The youngest son is likely to be the favorite of parents, if the family is large, because he is the little one of the whole flock, and it is not often that he grows to man's estate while his parents are living. And David, even after he was grown, was small compared with his oldest brother, Eliab, as even Samuel thought.

But let us look in upon the rest of the children.

First, there were David's two sisters. The fact that their children were David's familiar companions and attendants after he became king seems conclusive that they were either the oldest of the family or among the oldest. The mother of such men as Abishai and Joab and Asahel could have been no ordinary woman. She was Zer-u-i-ah, the first-mentioned of the two. Let us suppose her next to Eliab in the family. Perhaps it was because her father Jesse's Hebrew name was Ishai that she named her first son—perhaps the first grandson in the family—Ab-ishai, *father of firmness or of uprightness*, if we rightly interpret Jesse's name (as the name of a son of Ner was Ab-ner), the prattling playmate of little David, as afterwards in camp and flight and battle, his faithful friend and defender

---

* David must have been a new name, for it does not appear in the Bible before. The custom, long before this time, was in use of naming children from some special circumstances of their birth or appearance. See reasons for names, in Gen. xvii. 5, 15, 17, 19; xxv. 25, 30; xxvii. 36; xxix. 32–35, etc.

all his life. We may be sure that the fierce, impulsive, stout-willed Joab, who was afterwards the general of David's army, and blood-avenger of Asahel, and who dared disobey the king's express orders, even up to thrusting his darts through Absalom when he was caught in the oak— we may be sure that Joab, who was a great trouble as well as a great comfort, was sometimes an uncomfortable playmate in the court of Jesse's house. Many a wrestle and tumble and wordy contest, if not boyish battle, the young king and the young general must have had in house and street and hill-side. How their shouts in the court sometimes brought out Jesse or Zeruiah from some near apartment, or down from the house-top, with a sharp word following! As for Asahel—*God's creature* is the meaning of his name, perhaps for his lightness and fairness—he was as light of foot as a roe in the field. Valleys and hills and mountains were alike to him, as he outsped his brothers or his uncle down the ravine, and up the heights for a look at Jebus, or cooled his panting body in the warm waters of the Jordan, or on the dull shores of the Salt Sea. These three grandsons and their uncle David, are four far more important members of Jesse's house than any four sons of the family. And three sons so varied and so marked in character, show clearly that the mother, whose name is, no doubt, for that very reason connected with her sons, was a woman of varied accomplishments of mind and person. Picture to yourself a dark-haired, sharp-eyed, quick-spoken, nimble-footed Jewess, whose reasons and manner carry weight with Jesse and the older brothers, and whose strong womanly nature corrects and nurtures her three sons, and her little brother David; see her in her own house, near at hand in the village, and almost as often moving in and out through the inner apartments of her father's house, preparing the meals, spinning with the distaff, making ready the robes of the numerous family, despatching a servant, or herself bringing on her shoulder a skin or an earthen jar of water from the good well of the city, and with lively decision and energy, making the whole family feel her force; and you see some such person as David had in mind when he thought of Asahel's death, and Joab's bloody revenge, and their mother together, and said: "I am this day weak, though anointed king; and these men, the sons of Zeruiah, be too hard for me."

David's other sister, Abigail, strangely enough, had taken as a husband an Ishmaelite.* And her son, Amasa, grew up to be an Ishmaelite too. For he was ready, when his uncle David was old, to be the rebel Absalom's captain, when he ought to have given better advice to that young man. The story looks as if Amasa and his cousin Joab did not get on well together. There might have been envy or jealousy of each other's power; for, when Joab slew Absalom, King David appointed Amasa captain of the army in Joab's place—an affront which Joab could not brook, and for which he miserably and treacherously slew his cousin. With features and habits which revealed the blood of the Bedouin, David must have looked in wonder

---

* 1 Chronicles ii. 17 says Jether, an Ishmaelite; but 2 Samuel xvii. 25 says *Israelite*. "Israelite" seems to be an error in copying the manuscript, as there seems to be no reason for saying that Jether was an Israelite when all were Israelites; but the fact of her marrying an Ishmaelite needed to be noted. In 2 Samuel xvii. 25, Abigail is called the daughter of *Nahash*. There are four ways of explaining the name Nahash. 1. The common tradition of the Rabbis that Nahash and Jesse are the same person. 2. That Nahash may be the name of the wife of Jesse. There is nothing to prevent the use of the name by either sex. 3. That Jesse may have had two wives, one of whom was the mother of Abigail, or of Zeruiah and Abigail. 4. That Jesse married the widow of a Nahash of Ammon, and that she brought with her the two sisters, the oldest members of the family.

and in sorrow at conflicts of interest and of feeling between Amasa and his three cousins, between whom it is natural to suppose the warm-hearted and boyish uncle sometimes to have been peace-maker.

Eliab and Abinadab and Shammah, the three oldest brothers, were so much older, and so much more imposing in appearance than David, that David, as he became a lad, was kept under by them. This is fairly implied in the allusion to the stature and countenance of Eliab, in the fact that David was not called in at all when Samuel asked for the sons of Jesse, and in the fact that Eliab—and Abinadab and Shammah say nothing against it—despised and upbraided David the stripling in the army. Josephus says that Eliab was a "a tall and handsome man," and that the others "were in no way inferior to the eldest in their countenances," which shows what was the tradition in Josephus's time. It was after David was anointed by Samuel in the presence of Jesse's family, that these three brothers went to the army of Saul. It could not have been *long* afterwards. There may have mingled in their minds a remembrance that they were set aside, that David was anointed by the prophet—the envy of his brothers against Joseph re-enacted — when the indignant Eliab taunted the stripling for coming to the army at all, much less to fight the giant of Gath. He was not satisfied to say, "Why camest thou down hither, and with whom hast thou left those few sheep in the wilderness?" but he must impeach his motives: "I know thy pride and the naughtiness of thine heart, for thou hast come down that thou mayest see the battle"—a little speech which lets in a beam of light upon his character. The suspicion of haughtiness and of a bad heart arose out of the existence of the same bad things in himself. Brothers, too, who would stand by and not defend a younger brother who was moved by a lively and innocent curiosity to see a battie, and by a patriotic courage to fight, when themselves and all the army were sore afraid, must have shared the same invidious spirit. And in the camp in the valley of Elah, we have a mirror, no doubt, of like relations in the home at Bethlehem, whenever the smooth waters of that tranquil life were ruffled by any excitement of feeling. Yet Shammah must have been a man of some power and courage, otherwise he would not have borne a son Jonathan, who afterwards slew a giant of Gath when he defied the armies of Israel.* It may have been in admiration of this deed, or in admiration of some generous qualities, that David named his first son born in Jerusalem Shammah,† which seems to be the same name. Nor unless Shammah was a man of some sagacity would he have had a son Jonadab, with a wise and subtle mind, which, however, he might have turned to a better use than he did.‡ Eliab seems, too, to have become the prince of his tribe while David was king.

We know nothing of the other sons of Jesse but their names, and of one of them we do not know even the name. We are distinctly told that there were eight sons, although the genealogical table enumerates only seven. We will try in vain to obtain special features for Nathanael and Raddai and Ozam and the nameless one; but it is something to think of them as the playmates of David himself in his childhood, leading the little child as he first walked, trying his skill as he first syllabled his words, singing him a strain or filling the notes of a rustic pipe, as they watched the quickness of his musical ear and heard the quick imitation of his voice; carrying him off to the houses of their sisters and nephews, or bringing him in his misfortunes and mischief to his mother or to the resolute Zeruiah, who chided or comforted him as he needed.

---

* 2 Samuel xxi. 21, 22.
† Shimea and Shimeah are other forms of the two names in 2 Samuel xiii. 3 and 1 Chronicles iii. 5.
‡ 2 Samuel xiii. 3, 32, 33.

Third Sunday.

THE TRIBE OF JUDAH.

LESSON.

Joshua xv., xviii. 11, 15-19 ; Psalm lxxviii. 60-69 ; I. Samuel xxii. 3, 4.

WE need now to know something of the tribe of which Jesse's family was a member. We must know something more carefully of the territory of Judah : we must know something of its social and political position in the nation, in order to be prepared for David's kingly career. For the tribe from the beginning was the largest and most powerful of all ; and foretokened the strong kingdom which would one day, with a single other tribe, perpetuate the succession of David, when the other ten were shattered by conspiracies and usurpations.

The northern line of the territory of Judah, which separated the tribe from the territory of Benjamin and of Dan, can be pretty distinctly traced from the descriptions of Joshua. Most of the ancient towns noted in that survey are now sufficiently identified to show the probable line. From the mouth of the Jordan* it ran through or touched the valley of Achor, where Achan was stoned, and which was not far from Jericho ; then up the steep, twisted hills, no doubt by the road of all centuries between Jericho and Jerusalem, to En-Shemesh, "the traveler's first halting-place" from Jebus down ; then over the Mount of Olives down to En-rogel, at the junction of the two valleys, in the fork of which Jebus sits mounted on her throne ; then

---

* Compare Joshua xv. 5-11 with xviii. 15-19. The line is twice described—once from east to west, as the northern line of Judah, and once from west to east, as the southern line of Benjamin, part of which became afterwards the southern line of Dan.

winding with the ravine of Hinnom northward around and beneath the precipices of the city; then climbing the northwest hills two and a half miles to the waters of Nephtoah; then over the ridge between two ravines and up to Kirjath-jearim; then following

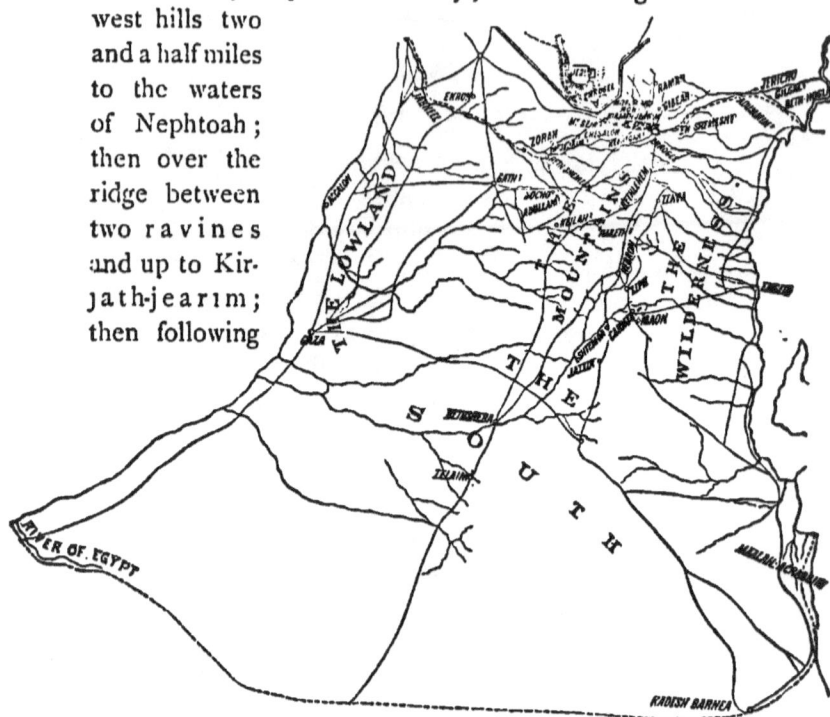

the side-ridge or the valley of a twig-ravine, a bough-ravine, a branch-ravine, where it takes Beth-Shemesh and Timnah in course, and a trunk-ravine leading to the sea, where are Ekron, and Jabneel on the east and west of the main torrent at its "goings out."

The southern line of the tribe ran from the southern end of "the Salt Sea," by a grand sweep southward, to Kadesh-barnea, and then westward or north-westward through desert and wilderness to "the great sea," at "the river of Egypt," far down below Gaza.*

---

* It is possible that "the river of Egypt" was the east branch of the Nile.

Within this little territory—about forty-five by fifty miles in average length and breadth—about the size of the State of Rhode Island—Joshua gave to the tribe one hundred and fifteen "cities with the villages," and separated them into four divisions. Think of one hundred and fifteen cities with their villages in the State of Rhode Island or of Delaware,* and you obtain some conception of the population in that early time. Three centuries of peace and war in the times of the Judges, in which neither Canaanite nor Israelite had remained sovereign master, and during which fortified towns must have been built up by one as fast as they were pulled down by the other, had not essentially changed the number and position of the towns down to David's time. The abundant ruins on every hillside to-day, show that at once there was a dense population there. The four divisions show what was the face of the country.

"The south"—for they had "the south" and "the north" as well as we—was the undulating pasture country which lay between the central hills and the wastes of gravel, sand and rock which lapsed away into the southern wilderness. Beer-sheba, some forty-five miles south of Bethlehem, with its wells and stone water-troughs and flocks of camels, sheep and goats, surrounded by gentle hills, clothed with grass in the rainy season, without a precipice or a tree in sight, where Samuel the Seer's sons had lately been judges when David was born—and Ziklag, where David afterwards lived more than a year, are the best-known to us of the thirty-eight "cities and their villages" in that region. And these two cities, with fifteen others from "the south," were classed together by the surveyors† of

---

* Colton's Atlas gives us in all, sixty towns in Rhode Island and sixty-five in Delaware.

† Joshua xviii. 4-6, 9.

Joshua as one of the seven shares into which they divided the land, after Judah and Joseph had received their portion. This one share taken from Judah's territory was drawn as the second lot by the tribe of Simeon. The area of Judah then became about one-fourth less than at first, something in size like Rhode Island with its important bay and islands taken away.

"The lowland," * which had forty-two towns with their villages, was "the garden and granary of the tribe," but a garden and a granary of which they never obtained a full possession. For this was the Philistine plain, with its fringe of sand along the sea-shore, midway in which was Askalon perched on the rocks, and its fifty-mile plain, always thick with fields of grain in the season—as it now is—and stretching from the sea right up to the hills and mountains. If they are Hebrew, the very names of the towns seem to show the nature of the country; for Zorea is wasps, En-gannim is springs of gardens, Tappuah is apple - (region), Enam is two-fountains, Socoh is boughs, Gederah and Gederathaim are sheep-folds, Terran, a place of flocks, and Dilcon, cucumbers. Three only of the five chief cities which we meet with in the history of the kingdom are mentioned here—Gaza, Ashdod, and Ekron. These, with Askalon and Gath, from six to twelve or fourteen miles apart along the plain, each on a swell or hill of land, were surrounded with suburbs, and stood among stocks of grain, groves of olives,† figs, and cypresses, and vineyards and orchards and palm-trees and sycamores,‡ with murmuring bees and cooing doves, and were then even more than they are now "remarkable for the beauty and profusion of the gardens which surround them, the scarlet blossoms of the pomegranates, the enormous

---

* Joshua xv. 33. "Valley." In Hebrew "low country."
† See Judges xv. 5. ‡ 1 Chronicles xxvii. 28, 29.

oranges which gild the green foliage of their famous groves." Then even more than now, so dense was the unbroken stretch of waving crops that the inland cities on their gentle heights, with their green gardens and orchards around them, seemed from the hills above like islands in the undulating sea. These rich harvests and this rich soil are the secret of the stout resistance of the Philistines to the Judeans. From these rich plains, the Philistines ran up the ravines to the mountains above in their raids upon the Hebrews. Gaza, too, was a commercial city, also one of the great towns on the road from Damascus to the Nile. "Grains and fruits of every kind and of the finest quality supply the bazaars. Those traveling towards Egypt naturally lay in here a stock of provisions and necessaries for the desert; while those coming from Egypt arrive at Gaza exhausted, and must, of course, supply themselves again." Here, too, from Abraham downwards, came the princes of men and kings of the earth—as centuries later, in the days of Jeremiah, a Pharaoh came against "Gaza the strong," and, centuries later still, the mad Cambyses, the Persian, is said to have left his treasures here on his way to Egypt.

"The mountains," with their thirty-eight cities, were a region rough and ragged—the largest of the four entirely natural divisions of Joshua. Below Hebron, the range mounts at once into high air, and it keeps its long, undulating, notched level to the very bounds of Jebus and of Benjamin. Swelling hills and hollows, then covered with forests, with abundant turf and sward and plants, made its lofty heights attractive, while its fastnesses were immovable walls against an enemy. Torrents pour down the thousand ravines to enrich the dead and the living seas, and as the thunder-storm bursts along the mountain plateau; and pebbles and limestone chips lie in these dry beds, when the summer sun beats down their torrid sides. The two important cities in the mountains are evidently Hebron and Bethlehem, as their long antiquity indicates. It is curious that the name of Bethlehem or Ephratah is

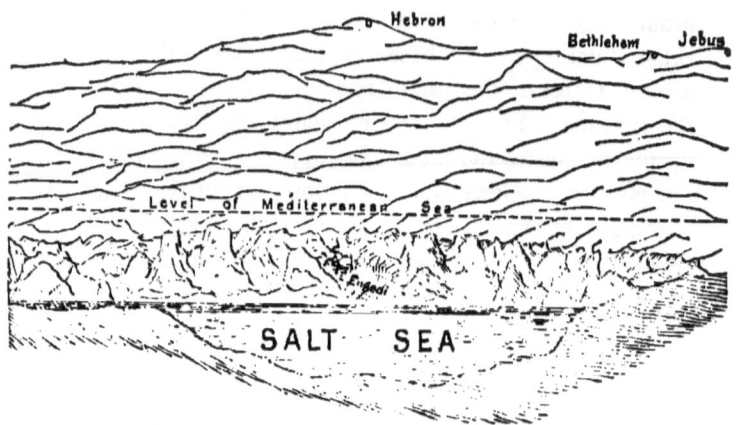

not mentioned at all among these cities. But in the Greek Septuagint translation it is metinoned, and with ten other towns inserted after the fifty-ninth verse of our English catalogue. These eleven names may have escaped the attention of some Hebrew copyist, and if they are inserted the whole number is forty-nine. At any rate, we know that Bethlehem was there long before. Hardly a hill in all this region but that has some fragments of stone buildings. These loose-lying stones on every hill-top we must restore into a town or city or village, and people with the stir of Jewish forms and features, if we would see the hill-country of Judah in David's boyhood.

"The wilderness" must have occupied the only space left in the tribe—the sunken strip along the Salt Sea, and the headlong slope of cliffs between the sea and "the mountains." These tumultuous bare limestone rocks burn beneath an unclouded sun for seven or eight months in each year. They open around the southern end of the sea into a little plain. Here and there fountains turn the universal stillness and solitude into luxuriant and rustling vegetation. Frogs croak amid the cranes and reeds of two or three brackish marshes along the northern half of this sea-coast—one of the most copious marsh-fountains being not far from the mouth of the Kidron ravine. Here, in this region, were six cities,* most or all of them in a climate and among plants quite like those of Sinai and "the great and terrible wilderness." The only one of them which we shall meet is Engedi, half-way down the length of this sea-ledge, where the wild shore-road from Edom and Moab and the *great* wilderness heads westward up a zigzag path through a steep, terrific pass of smooth limestone rock.† Far above the city, among the rocks, the gazelle, the jackal, the wild-goat, and multitudes of pigeons‡ may be seen, themselves far below the hills of Judah. High up the zigzag, so steep that, as you look from Engedi, it seems impossible to climb, you reach a point that is on a level with the great sea at Askalon; and down from the shelf on which the town is, you go four hundred feet before you reach the green waters of the Dead Sea. Desert shrubs are among the rocks above; but a beautiful sweet fountain at Engedi rippling down the rocks quickens a little plain nearly half a mile wide, at the foot, into tropical luxuriance. The sides of the de-

---

* "Beth-arabah," one of the six cities (xv. 61), was near the northern end of the Sea (see verses 5, 6), and "the City of Salt" will naturally be located in the salt region around the south end of the Sea.

† "My companion had crossed the heights of Lebanon and the mountains of Persia; and I had formerly traversed the whole of the Swiss Alps; yet neither of us had ever met a pass so difficult and dangerous"—*Robinson* i. 503.

‡ Robinson i. 500. There can be no question that the scene was substantially the same in David's time.

scent were no doubt in David's time terraced for tillage and gardens—a fresh oasis, fountain-formed, in the wilderness of the salt sea. There is nothing pestiferous in the climate, except that its Egyptian heat in the summer breeds from the marshes intermittent fevers. The shores and this cliff at Engedi have been inhabited from time immemorial. Far across from these rocks to the southeast—see the birds flying over the lake as you look across—over yonder opposite shore, the eye goes up a straight gorge which opens into the long wall of Moab. That is Kir-Moab, on a high, perpendicular rock, near the summit of the mountains; from which region comes that sweet and faithful woman Ruth, and to which region David will one day bear his parents beyond the reach of Saul, while he himself is a fugitive and an outlaw all through this wilderness.

And this takes us to the social and political position of the family and the tribe.

Fourth Sunday.

THE FAMILY AND THE TRIBE.

LESSON.

Ruth i. 1-6; ii. 1; iv. 17-22; Numbers xxii. 1-6 : xxi. 13; Deuteronomy xxiii. 3-6; 1 Samuel xi. 1-11; Numbers xxvi. 22, 37; Psalm lx. 8; cviii. 9; Matthew i. 5; Numbers i. 7; ii. 3; x. 14; 1 Chronicles ii. 10-12, 51.

OFTEN had David already heard the story of Ruth, the mother of his grandfather; of the famine of Moab, of Boaz and his barley-harvest. But it is not till the mind of the child quickens into the more thoughtful youth that this family history expands into a tribal and national significance. Many times as those bright eyes watch the changing blue and purple of yonder mountain-range, or as his mind dilates at the glory of the sunrise over that eastward-reaching table-land, does he revolve the particulars which his eager questions have drawn forth at home. Many times does he point out to himself the road to Engedi or the road to Hebron—whichever it was—as the path on which Elimelech and Naomi and their sons went southward around the Dead Sea. Many times did Abishai and Joab and himself discuss the battles of Moses straight across in Bashan. Often did they glory over the fear of Moab, who were afraid the multitudes of Moses "would eat up the land, as an ox eateth up the grass of the field," and over the left-handed dagger-stroke of Ehud, which sent the tyrant Ammonite and Moabite home again kingless. Little by little it all became clear that Ammonites and Moabites, the children of Lot and of Lot's daughters, were not to be received into the nation of Israel, and that God had separated the children of Lot and the children of Abraham by this deep chasm and cauldron, the vapors and clouds from which now sometimes concealed one from the other, as at first the smoke of Sodom and Gomorrah separated Abraham at Mamre from Lot at Zoar. Strange enough, the northern boundary now of Moab—the river Arnon—was straight across from the oak where Abraham sat and the place where he received the three angels at his tent-door. Just below that headlong river, between it and Kir-Moab, which from Engedi you may see at the head of the steep gorge, are the sepulchres of the Bethlehemites, Chilion and Mahlon. There, in a rich and undulating pasture-land, so high that the people look down on us at Bethlehem, and so fertile in meadows—like the Philistine lowlands—that the famine here was not felt there, Naomi, the widow, lived with her two sons for ten years; there, as she looked down with longing eyes on the Hebron and Bethlehem hills, she heard that the Lord had made us again a *house of bread;* there the faithful Hebrewess taught her Moabite daughters the story of the growing wickedness of the children of Lot, and the promise of God's blessing on Abraham's faithful descendants; and there the widow and her widow-daughters came to yonder mountain-town, and were ready to leave Kir-Moab for the ravine-path down and homeward, when Orpah kissed Naomi, and Ruth forsook her gods for the God of Jacob. Such, we suppose, was the general form of the events to young David, whose heart swelled with indignation or affection, as he thought of the crimes of Moab or the sweet virtues of his lovely ancestor.

Which sentiment was then prevailing—anger or affection—toward those kindred highlanders across the chasm? The question is easily answered. We have supposed that when David was a boy—at sometime from his infancy to his youth—Saul was anointed king. We suppose it true also that the names Ammon and Moab are used interchangeably for one people—the two being closely allied by blood and interest. Now, it was just after the anointing that King Nahash of Ammon resolved to put out the right eyes of the people of Jabesh-Gilead as an insult to the whole nation of Israel; and it was in a lofty indignation at the indignity put on his relatives—for the Benjamites, from whom Saul came, and the Jabesh-Gileadites, we must remember, had married to preserve the tribe of Benjamin*—that the young king had sent his slaughtered oxen from Gibeah throughout the land, and mustered thirty thousand men from Judah, and nine times as many from the rest of the tribes, and slew the Ammonites in mighty havoc as the sun rose next morning. From this time onward, in the mind of David as truly as in the fiercer Joab's mind, we may assume a settled hostility to the land of Ruth's ancestors. From that day of his boyhood, when King Saul's slaughtered oxen, brought by panting messengers to the city gate, summoned Eliab and Aminadab to the bloody defence on the other side Jordan, we may see that righteous contempt in which David afterwards wrote, "Moab is my wash-pot."

This battle, at which Judah furnished one-tenth of all the army of Saul, from which the oldest sons of Jesse must have brought back the admiring account of the new king's exploits, takes us now to the relation of Judah to the other tribes.

The twelve tribes were equal States united in a government which was at first representative or republican in character, with God for a national King, and a high-priest or a judge extraordinary as his prime-minister. From

---

* Judges xxi. 6-10, and 14, 15.

the oracles of the sanctuary, the prime-minister brought the King's directions to the people of the United States of Israel. This was the theocratic government. Judah was at the beginning the first and foremost of the twelve States. Fifty thousand warriors was then about the average strength of a State, for there were six hundred thousand when they entered the land. But Judah had seventy-six thousand, and only three other tribes, stretching to the north, Issachar, Zebulun, and Asher, had more than the average. Simeon was at that time weakest of all, and its divinely-drawn lot sheltered it under the wing of Judah. Entering the land, therefore, at the head of the army—the army itself conquering first the southern part of the land; assigned its portion before the others; divinely appointed after Joshua's death to go first against the Canaanites; and inheriting so large and so valuable a territory, Judah was already mighty and independent. Its dense population, descended from over a quarter of a million people at the conquest,* swarmed from towns on every eminence. Its counsels were mighty in the assemblies of the nation. Its warriors were intrepid—who swept the mountains at once clear of foes—a fit people to knock their power against the Philistine cities and the rocky Jebus of the Benjamites.

One tribe—small at first, only the *eleventh* in warriors at the entrance—proved the strong rival of Judah. This was the energetic and sensitive tribe of Ephraim, whose sharp "Why went ye without us?" Gideon and Jephthah had felt, and who in later generations envied Judah as Judah vexed her. Two things helped to make Ephraim conspicuous; Joshua was of that tribe, and the tabernacle was confided to the protection of her city, Shiloh. The

---

* If we reckon only three to every warrior, we have 228,000 at the conquest. The population of Rhode Island in 1870 was 217,000, and of Delaware 125,000.

jealousy of Ephraim will be seen in the refusal of the tribe to submit to David after Saul's death ; in "giving aid and comfort" to Absalom against his father ; in sustaining the revolt of Jeroboam, who was of that tribe ; and in the remarkable fact that, after the kingdom was rent in two, every king of the house of Israel came from the tribe of Ephraim. "With the single exception of Saul, all the Hebrew kings were natives of one or the other of these two rival tribes."

But just now, in David's boyhood, in the relations of these two leading tribes, that transition had begun to take place of which Asaph sung in his psalm of lament :

> " So that he forsook the tabernacle of Shiloh,
> The tent which he placed among men.
> Moreover, he refused the tabernacle of Joseph,
> And chose not the tribe of Ephraim,
> But chose the tribe of Judah,
> The Mount Zion which he loved."*

With Manasseh—own brother—next itself on the north, Ephraim was doubly strong ; and, owing to the genealogical and clannish way of thinking among the Hebrews, Benjamin, which lay between Ephraim and Judah, and was descended from their own mother, Rachel, would follow the tribes of Ephraim and Manasseh, rather than the descendants of the son of Leah.

Without further anticipating the political history which we are pursuing, let us turn back now to the family of Bethlehem, and gather some idea of its position in the tribe.

The ancestral family of Jesse, if not Jesse's own household, must have been known beyond the walls of their own city. The wealth of Boaz and his power in the town were

---

* Psalm lxxviii. 60, 67, 68

not shown simply in the express statement of the fact. His fields, his reapers, his observation of Ruth and knowledge of her previous character, his generosity, his hospitality, his resolution to marry the stranger, his influence at the gate, his ready purchase of Elimelech's estate, the gathering of "all the people" with the elders at the gate, their good wishes for his prosperity—all these things exhibit an influence which must have been associated with Bethlehem itself. That Boaz should have been willing to marry a wife of the forbidden Moabites may be explained by two reasons: first, that he was himself a descendant of a Canaanite woman, for his mother was none other than the famous Rahab of Jericho, whom his father Salmon married; and secondly, that Ruth, like his own mother, was a voluntary convert to the Hebrew faith, sincere, earnest, and profound in her entire devotion to the true God. Salmon, it has been conjectured, was one of the spies who visited Jericho.

We must notice, here, that the grandfather of Boaz was a man of power not only in the tribe, but in the nation. This was Nahshon, whose sister was married to Aaron, the high-priest, who was prince of the tribe of Judah, one of the twelve from the tribes, the renowned of the congregation, and who was the captain of the host of Judah through the wilderness. He was, therefore, the first man of the first tribe, so far as honor and station in civil life are concerned; and, aside from the priestly and Levitical offices, next Moses and Aaron, ranking with Caleb and Joshua. Salmon, the son of Nahshon, was also a leader on the circuits about Jericho and the upward march; for he became the founder or the father of Bethlehem,* and he

---

* In 1 Chronicles ii. 50, 51, "Salma the father of Bethlehem" is called the son of Caleb. "It arises from the circumstance that Bethlehem-Ephratah, which was Salmon's inheritance, was

may have honored God's approval of Rahab by taking her at once before all Israel to an honorable station in his own house. Little did he think that he was establishing the royal house of the nation, and both the lineage and the birth-place of the Messiah.

An ancient Jewish tradition says that Jesse was a weaver of the veils of the sanctuary. It is certain that Bezaleel, the embroiderer of blue and purple and scarlet and fine linen, was one of his ancestors. And in the East a trade is transmitted from generation to generation. We lift up our eyes to see Shammah and Nethaneel busy with the ass's load of fleeces from the valley, where Eliab and Raddai are at the shearing, and where young David and his growing nephews make merry with catching the sheep. We look again for the spindle and the distaff in Zeruiah's and Abigail's hands, the web and the weaver's beam as the pious father prepares the refined wool for the sanctuary service, or, as the mother mixes the dye,* and David again finishing for himself the finger-holes of a rustic pipe. It matters little that it was or was not precisely so. The spirit of piety was in the house, and the occupation was something similar. And, at any rate, the family was a most honorable one in the thousands of Judah, and, it is altogether likely, had even then a national reputation.

---

part of the territory of Caleb, the grandson of Ephratah, and this caused him to be reckoned among the sons of Caleb."— *Hervey.*

* Bethlehem was famous for dye-ing.

Fifth Sunday.

RELIGION AND EDUCATION IN BETHLEHEM.

LESSON.

Deuteronomy xii. 4-7, 13, 14, and 18, xiii. 6-15; 1 Chronicles xiii. 3; 1 Samuel vii. 2-17, x. 8, xi. 14, 15, xx. 6, xxi, 1, 6; Proverbs i. 8, 9, iv. 3-10; 1 Kings ii. 3, 4; 1 Chronicles xxviii. 9; 1 Samuel ix. 9.

THERE must have been perplexity and sorrow in Jesse's family when they thought of taking their young children to the house of God. Where could they go, with bullocks and an ephah of flour, and a bottle of wine, as Elkanah and Hannah did, to offer their child unto the Lord? As every year brought the feasts of Tabernacles, and of Passover and of Pentecost, where should the celebration be? As child after child grew, how could he be clearly taught to love the public worship of the God of his fathers? There must have been embarrassment and pain in every pious family.

On the one hand, the command of the law was clear. The only place at which sacrifice was to be offered was to be a place chosen of God. Gifts devoted to God and chosen vows, as well as burnt offerings and tithes, were to be made only there. Children were to be taught that *that* was the only place consecrated to the public worship of God. The command was explicit that children were not to be taken to other places to worship. And any city that should worship at other altars was doomed to destruction.

On the other hand, all the arrangements for the public worship had been broken up. The ark was in one place

—perhaps at Kirjath-jearim, about six miles north-west of Jebus. The tabernacle was in another place — later it was at Nob, which was probably about six miles north-northwest of Jebus. Altars had been erected in this place and in that, and sacrifices had been offered here and there in the land. There had been a wide corruption of the people in idolatry, from which many sincere, true-hearted Israelites kept themselves. Yet God gave his approval to special sacrifices and special places. Samuel the Seer had offered—it must have been in David's childhood—burnt offerings in Gilgal, when, by the direction of God, he anointed the son of Kish King of Israel. And he had before sacrificed at Mizpeh, when the Lord thundered on the Philistines, and in another city of Benjamin, which now is lost to us, on "a high place." And at home at Ramah he had an altar. Pious families, no doubt, therefore, did what Jesse and his house did. They established a family sacrifice, as in the patriarchal times. They called a priest; or the father prayed as Job did, offering burnt offerings for the children, and saying: "It may be that my sons have sinned and cursed God in their hearts;" or the oldest son was priest by birth-right, as in patriarchal times.* And once a year a most solemn offering was made for the whole assembled family, for an atonement for their sins. We have good reason to believe that Jesse was such a pious man. The special honor given in the Scriptures to Nahshon and to Boaz, and the prediction of Isaiah that the Messiah should grow not out of the stem and the root of David, but of *Jesse*, show that it was a family true to the God of Israel. The example of such a man as Jesse would affect all Bethlehem, especially as acts of sacrifice must, in the nature of the case, be public.

And these were the vivid object-lessons which impressed

---

* Numbers viii. 18.

on David's youthful mind the spirit of piety—the altar and the ascending flame in the open air, the running blood of the slaughtered sheep or ox, the gifts and tithes to priests or Levites who made the offering. Here he was taught what the wickedness of idolatry was, and what was the right heart which served God sincerely. The wickedness of Eli's sons, the destruction of Eli's priestly family, the voice calling at Shiloh to the child Samuel, the purity and power of the seer in the land—these, we may be sure, were used as illustrations of the good and the evil to David as a mere child.

His education of course was rude, fragmentary, and mainly religious. But as King David's "recorder" and "scribe" are ranked with the captains of his army and with the high-priest in the enumeration of his chief officers, and as he became a composer of psalms, and held in his hands the reckonings and administration of his kingly power, we must suppose that he was as a child, quick to gain the simple rudiments of reading, writing and reckoning. We may be sure Jesse taught David the substance of what David taught Solomon when he said: "Wisdom is the principal thing; therefore get wisdom: and with all thy getting get understanding." In the house where such persons as Naomi, and Boaz, and Ruth had lived, how often did lips of grace from the benignant face of the aged, say to the children and grandchildren: "My son, to hear the instruction of your father, and to keep your mother's law, will be ornaments of grace to your head, and chains about your neck." And the model for a daughter in Jesse's house was not unlike that fair woman of King Lemuel, in Solomon's time — seeking wool and flax, laying her hands to the spindle and to the distaff, opening her mouth in wisdom, and in her tongue the law of kindness —the description of whose character applies to no woman of the Scriptures better than to Ruth, the mother of Obed.

Of religious instruction in the time of David's youth, we may judge from three things: First, the general instructions of the law of Moses; second, two or three statements in respect to the general period of Jesse and David; and thirdly, from David's own instructions to his son Solomon.

I. Fast and festival, sacrifices and offerings, rites and ceremonies—and the answer to the ever-repeated question of childhood, "What mean ye by this service?"—these were the outward part of education in Moses' law. The statutes and judgments, the commandments and the testimonies—righteous and holy, as a law glorious and fearful in their historic and miraculous authority—which made their great nation a wise and understanding people in the sight of all the nomadic nations of their day, and even of Egypt herself—these were the inward and essential part of Moses' law, illustrated by the patriarchal history, and the escape from Egypt, Sinai, the Wilderness, the Conquest, and the Deliverers of the last three centuries. These the pious parents taught diligently to the children, talking of them as they reclined in the house or walked by the way, at evening and at morning, in work-hours and rest-hours, as if they were visibly bound on their hand to arrest their own attention, and between their eyes, to catch their children's notice, and written on the door-posts of Jesse's house, and gates of Bethlehem. The Levites, too, taught in every city with a diligence measured by their individual piety. Family history and local incidents and tribal exploits, as we have seen already, would give emphasis to this instruction.

II. Three things modified the power of these instructions in David's early life. The first was that the tabernacle service at Shiloh had been broken up when the ark was captured by the Philistines. The ark was brought back by Beth-shemesh, and to Kirjath-jearim, and a priest was consecrated to the special care of it there; but we have no notice of a reunion of the ark and the tabernacle till long afterwards. "All the house of Israel lamented after the Lord" during the twenty years when the ark was at Kirjath-jearim, separated from the tabernacle. If this twenty years expired before David's birth, still there was no fixed central place of national worship. If the lament of the people was simply for the outward ceremonial worship the truly pious felt it the more deeply. And as long as this was so, family instruction everywhere felt the loss of this powerful public support. The second thing was that the ark itself was not publicly inquired at in the days of Saul, that is, while David was growing to manhood. The fact shows that the priests and Levites, who were the educating life of the nation, were lax and negligent in their duties. The third thing was the extraordinary influence of the Seer. The renovating effect of Samuel's early life had been intensified at his first public appearance at Mizpeh. From the time of that open divine approval—as significant as the night vision of his childhood — Samuel was accepted as Judge and Deliverer of the nation. His piety is marked; his wisdom is undoubted; his speech is weighty; his decisions equitable and prompt; his form and features venerable and impressive; his spiritual insight and communion with divine purposes, past and future, make him everywhere known as "The Seer!"

There are four places where he holds his court on the days appointed in regular circuit: Bethel, twelve miles north of Jebus, where the ark was in the days of the war against Benjamin; Gilgal, between Jericho and the Jordan, where was the heap of twelve stones taken from the Jordan when Joshua entered the land, and where the manna ceased after they had eaten of the old corn of the land; Mizpeh, where the burnt-offering was answered by thunder, and where the son of Kish had been anointed king; and

Ramah, his own home, somewhere in Mount Ephraim, where was his house and his altar. "A man of God," honorable in the eyes of all, his character revered, his presence welcomed at the sacrifice, his blessing sought, a Levite, accepted by God as if he were a very priest, a truth-speaker to the face, honest from his childhood, as he goes from place to place, he is growing great in venerable power and dignity before all the nation.

This "Seer," whose rebukes the land feared, whose directions the nation prized, David the lad no doubt had seen when he had happened with his father at Mizpeh on a court-day, or when the flowing locks and flowing robes of the Nazarite had moved down the street of Bethlehem, or passed along yonder ridge-path, where David kept the sheep on the mountain-side. His circuit as a judge was not large, but the power of his character pulsated to the remotest corner of the kingdom, and elevated the spiritual education of every child of every tribe.

III. The instruction of David to Solomon in respect to the law of Moses confirms the impressions of Jesse's instructions to David himself in these single matters of religion, and they show how the Israelites understood the *spiritual* meaning of the Mosaic system in those early days. "Keep his statutes and his commandments," said King David to King Solomon, "and his judgments, and his testimonies, as it is written in the law of Moses: that the Lord may continue his word which he spake concerning me, saying, If thy children take heed to their way, to walk before me in *truth with all their heart and with all their soul*, there shall not fail thee (said he) a man on the throne of Israel." "Know thou, Solomon my son, the God of thy father, and serve him with a *perfect heart* and with a *willing* mind: for the Lord *searcheth all hearts, and understandeth all the imaginations of the thoughts:* if thou seek him, he will be found of thee; but if thou forsake him, he will cast thee off for ever." These spiritual instructions to his own son, in his old age, so in harmony with the psalms written from early to later life, are a pretty sure index of the pious spirit in Jesse's house, which was daily food for David as his impressible and tender soul expanded. Wonderful and strange and good were the ways of God to the opening mind of that youth who was afterward to be openly commended by him as "My servant, who followed me with all his heart, and did that which was right in the sight of the Lord."

Sixth Sunday.

FROM THE OLD GOVERNMENT TO THE NEW.

LESSON.

Deuteronomy i. 13-17, viii. 7-10, xxxi. 24-26 ; Joshua xxiii. 11-13 ; 1 Samuel viii., xvii. 12.

THE chronology of the times of Jesse, Eli, Samuel, and Saul is obscure. But we cannot go far astray, if we suppose that the difference in age between Jesse and Samuel was from ten to twenty years. Jesse "went for an old man in the days of Saul," when the Seer came to anoint David to be king. When the persecutions of David followed one, two, or three years later, David took his parents to Moab out of harm's way. It was just at the end of that one, two, or three years that Samuel died, venerable and full of years. The supposition, therefore, that Samuel was from ten to twenty years older than Jesse will harmonize with the events of Saul's and David's life.

As Saul was in his prime when David was privately anointed at Bethlehem—he had already been weighed as a king and found wanting—we assume that Saul was from ten to fifteen years younger than Jesse. This supposition is sustained by the fact that David, the tenth child of Jesse, took for his wife Michal, the fifth child of Saul. Michal we may safely assume to have been younger than David. If we suppose further that Michal was born when her father was from thirty-one to thirty-five years of age, we may take David to have been born from the twenty-ninth to the thirty-third year of Saul's life. And as we know that David was thirty years old at Saul's death, Saul must have been about sixty when he was slain. And if we further assume that David was from fifteen to twenty years old when Samuel anointed him, then Saul, in mid-career, was about forty-five or fifty years of age. How long Saul was king we do not know—a shorter time than David's forty years certainly!* We think that there is nothing to contradict the supposition that Saul might have been crowned at Gilgal in David's childhood. With these suppositions we go on with the story.

David is now a young man, with a mind of uncommon quickness and penetration—as his alertness of action throughout his life, his comprehension of the situation wherever he was placed afterwards, the vigor and variety and depth of his thoughts in his psalms, prove. We do not stop now to prove it. We shall see, as we go on, the evidence of character and abilities unusually attractive in speech and address, on his first public appearance.

No sooner, therefore, was he well acquainted with the character and career of Samuel up to his own day, with the rising spirit in the national life which, for twenty or thirty years, Samuel had been exciting, and with the new extraordinary fact of a human king in the son of Kish, than his mind must have grasped eagerly and dwelt long on the facts and principles involved. The man whom God was preparing for his chosen king would not be de-

---

* "And afterward they desired a king, and God gave unto them Saul, the son of Cis, a man of the tribe of Benjamin, by the space of forty years." Acts xiii. 21. This does not say that he was king forty years. It is supposed to include the general round period of Samuel and of Saul's public career.

ficient in historic penetration, or in now and then forecasting whither the future would tend.

We need, therefore, to understand the Theocracy a little more in detail, if we would understand the kingdom. That is, we need now to form in our minds such a conception of the old government as David had at that time in his mind.

It is a very remarkable fact that at that time in the world the Hebrew state was composed of a *free* people. Other nations—Egypt, Mesopotamia, the tribes of Canaan, and other nations—were ruled by kings who were absolute tyrants in power. "All other ancient oriental nations," says John Quincy Adams, "were founded on force; this only on consent." For more than three centuries, the Hebrews had no human king. This or that tribe warred against its enemies within its boundaries, or went abroad, but there was no king but God himself. Since Joshua's day, there had been long times of peace and prosperity. Under Othniel, the land had rest forty years; after Ehud's bloody slaughter of the tyrant Eglon, there were eighty years of peace; forty years the country was quiet in the days of Gideon; twenty-three years in Abimelech's reign; twenty-two years in Jair's days; and for twenty years Samson fought off the Philistines. But neither one of these Judges and Deliverers had perpetuated his reign in a succession. The people wished Gideon to be king, and to found a royal house, but he would not.* The people *elected* Jephthah to be Deliverer, and he consented.† Deborah rose up in extraordinary abilities, and they yielded to her.

And everywhere in the course of the history there is evidence of an unrestrained choice and action, and no evidence of a tyrant who succeeded in maintaining power.

---

* Judges viii. 22, 23. † Judges xi. 5, 6.

Abimelech, the son of Gideon, who attempted to be king, met with a ignominious death. His ambitious disregard of his father's noble example, his fratricidal usurpation, his uneasy three years' reign, and his contemptuous end, must have been an illustrious precedent against royalty in the lips of all the people for nearly a century before Saul was born. The Lord Jehovah was the national king in his holy cloud. Under his healthy, restraining laws of liberty, the people were as free as any nation to this day has been—their liberty in marked contrast with the surrounding nations, who were under despots who might be gracious and who might be monsters.

The people were also *equals* under the old government. The mode in which the land of a nation is held is a certain test of the people's rights. The land of the nation was not divided among a few, but among all. No king, no aristocracy, no privileged class owned the territory and towns. The tribes cast lots, the families took their shares in proportion, not to any rank or abilities, but simply in proportion to numbers, and "extreme poverty and overgrown riches were alike impossible." Every fifty years, too, his own land—no matter what were the debts or burdens on it—returned to each man or to his family. Sales and debts were made with reference to this. "The rich could not accumulate all the lands. The fiftieth year, beyond which no lease could run, was always approaching, with silent but sure tread, to relax their tenacious grasp." "At the return of this day, the trumpet peal was heard in street and field, from mountain-top and valley, throughout the length and breadth of the land." "The family mansion and the paternal estate again greeted eyes from which misfortune, through many a weary year, had divorced them." Labor, therefore, was honorable, the work of a citizen, and not of a slave or of a servile condition. Justice was to be impartial, without respect of rich or poor, great or small, without fear of the face of man.

The nation was a *representative* government. They *elected* their officers. Jehovah himself was elected at the first to be their nation's king, before he gave his law. He said, "I have brought you out of the land of Egypt. If ye will obey my voice, and keep my covenant, ye shall be my kingdom and my nation." The people said, "We will do what the Lord has said." And God their king then promised to speak with his nation from a thick cloud, the Shekinah.* The magistrates and elders were elected. "Take you wise men known among your tribes," said Moses to the people, "and I will make them rulers." They were to be "captains or leaders over thousands, captains over hundreds, captains over fifties, and captains over tens, and officers among your tribes." "Give out from among you three men for each tribe" to survey the land, said Joshua to the people. When Jephthah was made judge, it is said, "The *people* made him head and captain over them." Elders were chosen in tribes and in cities. There was no select or privileged class from whom the civil officers were taken. Clearly only some one on whom the people could agree might be elder at the gate in Bethlehem.

---

* Read carefully Exodus xix. 3-9. Notice the steps of progress: Moses comes down with the proposition; he gathers the people in a formal assembly; he receives their reply; he goes back up the mountain; he comes down again with the appointment of a place from which God will speak to them. Many of the most eminent writers who have written on this subject—Jahn, Dean Graves, Lowman, Michaelis, Warburton, Bossuet, Dr. Lyman Beecher, Dr. Spring, Professor Wines—agree in considering this action a voluntary contract or agreement between the people and God, by which God became the Theocratic King. See Professor Wines's "Commentaries on the Laws of the Ancient Hebrews," from which many of the suggestions of this lesson are taken.

Neither Jesse nor any son of his, illustrious as his house may have been, could inherit the office if the people chose otherwise. It seems probable that there was a general system of divisions and sub-divisions from the central power of the divine king, through tribes, cities, villages, and families in which officers and sub-officers were selected by the people for greater and smaller trusts.

Here, therefore, in this free, equal, representative government, long before the republics of Greece and Rome had risen—long before the republics of Switzerland and America, which we so often consider the ripened fruit of the slow-growing centuries—the Hebrews had a republic, secured for three centuries by a divine presiding King, who guided and moulded their human democracy, and who by his perpetual life preserved the government and the nation unbroken.

Two or three other characteristics of the old government may be alluded to. The nation was to be *peaceful in spirit.* There was no standing army. There, the sturdy yeomanry took up their weapons at the cry for self-defence, or at the divine call for retribution and punishment. Infantry was all that was needed for home contests; there was no cavalry for foreign conquests of Egypt or Syria or Asia Minor, and no ships for warlike expeditions to western lands or islands. Every conquest at home even, was not to be for ambition, but as a punishment, often under the direction of God, and depending on his power.

The nation was to be an *agricultural people.* All their commerce was domestic. They were bound together by their great religious festivals, which brought together a vast concourse of people, and which promoted a happy intercourse and a domestic trade. But Moses wished the people to understand that their country was united not to commercial, but to agricultural pursuits. It was "a land of brooks of water, of fountains and of depths that spring out of valleys and hills ; a land of wheat and barley and vines

and fig-trees and pomegranates, and oil-olive and honey, and iron and brass; a land of bread without scarcity."
"By a provision in the constitution before explained, no Israelite could be born who did not inherit a piece of land from his progenitors."

But after the varied experience of over three hundred years, during the general course of which the multitude of the evils of the surrounding sensual tribes had been kept from the land, the government and the nation had become degraded. Eli and Eli's sons had debased their office. The Theocratic King was wearied with the infidelity of the people to their compact. And—vain, alas! is the help of man—Samuel's sons had abused their trust. In the South, at Beersheba, for money they winked at injustice. God's guidance withdrawn in the days of Eli, the ark had been taken, and the nation had been on the verge of dissolution. Samuel's sons false to their trust, Samuel himself, their only stay, once dead, it was easy to see what the end would be. The people, therefore, made use of their occasion, and clamored for that which they had long desired. They would have a king, like all the nations! They put aside the Seer's remonstrances. When he said, "He will take your sons for his chariots and his horsemen, and as servants for his harvest and his army, and your daughters for confectioners and cooks and bakers, and your best fields and best flocks for his; it will be a heavy burden," their weak vanity could see only the glory of the royal court and the splendor of royal renown, such as came borne to their ears from the world around. The wise Seer, displeased, was overborne. Perhaps he felt it to be a personal insult to his life-long work for them. The Theocratic King said to him, "They have not rejected *you*, but they have rejected ME that I should reign over them. Hearken to their voice."

Did Jesse and his house share in the nation's vain desire? We shall find his three sons in Saul's army.

Seventh Sunday.

THE KING.

LESSON.

Deuteronomy xvii. 14-20; 1 Samuel x. 17-27, xi. xii.

THE stirring news which went through the land when David was a child, was, "The Divine Oracle has consented to a king! The Seer has told the elders so, at Ramah!" In every tribe and town and family the next thought was, "WHO will be king? From what tribe? From what house?" The Hebrews were not so much unlike other nations that they did not canvass the historic record of the tribes and of leading families, as well as the character and fitness of every man in any way eminent. The next question everywhere was, "In what way will the king be appointed?"

If now we go back to the directions of Moses on the heights of Moab, we shall find that he foresaw this very time in the nation. In the seventeenth chapter of Deuteronomy we shall find inspired preparation for the kingdom; and if we compare these directions with the history of the elevation of the son of Kish to the throne, we shall have reason to believe that this was the "manner of the kingdom" which Samuel "told the people" and "wrote in a book"—the transcribed constitution of the kingdom.

Now let us see how Saul was made king in accordance

with the inspired law, three and a half centuries before provided for a kingdom.

The following are the characteristics of this special law of Moses:

The people *might* at some time *have a kingdom*. It was not absolutely forbidden, if the nation should insist on desiring it.

The king must be chosen *both* by the *people* and by *God*. This choice of God and the choice of the people must unite in the person.

The king must be a *native Hebrew* and not a foreigner.

The king must not *multiply horses*. He must not be a warrior for foreign conquest, which would be the only use of horses or cavalry. Horses were not used for agriculture; cavalry was not necessary for defence, for the sea was west, the deserts were south and west, the Lebanon range was north. Their first natural communication to foreign parts was to Egypt, but they must not go back to Egypt for them.

The king, in royal marriage, must not have *many wives*. Many queens would be likely to involve alliances with royal houses abroad, or with women of beauty and of note in surrounding nations. There would come in, in the most subtle and powerful forms, the customs, the religious habits, and the gods of those nations—as they did in Solomon's time. And *then idolatry*, the very thing which the nation was organized to destroy, would be established at the head of the nation.

The king must not aim at *great personal wealth*. If God should choose to give it to him, it might be well, for He could protect him from its evils, but he was not to *aim* at it. And if riches increased, they were not the king's, but the people's.

The king must be a *defender of the faith*. From his throne throughout his dominions he must maintain resolutely the law of Moses against the religion of other nations.

The king must consider this *law* to be *supreme*, and not himself supreme. Before the majesty of that law transcribed by the Levites from the Divine Rolls, he must consider the people his equals.

If the king should observe these conditions, then the throne might *continue in his house.* If he violated these conditions, then the throne might be given to others.

The time having come, therefore, when the kingdom was to be established, let us turn to the Seer as he introduces the kingdom. As Saul now appears, let us notice the four inferior conditions of the kingly office first.

Saul was a native Hebrew, as the chronological tables carefully show. His grandfather, Ner, was one of ten brothers, and they, or Abiel, their father, the father and founder of *Gibeah*, must have had to do with the Benjamite war, when the people of Gibeah would not give up the murderers of the Levite's concubine.*

Some of the family too must have married the women of Jabesh-gilead or of Shiloh, when the tribe was preserved from destruction.† It was bad blood from which to come, but it was purely Hebrew.

Saul had no cavalry. During his reign we have no trace of numbers of horses in peace or war, although the Philistines came up with thirty thousand chariots against him.

---

* Judges xix. 1. See margin, a woman, a concubine, or a wife, a concubine. " The position of these two among the early Jews cannot be referred to the standard of our own age and country: that of concubine being less degraded, as that of wife was, especially owing to the sanction of polygamy, less honorable than among ourselves."—*Hayman*, in Smith's " Dic. of Bible."

See, too, verses 27–30 and xx. 13.

† See Judges xxi.

King Solomon began the introduction of horses. David in his war song, sang,—

> "Some trust in chariots, and some in horses,
> But we will remember the name of the Lord our God."

Saul did not make many marriages. His children were seven sons and two daughters; we have notice of only one wife and of one concubine, who watched the bodies of his children after they were executed.

Whether Saul aimed to make the kingdom increase his personal wealth or not, there is little to indicate. His father was a "mighty man of substance." At first he was modest, but afterwards vanity and love of display became passions with him, as when he spared Agag and his spoil for his own personal glory.

So far, therefore, as these four requirements of the constitution were concerned, the Seer would find in this goodly young man an entire outward compliance.

Let us look now at the three higher conditions: the united choice of the people and of God, defence of the faith, and submission to the law.

At the grand assembly of the nation at Mizpeh, one of the Seer's shire-towns, as we would call them,* the public choice was made. Saul already knew that he was to be king, for Samuel had already anointed him privately.

"The Mighty King that delivered you from Egypt and from all kingdoms," said the venerable, grey-bearded, solemn Seer, "who made you warriors and deliverers in the Judges, you have rejected. He now grants you a kingdom. Both he and you to-day choose the king. Let the tribes appear before him in their order." This was probably after

---

* Authorities debate on which one of the two heights was Mizpeh, *the Watch-Tower*, the height a mile north, or on the higher hill five miles north-east of Jebus.

solemn sacrifice. One by one they pass before the prophet. Neither Judah nor Ephraim is honored that day. By general lot, the tribe of Benjamin—once cut almost off from the nation—is chosen. Family by family comes the little tribe, and the family of Matri is chosen. House by house comes the family, and Kish is chosen. Name by name, as the growing excitement deepens, Kish's sons are brought before the Lord, and at last the name *Saul* leaps from lip to lip throughout the vast multitude. The young man, knowing the result, and abashed by the deepening curiosity of the occasion, is hid among the heaps of tent-cloths, saddles, and other luggage of the gathered nation, until the Lord points him out. Stalwart and tall he walks as they bring him forward, well-formed, and good-looking, a head and shoulders higher than the throng—the very figure for kingly pomp, the very strength for a valiant warrior. "Live the King!" the welkin rings. And yet a certain bashfulness—unbecoming such a position, as if he could never be quite at home as the nation's leader—provokes distrust. Some perhaps remember the tribe, and *Gibeah!*

The nation assent to the Lord's choice, and yet there is not a free and full consent. Saul, therefore, goes home to Gibeah, accompanied by the fighting men. And as the fault-finders say, "How can this man save the nation?" he goes back to his father's herds.

But soon come tidings which touch his heart to the quick and drive off his timidity. The wild wail as of a great calamity strikes his ear, one day, as he follows his cattle home. The whole town is in deep distress. "What aileth the people?" "Nahash taunts our kindred* of Jabesh-gilead, and puts out their right eyes as an insult to us all." The fire kindles! Saul is another man. The slaughtered oxen are despatched in pieces, and in haste to the

---

* Judges xxi. 14.

tribes! Memories of the Levite's concubine wake again. But now the Lord's Chosen summons. Over every hill they come, as Saul's messengers make speed across the Jordan with news of help. And by the next day's light three hundred thousand warriors—thirty thousand from Judah—are at the heels of the Ammonites till there is an utter rout and a victory. There is now no more question about the king. "Bring forth to their death those murmurers against the king—the children of Belial!" But the new king is as great in magnanimity as in conquest. "The Lord alone has done it. No man shall die for me."

And then at Gilgal, in another national assembly, the whole people solemnly confirm the divine choice with sacrifices, peace-offerings, and joyful, unanimous, and triumphant agreement. The people's choice and Jehovah's choice agree.

The venerable Seer makes his farewell address. Pointing out their king, the united choice of the nation and of God, he solemnly repeats the faith of their fathers and the law of Moses, to which they must adhere, re-enforces it by the mighty history of the past, and seals its authority anew by calling thunder and rain on the harvest—a thing as incomprehensible as snow in summer to the Hebrews. The people tremble, and before their king confess their guilt in asking for him. The Seer in the name of God, bids them support the kingdom in the faith and law of God. They assent, and the son of Kish, honored by all the tribes, takes up his royal state at Gibeah.

"This was the way it came about," we may imagine Jesse saying to the young shepherd from the valleys, as they return past Rachel's sepulchre, where more than once they had stopped to comment on historical events,* "when you, David, were a child upon your mother's knees, and when we of Bethlehem came home to tell the wonderful story!"

---

* Genesis xxxv. 19, 20. 1 Samuel x. 1-2.

Eighth Sunday.

THE KING'S SON.

LESSON.
1 Samuel xiii. xiv. 1–46; x. 8.

LET us suppose now that David is about twelve years old, accustomed, like Joseph in earlier days, to visit his brothers in the fields. Saul has been king two years. Since Samuel's retirement, the Philistines have made rapid strides again. They have succeeded is disarming the people. They have captured the smiths or broken up their forges. Whoever would forge or sharpen even a plough-point or prong-fork, unless he takes the slow file to do it, must go down to the Philistines. Good weapons are few. The nation is distressed at its weakness, and in terror at the power of the enemy.

A double wave of news comes to Bethlehem, and flows through the land, first elevating and then depressing the people: first, "The king's son has routed the enemy at Geba;" and then, "The Philistines have heard of it, and are rallying for revenge." The *king's son?* The mind of David is alive. Jonathan must have been at least twenty years old; six or eight years older than David. And this shows that, if Saul had a full-grown son two years after his inauguration, Saul himself must have been about forty years of age when crowned at Gilgal.

Much is meant by the news—much to stir the heart of young David—first, with enthusiasm and admiration at the valor and piety of Jonathan, and then with sympathy for him in his trouble. For King Saul has had three

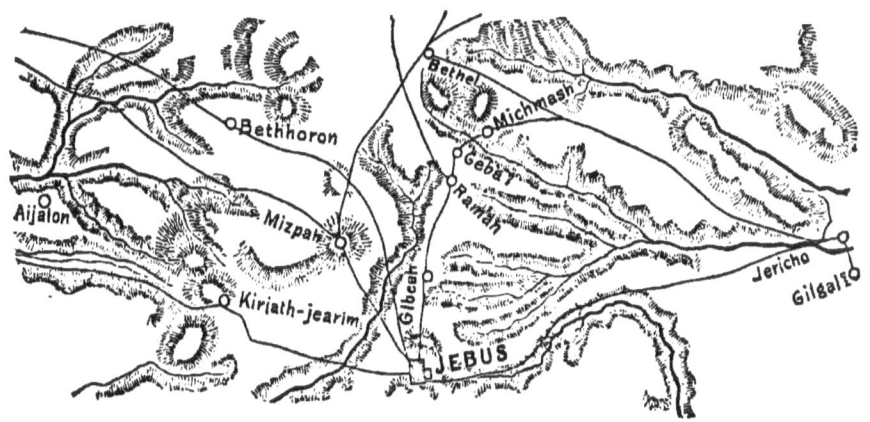

thousand chosen warriors in the heart of Benjamin; his army line lying along the hills from Michmash, seven miles north of Jebus, to Bethel, some three or four miles further north. The heights command the principal road to the northern tribes, and one principal ravine down to the Jordan. One thousand of the three is under Jonathan at Gibeah. Whether it was a *military post* at Geba, on the opposite edge of the rough ravine, south-west from Michmash, which Jonathan took, or an *officer* stationed there—the Hebrew word may mean either garrison or officer—the enemy is exasperated. Timid hearts condemn the son of Saul as more rash than brave in his valor. Let them wait and see!

Thirty thousand chariots gather on the plain, and six thousand horsemen. And an overpowering army, fully armed and fully aroused, swarm up the gorges and along the mountain-paths. Saul sends the trumpet throughout the land to signal all the tribes. The people come in mass to support the three thousand souls smitten with panic. They clamber down the rough way to Gilgal below, whither the king has summoned the people. They hide in the limestone caverns, and in the thickets, and on mountain-tops. Some flee even to the eastern tribes. The Philistines pitch on the deserted field. They look down on the trembling flock around Saul, content enough to hold those important heights.

Another prediction of the Seer has come true, confirming to Saul the kingdom. For Saul finds himself in Gilgal, where Samuel foretold him that he would come, and where he bade him wait seven days, till he should offer sacrifices for him and give him God's word and order. But in his dismay at the desertion of the people, and fearing the descent of the Philistines, like Peter in the winds and waves, the king loses sight of the divine power, and himself orders the burnt-offering. By so doing, he himself assumes the conduct of the war, disobeys the instructions of the prophet, and virtually puts himself *above the law.* The prophet denounces a woe against his royal succession—a thing which was, perhaps, not known to Jonathan at the time, since he and his thousand may have still held possession of Geba. To Geba or Gibeah, Saul and his six hundred remaining men climb back, inspired by the Seer's holy courage. Across the rough and deep ravines they encamp face to face—Gibeah to Michmash, Hebrews to Philistines. There the Hebrews see the Philistine raiders ravaging the country. Three companies of "spoilers" go, one to the west, towards Beth-horon; one to the east, towards the Jordan, as probably "towards the wilderness" means, and one probably towards the north, although we know nothing of " Ophrah, or the land of Shual." " While," Josephus says, " King Saul and his son Jonathan saw what was done, but were not able to defend the land."

The Septuagint says "they wept aloud" at the misfortunes which they saw, but could not help.

Now appear the pious faith, the brave spirit, the direct energy of the son. He had provoked the incursion by taking this hold of Geba. In the name of the God of battles he would drive the enemy out. He plans an attack, in which he will trust, not to his own royal assumption, as his father has done, but to divine assistance. He agrees with his armor-bearer on a day. They would climb down the sharp precipice Seneh, and up the sharp precipice Bozez, and would come on the enemy from an unexpected quarter in an unexpected moment, and would, in God's strength, gain foothold for others to follow. There God should set up their banner to rally the timid! The description of the situation by Josephus cannot be far from the general truth: "Now the enemy's camp was upon a precipice which had three tops that ended in a sharp and long extremity, while there was a rock that surrounded them like the lines made to prevent the attacks of an enemy. There it so happened that the outguards of the camp were neglected, because of the security that here arose from the situation of the place, and because they thought it altogether impossible not only to ascend to the camp in that quarter, but so much as to come near it." God favors them. They surprised the camp from their very strongest side, Josephus says while the army was sleeping. Like their brethren of their tribe and house, who, "armed with bows, could use both the right hand and the left, in hurling stones and shooting arrows out of a bow" (1 Chron. xii. 2)—"swift as eagles, strong as lions," as David in his elegy afterwards said Saul and Jonathan were—they "discharged a flight of arrows, stones, and pebbles from their bows, crossbows, and slings, with such effect that twenty men fell at the first onset. A panic seized the garrison, then spread to the camp, and then to the surrounding hordes of marauders; an earthquake combined with the terror of the moment, the confusion increased; the Israelites who had been taken slaves, as the Septuagint says, by the Philistines during the last three days, rose in mutiny; the Israelites who lay hid in the numerous caverns and deep holes in which the rocks of the neighborhood abound, sprang out of their subterranean dwellings."* Like the victory given with thunderings to Samuel at Mizpeh, is this victory given with earthquake and panic to Jonathan.

At one step Jonathan rises into favor on the enthusiastic admiration and thanks of the people; and but for another folly of the blundering Saul, would have inspired the nation with noble thoughts of the royal house—a folly divinely overruled to prevent too strong an attachment to the house of Saul.

No sooner do Saul's watchmen discover the retreat of the enemy, and his army rouses the country in full pursuit after Jonathan to the victory, than Saul proclaims a solemn curse on all eating till nightfall, till the enemy is routed and slaughtered. From morning light, if Josephus is right, through the livelong day till evening, from twelve to fifteen miles westward, over the mountains of Ephraim, the fighting goes on, over rocks and headlong precipices, in chasms and valleys, down to Aijalon, on the borders of their lowland. Flushed with victory, Jonathan breaks an order which was indeed foolish, but which was a royal military order, issued by the authority of a king divinely appointed. He takes advantage of the fact that the king is his father. He even justifies the people in breaking it, telling them the victory would have been greater if no such order had been given. The heated and wearied people rush into excess upon the spoil, and break the Levitical law which forbids the eating of the blood upon the meat. The Lord

---

* Stanley.

shuts off the full success of conquest. There is an Achan in the camp by the Lord's word. Saul swears before the altar that the guilty man shall die. By division and by divine lot, Jonathan is taken. He confesses his folly and his sin before the people; he acknowledges the just punishment; he listens to the dread sentence of his father, who stands solemnly committed to the holy execution of the law.

And had not the people, full of astonishment both at the victory wrought by God through Jonathan, and at the divine arrest and sentence of Jonathan as a criminal, been ready to explain all the unfortunate circumstances of that peculiar crime before the altar to God, had they not confessed their own guilt and their repentance, and honored the law itself by solemn sacrifices, as we may reasonably suppose, Jonathan must have died by the law of the kingdom and the law of God. "By which means," says Josephus again, "they snatched him out of danger he was in from his father's curse, while they made their prayers to God also for the young man, that he would remit his sin."

What a strange mixture have we here in the intelligence which throbbed along the avenues to all the tribes! The king's son's first attack; the king's first panic; the king condemned, his succession denied; the prince-royal rescuing the land, the prince-royal condemned to death; the people guilty; the penitent people rescuing the guilty prince; pardon and peace by the altar and by the law. How the heart of David throbbed at all this, as he hears, perhaps for the first time, of this generous, valiant, pious, impulsive youth of the royal house, bringing in the same hour the victory and the blame of God! How he longed to be by his side in the fight, in the place of that armor-bearer, with their trust in God! Might not David have been that armor-bearer? No; he was too young. Jonathan is only just grown, we must suppose, and his sister Michal, between himself and whom were three children, was nearer David's age.

Ninth Sunday.

THE RISE AND THE FALL.

LESSON.

1 Samuel xiv. 47-52; xv. 1-23, 32, 33; xvii. 34-37; Deuteronomy xxv. 17-19.

A NEW energy now sprang up in the nation. The king and his son were towers of strength and engines of destruction against their enemies. There was strenuous war all the time with the Philistines. For six or eight years the king was gaining in power. Saul was in his prime. The reverse which Jonathan had given to the Philistines held them in check. At length the nation had champions who cleared their coast. The Hebrews learned anew the power of their rocks and mountains. The wolves bayed at the sheep in the distance. Nahash with his Ammonites and Moabites was forced to keep well behind the Salt Sea. Marauders of Edom were kept below Beersheba. The kings of Zobah—a country or district undefined to us, lying somewhere in the region of Damascus and Lebanon —were compelled to retire behind the north-east plains and mountains. Wherever he went, north, south, east, or west, the valiant king gained his cause—and God was with him. The Amalekites, roving in Bedouin license along the southern border—once in league with the Moabite Eglon and driven out by Ehud, once overrunning the country with the Midianites, like locusts in multitude, into the very north, and thrown into panic by Gideon's trumpets and lamps—these fierce and lustful plunderers King Saul swept back in mighty valor.

The king was learning, too, how to strengthen his royal power internally. He watched for men who developed abilities. When he saw them, he took them to himself. The consequence must have been a court of military strength in the eyes of the people. Abner was at the head of the army, that uncle of Saul—yes, no doubt that very uncle whose eager mind was first to ask, on his return home, what the Seer said unto him when he was in pursuit of the asses.

The annals of peace are always shorter than the annals of war, and there is little information, therefore, given us in respect to this important time of Saul's life. But we can see that the surrounding nations were held in check by the valiant king. Vineyards are trained again on the hillsides. Flocks again graze freely in the valleys and fresh ravines of spring. Grain waves in the fields. Home is peaceful. No alarm thrills the house by night or by day. The story of battles is the calm story of even success, and no longer the palpitating story a life-and-death struggle. Beneath the royal shepherd, the wolves fear and the sheep are safe.

Meanwhile, David himself has grown to be a shepherd. He takes his flocks down the valleys about Bethlehem, some of which to this day are fresh with verdure. He leads them along the dark ravines, perhaps through the evening shades when the short twilight shuts out the sun. He stretches the strings over a piece of cypress or juniper, or tunes a pipe from a Jordan reed. His frame grows solid with strength. His limbs develop in agility and in feats of clambering up and down the rocks. The sharp limestone chips he hurls with precision and with a powerful arm against yonder growling bear that peers through the stony ledge. And that day comes and passes when, with a roar and a spring, a lion is upon the flock, and the *test* is *on him* whether he will play the hireling or the good shepherd. Quicker than that shepherd whom the prophet Amos describes, who rescues from the lion's mouth only "two legs or the piece of an ear," the lion-hearted youth is on him. Like a flash he clutches him, and like a flash his spear or his knife finds the vitals. Yonder growler comes another day; the young shepherd prowls for him as he prowls for the lamb; his challenge is accepted, his burly body stretched on the rocks for the wheeling eagles and sly foxes, and the bleeding lamb snatched from his teeth.*

Awe-struck at the danger and the deliverance, he ascribes his success to God, and treasures in his grateful heart that vivid picture which afterwards, when in danger from human enemies, he paints in his psalms:

> "O Lord my God, in thee do I put my trust:
> Save me from all them that persecute me, and deliver me:
> Lest he tear my soul like a lion,
> Rending me in pieces while there is none to deliver."

> "They have set their eyes bowing down to the earth;
> Like as a lion that is greedy of his prey,
> And as it were a young lion lurking in secret places."

> "They gaped upon me with their mouths,
> As a ravening and a roaring lion."

But these dangers from wild beasts were less to be feared than dangers from fiercer foes who had been accustomed to steal from the southern desert around the ends of the Dead Sea, to file up the torrent-beds from the west, and to pour down the Jordan channel from the north, and whose corruptions were worse than their cruelty.

---

* "Thevenot says: 'The Arabs are not afraid of lions, but if armed with a good stick will pursue them, and kill them if they can catch them.'"

While David is looking for fresh pasture by day and keeping his shepherd's lodge by night, and occasionally returning to Bethlehem, King Saul has a new commission from the Seer. Strong now in his kingdom and in the esteem of his people, he is in just the position to execute the long-deferred and righteous purpose of God. Those fierce Amalekites whom he has begun to chastise have long deserved the full measure of the divine judgment. Cruel and merciless, they played the *guerilla* on the army of Moses. The feeble, who, faint and weary, could not keep on the march, they flew upon and killed. A roaming tribe themselves, they hated and murdered the Hebrew wanderers of the desert. There can be little doubt that they were as sensual as they were cruel. Therefore God revived to Saul the curse on Amalek which he first uttered to Moses. As for the command to inflict execution, Saul had no responsibility. Jehovah himself assumed the justice or injustice of the act. " Go and utterly destroy the *sinners*, the Amalekites, and fight against them till they be consumed," is his order. The command is given in particulars. Spare no man nor woman, not even the infant. Destroy oxen and sheep, camel and ass. Leave nothing to infect the people by even remote association with their fierce and beastial wickedness. Let no fairness of appearance or of wealth give power to their temptations to cruelty or lust. As for thyself, remember only " that which Amalek did to Israel when he laid wait for him when he came out of Egypt, and that for this long-deferred work of justice and judgment on the wicked I have given thee royal power and position."

Forthwith the king accepts the commission. He gathers two hundred thousand men, ten thousand from Judah —Bethlehem and every other city of the tribe must have been astir—at Telaim, which is supposed to have been in the extreme south, beyond Beersheba. Many of the troops must have filed past Bethlehem and the flocks of David. The city at which they make a stand Saul takes; their army he pursues from Havilah to Shur, from one end of the desert to the other, east to west. The homeward march is sounded, King Agag a prisoner, and the spoil rich and splendid.

Noble is the king's prowess in the eyes of the people, but terrible his crime in the eyes of God. The very man that stands as the champion of the tribe and its wickedness, the king and leader, he spares. He destroyed everything that was refuse and vile among the animals—that is, everything that would have excited contempt for the Amalekites. But the *best* of the sheep and oxen and lambs, and all that was good—that is, everything which would provoke the people to admire the Amalekites and their possessions, these he spared. The supposition seems probable " that Saul spared the king for no other reason than that for which he retained the spoils, namely : to make a more splendid show at the sacrificial thanksgiving." The king's vanity and self-will were overruling his respect for the supreme law. Josephus says that Saul "admired the beauty and tallness" of Agag so much that he thought him worthy of preservation. It is quite likely, therefore, that Saul came back to Carmel, below Hebron, and then over to Gilgal, to make a great sacrifice before the assembled people, a grand thanksgiving and *Te Deum* for the splendid victory.

Here at Gilgal, in what he considers the very height of his glory, the Seer meets him to let in the flood of truth upon his vain and self-willed mind. The very pomp of his victory is teaching disobedience to God, in the very place where holiness and wickedness are in conflict. He has thwarted the very object which God sent him to accomplish. He was to shut off for ever from the people's mind all associations with the Amalekites, and he had brought this stately and handsome king into the heart of the land with the best of his flocks to the great gathering of the people. On a grand scale, he had assembled his troops and made known the express command of God. On a grand scale, he has deliberately assumed superiority to God's orders, and has made his disobedience splendid and attractive. What he did in adversity at Gilgal when the Philistines pressed him hard, he now does at Gilgal in the height of national prosperity and victory. How can he be longer trusted with the nation and the law?

Samuel has cried unto the Lord all night, that he would spare Saul; but he sees clearly now that the king or the law must be sacrificed. The sentence is therefore prompt and unsparing. "It was not sacrifice, but display which you sought; not burnt-offerings, but the pomp of heathen self-will; not God's glory, but your own. In what does the Lord delight: in offerings or in obedience? in flocks for sacrifice or in attention to his word? in rebellion or in law? Which does he consider the better, the wickedness and idolatry of Amalek, or the stubbornness of Saul, which will lead to them? Because thou hast rejected the word of the Lord, he hath also rejected thee from being king."

Tenth Sunday.

THE SEER AT BETHLEHEM.

LESSON.
1 Samuel xv. 23-35; xvi. 1-14.

IT is an interesting question now, as we come to the private anointing of David, how far it was known throughout the nation that the house of Saul was deposed from the kingship. Did it thrill, like the news of his coronation, to the remotest villages of the land? Did Jonathan know it? Did the people of Bethlehem know it? Was what Samuel said to Saul, "Hath given it to a neighbor of thine that is better than thou," common news?

On the one hand, if it should be commonly understood that the family of the son of Kish had been deposed, would it not harm the nation as well as the king? If Saul himself was to continue king for some years, would not the kingdom be alienated from a man for whose unfaithfulness his house was cut off from the royal succession? Would there not be danger of the nation turning their thoughts to some way of ridding themselves of the reproach of a condemned king? Would not the office be weakened, while the people clung to its form, and while they discussed the claims of this family and that to the throne? In this way the very stability of the kingdom would be shaken.

On the other hand, if the condemnation of the royal house was a secret sentence known only to Saul and Samuel, how could the proper disapproval of Saul's character be shown? If he was a divinely-chosen king, and the people believed him divinely maintained in office, then they would copy his corrupt example and relapse into their old decline from virtue.

We must take a middle ground; that the deposition of his family from the kingship was not known to the *whole* nation, perhaps not even till after Saul's death; that it was not widely known among the people, except so far as it gradually filtrated down to them through the limited circle which at first learned the important secret; and that a limited circle did know it from the first. The people could not fail to notice the change in the Seer. He separated himself from the king. He evidently disapproved the king's spirit, and did not hesitate to have it known. He mourned over the king's wilfulness and temper. It is altogether likely that the king began to show at once, as he certainly did afterwards, a consciousness of the loss of divine favor. It was perhaps—in the exact knowledge of the facts—the dread state secret of that young kingdom, guarded, it may be, with oriental jealousy, but sufficiently ascertained by the well-informed in the gates of the land.

Let us notice how the Scriptures support this view of the matter.

1. So far as we have already come, there has occurred nothing which Saul and the prophet might not have known exclusively. The rebuke to Saul, at Shiloh, the first time for assuming to offer the burnt-offering, might have been communicated to Saul alone. "Saul went out to meet him." The rebuke and the denial of a successor on the throne is evidently a private communication to Saul, or in the presence of his military body-guard. And it was just

so the second time at Gilgal, up to the point of the Seer's rebuke. Saul's request that Samuel will honor his kingly office "before the elders of my people" shows that the communications between the two were not open and public.

2. But with the execution of Agag at this second visit of Samuel to Saul at Gilgal, there is a public and awful manifestation of disapproval, which all the assembly see, and all the nation must have felt. When Saul confessed his sin he begged the prophet yet to honor him before the people. Samuel does go and offer sacrifice before the people. He still supports publicly Saul as the anointed king, but it is at that very same sacrifice that he strikes down Agag the murderer with a swift and terrible death— Agag whom the king had spared and who thought the bitter sentence of death passed by, so weak and lenient was the king. Putting aside, as he must have done, the flocks and herds of Agag, he made a great change in the sacrifice that day. It was a very different offering from the grand *Te Deum* which the king intended. And the change must have been as marked in the minds of the people as it was humiliating to the king.

3. Samuel's withdrawal from Saul after such a solemn and signal act must have been observed. He mourned for the king. This must have been known at Ramah and in the rude court-life at Gibeah, to which Saul returned. There was a lasting breach. It is hardly possible that the discerning did not see that the king was no longer in favor, and that the irreconcilable breach was not so much between the Seer and the king, as between the king and the Lord of hosts.

This secret, if not at first known to the prince royal, who was the most interested, soon became known to him. The counsellors of the king saw in the king, as time went on, the development of a stubborn will which would not brook even the direction of God. For this it was by which God had virtually put him off his throne. The elders of tribes and of cities became acquainted with the king's temper and the king's rejection. During all this time the matter would not be spoken of to the king. Delicacy forbade. Fear forbade.

But the king's mind was haunted. "*The Lord hath rejected thee; hath rent the kingdom from thee; given it to a neighbor of thine.*" How his mind brooded gloomily on these thoughts at times! We know what his resolution was afterwards. It was to maintain himself resolutely in the kingdom; to be ready for the new upstart—this neighbor—and to make way with him as soon as possible. And these very dark and gloomy thoughts were soon to bring into his very presence the stripling who was to sway the kingdom with great and holy power.

Samuel himself feared Saul's malignity. When he said, "If Saul hear it, he will kill me," he could hardly have feared that Saul would have put him to death legally for treason in anointing another king, but that his deadly malice was fully set, like the jealousy of oriental tyrants, against even the prophet whose office it might be to select a new king.

And so Samuel goes to Bethlehem to anoint a king from Jesse's house, under cover of a sacrifice. The anointment of David is therefore private—as Saul's first anointment had been—confined to the family of David, the act not known even to the town.

The little city, however, is moved by the coming of the great and good man. The elders tremble at the announcement of the visit, and, when they hear that the Seer is coming up the Jebus road, solemnly driving a heifer before him, they recall his last public act—a few years before—the righteous vengeance on Agag at the sacrifice. What now has called him from his retirement? Why does he come in this formal manner to Bethlehem? What woe has he for us? Some of them no doubt helped to drive home the fair flocks of Agag. But "Peace!" is his salutation. "I have come to sacrifice for sin, and to honor the Lord. Sanctify yourselves, and come." He gives special attention to Jesse and his family—by ceremonies of purification preparing them for the sacrifice. The public offering is over. Flesh from the sacrifice is taken home to the houses for the after-feast. Samuel goes with Jesse's family. And there and then, before the home-feast begins—in the court, or a room off the court of that house on the street of Bethlehem—transpires the scene of anointing. Jesse is made acquainted with his errand—and his sons. Eliab, like Saul in goodly proportions and features, has moral features like Saul. Neither he nor any one of the seven is acceptable to Him who looks not, like the nation, on the bodily presence, but on the heart. "Are these all thy children?" No; there was one whom it was not thought worth while to call in to the sacrifice, nor to see Samuel that day—the least important. "No; there is the youngest, who is looking after the sheep." "Send for him. We will not taste of the food till he is come." A messenger goes—a son or servant. A flush is on the cheek of the quick-footed young man as he comes from the narrow entrance into the court.

"This is he: arise; anoint him!" is the secret voice of the Lord.

There, in the presence of the family—his mother,* Zeruiah, and the women, of course, not with them, but in the women's apartment, if at home at all, perhaps peering through a lattice—the prophet pours his sacred oil on his head; and David the Darling is henceforth in the family David the Anointed.

---

* David's mother was living after this time. See 1 Samuel xxii. 3.

What instructions the prophet gave that day may be easily imagined: the reasons why he anoints David; the king deposed; the Lord's direction; the future time when God will call him openly to his throne and to his own work. *Secrecy* was an important part of all this transaction. It indicated God's secret purpose, which was not yet to be made public. Samuel need not urge reasons why the anointment should be kept secret. The safety of the family, as well as the safety of the son, would secure this. For the king would not scruple to take the life of one son or of all the sons, if he suspected that one of that house was aspiring to the throne. Indeed Samuel himself said, when the Lord directed him to Bethlehem, "How can I go? if Saul hear it, he will kill me."

Eleventh Sunday.

THE KING SENDS FOR DAVID.

LESSON.
1 Samuel xvi. 14-23.

TWO or three, five or six years may have passed after Jesse's family were possessed of the important secret before the next important event came to pass. The Spirit of God is upon David, enriching his natural gifts with supernatural endowments. As he goes before the sheep, and his quick eye runs from this side to that for pasture and for beasts, his quicker thoughts run over the national history, the laws of God, the Theocracy, the kingdom, and that private anointing of the venerable man of God. He knows that he is called of God to some important work in life. Songs of praise and of thanks, and of loyalty to God's love, and God's law escape his lips. They strike the ear of the passer-by, who waits to listen to the sweet voice and the harmonious accompaniment of the well-thrummed lyre. His daring and his prudent speech, his handsome person, and the sincerity of his piety, become known.

If Eliab and Shammah are jealous, as Judah and Simeon were jealous of Joseph, they dare not tell the dangerous secret of the anointment, for the risk is as great to the whole family as to him. And as for his nephews, Abishai, Joab, and Asahel, and Amasa—those daily companions of David's work and recreation—while their exploits challenge and sharpen his abilities, his loving temper subdues their fierce and turbulent nature. Perhaps they suspect what it was for, that the prophet called David away from them at the sheep-fold. Possibly they too have been entrusted with the sacred message, and exalted prospects of their young and gracious uncle. If the town becomes possessed of the knowledge, honor and fear guard the secret.

At length, one day, a messenger from King Saul himself arrives: "Send me David thy son who is with the sheep." *Has King Saul heard?* No! It was only a *sacrifice* which Samuel made at Bethlehem! It is a friendly and not a hostile message. The king desires his musical skill and handsome speech. Forthwith an ass is led out from the court; a skin of wine and a goodly kid are thrown across his back, with a leathern bag or a basket of bread-patties or bread-cakes from the oven (bread is baked every day in the East), and with the king's messenger David leaves his homes for—the Kingdom! In Jesse's gift are both courtesy and expediency.

But at Gibeah a different house waits for David. While the Spirit of God has come upon David, that Spirit has departed from Saul. His endowments, which have been roused to extraordinary power under God's blessing, have failed him under God's frown. Inspiring thoughts—such as are sent into good men's minds by God—no longer animate him. He is troubled by him against whom he has turned.

It is not of very high importance that we should know precisely what is meant by "the evil spirit from God" which was upon Saul. Some persons have imagined it to be nothing more than bodily disease which preyed upon his mind; a spasmodic lunacy or deep melancholy. Others think it the frenzy of a high temper, stung by disappointment and obstinate by resistance. It is better to take the Scripture plainly as it stands. The doctrine of demoniac possession of the human soul is plainly taught in the Scriptures. The devil not only entered into Saul, who betrayed God's kingdom, as he entered into Judas, who betrayed our Lord, but was there as a direct possessor and troubler of his soul. As all men who oppose themselves to God are taken captive by the devil at his will, so some men who, in the midst of great and plain opportunities to do good and to be good, have become stubborn instead of docile, are *given up* to the full possession of Satan. The existence of Satan is an awful certainty; and just how or when Satan or a minion of his takes full possession of an utter apostate, we cannot discern.

Probably, however, the outward manifestation of this possession soon became clear. His heart, haunted by the prophet's woes and by the sense of the divine withdrawal, grew dull and hard. Like Satan, he gave himself up to a vain and desperate self-assertion against God's decree. His subsequent career shows it. He became mad and raving at times in his passions, suspecting very likely some one of his court to be conspiring against him, or watching for that "neighbor" to whom the kingdom would be given. Reason and good sense and kindly thoughts returned at times—as they do occasionally even in abandoned men—when his courtiers endeavored to soothe and subdue him. And when his self-will could be overcome by pleasing reasons, they argued that pleasing sounds addressed to a selfish fancy might lull to rest the beast and the serpent in him. And, therefore, they recommended a skilled musician or minstrel. The selfish will of the king was pleased, and, when one of the servants said that he knew such a man, little cared he who or where he was. "Send for him," was his order. The very essence of demoniac possession consists in the co-operation of the demon's self-will and the self-will of the soul possessed; and, therefore, satanic and human self-will may be soothed at the same time by the gratification of any self-willed fancy. And when "David came to Saul and stood before him," his will was much pleased. The grace and beauty of the youth, his music, his address and compact strength, his stature, which disarmed the king's mind from the suspicion that he could be his successor; these pleased and soothed him through his taste. He at once appointed him his personal attendant; to bear his armor and wait upon his person.* He was delighted with him. When his paroxysms of kingly jealousy and desperation came on, the unknown king before him, with song and harp, diverted his self-will from jealousy to pleasure. "So Saul was well and was refreshed, and the evil spirit departed from him." The towering rage of jealousy and of selfish will no more appeared. The intensity of his mad temper, superinduced by satanic possession, relaxed and passed away, as he gazed in astonishment on the performance of the musician.

Another young man must have been silently observing—Jonathan! What friendship here began, as those gentle and brave eyes met, and courteous addresses challenged each other's admiration in that royal house!

We cannot tell how long David was at Gibeah—a few months perhaps. He was only a temporary charmer. He shortly went home—it may have been at his own request.

---

* The words translated "armor-bearer" mean literally, "the one bearing the prepared (things)," that is, bearer of apparatus, whether weapons in the army, or clothing, or furniture in the house. Perhaps "armor-bearer" really includes all these.

The revelation of royal life made to him could not have been agreeable. Gibeah! the name was offensive! The well and walls of Bethlehem were full of peace and strength to him. It may be that Saul grew sufficiently indifferent to let David depart.

Twelfth Sunday.

THE PUBLIC INTRODUCTION.

LESSON.

1 Samuel xvii.; 2 Samuel xxi. 15-23; Deuteronomy ii. 10-12, 20, 21; ix. 2; Joshua xv. 8; xviii. 16; 2 Samuel v. 18; xxiii. 13; 1 Chronicles xi. 11-14.

THE time had come for God to bring David out into public life. The broken power of the Philistines rallied again. The Israelites anticipated their ascent. The king and the army met them well down the ravine towards their own country. There the two armies encamped again face to face, as at Michmash a few years before, the Hebrews on the south side, the Philistines on the north side, and the valley between. This time the valley is not a gorge of steep and broken rocks, but a little, fertile plain, still partly covered with fields of grain, and where still grows the terebinth-tree, from which comes the name "Valley of *Elah*," or "Valley of *Terebinth*." On the opposite hills were the tents of the armies. Remembering, perhaps, the achievements of Jonathan at Michmash, the Philistines put forth a challenge to personal combat, and lay the wager of victory on the single fight. The challenge is thundered forth with such audacity and boastful defiance that Saul and his army are abashed. The champion is a giant. His stature is a tremendous challenge to Saul personally. He is from a family of giants, of whom there are at least a father and five sons. His powerful body, towering to ten feet three and a half inches,* bearing his ponderous coat of brazen mail, takes every soldier's mind back to the Sons of Anak—the giants conquered by Joshua. Here before them the soldiers see a remnant of those huge and terrible men whom the Moabites called Emim; the Edomites, Horim; the Ammonites, Zuzim, or Zamzummim; and the Hebrews, Anakim;† and who were all, no doubt, clans of the tribe of "the Rephaim," or "the Giants," the fragments of which still dwell in the land.

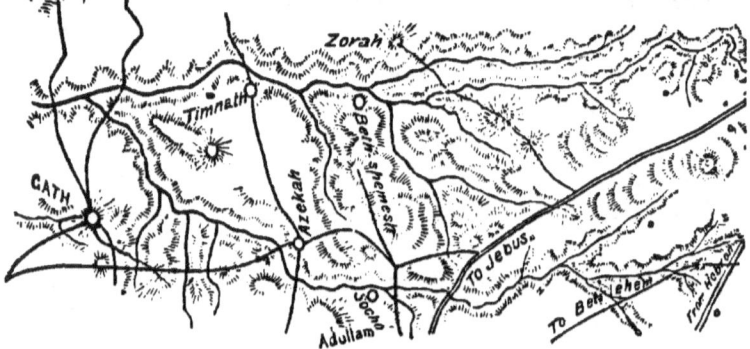

The power of these associations must have affected the soldiers' minds fully as much as Goliah's fierce look and challenge. And as every morning and even-

---

* Six cubits and a span, reckoning the cubit at nineteen inches, and the span at half a cubit, make ten feet three and a half inches. There are other instances on record of men of similar height in different nations. "Pliny says that in the time of Claudius Cæsar there was an Arab named Gabbaras nearly ten feet high, and that even he was not so tall as Pusio and

---

† The same termination of these names in *im* signifies the plural number, like cherub*im* and seraph*im*. Anakim is, sons or children of Anak.

ing the giant rent the air with his insolent shouts, the Hebrews' fear grew into dismay. King Saul offered great riches to the man who would kill him, but no one ventured. He offered to make the man his son-in-law, but no one dared. He offered besides to make his father's family perpetually free, but no one stirred. "Give me a man to fight," was his insolent challenge. The defiance was flung in his face a month, for forty days, as the terrible monster descended into the arena between the two armies; and not a man, neither Jonathan nor Abner, nor the fierce warriors of Bethlehem, among whom were Eliab, and Abinadab, and Shammah, nor the King himself, took his life in his hand to meet the foe. God was preparing to introduce his king!

Jesse, now an old man, twelve miles off at Bethlehem, east from Elah, keeps his eye upon the army. Rumors of the champion and the challenge have no doubt come up to the city-gates. At length, he directs David to go down for the news. He loads him with a bushel of roasted wheat* and ten bread-cakes for his three brothers, and

---

Secundilla in the reign of Augustus, whose bodies were preserved. Josephus tells us that, among other hostages, Artabanus sent to Tiberius a certain Eleazar, 'a *Jew*, surnamed 'the Giant,' seven cubits in height."—*Farrar* in Smith's "Dictionary of the Bible." "One of the King of Prussia's gigantic guards, a *Swede*, measured eight feet and a half; and a yeoman of the Duke John Frederick, at Brunswick, Hanover"—an Englishman —"was of the same height. Several *Irishmen*, measuring from seven to eight feet and upwards, have been exhibited in this country. The most celebrated was Charles Byrne, who died in 1783, at the age of twenty-two, and measured eight feet four inches. His skeleton in the museum of the College of Surgeons in London is eight feet in length."—*English Encyclopædia.* The average height of the Patagonians is from six and a half to seven feet.

* The reapers and gleaners "offered us some of their parched

with slices of milk-curds for the colonel of their regiment, and bids him bring back a token of how they are. David's heart had been stirred, no doubt, already with the impious affront to God and to the nation, of which his quick ear must have heard, for it had been continued a whole month, only twelve miles away. And his temper does not cool on the way down as he thinks of it — reflecting, perhaps, on Samson's fights with the Philistines just beyond Elah at Timnath, and on the cruel crimes of these heathen monsters from the days of Adoni-zedek. As he comes up to the baggage-circle, which formed, as in Arab settlements, a rude defence around the camp, he hears the well-known war-cry. He leaves his bag of wheat with the baggage-master, and hastens forward to see the array and the battle. As he salutes his brothers, the shield-bearer and the giant appear in the arena below. The sound of Goliath's voice nerves him like the growl of a bear or the roar of a lion. "No one to take the king's offer! Defy the living God!" are the outbursts of his patriotic and holy passion. And when Eliab kindles at the verdant hardihood of his stripling brother, fresh from sheep-leading, his spirit is the more aroused. "Is there not a cause for speaking? No one to fight this uncircumcised Philistine?" he says, as he turns from one to another. His undaunted speech creates a commotion. Word comes to Saul. The king sends for him. And to the king he says, "Let no man's heart fail; thy

---

corn. In the season of harvest, the grains of wheat, not yet fully dry and hard, are roasted in a pan or an iron plate, and constitute a very palatable article of food. This is eaten along with bread, or instead of it. Indeed, the use of it is so common at this season among the laboring classes that this parched wheat is sold in the markets; and it was among our list of articles to be purchased at Hebron for our further journey to Wady Musa.' —*Dr. Robinson, on the road from Gaza towards Elah*, vol. ii. 50.

servant will go and fight this Philistine." He tells the story of the lion and the bear, and that it is not himself but *God* who will fight. The armor of Saul he puts aside. His staff, and his sling, and five smooth stones from the brook are his weapons, as he advances into the arena, in the sight of the double audience of spectators. With rage and disdain, and curses by his gods, Goliath greets the little champion, so much smaller than even Saul, whom he would have met, so much more greedy of death than Saul dared to be. In the name of the living God, in behalf of the wide earth—little knew he how wide his words would ring—David accepts the challenge. His soul swells with holy fire. He runs to meet the swearing, swaggering foe. Quick as a thought, he has a pebble in his sling. His strenuous arm and body let fly the stone, with every muscle rushing to the work. Look! he staggers! See! the giant falls on his face. The coming general and king knows how to follow up a victory. He runs. The armor-bearer flees. He mounts the stunned body. He pulls out the sword from the huge sheath. The blood runs from the vulnerable neck. And amid the wild shouting, the thunder-struck panic, the rush down the valley, the cry for pursuit, he brings off Goliath's head and armor.

The rout is complete. The slain line the way to the very gates of Gath and Ekron. The Philistines are shut up on their own plain within their own walls, while the Hebrews leisurely plunder their slaughtered and their tents.

The king was in amazement when he looked at that youth hastening alone out upon the plain. He had been accustomed to mark men of valor and of daring. "Abner, *whose* son is this youth?"* Although he has known him

---

* The two descriptions of Saul's acquaintance with David in chapter xvi. 14-23 and in chapter xvii. 12-31, 55-58, have been

as a young man, pleasing in song and harp and arts of address, here are higher and heroic qualities worthy of definite enquiries. But the king's man of war has taken no pains to enquire about a charmer of evil spirits. "*Enquire!*" said the king.

As the army are gathering the spoil, Abner seeks out David and brings him to the royal tent, the giant's head in his hand. There is in him none of the diffidence of

---

supposed to be a disagreement or a contradiction. One statement is that David was beloved by Saul and therefore wellknown, and was made his armor-bearer before the battle of Elah. The other implies, it is said, that Saul did not know David, and that he had no connection with the king's army before that battle. Horsley transposes the passages. And the Vatican MS. rejects chapter xvii. 12-31, 55-58, as spurious. But is there any necessary contradiction? According to the interpretation which we have given above, Saul in the intervals of his frenzy assented to his courtiers' or servants' advice to seek for a skilled musician.

That being settled, a certain young musician was recommended without special note of who he was or where he came from. He said, "Send for him." Observe that, in the sixteenth chapter, *Saul* does not once *speak Jesse's* name. *The writer of the book of Samuel*, knowing the facts, says it was Jesse to whom he sent. Saul knows that the *young man's name* who is recommended is David. And so far as the record reveals Saul's mind or Saul's words to us, the thought and message may have been, "Tell the young man's father, 'Send me David, thy son, that is with the sheep.'" Then, when Saul saw David and was pleased with him, he assigned to him the office of armorbearer—words which may mean keeper of his wardrobe or apartments, as much as bearer of his armor. At any rate, if he was armor-bearer, so far as the history goes, David had departed home before any battle or campaign occurred.

The seventeenth chapter says particularly (verse 15), "David went and *returned from Saul* to feed his father's sheep at Bethlehem." The thirty-third verse as much implies previous acquaintance with David as lack of acquaintance. When David's

Saul when he hid among the stuff at his anointing, but a divine courage and a modest but heroic self-reliance in his bearing. Jonathan, glowing with admiration—none but the brave can admire the brave—looks on. "Whose son art thou, thou young man?" Did ever psalm syllable itself more sweetly than the beautiful and modest answer: "I am the son of thy servant Jesse the Bethlehemite"? Did ever lips of grace and a warrior's arm blend in spoken

sublime bravery impressed Saul and he saw his conspicuous part before the whole nation, his interest in David was wholly changed. It was at once intense and particular. If he had known nothing of Jesse before, his question was, "Abner, whose *son* is this youth?" If he *had* known something of Jesse, the question may have been, "*Whose* son is this youth?" And this question is capable of two constructions: the one, "*Whose* son did I understand this youth is?" the other, "Is *this* young man really the son of Jesse of Bethlehem? Enquire particularly." If he knew *nothing* of Jesse, then Saul said to David, "Whose *son* art thou, thou young man?" If he *had* known Jesse to be his father, he may have said with a profound and particular intensity, a king's interest bounding in the thought, "*Whose* son art thou, thou young man?"

If we interpret it in this way, the order of the history is natural. The interpretation is easily admissible, and relieves the necessity of transposition or erasure—too dangerous a resort even to relieve a perplexity, when three thousand years have intervened since the events transpired.

It may be said besides, that on the first occasion Saul was half, or wholly out of his mind, but on the second occasion quite sober.

Thomson says: "It is a fact that lads of this country, particularly of the higher classes, are often very fair, full-faced and handsome until about fourteen years of age, but during the next two or three years a surprising change takes place. David had become a shepherd after leaving the king's palace, an occupation which, of all others, would most rapidly change his fair complexion into a dirty bronze. He appeared in his shepherd's attire, not in the gay dress of a courtier."

and mute eloquence, as when Goliath's head and David's words addressed the stalwart Saul?

Jonathan confessed to himself his exploit at Michmash, surpassed in courage, piety, and completeness. He was absorbed in admiration. No wonder that from that day he loved David as his own soul. Yet it *is* a wonder. For Jonathan was the prince-royal; and he was mature enough to know what such a victory in the eyes of all the kingdom foretokened.

King Saul at once identified David with his court, and sent word to Jesse.

Thirteenth Sunday.

AN EVIL EYE.

LESSON.
1 Samuel xviii., xix. 1-17.

WE now enter upon a new and distinct period of David's life. We can define the period with tolerable exactness. The word "youth" or "young man," describing David at the battle of Elah, includes the time of life from the end of childhood up to the marriageable age—from about eight or ten to about twenty years of age. It is applied to Joseph when he was at least eighteen years old, (Genesis xxxvii. 2 ; xli. 12), and to the "young man" Absalom after he led the rebellion against his father, to young Amalekites who were mounted warriors, and to the young prophet who anointed Jehu king. The general meaning seems to be a young man pretty well grown. We may safely assume that David was now about twenty years of age, possibly eighteen or nineteen, but more likely from twenty to twenty-two years old. We know that he was thirty years old when he was publicly anointed king. We have therefore a pretty well-defined period from eight to ten years during which his persecutions by King Saul took place. We have already assumed that Saul is now about fifty years of age, and has been king ten years or more ; and that Jonathan was six or eight years older than David, that is, from twenty-six to thirty years old. For convenience, it will be well to lay up this period of persecution in the memory as a round ten years.

After the victory, King Saul at once promoted David. He set him over his men of war. He was probably next in rank or equal in rank to Abner, who, though Saul's uncle, was probably no older and may have been younger than Saul, for he is vigorous for years after Saul's death, and seems but a companion-in-age to Joab. The relief from his dread enemies and the universal joy at the victory were too great for Saul on the instant to become suspicious of the mere youth who had delivered the nation. But by the time the short campaign was over and the triumphant army came home, the people from every city and village poured forth. We must remember that the thickly strewn ruins show a dense population. There has been no such victory since the days of Samson! Everything produces excitement and enthusiasm. Dismay has been turned to triumph. Defiance of God has been avenged. Taunts of the people's cowardice have been answered by heroic bravery. David has done it!—with a sling and stone!—a mere, ruddy, rosy boy! The victory is so complete. Ekron and Gath shut fast!

The welkin rang with shouts of relief and joy. The women poured out from their seclusion. The tide of rejoicing burst all bounds of common restraint. With tabrets, that is, tambourines, and "cymbals," Josephus says, and stringed instruments (rude guitars), they poured along, singing and dancing, to meet the conquerors as they mount up towards Gibeah. They sing in responses. Josephus has it: "The wives said, 'Saul has slain his thousands!' The virgins replied, 'And David his ten thousands!'" Every demonstration of tumultuous joy mingles in the welcome.

But all this gave a terrible start to Saul. Instead of saying to himself, like a secure and generous monarch, "The victor is worthy of his praise; let him have his day of glory, and then let him take his place. How can the people feel otherwise toward the brave little man?" he thought he saw his royal fortune changing. "They put David in their minds higher than myself! And what can he have more but the kingdom?" The haunting thoughts must come again : "*Thy kingdom shall not continue! The Lord hath rejected thee! A neighbor of thine, that is better than thou! Bethlehem? the son of Jesse?*" "And Saul eyed David from that day forward." His gloom and desperation against the decree of God returned. The demoniac spirit was upon him. He would see that no upstart should take the throne from *his* house!

David was now another man to the gloomy king than a mere charmer with music. Saul's self-will was now so far from being pleased with David's voice and skill that every tone roused his hate and will. His very acts of address would win the people. Twice he let fly his spear at him to nail him to the wall. Yet Saul was the coward. *God* was with David, and Saul knew it. God had left *him*, and he knew it. He bethought of another way to dispose of David—no uncommon way with kings to rid themselves of able and ambitious aspirants. He would give him a command which would peril his life. He ordered him, therefore, from the military court to the command of a thousand—a regiment. He played false with him with an offer to make him a member of the royal house by marriage. He offered him his daughter if he would fight valiantly the Lord's battles against the Philistines; and, when the time for the marriage came, he had given Merab to Adriel. When he saw that David had no strong ambition to be a member of his royal house, he made use of the love of Michal for David to take David's life. He bade his attendants represent to David the love of Michal for him, and his own love for him, and the love of all his court for him —to induce him to become his son-in-law. Openly and outwardly, it would seem as if the king saw the wisdom of a royal alliance with the coming king. When the ingenious David—possibly thinking that this was his motive—said that he was poor and could bring no dowry, he said, "A hundred Philistines shall be counted for dowry." When by this the martial ardor and pious valor of David were stirred against the doomed criminals of God's kingdom, and he brought the proof of *two* hundred slain Philistines as a dowry for his daughter, and Saul saw that God had saved him from his own "snare"—when Michal became his wife and a house was made theirs, and the king saw that it was a true and loving marriage, and now knew that, however the succession might go, it was certain that it would be in his own family, he yet turned the more fiercely against David. A *male* descent is, to be sure, the rule in all oriental kingdoms, but it is evident that the feeling in Saul was now that of a narrow and bitter envy. He grew every day more afraid and more jealous of the man whom God had blessed. David's discretion, his speech, his bravery in the very midst of all this, were winning the people and making him prominent in the land.

It is a sufficient proof of the guilty stupidity and mad desperation of Saul's mind that the members of his family became David's friends. Michal admired and loved David before he made love to her. Jonathan seems to have understood the real situation from the first. God had decreed that himself should not be king. To that decree he bowed, and in pious obedience waited for the new appointment. The graces and abilities of David challenged the love of his own heroic nature. Extraordinary gifts of God were on him. He evidently saw in him the "neighbor" to whom the throne belonged by divine bestowal. He sought a covenant with David, and made it. The nature of the covenant we may infer from the symbolic acts with which Jonathan sealed it. He took off his robe, and put it on David. He gave him his own prince's garments, girding him with his girdle and arming him with his sword and bow. If any prince-royal now should do the like to his friend in circumstances like these, there would be only one inference for us. These acts must signify that he understood that David stood in his own place as successor to the throne. Perhaps by this symbolic language—a language common in the poetic East—he delicately signified to David that his friendship fully comprehended the fact of his becoming king. Like an older brother to a younger, he advised David to keep out of Saul's way. In David's absence he intercedes with Saul for him. He rehearsed the wonderful victory over Goliath, and magnified the Lord's mighty salvation by David's daring. He kept David informed of Saul's temper towards him. And he brought him back again, the king mollified, and David glad for Jonathan's sake.

An equal test of Michal's devotion came. David came back victorious from another rout of the Philistines; and the "evil spirit" glared again in the king's jealous eye. As David played with his hand, the king lifted his huge form and hurled his spear to crush the young warrior. The power exerted set the spear fast in the wall; but David escaped to his own house. Now came Michal's turn. Will her love for her father or her devotion to her brother as the royal successor, or her love for David, prevail? Her evasions and falsehoods and artifices to save David are perfectly characteristic of oriental royal life, such a mixture is there of duplicity in time of temptation, of ambition, of wit, and of affection. Perhaps, after all, since David is hers, she would rather her husband than her brother would be king. And she is true to David, and her father is too willing to believe her when she says, "He said to me, Let me go: why make me kill you?"

And thus the malice of an evil eye and the love of ripening friendship grew on during that first year at Gibeah!

Fourteenth Sunday.

DAVID'S FIRST PSALMS.

LESSON.

1 Samuel xix. 11-24; xx; Psalms xi. lix. (see titles.)

THE eight or ten years of David's persecution by King Saul may be divided into three parts: the first, one year or thereabout at Gibeah, when Saul's jealousy was inflamed; the second, the period of his flight, comprising about six or eight years, during which Saul kept up his pursuit; the third, the year or so when he went over to the Philistines to save his life. We have already watched the growing jealousy of the evil eye. We now come to the flight and persecution, during which the persecuted David, bruised and mellowed by providential afflictions, sang many a psalm of praise and thanks to God for marvellous protection and deliverance. *Some* of these psalms —we cannot suppose them to be all—we now have, sublime and beautiful in the pious trust of a high-tossed and deeply troubled soul.

After David's flight from Michal's window, to whom should he go, in the heavy troubles which began to press down his young spirit, but to the aged prophet and Seer. We suppose Ramah to have been not more than a mile or a mile and a half north from Gibeah." * Samuel takes him to "Naioth." Where was "Naioth in Ramah," to which David and Samuel went together?

---

* See map on page 51.

The word "Naioth" means "habitations," and has long been interpreted as meaning the *dwellings* of a school of prophets over which Samuel was "father" or "master." There is no difference of opinion now in respect to this. Elijah afterwards had such a school at Gilgal and Jericho.* Music and sacred minstrelsy were practised and no doubt taught, as well as the civil, ceremonial, and spiritual law and its interpretation. The "company of prophets" that met Saul after he was privately anointed came down "from the high place, with a psaltery and a tabret and a pipe before them" as they prophesied. Here at "Naioth in Ramah," that is Naioth at or near Ramah, was such a company, and Samuel "appointed" over them. Here these younger prophets prophesied.† Into their company David now came, with the aged "father" of the school. Here, perhaps, he indited the "good matter" of a psalm, the first of his own, preserved for the church, as we shall soon see—the gifts of music and of song uniting with the divine inspiration of his poetic genius. To this place, not two miles away, if our conjecture be right, the king sent over his messengers when he heard that David had fled thither from Michal's house. God has his defence for his servant! Once, twice, three times he pours upon the king's messengers the prophetic spirit, so that while they come to take David they are put into sympathy with the prophets. Saul himself comes, first to Sechu—on the way to Ramah, we suppose—where was "a great well," asking for *Samuel* and David! and then to Ramah, then to the prophets' house. His attendants, of course, accompany him. He too is disarmed of curses and of weapons, like Balak and Balaam, by the compelling prophetic gift, until

---

* See 2 Kings ii. 3, 5, 7.

† Compare these prophetic gifts with the prophetic gifts of the New Testament in 1 Corinthians xii. and xiv.

the amazed people ask again, as they did years before, "Is Saul also among the prophets?"

In the midst of such elevating influences as these, we may find the answer to the question: When were the first psalms of David written? A nature so poetical as his must have found expression at an early age. The "youth," so independent and resolute in defence of his flock and in attack of the nation's enemies, could hardly have been less independent and vigorous in the use of his undoubted poetic abilities. It was his cunning in playing and his prudence in speech which brought him the first invitation to the king's court. Many a fragmentary strain and hymn must then have floated for ever away with the zephyr upon which they were breathed. The anointment also to a lofty career appointed by God, must have defined more clearly and aroused more fully every faculty of mind and soul. Many a spiritual song, sung only to the rocks and to the sheep, was laid up in the associations of his poetic mind, to be drawn forth again by future events and occasions.

We are not at loss, however, for some of his first *public* hymns of praise to God; or, perhaps, rather for some of his first hymns which afterward were adopted into public use.

Among the seventy or eighty psalms of David's composition in the book of Psalms, are three which *may* be referred to his early life. One of the three was certainly written or substantially composed just at the time of his life at which we have now arrived. Two of the three are conjectured to have been written during his shepherd-life; and the third to have originated just before his flight from Saul.

It will be impossible for us, as we go on, to fix *certainly* the *precise* place of every psalm in the life of David; but it will be a real service to ourselves if we can locate some of them with *tolerable* exactness.

Let us see whether these three psalms belong to this early period of David's life.

First, let us look at the psalm which, most of all, is associated with the thoughts and feelings of his shepherd-life :

"The Lord is my shepherd, I shall not want," etc.
—*See the Twenty-third Psalm.*

This exquisite psalm is beautifully appropriate to David's shepherd-life. It seems like the spontaneous and natural outflow of such a period. There is nothing in it too mature for that early time; for poets in all ages have commenced in youth to express mature thought in musical cadence. And if it should be said that psalms for the public worship of the universal church were *inspired*, and surely, therefore, no person would have been permitted to compose them until he had reached the priestly age, there is a twofold answer: first, that from the time of Samuel's private anoinment at Bethlehem, "the Spirit of God came upon David from that day forward;" and secondly, that the titles of some of his psalms show that they were composed before he became king at the priestly age. One was composed "when the Ziphim came and said to Saul, 'Doth not David hide himself with us?'" (liv.); another, after Doeg came and told Saul that David had been to Ahimelech's house (lii.); another, "when he fled from Saul in a cave" (lvii.); and another, "when the Philistines took him in Gath" (lvi.); all of which events happened before he reached the mature and priestly and kingly age of thirty years.

Beautiful, however, as it may be to associate the *composition* of the Twenty-third Psalm with David's shepherd-life, and to think of it as the first sparkling spring from which the deep, broad river of his psalmody flowed, there are one or two expressions which forbid us to locate it there.

It would hardly have been natural for him at that early day to say, "I will dwell in the *house* of the Lord for ever," while the tabernacle was at Nob and the ark at Kirjoth-Jearim and the worship scattered and broken. And we cannot think that he would have sung in calm and happy triumph, "Thou preparest a *table* before me in the presence of mine *enemies*," when the only enemies which he had yet encountered were the lion and the bear. When, however, he had established the worship in Jerusalem years afterward, and had been through the terrible flights and fights into which he was forced by Saul, and God had many times spread his table when Philistines and Amalekites would have snatched away his life, then he could gather up the happy and fearful memories of the sheepfolds and hiding-places about Bethlehem and Judah, and write in the abundant calm of his tranquil soul:

> "Thou preparest a table before me
> In the presence of mine enemies;
> Thou anointest my head with oil.
> My cup runneth over.
> Surely goodness and mercy shall follow me all the days of my life.
> And I shall dwell in the house of the Lord for ever."

We prefer, therefore, to dismiss the Twenty-third Psalm to a later period of his kingly life, when the brooks and fields and dark ravines and lurking-places of Bethlehem and Judah gave his memory happy imagery for his sweet song of repose on God.

The Eleventh Psalm is a hymn of confidence in God, when timid and dejected friends urged David to flee. It has been supposed to spring from Saul's or Absalom's first persecutions, when David's friends represented his affairs as desperate. If we connect it with one of these persecutions, we see in it an expression of sublime confidence in God as a sure Defender of the righteous and a sure Punisher of the wicked. Although we cannot be *sure* that it was written then, yet we may be sure that we do not magnify too much the spirit of trust in God which David already showed, by locating this psalm just at this point in his life. We must recall the short history of David at Saul's house. During that short time, acquaintances and friends have increased around him. They remembered his musical charms over Saul at the first. They saw his valor and abilities as a champion at Elah, and they saw Saul's estimate of them. They detected the king's evil eye. Even the people of Gibeah, not intimate with the internal house of the king, became aware of it. The public attention which David received in the first rejoicing; the promotion with which he had been honored; his station afterward nearer the people, at the head of his own regiment; his bearing and wise behavior "as he went out and came in before the people"—which probably signifies a greater familiarity with them than the haughty Saul had shown—and for which "all Israel and Judah loved him;" the story of his betrothal to Merab, and of his betrayal by Saul; and of his marriage to Michal, and the dangers by which he won her dowry—all these created a quick and growing personal interest in him, and brought many persons into personal relations with him. The increasing jealousy and deepening malice of the king, his snares and strategems to take David's life, his directions to his servants and to Jonathan to kill David, alarmed and terrified those who loved the young man. Even Jonathan told him to hide himself in a secret place; and we can imagine what the advice of more timid souls would be. Flight they thought the only safety, and that quickly. But in David's heart was a profound security, both in respect to himself and in respect to God's sovereign care over kingly haters and ungodly conspirators against his divine plans, when he sang in reply to these timid counsellors:

> " In the Lord, do I put my trust. Why say ye to me,
> ' Flee like a bird to your mountain ;
> For, lo ! the wicked bend their bow,
> They make ready their arrows on the string,
> To shoot in secret at the upright in heart.
> If the pillars be broken down,
> What can the righteous do ' ?

> " The Lord is in his holy palace :
> The Lord's throne is in heaven :
> His eyes behold, his eyelids prove the children of men.
> The Lord trieth the righteous ;
> But the wicked and the lover of violence his soul hateth.
> Upon the wicked he will rain lightning.
> Fire and brimstone and a burning wind shall be the portion of their cup.
> For the Lord is righteous ; he loveth righteousness ;
> The upright shall see his face."—*Noyes's Translation.*

If this was the first of David's psalms which was afterward adopted into public use in the tabernacle service, David's spirit of pious confidence begins to do its important work at the very time that he becomes a public and noted man. Persecution makes conspicuous both the man and his piety; and Saul's malice was made to do God's beautiful will.

But as we cannot be sure that this psalm was written just at this time, we may take another psalm which does stand at the very extrance of his public career. The title of the *Fifty-ninth* Psalm gives us a hymn composed by David "when Saul sent and they watched the house to kill him." In this psalm is the same sublime and pious confidence which David expresses in the Eleventh. The thoughts are thoughts of trust in God, of personal innocence, of certain victory over enemies, of necessary justice upon malicious and obdurate foes. The king's messengers came at night ; they took up their watch outside the door ; they must have been of Saul's own temper, for Michal saw that they were in earnest ; perhaps they were turbulent and insolent, as such messengers in the East sometimes are, as they pace the streets, boasting of their prey ;

the morning light—curses upon him!—would put him in their power. "Through a window"—it may be within the rough sound of their voices and oaths—"Michal let him down, and he went and fled, and escaped," with that solemn feeling in his heart which was already forming into words as he took his way to Ramah:

" Deliver me from my enemies, O my God!
　Defend me from them that rise up against me!
　Deliver me from the doers of iniquity,
　And save me from men of blood!
　For lo! they lie in wait for my life:
　The mighty are gathered together against me,
　Without any offence or fault of mine, O Jehovah!
　Without any offence of mine, they run and prepare themselves.
　Awake to help me and behold!

" Do thou, O Jehovah, God of hosts, God of Israel,
　Awake to punish all the nations!
　Show no mercy to any wicked transgressors!
　Let them return at evening;
　Let them howl like dogs,
　And go round about the city!

" Behold! with their mouths they belch out malice:
　Swords are upon their lips,
　'For who,' say they, 'will hear?'
　Yet thou, O Lord! wilt laugh at them.
　Thou wilt hold all the nations in derision!
　O my strength, to thee will I look!
　For God is my defence.
　My merciful God will come to my aid:
　God will let me look with joy upon my enemies.

" Slay them not, lest my people forget.
　Scatter them by thy power, and cast them down,
　O Lord, our shield!
　All the words of their lips are sin.
　Let them be overtaken in their pride,
　For the curses and the falsehoods which they utter!
　Consume them in thy wrath: consume them that they be no more,
　That they may know that God ruleth in Jacob,
　Even to the ends of the earth!
　Let them return at evening;
　Let them howl like dogs:
　Let them wander about for food,
　When they have passed the night unsatisfied.

> "But I will sing of thy power:
> Yea, in the morning will I sing aloud of thy mercy;
> For thou hast been my defence,
> My refuge in the day of my distress.
> To thee, O my Strength! will I sing;
> For God is my defence: a God of mercy to me."—*Noyes's Translation.*

It is highly confirmatory of the composition of this psalm at that time that David went immediately to "Naioth" in Ramah. It was the next morning or the next day, there can be no doubt, that he found the way to Ramah to Samuel; and perhaps it was on the same day, while the king was wrangling with his daughter over the sick image and bolster in the bed, Samuel and David together went to Naioth. There in the midst of the prophets and the inspired and prophetic gifts of that school, where soon afterward the Spirit of God compelled even Saul's messengers and Saul himself to prophesy, nothing is more appropriate than to suppose that David also was unusually inspired. The thoughts which he had had the night before in Gibeah and when he fled over the hill to Ramah, when God was his profound support, may have been put then into verse. And when the tabernacle service was fully reformed by him after Jerusalem was taken, the psalm may have been retouched by the kingly poet, and delivered to the chief musician of the tabernacle-choir, with directions to sing to the tune of "Do not Destroy," or "Al-taschith;" and entitled like others a "Golden psalm," or "Michtam"?

Who can tell but that from the young prophets then in the school at Ramâh came Asaph, and Heman, and Ethan, and Jeduthun, and the sons of Korah—one, or some, or all of them?

Fifteenth Sunday.

DECEPTION AND FALSEHOOD.

LESSON.

1 Samuel xxi.; Matthew xii. 3, 4; Mark ii. 25, 26; Luke vi. 3, 4: Psalm xxxiv.

WHEN David left Jonathan, he went to Nob, a "city of the priests," where Ahimelech was high-priest. Four things seem to show that the tabernacle was now at Nob. The first is that Ahimelech wore the ephod, for he had it there. The ephod was one of the most sacred vestments of the high-priest, covering the body from the shoulders to the waist, and supporting the breast-plate with its twelve stones, with the blue-bordered "*robe* of the ephod" under it next to the white tesselated shirt or tunic. "The ephod" sometimes means *all* the upper dress of the high-priest—that is, the ephod, the blue robe of the ephod, the tunic, and the breast-plate, which were, in fact, the distinctive dress of the high-priest, the mitre only excepted. The second thing is that there were at Nob at least eighty-five priests who wore "the *linen* ephod," and who were held in reverence by the people, as is shown by the fact that Saul's own soldiers held them in reverence. The third thing is that the table of shewbread was at Nob. And the fourth thing, that the shewbread was "before the Lord." These things seem to show conclusively that the tabernacle was at Nob, the ark itself remaining at Kirjath-jearim till several years after David became king.

Where, now, was Nob? It is quite certain that it was near

Jebus, and on the north of it, but no historian or traveller at present can tell us where. It has been located about a mile north or north-east from Jebus, somewhere on the range of Mount Olivet, as that range sweeps around to the north; but the most probable supposition now is that Mizpeh and Nob were the *same place*, four miles north-west of Jebus.* From Nob you could see Jebus; for at Nob, in later days, the Assyrian shakes his hand at Jerusalem.† It must have been from three to four miles from Ramah to Nob; and when David came, with some young men with him, he was weary and hungry. When the high-priest saw that David and his party were without any other officer of Saul's court, observing, no doubt, too, their fatigue and haste, he was afraid. He knew too well what was the general posture of affairs over at Gibeah. It was his duty to know what was the situation of the government. He knew, therefore, what Saul's attitude was towards David; and he feared lest David would involve him in the alleged treason against the king. "Why art thou alone, and no man with thee?" he demanded. David boldly told him that he had come on the king's business. It was a secret errand; and the high-priest must give him food. On the

---

* Lieutenant Conder, of the English Palestine Exploration Expedition, has recently assigned strong reasons for the identity of these two places. Mizpeh means a watch-tower, Nob a high place. The two names never occur in one passage. Both are described in a like manner as places of military and religious importance, near Ramah and Gibeon. One name might easily have been applied at one time, and another at another. The Hebrew word *Nob* is simply *N'b* with the vowel, and may easily have become transmuted into the present Arabic Neby, applied to the high lookout mountain, *Neby-Samuel* (*the Prophet Samuel*), from which Jerusalem is visible, and which is supposed to be Mizpeh. The two names are therefore attached to the same place on the maps on pages 16 and 51.

† Isaiah x. 32

assurance that they were all ceremonially pure, the priest gave them the only bread which he had—the hallowed bread which had been removed from the shew-table, and which no one but the priest could lawfully eat—an act which the Jews afterwards so justified that our Lord could appeal to it confidently as an argument for the proper observance of the Sabbath.

But what shall we say of David's representation to Ahimelech? Was that a bold falsehood—that he was on the king's business? Was there some way in which he justified his representation to his conscience and to God? We can conceive that David might have said to himself: "It is clearly God's design that I shall be king. I command myself on this business, and say, Let no man know where we go. I appoint my servants to places as I please. It is true. Independent of Saul, I now act in God's name as king." Or we can conceive that David might have said, "God is king according to the old government. He has rejected Saul. What I have done, I have done for him. And he hath commanded me here and onwards; and even his sacred bread is for my sustenance." But whatever may have been his specious reasoning—even if such reasoning might have run quick through a fertile brain —David did deceive Ahimelech—a deception which cost the high-priest his life. We must not justify David in a falsehood, even where he falsified to save his own life, particularly when to save himself he brought death on another person. It is more probable that the plain truth is, that under the pressure of great danger he forgot the God in whom he had trusted, and spoke falsely. If he was innocent at heart and God could approve of it, he approved. If he was guilty of sin, he repented of it, and God approved of his repentance; for soon after, as we shall see, he composed another psalm which took its place in the inspired psalmody.

David, however, carried out the deception. "Have you weapons here," he said, "spear or sword? The king's business requires haste, and I came without my own." "The sword of Goliath, whom you slew in the valley of Elah, lies, wrapped up, behind the priests' robes —the trophy of the Lord's triumph."

David grasps at any hope of defence. No time is to be lost. The stripling for whom Saul's armor was too heavy, now is eager for Goliath's sword. "There is none like that; give it me." But before he hastened away, he noticed there, looking on, one of Saul's officers, the chief keeper of the king's flocks, detained at the tabernacle by some vow or ceremonial purification—an Edomite, probably a proselyte—from whom David feared mischief might arise.

Was it now this very sword which turned David's thoughts to Gath, where Goliath lived? Saul was on his track, he was sure. Where could he go to get out of his power? Not to Bethlehem, to involve that city in revolt against the king, and his family in destruction. A bold and brave man, Goliath's sword in hand, he took his way to Goliath's city. Down the hills he went, he and his trusty few, past the strong walls of Jebus and its defiant people, past the Zorah and Timnath of Samson, past the valley of Elah, not doubting that the God that delivered Samson from Gaza could deliver him from King Achish and the walls of Gath. It may be, that he thought he would "pass for one of the many Hebrew fugitives who for one cause or another were continually falling away to the Philistines." Perhaps he offered himself as a servant or a minstrel at the court of Achish. And he laid away among the rocks perhaps, or gave to one of his friends Goliath's sword, until he should know what to do.

But now it was David's time to fear. He had in him the guilty "conscience which makes cowards of us all."

He must have thought of Doeg looking on at Nob; of the danger to which he had exposed the high-priest. The consciousness of his falsehood at the very time when he took the sacred bread for his life, took away his courage, as Samson was shorn of his strength when he forsook God. The servants of King Achish suspected who he was. They had either seen him in one of his fights against their people, or they detected him from his bearing or the communications of his party. When they said, "Is not this David, the king of the land"—mark their version of the contest, "the king of the land"; the story which had gone abroad and had come down to them—"did they not sing in their dances, saying Saul hath slain his thousands and David his ten thousands?" David saw their suspicions, and he was afraid. But his quick wit saved him. If it was David, it should be David befooled and mad! And so he diverted their suspicion, and behaved so much like a fool that the king was vexed with his servants for bringing him in. "Ye see the man is mad. Do I need a mad man? Why do you bring him to my house?" And so glad enough he got away from the city.

After he had escaped, however, and had once had time to reflect upon his dangers at Gibeah, at Ramah, at Naioth, when with Jonathan, and while waiting for three days rest at Nob, and at Gath, when he had had time to think upon his own sins under the pressure of terror, and upon the misery in which he was "*sore afraid*" of King Achish, and had received the pardon given to the contrite spirit; he gave his grateful acknowledgment of God's goodness, in the form of

A PSALM OF DAVID,
When he feigned himself mad before King Achish,* who drove him away, and he departed.

    I will bless Jehovah at all times;
    His praise shall continually be in my mouth.

---

* Ahimelech, in the English version, is by some writers considered a corruption for Aki(sh)-melech, *i. e.*, Achish-king. (See the margin in the English version.)

In the Lord doth my soul boast,
Let the afflicted hear and rejoice!

*　　　*　　　*　　　*　　　*　　　*

I sought the Lord, and He heard me,
And delivered me from all my fears.

*　　　*　　　*　　　*　　　*　　　*

The angels of the Lord encamp around those who fear Him,
And deliver them.

*　　　*　　　*　　　*　　　*　　　*

The righteous cry and the Lord heareth,
And delivereth them from all their troubles.
The Lord is near to them that are of a broken heart,
And heareth such as are of a contrite spirit.
Great are the afflictions of the righteous,
But the Lord delivereth him from them all;
He guardeth all his bones;
Not one of them is broken, etc.

Thirty-fourth Psalm; Noyes's Translation.

Sixteenth Sunday.

OUTLAWS AND CAVES.

LESSON.

1 Samuel xxii. 1-4; 2 Samuel xxiii. 13-19; 1 Chronicles xi. 15-21; Psalm lvi.

BOTH Gath and Adullam are places not certainly known in our day. But they were both in "the low country," for Adullam is one of the cities of the low country in the time of Joshua,*, and Gath and Adullam are mentioned together as "fenced cities" which King Rehoboam, Solomon's son, built, that is, rebuilt. Modern travellers, however, are pretty well agreed that Gath is where it is located on the map. (See page 74). A mile or two south from this place is a labyrinth of caverns and pits, and six miles farther south are still larger excavations of the same curious character. But M. Ganneau, of the English Palestine Exploration Survey, locates Adullam, with great probability, at *Aid-el-Mia*, on the hill-side near Socho, where natural caves have been enlarged by human excavations—six or seven miles east, up from Gath. Another immense cavern over the mountains, between Bethlehem and the Dead Sea, south-west from Bethlehem—a labyrinth of chambers—the monks say is the Cave of Adullam. But the Scriptures plainly place it with Gath in the "low country of Judah." It is, therefore, much more likely that the hill-side near *Elah* was the place to which

---
* Joshua xv. 35.

David hastened when he left Gath. Here he would have been on the border of the Philistine country. If the king should come here, he might have the Philistines to face as well as himself. Here, in his desolation and distress, we may place the psalm composed "when the Philistines took him in Gath," or *had taken* him in Gath! It must have been either just after he first gained a residence in Gath, fearing and trembling at the hazard, or more likely when he had escaped to Adullam, driven and at his wit's end, from foes above and foes below.

A PSALM OF DAVID, WHEN THE PHILISTINES TOOK HIM IN GATH.

Afterwards dedicated to the leader of music, " to be sung to the tune of ' The Dumb Dove among Strangers."

Have pity upon me, O God, for man panteth for my life;
My adversary daily oppresseth me!
Mine enemies daily pant for my life,
And many are they who war proudly against me.
When I am in fear
I will put my trust in Thee!
I will glory in the promise of God.
In God do I put my trust; I will not fear:
What can flesh do to me?
Every day they wrest my words.
All their thoughts are against me for evil.
They gather themselves together, they hide themselves, they watch my steps,
Lying in wait for my life,
Shall they escape by their iniquity:
In Thine anger cast down the people, O God!
Count Thou my wanderings!
Put my tears into Thy bottle!
Are they not recorded in Thy book?

When I cry to Thee, my enemies shall turn back;
This I know, that God is for me.
I will glory in the promise of God,
I will glory in the promise of Jehovah.
In God do I put my trust; I will not fear;
What can man do unto me?
Thy vows are upon me, O God!
I will render praises unto Thee,
For Thou hast delivered me from death,
Yea, my feet from falling,
That I may walk before God in the light of the living.

—*Noyes's Translation.*

The news of David's flight has gone quickly to Bethlehem. Either David himself has sent hasty word, or the story of alarm to Jesse and his family has quickly run from Nob or Gibeah to the little city. Nothing was more probable than that the enraged king would seek David at Bethlehem. Indeed, Jonathan had left the king to infer that David had gone there. The king's madness would certainly strike at the whole family. So soon, then, as they knew that David was hiding at Adullam, the whole family hastened down, his father and mother, brothers and sisters, and his old playmates, his nephews.

Meanwhile, at the spreading of the news, the people flocked to him by scores, and at length by hundreds; but a motley and disagreeable crowd of them at first. The malcontents of the kingdom were the first to rally to the new leader. They were not those who stood for a principle nor for the new Anointed, but those in distress and in debt, and in a bitter and discontented mind. They selfishly hoped for relief from a new state of things. At length David found himself surrounded by about four hundred men, a good portion of whom would, no doubt, have been glad to take up a wild life under a captain like him who had killed Goliath. This must have been painful and disagreeable enough to David; for, besides being forced to be at the head of a band of outlaws, there would be some reason to charge him with sedition and treason. The whole four hundred could have been hidden away, upon an occasion, in the caverns which we have described.

Among the four hundred at these "caves," Abishai, Zeruiah's son, is mentioned, and two companions of his. This large company David probably organized—in the usual organization of the kingdom—with captains over hundreds and over tens. To this there may be allusion, when it is said that "three captains over the thirty" went down to David in the cave.

While David was in Adullam, as we discover from the second book of Samuel, and the book of Chronicles, there was some stir among the Philistines. A troop of them went up and encamped in the valley of the Giants, which is supposed to be a little valley just south of Jebus, along the west side of the Bethlehem road. They had even penetrated to Bethlehem, and made a military post there before the city, a thing not very difficult to do, as Jebus was a Canaanite town. Very likely the removal of so strong a family as that of Jesse had uncovered that place to attack. It was now harvest time. Brave as David was, he was hot and faint. He longed for the place of his childhood. "Oh!" said he, "that I might drink of the water at the well of the gate of Bethlehem." It was a wish to arouse the fierce bravery of the Bethlehemites. Forthwith, Abishai, his nephew, with the all-conquering energy of his mother, leads off his two fellow-heroes, and, defying the Philistines before Bethlehem, bring the identical water down the hills for David to drink of it. "May God forbid," said David, "that I should do this thing. Shall I drink the blood of those men who have put their lives in jeopardy for me?" He saw that it would be not only an unwise but cruel thing to establish such a precedent—to peril the lives of brave men to gratify a mere passing wish. As a precious thing, therefore, representing human blood and human life, he poured out the water as a free libation unto God.

Bethlehem, no longer home! What shall he do with his aged father and mother, if Saul, with a troop, should come? The conflict is no longer a conflict with David, but with David's house. He quickly decides Adullam is no place for them. The land of Ruth! Naomi, in famine, found refuge there, and so may Ruth's grandchildren in *their* son's distress. Imagine the hasty company, then, in oriental robes and turbans, with long spears, and ill-assorted weapons, the women veiled and on mules, perhaps a camel or two and a good *number* of mules in the company, making their way southward; first crossing the frequent and shallow ravines, then along an open valley, then westward up a narrower valley over gravel and rock, and between terraced slopes and up deep glens and steep zigzags, along ridges looking down on green fields—to Hebron; stopping after their half-day's journey for hasty rest and food; then filing southward, cutting the hills obliquely, crossing an elevated plain shut in by higher hills, except where it looks off toward the Salt Sea, passing the busy harvesters in the wheat-fields—for there is one of the finest regions of "the hill country," and it was harvest-time—past Ziph and Carmel, to which David is soon to return; over a ridge from which the deep chasm but not the water of the Salt Sea can be seen; through a dried and wilderness region, in which we may imagine them after another half-day's journey encamping for the night, and discussing how many or how few shall go on out of the boundaries of the tribe into the land of Moab. In the morning, see a smaller company, at easier pace, mounting a small swell of barren land, from which they take backward glances at the spreading desert region of "the south," then making their slow and circuitous way down a steep declivity seven or eight hundred feet, and across another broad tract from which Moab, with its peaks and green ravines, becomes more distinctly visible as they look over the white hills and fantastic ridges of chalk and limestone between them and the Salt Sea; then across that "frightful" and "hideous desert"; then down another steep, rocky ledge seven or eight hundred feet, to the whitish, marly bottom which borders the Salt Sea, keeping a sharp lookout for Edomite and Amalekite Bedouins, as they hide their camp-fire in a wild gorge shut in by cliffs of hardened marl; then along the salt region, the mountains and hills salt around them, their path salt beneath them, until turning the end of the Salt Sea, with fragments of traditions about Zoar and Lot from the aged Jesse, as his mule stops to crop the verdure of the Salt Sea peninsula, they mount up the steep path along the green ravine, at the head of which was Kir-Moab. There they look back on the rocky terraces rising one above another from the Salt Sea to Hebron, along the elevated table of which lies the strength—now, alas! the cruel strength—of Israel's king.

This city of Kir-Moab was, we suppose, the Mizpeh (watch-tower) of Moab to which David took his aged parents, and to the king of which he said: "Let my father and my mother, I pray thee, come forth and be with thee, till I know what God will do for me." What reference David or Jesse may have made to Chilion, and Ruth, and Naomi, or whether descendants of Mahlon and Orpah, or of her father's house, took interest in these Israelite kindred we cannot know. But with oriental hospitality, the king received the aged pair, who were thus made safe from Saul's mad jealousy and hostility.

Seventeenth Sunday.

THE HIGH-PRIEST TRANSFERRED TO DAVID.

LESSON.

1 Samuel xxii. 5–23; xxiii. 6; Psalm lii.

HERE in Mizpeh of Moab, where, in peace and security, he can look down upon the distracted land of yonder miserable ruler, David seems inclined to stay. But God has put into his company one of his own messengers to instruct him. The prophet Gad, afterwards called "the King's Seer," and "David's Seer," has been compared to Elijah, so suddenly does he appear here in David's presence. Whether he continued with David in his wanderings or not, we know that he wrote a book of the acts of David, and that he was sent to David in his old age, with the choice of one of three punishments for the sin of numbering the people. It is natural to suppose, therefore, that he was in later days connected in some way with the royal establishment.

Did "Gad the Seer" come from the school of Samuel the Seer at Naioth in Ramah? It is quite possible. As David's flight was so intimately connected with Naioth, and David came to Nob in company with young men, Gad might have been one of the "young men." Perhaps Samuel sent him privately to Mizpeh. He could not have been much older than David, for he was living when David was old. He might have gone with him to Gath or to

Adullam, or for David on some side errand, like an errand of alarm to Bethlehem. At any rate, he had already joined David when he was at Mizpeh of Moab ; and he spoke as a prophet, and as if by divine authority. " Abide not in the hold "—this high and strong fortress, either of the city or the wilds of Moab—" depart, and get thee into the land of Judah." It was not seemly that a man, anointed by God to be king over His people, should hide in a land expressly given to strangers. So " David departed, and came into the forest of Hareth."

Where the forest of Hareth was, is not known. As David undoubtedly came from Moab around the lower end of the Salt Sea, and as Keilah, the next place to which he goes, was not far from Adullam, and as David is directed to "go *down* to Keilah," which would have been the proper direction for advancing from the heights about Hebron towards Adullam, we may assume that the forest of Hareth was an abundant woodland somewhere well up the heights, between the Salt Sea and Hebron.* Here, then, in the wood and wilderness, was the encampment of David, the four hundred gradually swelling in numbers, as others made their way to him ; for at Keilah he had six hundred men. David is firmly resolved to act on the defensive ; but for this, and for attack on the common enemies of the nation, we may suppose the military organization and drill go on.

Saul, who is never alert, except when mightily aroused, is still in Gibeah. He is ready now to pursue David. His headquarters are under a tamarisk tree just over at Ramah. He has his spear in his hand—symbol of war—and his captains stand about him. He could not have failed to

---

* M. Ganneau thinks the proper rendering, " *City* of. Hareth," and locates the City of Khorith at *K'horas*, half way from Hebron to Adullam, as on map on page 16.

learn of David's increasing party. And he makes his address to stimulate personal loyalty, and to rouse the pursuit. His speech is wholly personal and selfish. He appeals to them, not as Israelites, but as Benjamites, as if he had said: "Will a Bethlehemite of the tribe of Judah do better for you than a man of your own tribe?" He appeals to their love of riches and of military station. "How can the son of Jesse give more than myself?" He suspects even them of conspiracy, and has no deep confidence in their loyalty. By their selfish fears and their selfish interest, he appeals to them to tell him the extent of his son's league with sedition against himself. He accuses Jonathan of having stirred up David, a mere servant, to lie in wait for the throne. There is not a syllable of high-toned passion for God and for God's people and the maintenance of God's kingly government, such as Samuel would have shown.

No one, however, is willing to testify against *Jonathan*. But Doeg, a man of influence, of station, and of wealth, as the Fifty-second Psalm fairly implies, the chief over Saul's servants, is ready to testify falsely against the high-priest. He tells Saul what he saw at Nob, and puts the construction of treason on the high-priest's act, as if the high-priest had welcomed and blessed David as a rising king, and as if he had put Goliath's sword in David's hand as a symbol and prophecy of victory. The king sends for Ahimelech and for all the priests. He accuses Ahimelech of conspiracy. Ahimelech answers, in surprised innocence, that David was on the king's errand; that he came as the king's servant and the king's son-in-law, faithful to the king's honor and interest; and that he did not "begin to inquire of God for him." The suspicious king does not credit the answer. He insists that he and his priests had conspired with David. They knew of David's flight; they did not tell the king of it nor arrest it; they blessed him in the name of God. His decree was peremptory : "*Thou shalt die, thou* and thy *father's house.*" The sentence was executed with oriental despatch ; and it was not the only time when Saul's cruel jealousy and anger crushed an innocent people.* But the soldiers refuse to slay the priests. Their reverence for the priests and their confidence in their innocence are greater than their fear of the king. He commands Doeg. He is base enough to comply. He takes his soldiers. Bedouin himself, his Bedouin soldiers care no more for the Lord's priests, than for sheep and oxen. Ahimelech, of course, is first slain. They hasten to Nob. They strike down the whole city, more severely than Saul the city of the Amalekites when wicked Agag was fair and comely. Men, women, children, infants, oxen, asses, sheep, the city were destroyed, except only one priest, Abiathar, the son of Ahimelech, who escapes and makes his way to David, bearing with him the sacred vestments of his office. But God again overrules the wrath of man, for by this very act Saul has transferred to David both the high-priest of the nation and the divine insignia of his office.

The awful tidings were told David. "I foresaw it," said the noble-hearted man. "I saw Doeg there. I have occasioned the death of all thy father's house. Do you stay with me. The king seeks both your life and mine ; with me you shall be guarded." What a tumult must have filled young David's soul ! To be reckoned a traitor when he was conscious of innocence ; to be put into straits in which he had been betrayed into falsehood and lying ; to be the death of the innocent priests who had saved his life ; to be lied about by this son of Esau ! Grief over his own sins, and righteous indignation and anger at the atrocious gilt of that miserable place-seeker, and a sense

---

* 2 Samuel xxi. 2.

of innocence in respect to the government and the king—how his heart was swept by emotions of sorrow and holy rage and conscious innocence, as when the joyful and plaintive music flowed beneath his own hand from the lyre!

It is in this mood of innocence and penitence, mingled with overpowering wrath at the superlative wickedness and malicious delight of a base sycophant and time-server, we suppose, that he poured out his soul in the Fifty-second Psalm. In the psalm there may be an allusion to his own falsehood and to the hideous lying of Doeg:

> Why gloriest thou in mischief, thou man of violence?
> The goodness of God yet continueth daily.
> Thy tongue deviseth mischiefs
> Like a sharp razor, thou contriver of deceit!
> Thou lovest evil more than good,
> And lying more than to speak truth.
> Thou lovest all devouring words,
> O thou deceitful tongue!
>
> Thee also shall God utterly destroy!
> He shall seize thee and tear thee from thy dwelling-place
> And uproot thee from the land of the living.
> The righteous shall see and fear,
> And make him a subject of scorn:
> "Behold the man that made not God his strength,
> But trusted in the abundance of his riches
> And placed his strength in his wickedness."
> But I shall be like a green olive-tree in the house of God;
> I will trust in the goodness of God for ever and ever.
> I will ever praise thee for what thou hast done;
> I will trust in thee on account of thy goodness
> Before the eyes of thy worshippers.
> —*Noyes's Translation.*

A subtle and keen contrast between his own sensitive grief over his sin and Doeg's wicked exultation in *his* guilt may lie in the words:

> "*Thou lovest* evil more than good,
> And *lying more* than *to speak truth.*"

"Why dost thou expect success, thou wicked man! It is God in whom I trust, and not in place or riches. My kingship is his plan, and I wait on him and not on man to develop it."

The seer who wrote the "Acts of David," and who had bidden him depart from Mizpeh, may have caught this tumultuous lament in the woods of Hareth, and preserved it by divine guidance for its proper use in the tabernacle and temple psalmody.

Eighteenth Sunday.

RESCUE FROM GOD.

LESSON.

1 Samuel xxiii. 1-18; Joshua xv. 43, 44, 55; Psalm liv.

WORD came now to David that the Philistines were aroused again. They were in the general neighborhood of Adullam. Perhaps they had hope of regaining their old territory during the distraction between Saul and David. They may have been aroused by the challenge with which Abishai and his two fellows carried off the water from the well at Bethlehem. They heard, it may be, that David outwitted them at Gath and had a troop of men at Adullam. If they came to Adullam and found him and his four hundred gone south-eastward over the mountains, and followed on only six miles, they would have come to Keilah. The place was on the edge of the unconquered portion of the tribe. David's four hundred and more, were afraid to go down there to an open fight.

There at Keilah the Philistines had played an old game. The camels and asses have no sooner left their loaded sheaves at the threshing-floors, the mules and oxen no sooner trodden out the grain, than the Philistine troops sweep in, carry off the threshed heaps, and attack the town.

For the first time that we hear of it, David now makes a formal inquiry of God in his own name. Abiathar, we have supposed, has reached him with the ephod, by which he could appear before God in the order which God had himself appointed. For, although it is said that Abiathar fled to David to *Keilah*, the phrase may mean simply that Keilah was the first place they came to after Abiathar joined them; and the fact of the presence of Abiathar and the ephod is mentioned in connection with the inquiry of God *before* they advance on Keilah. A sacrifice is therefore offered; the high-priest, in his robes, presents the king's request; and in some way, by vision or sacred lot or voice, the answer in returned: "Go, and smite the Philistines, and save Keilah." David's motley troop, however, are faint-hearted, and he asks God again. He receives the more emphatic response: "Arise, go down to Keilah; for I will deliver the Philistines into thine hand." Animated by the courage of their leader, who excited in them memories of Goliath and of the lion and the bear, they rush down to the fight, overpower the enemy, raise the siege, save the harvest, and bring off the enemy's cattle.

But David's success is likely to prove his defeat. Received as a deliverer, he may now defy Saul within walls and gates. His little army is twice strong, for they have proved their valor. The news and the stir bring men flocking to him, till his four hundred become a full six hundred. Saul sees his opportunity. "He is shut up in a town," he said. "God has turned him over to me!" He called his warriors to the siege. He would pull the city in pieces. David heard of Saul's preparations and saw his danger. He calls for Abiathar. He bids him seek counsel from God in the divine mode, and to request information in respect to two points: first, whether Saul will certainly advance to a siege of the city; and secondly, whether the people of Keilah, grateful for deliverance, will stand by him in resisting Saul. Mark now the wisdom of the divine providence. "Saul will certainly come." "The men of Keilah will certainly deliver you up," are the answers of the oracle. This is intended to save David from an open conflict with the government. It is not by battles and sieges with Saul, and the spectacle of one divinely anointed king warring with another divinely anointed king, that David is to be brought to the throne. With his six hundred, therefore, he quickly left those dangerous walls. Saul does not catch him in the trap of Keilah; but where shall he go? North? That will be to surrender himself to Saul. West? That is to go among the Philistines whom he has just defeated. South-west, towards Gaza and the great highway to Egypt? That will put in peril his independence. Back over the mountains to the south-east—that is the safest, for from there he may escape to the Sea wilds or the southern desert, or even to Horeb and Sinai, as Elijah did afterwards.

But where is the wilderness into which David went? If we read the story on to the end of the twenty-sixth chapter, and gather up the various names mentioned, we shall find that, taken together, they define the region with considerable exactness. For during the time contained in these chapters, David was in a region in which were "wilderness" and "wood" and "mountain" and "strongholds" and pasture for sheep and farming-lands, and where were "Ziph" and "Hachilah" and "Jeshimon" and "Maon" and "Engedi" and the "wilderness of Paran" and "Carmel." Ziph, four miles away from Hebron, Carmel (quite another place from Mount Carmel) three miles further, and Maon another mile, are on the road south-east from Hebron, over which we have already seen David take his father and mother. These places are recognized and well-known. Engedi we know too, on the Salt Sea, nearly east from Hebron. The "wilderness of Paran" is the great wilderness, extending to Sinai on the south and beginning in the region of Ziph and Maon on the north. The hill of Hachilah is unknown, except that it was not far from Ziph and Moan.* It was on the south of Jeshimon; the margin reads, "on the right hand of Jeshimon," which is the same thing if you are on the road traveling south-east from Hebron. The word "Jeshimon" means "wilderness." As "the hill of Hachilah" was "*before* Jeshimon,* that is, in *front* of or in the *face* of Jeshimon, and as Pisgah and Peor also "looked towards Jeshimon" or the wilderness,† Ziph and Maon were on one side, and Pisgah and Peor were on the opposite side, and Jeshimon was between them. This makes it clear that Jeshimon was the wild region which lies between the plain of Ziph, Carmel, and Maon near Hebron, and the northern end of the Salt Sea—a vast, ragged, rocky slide, cracked and tossed at some past period by a convulsion of nature, gnawed by the tooth of winter torrents, which for centuries have plunged from the water ridge of Judah to the Salt Sea. Everywhere you see naked conical hills, "barren and rugged, patched with buff and brown, dotted with low black tents;" the ridges are hundreds of feet high; the deep ravines "start suddenly and fall steeply down" to the desert and the sea. As you go down, the shrubs with which the hills are sprinkled disappear, and only a dry, stunted grass, the growth of the rainy season, remains. Chalk and flint become mixed with the limestone. You find your rugged path between close walls of perpendicular rock a hundred feet high, or along the steep face of a hill, or in the dry bed of a torrent. On all sides the rocks are full of caverns. Here you start a gazelle; there a yellow jackall runs like a fox to his hole; along the opposite cliff bounds a mountain goat. The plain of Ziph and Carmel and Maon, "on the south of Jeshimon," is cultivated and fertile; but it was no

---

* xxvi. 1–3.   † Numbers xxi. 20; xxiii. 28.

doubt this wild region which lay so near, that was called, from the south-western side, "the wilderness of Ziph," or "the wilderness of Maon," and from the eastern side "the wilderness of Engedi." The waving plain about Ziph, now so fertile, may once have been a noble forest or a thicket-wood, which helped to hide David as he and his party kept ready to escape into the awful rocks and caverns of Jeshimon below.* Saul did not find him, although his spies and messengers looked for him every day. But hither Jonathan comes, taking occasion to escape his father, still at Gibeah, and seeking to support the fainting spirit of David. His faith is as heroic as David's; for he expresses the utmost confidence that God's anointment is certain. "Do not fear: you will escape: you will be king; I know it: my father knows it," says the generous youth, as the two friends pledge again their covenant in the wilderness, and separate for the last time.

Reassured by Jonathan, David is not, however, to be left to mere human assurances. God has a mode of showing him with whom he has a stronger covenant. The people of Ziph have watched the company of David as they have gone over to Moab, as they have come back to Keilah, and as, trembling, they have fled again into the wood and the mountain lurking-places on the wilderness

---

* The probable site of Hachilah is the high hill bounded by deep valleys north and south, on which the ruin of *Yekin* now stands. A large ancient ruin stands on the brink of the deep slope, and looks down on the white marl ridges of the Jeshimon. On the north, the two peaks above and beyond Engedi are separated by the gleaming thread of sea, scarce seen in its great chasm. Below are the long ridges of Moab, the iron precipices, the thousand water-courses, the great plateau of Kerak, the black volcanic gorge Callirrhoe all lying in deep shadows under the morning sun or brightened with a crimson-flushed sunset.—*Lieutenant Conder.*

edge. Saul's spies probably brought some of these Ziphites to Gibeah, or they volunteered the twenty-mile journey to tell Saul of David's hiding-places, and to offer to betray him to the king. At first the king wishes them to bring word again, particularly of his strongholds, but at length he arouses himself, and starts with them, determined to search him throughout all the thousands of Judah. As the Ziphites were of Judah, it is plain that there was not yet awakened any general sympathy of the tribe of Judah with one of their own number, either as a persecuted innocent or as an expectant king.†

Now begins the pursuit in earnest. David's scouts are on the lookout. He shifts his place from one point to another—from the lofty rock or the cliff cavern to the forest or thicket. Saul's men plunge into the very wilderness. David for his life, like a partridge, flees along the mountain-side. On the opposite side of the mountain, Saul and his men so divide themselves that they are on the point of surrounding David when God calls off the pursuit. A runner comes in panting from Hebron. "Haste thee and come. The Philistines have invaded the land." Recovered from their defeat at Keilah, they are pushing up the mountains. No time is to be lost, or between divided opinions the kingdom will be lost. In an hour, the king has wheeled and gone, and David breathes free, saved by the Lord's providence.

He falls back with his little army into the lower wilderness, and finds a rocky refuge in the cliffs and caverns about Engedi.

Here we may suppose—since we know it was about this *time*—as he thought of the walls and bars of Keilah, and of this stranger providential deliverance at the hill of Hachilah, he sings the psalm which bears the inscription:

---

† The treachery of the Ziphites forms a striking contrast to Jonathan's treatment of David.

A PSALM OF DAVID,

When the Ziphim came and said to Saul, "Doth not David hide himself with us?"

Save me, O God, by thy name,
And by thy strength defend my cause!
O God hear my prayer,
Give ear to the words of my mouth.
For enemies have risen up against me,
And oppressors seek my life;
They have not set God before them:
  Behold! God is my helper;
The Lord is the support of my life.
He will repay evil to my enemies;
For thy truth's sake, O God, cut them off!
With a willing heart will I sacrifice to thee;
I will praise thy name, O Lord! for it is good;
For thou hast delivered me from all trouble,
So that my eye hath looked with satisfaction upon my enemies.

—*Noyes's Translation.*

Nineteenth Sunday.

A SOFT ANSWER.

LESSON.

1 Samuel xxiii. 29; xxiv.; 2 Chronicles xx. 2; Genesis xiv. 7; Song of Solomon i. 14; Psalms cxlii., lvii.

THE region above Engedi has already been described. The two names, poetically descriptive, picture it to us—En-gedi, *Fountain of the Kid*, a fountain in the midst of wild rocks where wild goats have their haunts; and Hazazon-tamar, *The Pruning*, or *The Felling of the Palm*, on account of the palm-groves which surrounded the place, Josephus says. The Amorites and the Amalekites lived there when Lot came down into this "well-watered" "garden," and King Jehoshaphat at Jerusalem, a century and a half after David, was full of fear when he heard of a multitude from beyond the Dead Sea, gathered at the pass where the shore road heads up the cliffs toward Tekoa and Jerusalem. The fountain is now on a shelf of the rocky ledge, midway in the face of a perpendicular cliff fifteen hundred feet high. Ruins near the fountain and four hundred feet below at the bottom leave the traveler in doubt on which spot was the town itself. The fountain and its secure, defensive position perhaps decided the location. The path from the top down the smooth rose-colored limestone is by a sharp-angled zigzag, and is one of the most terrific passes in the world. The fountain bursts out of the narrow terrace, and rushes down, through a luxuriant thicket of trees and shrubs, to a little plain half a mile square on the shore. There grow the gum-arabic tree, thorn-trees with their acid apples, a large tree called by the Arabs *Fustak*, "with long, beautiful clusters of whitish blossoms," and the curious 'Osher, ten and fifteen feet high, its trunk six or eight inches in diameter, with leaves and flowers like the milk-weed, and, like the milk-weed, discharging a milky fluid when broken, and with fruit in clusters of three or four, the size of a large orange, yellow and smooth, "fair and delicious to the eye, but exploding like a puff-ball when pressed or struck." The palm, we suppose, grew there in David's time, but none are there now. Probably the whole descent was then terraced with gardens or vineyards; for it was famous in Solomon's day, and its appearance now indicates such ancient cultivation. The little plain on either side of the brook at the foot, now rich and cultivated, was then, no doubt, covered with tillage and prolific in tropical fruits and vegetables. On the north, a gigantic cliff, broken and gashed by a short ravine, the base of which juts out into the sea, stops all progress from the plain, in that direction; while on the south, the little plain is bounded by a larger ravine, through which the waters tumble in the rainy season, between lofty precipices, and past which the road from the lower end of the sea advances. Yonder David may escape into the land of Edom or of Moab, if King Saul shall venture down those long and ragged and terrible slopes, the bottom of which strike the tops of these cliffs.

Here was much to impress the soul of the young poet and warrior. From the tops of the cliffs as he came from the wilderness behind, he looked out upon a scene magnificently wild and stern. A vast solitude stretched around him, the silence of which was hardly broken by the voices of his few hundred men, or the gentle, heavy surge on the shore below, or the carol of the lark, the whistle of the quail, the call of the partridge, in air and tree and rock. As he and his company retreat from the sea into the wilderness of rocks, this awful chasm and these shattered mountains are to them, as they are to us, tokens of the wrath of God. The smoke of the doomed cities once went up as the dense vapor now rises from the waters, filling the chasm and spreading its haze along yonder mountains.

It is said that "David went *up* from thence, and dwelt in strongholds at En-gedi." It may be that when Saul was called away to the Philistines, David fled southwards from Maon, and came *up* to Engedi along the shore-path.

Will King Saul venture far down into these awful rocks, into these narrow passes where a score of men can hold a thousand in check, and where, from crags and cliffs and caverns, his chief men and the king himself may be slain? Yes! All warfare in those days, and certainly in that land of mountains, was hand-to-hand fighting, the scaling of impregnable walls, and the assault of rocky strongholds. In this spirit, stirred by the almost perfect success at Maon, and by the flight of the Philistines before him, Saul boldly descends with his three thousand, resolved to hunt David out through every ravine and cavern of Judah. On every rock where an ibex can stand, he will hunt him out! When he had hastened back to Ziph and had learned where David was, the three thousand chosen for this service in the gorges of the wilderness were picked* men from his army. Imagine them divided into small companies, exploring the ravines and caverns. Some climb the crags, some peer cautiously into the dark caverns from which a beast may spring. Every ridge and every gorge has its man or its party, Saul and his body-guard following

---

* Hebrew "tried," "proved."

their own pursuit; and thorough search is made so far as they go.

The two psalms written while "in the cave," must have been composed in the haunts to which David and his men at this time daily resorted—in daily expectation of the pursuers. From one cave-haunt we hear this plaintive and hopeful lament; afterwards revised for tabernacle-service, as

INSTRUCTION OF DAVID.

A PRAYER WHEN HE WAS IN THE CAVE.*

I cry unto the Lord with my voice,
With my voice to the Lord do I make my supplication.
I pour out my complaint before him,
I declare before him my distress.
When my spirit within me was overwhelmed,
Thou knewest my path!
In the way which I walk, they have hid a snare for me;
I look on my right hand and behold:
But no man will know me!
Refuge faileth me!
No man careth for me!
I cry to thee, O Lord!
I say, Thou art my refuge,
My portion in the land of the living.
Attend to my cry, for I am brought very low.
Deliver me from my persecutors,
For they prevail against me!
Bring me out of my prison
That I may praise thy name!
The righteous shall gather around me
When thou shalt show me thy favor.

—*Noyes's Translation.*

From the very cavern into which Saul shortly afterwards retired, comes this more hopeful psalm, afterwards set to the tune of "Do not Destroy,"—

"A GOLDEN PSALM OF DAVID,

WHEN HE FLED FROM SAUL IN THE CAVE."

Have pity upon me, O God, have pity upon me.
For in thee doth my soul seek refuge!
Yea, in the shadow of thy wings do I take shelter,
Until these calamities be overpast!

---

* The psalm may have been composed in the present tense and afterwards used in the perfect tense, the Hebrew verb admitting of either construction.

NINETEENTH SUNDAY.

I call upon God the Most High,
Upon God, who performeth all things for me;
He will send from heaven, and save me;
He will put to shame him that panteth for my life;
God will send forth his mercy and his truth.

My life is in the midst of lions;
I dwell among them that breathe out fire;
Among men whose teeth are spears and arrows,
And whose tongue is a sharp sword.

Exalt thyself, O God, above the heavens,
And thy glory above all the earth!
They have prepared a net for my steps.
My soul is bowed down;
They have digged a pit before me,
But into it they have themselves fallen.*

My heart is strengthened, O God, my heart is strengthened!
I will sing and give thanks.
Awake, my soul! awake, psaltery and harp!
I will wake with the early dawn.
I will praise thee, O Lord, among the nations;
I will sing to thee among the kingdoms!
For thy mercy reacheth to the heavens,
And thy truth to the clouds!

Exalt thyself, O God, above the heavens,
And thy glory above all the earth!

—*Noyes's Translation.*

David and a few of his men have advanced or retreated to the sheep-folds—a place "by the way," that is, on the worn path, were a circular wall of loose stones had been thrown up for the shepherds and their flocks at night, often built in front of caverns. As the shouts of the king's pursuers approach, they hide in a cave. "The cavern may have been full of sheep when they entered; nor would their presence have disturbed them."† The king's men come near. A form appears at the mouth of the cavern. It is the king himself! Strange providence indeed! His guard do not enter! He is alone! Blinded by the glare of the sun against the rocks, he cannot see

---

* From these two lines, it may be inferred that the psalm was written after David had caught Saul in the cave and after Saul's troops were withdrawn. If so, the psalm expresses his lack of confidence in Saul's professions and his entire confidence in God.

† Thomson.

five paces inwards; but, crouching back in the depths or turns of the cavern, they can see his every movement. His face is turned from them, and the skirts of his ungirded robe lie spread around him. "Now is God's time," whisper David's men; "for he said he would deliver him into your hands." Sword in hand, the youthful valiant approaches the king, his step undistinguished from the tramp or step of sheep. To the astonishment of his friends, he does not strike, but only cuts quickly off the end of Saul's robe. Even for this, his heart smites him. "After all," he says to himself, "I ought not to disgrace or demean the king." "He was anointed of God," he whispers to his men, amidst the rustling of the sheep. "The Lord forbid that I should strike him or do him harm." He keeps them back till Saul rises up and joins his body-guard outside, and hastens on, when David goes out, and cries, "*My lord the king!*" Saul looks, and sees David bowed prostrate in obeisance and reverence. And as the king returns, David rises with an appeal, every word of which went to the very soul of Saul: "Why dost thou hear the words of men, O king! when they tell thee David seeks thy hurt? Behold, this day thine eyes have seen how God himself delivered thee to my power. My men bade me kill thee; but my eye spared thee. I said I will not lift my hand against him; for he is the Lord's anointed. See in my hand, my father, the skirt of thy robe. Know then and see for yourself that there is no evil design in me that seeks thy hurt. Yet *thou* huntest *my* soul to take it.

"Let the Lord judge us. Let the Lord avenge me. But *my* hand shall not be on thee. From the wicked, saith the proverb of the ancients, comes wickedness: but my hand shall not be upon thee.

"And after whom has the king of the nation come in pursuit? a mere dead dog, a flea.

"The Lord be judge. Let him see, and plead my cause, and deliver me from thy hand."

The king looked on amazed! His hard heart melted, as the soft and loving words of David fell upon it, like gentle gusts of warm rain on the ice; and as he glanced at his royal robe, and saw the severed piece in David's hand, he filled with emotion, his eyes filled with tears, and he said :

"Is this thy voice, my son David? Thou hast been more righteous than I. Thou hast rewarded me good, while I have rewarded thee evil. Thou hast truly showed me that thou hast dealt kindly with me; for, when the Lord shut me up into thy hand, thou didst not kill me. If a man find his enemy, will he let him go? The Lord reward thee good for what thou hast done to me to-day. Now I know well that thou shalt be king, and that the kingdom of Israel shall be established under thy hand.

"Swear, then, to me, that thou wilt not cut off my seed after me, and that thou wilt not destroy my name out of my father's house."

What an oath was that for David to consent to take there in the wilderness—an oath of *protection* instead of fealty to Saul !

The king was overcome and confounded. His imagination and suspicion were disarmed. As his trumpets sounded through the glens the signal for retreat, and the long column of his chosen warriors wound up the defiles towards Tekoa and Bethlehem and Gibeah, the moody man did not doubt for the time that David was innocent of evil intent against the government or against himself.

Twentieth Sunday.

NABAL AND ABIGAIL.

LESSON.

1 Samuel xxv.; xxviii. 3. Psalms xiii., lxii.

IT has now been three or four years since David left Naioth in Ramah. Let us suppose that the time spent at Gath, at Adullam, where the four hundred gathered, at Mizpeh of Moab, and in the forest of Hareth, amounted to about one year. Let us suppose that the expedition against Keilah, and the time spent in that city and in the strongholds and wilderness of Ziph, consumed another year. Then, while Saul has gone in pursuit of the Philistines and is making ready his three thousand, during which time David is in the wild regions of Engedi, and the months which transpire after Saul left him at the sheepfolds, make up something more than another year. During the following autumn occur the events at Carmel and Nabal's possessions.

During this last year, besides the proof which Saul had that David was innocent of conspiracy against him personally, another cause gave David respite for a time. The aged Seer at Ramah died. The death of that pre-eminent man, God's accepted prophet, made a profound impression. "All the Israelites gathered together, and lamented him, and buried him." More than one told over his famous speech down at Gilgal, when he said, "Witness against me: whose ox or whose ass have I stolen?" and commented on its truth. More than one good man rehearsed Samuel's righteous indignation at Saul and his terrible punishment of Agag, and praised the justness of the Seer's character. In many a house, mothers to a new growth of children repeated the oft-told story of the little child in the tabernacle at Shiloh. "He set up the kingdom; he did it wisely and well: he told us of the sin and misery that would come from it; would God we had been content without this miserable Saul," was the conversation of wise men. The land was moved, and the people thronged up and along the mountains to bury him in Ramah. When Aaron died, the congregation mourned for him thirty days. When Moses died, there were thirty days of mourning and weeping. When Samuel died, therefore, the public lamentation was formal and protracted; attended with all the customary signs of grief, and of funeral honor:—the rending of clothes, sackcloth, dust or ashes, fasting, silence, the wailing of women, the beating of the breast, and the shrill dirge of pipes. For a month, in some form, the signs of respect and grief were maintained, the king and the elders of the tribe or elders of cities throughout the land formally abstaining from occupations inconsistent with grief.

David cannot join the mourning nation. It would not be prudent for him to appear. He knew the changing moods of Saul's mind too well for that. It were better to be entirely separate from the nation. He goes down, therefore, into the wilderness of Paran. "Goes *down;*" that seems to signify that he descended the steep at Engedi, and went down the shore-road to the end of the sea, and encamped in the wilds there or beyond; or if "goes *down*" signifies only the general direction downwards towards the great southern desert, the shortest and most secluded road was by the Éngedi pass and the sea-path. Here they cannot have the fruits and vegetables of Engedi, but must subsist on whatever they can find, as many a band of Bedouins have done since.

In some such respite as this, while in the solitudes of the wilderness, musing on the moodiness of Saul's temper, and perhaps on the death of Samuel, the soul which was always breathing itself forth in ejaculations of song and petition and praise, gave utterance to the Thirteenth psalm:

> How long, O Lord, will thou utterly forget me?
> How long wilt thou hide thy face from me?
> How long shall I have anxiety in my soul,
> And sorrow in my heart all the day?
> How long shall my enemy be exalted over me?
> Look down and hear me, O Lord my God;
> Enlighten my eyes lest I sleep the sleep of death,
> Lest my enemy say, I have prevailed against him,
> Let my adversaries rejoice when I am fallen.
>
> Yet will I trust in thy goodness;
> My heart shall rejoice in thy salvation;
> I will sing to the Lord, that he hath dealt kindly with me.

These men were not freebooters and bandits, like the present Bedouins; certainly David was not in any true sense an outlaw, for he was driven into this wild life against his will. He could not go back to a settled life at Bethlehem, if he would. God himself had compelled him to flee, nay, had told him that he must not stay in Keilah. The most, therefore, that he can do is to restrain his men from depredations as much as possible, and to gain food for his hundreds by whatever contrivances he can. This he had already done when they were up in the fruitful plain of Ziph and Carmel. Thousands of sheep and hundreds of goats were browsing on those pastures, but his men were not permitted to seize them nor to insult or annoy the shepherds. They even protected them from robbers or beasts for a considerable time. If such a chief as David had control of that region now, those dangerous regions would be safe for travelers.* Many of David's men very likely had some money at first. If it had not been entirely expended at Engedi, they could still purchase something for their wants. The shepherds and herdsmen too, no doubt, returned provisions for their good offices. It is at just some such time as this, we imagine, that David heard of Nabal's sheep-shearing in Carmel. Nabal was rich. Three thousand sheep were led by his keepers out to pasture, and a thousand goats were mixed with them, as on the self-same pastures sheep and goats are now mixed. He was "very great" in the hill country of Judah. But he was a hard, harsh man, quick in temper, ready to let fly his tongue when his interests were touched; who had no good reputation for his business transactions, and who was thought by some to be a very "son of Belial."

David heard in the wilderness that Nabal's annual sheep-shearing, which is something of a festival in the East, " a time of open-handed hospitality among flock-masters," was in progress at Carmel. He at once sends up ten of his young men to salute him, and to tell him of their need and their services to his flocks, to congratulate

---

* "That entire region is now almost deserted except by Bedouin robbers, who render it at least as dangerous to honest shepherds as it seems to have been before David and his company frequented it. The men of Carmel mention it as something remarkable that they were not *hurt*, neither missed anything as long as they were conversant with them in the fields. 'They were a wall unto us night and day all the while we were with them keeping the sheep.' It is refreshing to read such a testimony to David's admirable government over the heterogeneous and not very respectable band that followed him; and if there was now such an emeer in that same region, we might have safely extended our rambles down to the Dead Sea, at the famous castle of Masada, and then passed on northward by Ain Jidy to Jericho. As it is, we are only able to get some such view of these districts as Moses had from the top of Pisgah."—*Thomson in the Land and Book.*

him on his prósperity—"we come in a good day"—and to ask something generous for thy "son David" and his men. A modern sheikh of the neighboring desert would do the same thing.* The words of David's message conveyed fully to Nabal who it was that sent him, and that he had sent graciously and not by force for provisions in a time of need. He knew who David was, for the king's army had been hunting him almost over his fields; and he knew that, if David's men, pressed by need, had made a raid on his crops and cattle, no one would have condemned them harshly. But Nabal's answer is the petulant answer always of a mean and stingy disposition: "Who is David? and who is the son of Jesse? there be many servants nowadays that break away from their masters. Shall I take *my* bread, and *my* water, and *my* slaughter that *I* have killed for *my* shearers, and give it unto men whom I know not whence they be?" He turned away the young men with a coarse contempt.

David was stung to the quick by the answer, "Who is David?" Who is any one in need to a selfish, cold heart! And the fling at his men as runaways and outlaws was just the taunt to fire them. "Gird on your swords," he said. He took four hundred. Two hundred stayed by the camp.

But one of Nabal's young men had seen trouble and danger ahead. He told the story of David's kindness and protection and of Nabal's stingy spite quickly to Abigail. "Evil is certainly determined against him and against us all." Abigail's good understanding was quick to perceive and quick to provide. She ordered the asses. She piled on five dressed sheep, and five bushels of roasted wheat,

---

* "On such a festive occasion near a town or village, even in our own time, an Arab sheikh of the neighboring desert would hardly fail to put in a word, either in person or by message, and his message both in form and substance would be only the transcript of that of David."—*Robinson.*

and two skins of wine, and two hundred cracknels of bread, and a hundred bunches of dried grapes, and two hundred cakes of pressed figs. "Drive on," she said, "I will come behind myself." And like Jacob following his presents to Esau, she mounted her mule, and made haste down the hills. She was not too soon; for at a certain hiding-place in the hill she met David in his wrath. His generous spirit was stung by the contemptible meanness and bitterness with which he had been treated. "Is this the return he gives me for my care? Not a dog of his flocks shall see to-morrow's light."

But these presents and this woman! Abigail is bowed before him as he had been prostrate before Saul. And she poured out a gracious appeal, which glimpses of a fair face do not weaken: "On me let this wickedness be! Fool is this man's name, and folly is with him. Thine handmaid did not see the young men thou didst send. May thine enemies be as Nabal; but do not shed blood." And then with what handsome speech does she retract Nabal's taunt, "Who is the son of Jesse?" by alluding to her knowledge of his past career, of his innocence in the contest with the king, by declaring her confidence in his establishment as a ruler, and by delicately appealing to him not to mar his future success by a remembrance of having shed Nabal's blood.

The grace and beauty of her words and her address, even if the beautiful face was hidden by the veil, touched the heart as well as the gallantry of David.* He blessed God that she had come with her presents and her gracious words to keep him from blood. He took her presents, and said, "Go home in peace. I have harkened to thy voice."

While his discreet wife meets the angry troop in the wil-

---

* The *name* too may have touched him tenderly, for David's sister's name was Abigail.

derness, the stupid Nabal makes a feast for himself. With a passion for drink, the wine flows freely, and when Abigail at length toils up the steep road back to the shearing-place at Carmel, her fool of a husband is too drunk to comprehend the state of things. In the morning he is sober enough to be appalled at his narrow escape. As Abigail goes over the events as they occurred, telling him, no doubt, who it is whom he has insulted, and that David is certain to be king and Saul to be destroyed, it may be visions of future punishment from such a mighty man— an oriental tyrant—rose up before him. He sank into cowardly terror and abjectness. His heart died within him, and *he* became as a stone. " It was as if a stroke of apoplexy or paralysis had fallen upon him."† Whether it was the effect of this terror, or the continuance of a drunken debauch—continued, to drown fear—or some more direct infliction of the Almighty, ten days afterwards he died. "It was not without justice regarded as a divine judgment." David considered it a vindication of his own cause.

After the customary time of grief required by respect for her husband had expired—and that respect for Nabal could not have been profound—David sends his servants to propose marriage. He has had time to make enquiries in respect to her character and station. It is to be observed that, although David may be reckoned an outlaw in the wilderness, and she is the heir of large possessions, his message to her is not in the nature of request or solicitation, but of decision and command, and that she accedes to it as if made by one whose station authorized it. David was already allied to the royal family—a son-in-law to the king, although Saul had given Michal to a man named Phalti, of the town of Gallim, a town probably in the

---

† Stanley.

king's own tribe. Abigail's faith in David's prospects was, therefore, put to the test. Marriage with the outlaw whom Saul had twice pursued through this very region might endanger all her possessions and her life besides. She is confident that the soul of David is bound up in the bundle of life, and that, as from a sling, the Lord will sling out the souls of his enemies. She is attracted, too, by his beauty and address, as well as he by hers. She at once accepts the offer as an honor, bowing herself as a servant, and declaring herself happy to be but near him as a servant of servants; and hastening with five attendants to her future lord.

In the midst, therefore, of adversity, David has something of prosperity. But in prosperity, he is compelled to remember his insecurity and his oppressions. Easily moved to heights or depths, he can still keep the even balance of trust in God. It cannot be far from the true circumstances of its composition, if we assign the Sixty-second psalm to this time:

"A PSALM OF DAVID,
Afterwards delivered to the leader of the music of the Jeduthanites."

On God alone my soul reposeth,
From him cometh my deliverance;
He alone is my rock and my salvation.
He is my safeguard! I shall not wholly fall!

How long will ye continue to assault a single man?
How long will ye all seek to destroy me,
Like a bending wall or a tottering fence?
They study how to cast me down from my eminence:
They delight in falsehood;
They bless with their mouths, but in their hearts they curse.

. . . .

Truly, men of low degree are vanity,
And men of high degree are a lie.
Placed in the balance,
They are all lighter than vanity.
Trust not in extortion;
Place no vain hopes in rapine.
If riches increase, set not your heart upon them!

> Once hath God promised, twice have I heard it.
> That power belongeth unto God;
> To thee, also, O Lord, belongeth mercy,
> For thou dost render to every man according to his work.
> —*Noyes's Translation.*

From the neighboring town, Jezreel,* very different from the town which was afterwards Ahab's capital, David took also another wife, Ahinoam. Both these wives, his real and free choice, were his wives after he became king in Hebron, and Ahinoam was the mother of his first-born son Amnon. He did not recover Michal till he had been seven years king in Hebron.

---

* Joshua xv. 56.

Twenty-first Sunday.

"COALS OF FIRE."

LESSON.

1 Samuel xxvi.; xxvii. 1.; Psalm xxv.

OTHERS besides Saul himself affected the king's temper. How much had the Ziphites to do with King Saul's third pursuit of David, after he had solemnly assured David that he was innocent of treason or other crime? They had informed Saul twice before, for it was no doubt they who told Saul after he returned from the Philistines, that David was at Engedi. They had acquired a reputation as spies and informers, and could make it appear their duty to the government to be so. Their very appearance and presence at Gibeah would arouse Saul's jealousy again. They know now just the rebel's haunt. They tell him of Abigail and of David's alliance, and of his resort to his new home.

His family, and his chief counsellors too, with such reasons as courtiers can always find, may have urged Saul to maintain his kingdom. Abner, his general, and his uncle, we know, maintained Saul's cause against David for seven years after the king was slain; and we may, therefore, be sure that, while Saul was yet alive, he advocated the policy of putting down a rising usurper.

We have, therefore, reason to believe that these two influences—courtiers at home and Ziphite spies—helped on the decision of the king to hunt David again. The evil spirit is on him, and, forgetting his state of mind at the sheep-folds, he issues his orders to three thousand chosen men.

David could not have been greatly surprised. He was well acquainted with the moodiness of Saul's mind. Although he was now stronger than ever before, from his alliance with the towns of Maon and Carmel and Jezrael through his wives, still his power was very small before the thousands of the king. He kept himself therefore concealed, and sent out his spies, till he knew that Saul was actually come into the wilderness. At length, he learns that Saul's troops are at the very hill of Hachilah which he knew so well; and by night with a trusty few, he goes out to reconnoitre.

From some neighboring rock, they look down on the camp. The beasts and their burdens and the camp luggage lie in a circle as a rampart, just like a "corrall" on the western plains. In the centre can be seen a spear, stuck upright in the earth, showing where the king lies, just as an Arab sheikh's tent is to-day distinguished.*

Abner, the king's uncle and his general, lies next him. Heavy with sleep, without sentinel or guard, the soldiers lie around.†

---

* "I noticed at all the encampments which we passed that the sheikh's tent was distinguished from the rest by a tall spear stuck upright in the ground in front of it; and it is the custom, when a party is out on an excusion for robbery or for war, that when they halt or rest, the spot where the chief reclines or sleeps is thus desigated."—*Thomson, Land and Book*, p. 20.

† "The whole of that scene is eminently oriental and perfectly natural, even to the deep sleep into which all have fallen, so that David and Abishai could walk among them in safety. The Arabs sleep heavily, especially when fatigued. Often when traveling my muleteers and servants have resolved to watch by turns in places thought to be dangerous, but in every instance I

"Who will go down into the camp with me?" says David to his two leaders of his party—perhaps the only two with him. The same intrepid man that took water from the well at Bethlehem, perhaps when the Philistines were sleeping, is at once ready for another such excursion. The very peril fires his bravery. David and Abishai creep cautiously down the rocks, through the line of camels, asses, and baggage, past the sleeping soldiers, to the upturned faces of the general and the king. "Now God hath shut him up into your power," says Abishai, his hand on the hilt of his sword. "Let me strike him *once;* no need of a second blow." No! respect for God's anointment forbids it! "Destroy him not. It would be a guilty thing to do. The Lord himself shall smite him, or his day shall come to die. That will be soon enough for the Lord's purposes. Or he shall die in battle. The Lord forbid that I should stretch forth *my* hand against the Lord's anointed. Take his spear and his cruse, and let us go." *

---

soon found them fast asleep, and generally their slumbers were so profound that I could not only walk among them without their waking, but might have stolen the very *aba* with which they were covered."—*Land and Book.*

"We were just now in the track of the Bedouins' marauding expeditions. The fellah marched off indignantly to call on his friends to attack us during the night. All we could do was to keep strict watch all night. We awoke without mishap, but not by any means due to our watchers, for on waking once near dawn, I found all snoring fast, and could not disturb them by sticks or stones."—*Capt. Warren, of the English Palestine Exploration, in the Valley of Elah.*

* "No one ventures to travel over these deserts without his cruse of water, and it is very common to place one at the 'bolster,' so that the owner can reach it during the night. The Arabs eat their dinner in the evening, and it is generally of such a nature as to create thirst, and the quantity of water they

Strange conversation this, in that low tone, under the bright sky and over the sleeping general and the sleeping king, and among the sleeping thousands. A greater magnanimity than that shown in the cave! for Saul has come with aggravated injustice, since the demonstration which David had given him of his innocence and of reverence for the government.

Leaving the camp, they climb an opposite hill, which a deep chasm separates from the troops. Once mounted to that safe place, David cries out to the army. His musical voice rings out through the still night in the pure air, echoing from the rocks, "Abner!" "Abner!" "Answerest thou not, Abner?" until at last the general breaks away from his heavy slumbers, and confusedly cries, "Who art thou that criest to the king?" The king and the army are quickly all astir, and all silent to hear. Over the chasm a voice is heard, clear and cutting as Winter air: "ART not thou a valiant man, Abner? And who is there like to thee in Israel, thou, the keeper of the king? What hast thou done, thou keeper? An enemy came in to kill the king. *Ye all* deserve to die, because ye have not kept the king. Look! see! here! look where the king's spear is! and his cruse of water!" Surely, where *are* the king's spear and cruse? Yonder, held aloft in yonder hands!*

Saul understood. *It is David.* "Is this thy voice, my son David?" "It *is* my voice, my lord, O king! Why dost thou pursue after me? What have I done? What

---

drink is enormous. The *cruse* is, therefore, in perpetual demand. Saul and his party lay in a shady valley, steeped in heavy sleep, after the fatigues of a hot day."—*Land and Book*, p. 21.

* "There are thousands of ravines where the whole scene could be enacted, every word be heard, and yet the speaker be quite beyond the reach of his enemies."—*Land and Book*, p. 21.

evil am I guilty of against thee? Hear me, O King! What is the cause of your hostility? It must be God or man. If Jehovah stir thee up to pursue, let him smell a sacrifice; but if men only direct you, cursed be they before the Lord; for they have driven me from the land of the true God, and said, Go serve other gods." He thought how he had been driven to Gath and to Mizpeh of Moab. "Let not my blood fall to the earth; for it will fall before the face of God. For the king of the nation has come hunting a mere flea, a mere partridge like these that run along the mountains."

The second time! The king was amazed! "They are wrong—these miserable counsellors of mine—these petty Ziphite spies! *I* am wrong! He has twice spared my life!"

With a loud voice he calls to David—to reach David across the space the voice must have been so loud that the army heard the king—"I have sinned. Return, my son David. I will not do thee harm! never again! My soul has been precious in thine eyes. I have played the fool. I have erred exceedingly." Here is an open confession of his folly, and of David's innocence.

"See the king's spear! Let one of the young men come over and fetch it. The Lord render to each of us in justice and righteousness. For he delivered you into my hand to-day, but I would not stretch out my hand against the Lord's anointed. I have spared thy life tonight, and delivered thee: so let the Lord spare me, and deliver me from all my troubles."

Again the hard heart melted, and again the king himself is compelled to prophesy good things for David: "Blessed be thou, my son David. Thou shalt do great things, and shalt still prevail." With this prophecy, like John the Baptist's, "He shall increase, but I shall decrease," the king sounded his last retreat. The Philistines would next call him out to defeat and death.

David makes his way through the mountains and wilderness to his own troops, where, as the day wears on, the night's adventure is told abroad; and comments of admiration and indignation are made on the cave of the sheepfolds and the hill of Hachilah.

The earnestness, however, of David's cry to Saul, his solemn appeal to God, his warning to Saul not to shed his blood before the Lord, signify that David was in anxieties too profound for him to be affected by a light admiration. He despairs of any end to Saul's hostility. Saul will certainly catch him and crush him! His natural thought would have been, that his sins brought on him his afflictions! Deliverance, guidance, forgiveness, restoration of the nation from destruction and turbulence, are the topics which were uppermost,—the topics which we find in the Twenty-fifth psalm :

> To thee, O Lord, do I lift up my soul!
> O my God, I trust in thee! Let me not be put to shame!
> Let not my enemies triumph over me!
> Yea, none that hope in thee shall be put to shame!
> They shall be put to shame that wickedly forsake thee!
> Cause me to know thy ways, O Lord, teach me thy paths!
> Lead me in thy truth and teach me.
> . . . .
> Remember not the faults and transgressions of my youth!
> According to thy mercy remember thou me,
> For thy goodness' sake, O Lord!
> . . . .
> For thy name's sake, O Lord,
> Pardon my iniquity, for it is great!
> Who is the man that feareth the Lord?
> Him doth he show the way which he should choose.
> He shall himself dwell in prosperity,
> And his offspring shall inherit the land.
> Mine eyes are ever directed to the Lord,
> For he will pluck my feet from the net.
> . . . .
> Guard thou my life, and deliver me,
> Let me not be put to shame, for I have trusted in thee,
> Let innocence and uprightness preserve me,
> For on thee do I rest my hope.
> Redeem Israel, O God, from all his troubles.
> —*Noyes's Translation.*

Twenty-second Sunday.

"GONE OVER TO THE PHILISTINES."

LESSON.

1 Samuel xxvii.; xxviii. 1, 2, 4; xxix.; xxx. 26-31; 1 Chronicles xii. 1-22; Psalm xxxi.

DAVID was now nearly or quite twenty-eight years old; and it is the first point in his age that we have definitely marked. For when he left the land of the Philistines to be king, he was thirty years of age; and he was a year and four months in that country before he became king. We may assume that after Saul left him at the hill of Hachilah, some months passed away before he actually went over to the Philistines.

At the end of the thirtieth chapter, we have a list of at least thirteen cities in which David had friends during these eventful years of his wanderings. Now that we have come to the time when, as a persecuted refugee, he leaves that region, we may glance at what we know of these cities, and see something of David's resources then. Here and there, suddenly on this day or that, we may see David and a party, or David and his whole troop, or a party of spearmen, or a single messenger, at the gates of a city, on an errand of "aid and comfort." Three of these cities were directly south of Hebron: Eshtemoa, seven miles away, a priests' city, and for that reason in sympathy with Samuel and his school—on a low hill in the midst of olive-trees and pasture-valleys, and in the same elevated hill-surrounded table as Ziph, Carmel, and Maon ; Jattir, ten miles away, and Aroer in the wilderness, further south than even Beersheba. Bethel, South Ramoth, and Hormah were in the territory of Simeon. We know nothing further of them, except Hormah, which was twenty long miles through rocks and gravel below Aroer, a town guarding the pass up the first "step" from the lowest level of desert-wilderness southward, and situated on the side of a great ravine running north-east to the foot of the Salt Sea. To Hormah, David and his six hundred could have come when they "went down" to the wilderness of Paran, by a natural route from Engedi, without fear of molestation from Saul. In these vast solitudes he might have been, while the nation were mourning for Samuel, and before he sent up to Nabal's stingy shearing. The Kenites, old friends of the Hebrews from the times of Moses, lived "in the wilderness of Judah, south of Arad." Arad was about eight miles south of Hebron. "The cities of the Kenites," therefore, were in the region between Jattir, Hormah, and the foot of the Salt Sea. We know nothing of "the cities of the Jerahmeelites," except that they were in the very southern part of the tribe of Simeon, and that Jerahmeel, the ancestor of these inhabitants, was brother to the great Caleb who conquered and inherited Hebron. We must imagine, too, the families of his men with David, or joining them one after the other, for we shall find them with him in numbers when we come to Ziklag.*

It is not at all likely that David ventured to reside at any time in any of these cities. Gates and bars would attract Saul, as they did at Keilah, and his presence within walls would be a temptation to some of the town-people to betray him. The time was not come for the people of

---

* See, too, 2 Samuel ii. 3.

his own tribe to rank themselves openly on his side. It would have been treason, indeed, in David and in them, for a tribe to espouse his cause. Yet he was not without adherents, and strong men from his own tribe and from other tribes than his own, as the First Book of Chronicles shows. When a new company from Judah came to him, David, seeing among them Benjamites, and remembering the Ziphites, was at first suspicious. "If ye be come peaceably to help me, my heart shall be knit unto you: but if to betray me, as I am innocent, may God rebuke you." Amasa, his nephew, in a noble spirit, answered, "Thine are we, David, and on thy side, thou son of Jesse: peace, peace be unto thee, and peace be to thy helpers; for thy God helpeth thee."* They are taken into full confidence, and become captains of his troop. Some valuable helpers came, too, from the tribe of Gad, across the Jordan, lion-like men, fleet-footed, able to clear their way before them, who breasted Jordan when the waters were far over the banks. There were eleven of these captains, who perhaps brought men with them, and who "separated themselves unto David into the hold in the wilderness." These accessions, we may suppose, came after the affair of the robe at the sheep-folds, admiration for which exploit would naturally attract men to David, and kindle higher the wide-spread excitement.

David now saw that another return of Saul would be only a question of time. If he pursued him in the rocks of Engedi, he would certainly hunt him down to the further boundaries of Simeon. Sooner or later, he would be compelled to escape out of the land into Moab or the depths of Paran, or into the land of the Philistines. Of these three countries, the land of the Philistines belonged

---

* Yet Amasa, Ishmaelite's son that he was, afterwards in Absalom's rebellion forsook David, becoming Absalom's general.

by right to Judah and Simeon. If he put himself under the Philistine king, Saul would despair of him. He could make it appear the advantage of King Achish to receive him into his territory. When he feigned madness before Achish, he was a fugitive almost alone. Now he brought six hundred warriors, some of them "men of might," and all of them somewhat trained. This would be an accession not to be despised by a petty king whose sole possessions were a royal city and a few suburban towns. Achish would be glad, too, to take the occasion to draw off so much force from the Hebrews. And he must trust to providence, to God's definite directions, and to his own skill, to escape into Judah if Saul should die.

He, therefore, goes boldly down to Gath, and proposes allegiance to the king. He brings his wives and families into the royal city, which gives the Philistines security that these Hebrews are his own subjects. To the king, this is a desertion of his own country and alliance with an enemy. To David, it is simply a residence in his own rightful territory and city under compulsion, which the Philistine usurpers are just then enabled to enforce, and which he must resist by wile and strategem. To King Saul—we can see him as he hears of it—" Gone over to the Philistines! Aha! a godly man, indeed!" David gains favor by his demeanor and the demeanor of his people in the royal city. His request for a town of his own —indicative of his spirit and foresight—is granted. Such a permission we might at first think very remarkable, since it would give David an independent position; but we need only remember that such a vassal was liable at any time to be ordered out to war, and that then the families occupying the town would be hostages for his conduct and return, to see that Achish not only felt himself safe, but was *glad* to secure so powerful a subject.

Ziklag, where David takes up his residence for more

than a year, and which remained always afterward in his possession, is one of the unknown towns. But we can fix the region in which it was. It was in the "south" and in the tribe of Simeon, as the list of Joshua shows, where it stands next to Hormah. Centuries afterwards, when Nehemiah enumerates the officers of the restored kingdom and their cities-in-charge, Ziklag stands next to Beersheba. I seems reasonable to suppose, therefore, that it was not far from Beersheba, standing off on the south or southwest from the thirteen cities connected with the haunts of David, and some twenty or thirty miles from Gath. It was a city so far-off on the dangerous border that Achish probably had trouble enough with it. Here with his wives and with quite a population of the families of his increasing armies, David at last took up a residence within walls and gates. Here if Saul should attack him he would have the Philistines to contend with; and here there are no inhabitants who can betray him. Only the rovers of the great desert, and their incursions, need to be looked after.

Here David remains a year or more, for he spent part of the sixteen months in Gath. He rallies his confidence in God, but still as the weary months pass, he feels keenly that he is an exile from his own land. The Bethlehemites are fearful that he may bring vengeance on their city. The Ziphites, tribe-neighbors to them, have betrayed him. He is buried like a dead man, away and unknown, in the land of Ziklag. Yet the Lord has heard his cry; for he is not in the perils of mid-Philistia, but has a fenced city with a broad sweep of wilderness. Here David could not live so long without psalms and hymns through which to pray and praise. How often did he sing again, or gather some of the voices of his men around him to sing again psalms already composed during his troubles. New hymns, too, no doubt he added to those already written, one of which, expressing the feelings we have above supposed, may have been this

PSALM OF DAVID.

And "the leader of music" or "chief musician," to whom it was afterwards dedicated, may have been even then in the company at Ziklag.

> In thee, O Lord, do I trust; let me never be put to shame.
> According to thy righteousness deliver me!
> Bow down thine ear to me; help me speedily!
> Be to me a strong rock, a high fortress for my deliverance!
> For thou art my rock and my high-fortress!
> . . . .
> I will be glad and rejoice in thy mercy,
> For thou hast looked upon my trouble
> And hast had regard to my distress:
> And thou hast not shut me up into the hand of my enemies
> But hast set my feet in a large place.
>
> Have mercy on me, O Lord, for I am in trouble,
> For my eye is consumed with grief,
> Yea, my soul and my body.
> . . . .
> I have become the reproach of my neighbors
> And a fear to my acquaintances;
> They who see me abroad, flee from me;
> I am forgotten like a dead man.
> I am like a broken vessel,
> For I hear the slander of many.
> Fear is on every side,
> While they take counsel together against me
> They devise to take away my life,
> But I trust in thee, O Lord,
> I say, "Thou art my God."
> . . . .
> Blessed be the Lord,
> For he hath shown me his wonderful kindness
> In a fenced city.
> For I said in my haste,
> I am cut off from before thine eyes,
> But thou didst hear the voice of my supplication
> When I cried unto thee.
> . . . .
> Be of good courage
> And ye shall strengthen your hearts,
> All ye who hope in the Lord.   —*Psalm* xxxi.

The first signal act of David, after his families were established in Ziklag, was to *make* an incursion or raid upon the wandering tribes still further southward. Perhaps he felt it necessary to keep his troops in use, and at the earliest opportunity to make his power felt against the tribes condemned to extermination. Warfare was rough and savage. The nomadic tribes of the south were perpetual and merciless marauders. The law of retaliation was the international as well as the individual law. One of the special things in which David was to be a reformer was this work of just destruction. God's command to him was, as it was to Saul, to execute sentence on those incorrigible offenders. This David began to do by attacking and destroying certain bands of Geshurites, and of Gezrites or Gerzites, and of the Amalekites, who inhabited the wilderness on the road to Shur and Egypt. The road to Shur and Egypt was probably a road which, far below the country of these people, branched south to Shur, near the head of the Red Sea, and west to Egypt. Their clothing—and clothing is still a part of riches in the East—rich robes in part, perhaps, and their cattle of various kinds, David brought back to Achish, reporting that he had made a raid against "the south of Judah." And so it was, for Ziklag was far enough south. Possibly he kept within the letter of the truth, but he meant that King Achish should infer that his raid was against his own kindred. We cannot tell whether in those savage wars, and during the practice of oriental arts which were then accepted as honorable, such a deception would have been considered a violation of integrity. For more than in modern civilized warfare such prevarication, like the deception of espionage, was reckoned only a justifiable play of skill and wit. If we condemn it as a wicked thing, it was one of those strong temptations into which the impassioned David fell.

The object was gained, however; Achish gave him his confidence. When the Philistine army was summoned the next time to fight with the Hebrews, Achish sends word to his Hebrew vassal, "Be ready: thou shalt go the battle." With a wit and a manner which do not seem to be penetrated by the rude king, the ready captain says, "Certainly. Thou shalt see what thy servant can do." Relying on his recent fight against the Hebrews, and hoping to spur him on to greater achievements against his countrymen, and thereby to a wider separation from them, the king replies, "Then I will put you next my person, as keeper of my head."

David, therefore, reported himself and his men at the place of rendezvous, from which the Philistine army was to march to the valley Jezreel—to the very battle in which King Saul was to be slain. A watchful Providence would see to it that David the Anointed should not destroy Saul the Anointed.

There was a general gathering of the Philistines; for the word *lords* of the Philistines is a word peculiar in the lists of Joshua, Judges, and Samuel, to the five Philistine lords of the five strong cities, Gaza, Ashdod, Askalon, Gath, and Ekron. Achish seems to have been the leading king. Where Aphek was, we do not know, but somewhere on the way from Philistia to Shunem, outside of the Philistine land,* and more than two days' journey from Ziklag.† Shunem, to which the Philistine army marched, is supposed to have been on the slope of Little Hermon, in the valley of Jezreel, three miles north of the city of Jezreel, and five miles north of Mount Gilboa, whither the army of Saul was hastening. From both armies the large and beautiful valley of Jezreel could be seen stretching north-west down to the great sea. At Aphek, however, as the divisions of the army go past, and Achish, at the post of honor, comes last, the five lords see the Hebrews, and at once suspect David. "What do these

---

* xxix. 11. † xxx. 1.

Hebrews here?" The representations of David's fidelity for a whole year, by Achish, do not disarm their indignation and suspicion. Not without reason do they think that Achish is exposing not only the battle, but their own heads. "How will he get back to his king, but by turning against us in the battle—this very David, whom they put in their songs and dances higher than Saul himself?" They held a consultation, and decided against him. And so King Achish was forced to commend David and his troops, and to send them home to Ziklag with all despatch. At morning light they started. As they took their two days' journey southward, the army of Achish was winding the heights of Mount Carmel to the battle—Achish to a temporary but glorious victory: David to freedom from Philistine vassalage and to the kingdom.

From this very time onwards, David's troops increase until they become a great army. There was great excitement in the kingdom. Saul was weak in authority, and was himself in mortal terror when he saw the strength of the Philistines. The people were disaffected; for some mighty and resolute men of Saul's own tribe, twenty-five of whose names are recorded, skilled in slinging stones and shooting arrows with either hand, had either already come to David at Ziklag or now joined him. It may be the features of Benjamites in David's troops helped to alarm the five lords.

Seven captains, or, as we would say, colonels, for they were captains of thousands in their own tribe, joined him as he turned back from the tribe of Manasseh. They saw no hope in Saul, and turned their fortunes in with David's at that opportune moment when the lords of the Philistines demanded that David be sent home. While the Philistine army passed through their own tribe up Mount Carmel, they turned southward with David to Ziklag. From that very time, every day, new troops gathered to him.

Twenty-third Sunday.

TAKEN AWAY IN WRATH.

LESSON.

1 Samuel xxviii. 3-25 ; xxix. 1, 2 ; xxx. 1 ; xxxi. ; 2 Samuel i. 6-10 ; 1 Chronicles x. ; Deuteronomy xviii. 9-14 . Leviticus xx. 27 ; Exodus xxii. 18.

IF we take now a broad look over the whole kingdom, we see it full of excited action. At the south, the city of Ziklag is smoking with fire. The Amalekites who have kindled the flames during David's absence are beating their retreat, their captives on their camels, into the far distant wilderness. West from Jebus, now rapidly advancing to the dignity of a feudal lord, David pursues his leisurely way southward, little imagining the disaster at Ziklag. The Philistines suspect and fear his power ; and each day of his journey gives him fresh accessions of numbers. To the north-east the whole strength of the Philistines pours down the upper slopes of Carmel towards Shunem and Jezreel. Along the "back-bone" of the land towards the mountains of Gilboa, King Saul hastens the rallied tribes to meet the enemy on the old battle-field of Deborah and of Gideon. The eastern part of the kingdom across the Jordan seems the only portion at peace and rest ; and from there we shall soon see Saul's kinsmen, the men of Jabesh-gilead, coming on a kind and an awful errand.

We now follow the tragic fortune of the desponding king. Once pitched on Gilboa, the mighty forces of the enemy lie spread out on the plain below. It is less than five miles to the furthest line of their army. They are out in the solid power of all Philistia, every prince and town in their full strength. Saul is afraid. Trembling seizes him. His army has never had a lofty faith in their leader. Confidence in him as a man and as a king is utterly shattered. He is conscious that his power has departed. God has left him. No dream directs him. The sacred lot cannot respond, for he himself has driven the high-priest and the ephod over to David. No prophet approves him or follows him. The frenzied king sees a great battle and a great crisis imminent, and has no confidence in himself to direct the kingdom. Oh! for an hour of Samuel's wisdom and of Samuel's power! Yielding, therefore, again to the evil spirit which is upon him, he resorts to a wicked device which drives him on to his awful fate.

There are conjurers and diviners in the land who claim to communicate with the dead. Perhaps it is possible to gain access to the good Samuel. The pitiful and friendly prophet may take compassion on him in his strait; and for the sake of the king and the kingdom which he established he may direct him. Just then and there, the king, it is likely, passed through all that reasoning through which so many pass in our own day and in all ages have passed. He arrayed before his mind the alleged facts of spiritual communication from the unseen world, and the power to be derived from it, ignoring the subtle power of such spirits to deceive, and disregarding the command of God to seek Him only in his open revelation. Necromancy, enchantment, divination, and all the arts of the wizard were then associated with the sensual life of the heathen tribes, just as now much of modern spiritualism is associated with the doctrine and practice of "free love." These arts belonged to the very abominations for which God expressly ordered Samuel and Saul and David to punish those nations. And these things Saul had sternly prohibited, driving them out of the land, and making the diviners and conjurers tremble for their life.

But notwithstanding all this, Saul in his frenzy determines upon the desperate experiment. He will confront his own commands, defy his own conscience, that he may meet, through forbidden arts, information drawn from the unseen world. And God determines to meet him with information true and terrible.

He bids his servants find for him a woman who professed to communicate with spirits. Perhaps he had heard there was one in this north country. They bring him word that there is one at Endor, seven or eight miles across the valley, over a broken and difficult country, and beyond the army of Achish. The distress of Saul's soul is so great and his passion so headstrong that no risk or difficulty will stop him. He disguises himself, and, taking two men with him, threads the dangerous path by night and obtains access to the woman. The very first words with which she confronts the king are, "Why do you seek my life; for you know King Saul has made a capital decree against us?" The woman evidently supposes them to be spies—Hebrew soldiers intent on reward or in obedience to law—or else she takes her customary precaution against the betrayal of her illegal profession. On the solemn oath that she shall not be exposed, she asks whom they wish to see. When the king says "Samuel," and she secretly performs her incantations at so strange a request, to her consternation the actual form of Samuel appears before her. She recognizes at once the seer and the king, and cries out, full of alarm. Saul quiets her fear, puts her aside, and, proceeding to investigate the apparition, sees that God has truly permitted Samuel to appear. It is very evident from the description that Saul *saw* and *believed* the form to be Samuel's; that Samuel spoke to Saul in his proper character; and that Samuel made predictions for the next day which could be made known only by God. "Why hast thou troubled me, to bring me up?" says the august prophet. What a dismal confession does the king make, *"I am sore distressed; for the Philistines make war against me, and God has departed from me, and will not answer me by prophets or by dreams; therefore I have called thee, that thou mayest make known unto me what I shall do."* " Pity me, and tell me what to do," is the cry of this weakling who should have been strong in heroic faith and heroic valor. It is *too late:* too late for pity from Samuel, or for instruction from Samuel, for one who has turned his back upon the face of God. "Why dost thou ask of *me*," is the solemn voice of this supernatural person in the silence of the night, "since Jehovah has departed from thee and thou hast made him thine enemy? Jehovah has done what I declared he would do. He *has* rent the kingdom out of thine hand: he *has* given it to thy neighbor, to David. Thou knowest the reason. Thou didst not obey, thou didst not inflict his wrath on Amelek —in the crisis of thy character. Jehovah will also deliver over the kingdom, and thee its king, to the Philistines. To-morrow, thou and thy sons shall be with me."

Terrible was this volley of thunderbolts. Terrible accusations of his conscience! terrible reverberations down his guilty life! terrible sentence already in process of execution in the mustered armies! terrible doom of to-morrow! The huge form fell back on the floor, faint with sense of guilt, with fright and with fasting.

At length the woman and his servants aroused him. The woman saw that the king was in trouble and was faint. She had put her life in his hand, and now she wished to ingratiate herself by good offices. She killed her fatted calf; she baked hasty cakes of bread for him; she compelled the three to eat for their strength. And at length they silently and cautiously departed. What a night journey was that, as they took their way across the bed of the ancient Kishon, and as the stars were hastening from the morning light!

Dismayed or undismayed, there is no time for delay. The battle is pressed on in the morning by the enemy. With such a leader, the Hebrews have no spirit. With such tumultuous thoughts, Saul is no leader even to himself. He rushes, in sheer desperation, into the front, and the enemy make head directly against him. The chariots and horsemen press closely upon him. The arrows pierce

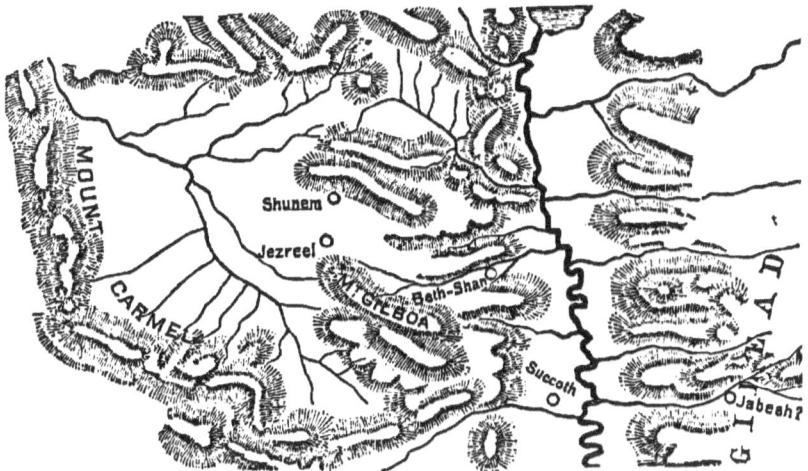

him. He is struck till he is "sore wounded" and ready to fall. In the very hands of these dogs, under their savage mockery, he is likely to die. "Thrust thy sword through me!" he cries to his armor-bearer, who either will not or dare not. He, therefore, falls heavily on his own sword, and his armor-bearer imitates him. Even then the king is not dead. As the margin reads, his coat of war hindered the fatal wound. Weltering in his blood and in anguish as he was, he calls to a man near to know whether he is Philistine or Hebrew, and, finding him an Amalekite, commands him to stand on him and kill him. And thus the ignoble king, anointed of God to be a reformer and deliverer and victorious ruler of his people, set on his high career by a great prophet who had already for him inaugurated the reformation and the victory, dies beneath the feet of an Amalekite, a representative of the very nation whose guilty life he had spared.

The Philistine army sweep past him and drive everything before them. Jonathan and his brothers fall. The citizens from Jezreel and Shunem and other towns, as well as the army, flee in utter rout. And the Philistines seize and hold the towns and the whole region. They even take and hold cities across the Jordan!

But the last disgrace is not yet offered to the apostate king. When, the next day, the Philistines come to strip the slain, in the barbarous practice of early war, they find the bodies of Saul and his three sons on the mountain-side. The king's head they cut off, as when David cut off Goliath's. They send it in triumph with his armor down through their own country, publishing the glorious news abroad, and were greeted, no doubt, on their return, by songs and dances—as David was when he went up to Gibeah with Goliath's head—carrying his armor to their idol-temples, and fastening up his head in the temple of their fish-god Dagon. This is for glory and for exultation at home. But for revenge and savage triumph over the hated Hebrews in their own land, they carried Saul's body to one of the conquered towns. There at Beth-shan, in the valley of the Jordan, where the road descends from the valley of the battle to the south in the river-gorge, and past which, no doubt, the Hebrews had fled, they nailed the headless trunk, with the bodies of his sons, against the gate,* as

---

* See 2 Samuel xxi. 12, where the statement is that the body was taken down from the *street*. The two passages harmonize, if we consider the gate-wall the entrance of the street.

a menace and taunt. The walls of Beth-shan were probably not more than twenty miles from Jabesh across in Gilead. Moved with horror at the spectacle, and with grateful remembrance of the king whose first exploit in his royal career had been to deliver their city and their right eyes from King Nahash, the valiant men of Jabesh arose as one man. They pressed across the twenty miles by night; they took down the bodies from the wall; they brought them over to Jabesh; they decently burned them there; they buried the bones under an oak, and fasted seven days in honor of the dead and in solemn sense of the awful bereavement.

The two sins for which King Saul is especially condemned, as we read the record of his death, are *disobedience to God* and *inquiry of unseen spirits.* His life had been a wilful departure from implicit respect for God's word, and it had culminated in turning away from God to seek counsel from a source forbidden by God and by his own commands. His whole career was that of a wicked man, who filled his miserable place in history and gave awful truth to that saying of Jehovah: "I gave them a king in my anger, and took him away in my wrath."

Twenty-Fourth Sunday.

THE CROWN AND THE BRACELET.

LESSON.
2 Samuel iv. 4, 10 ; 1 Samuel xxx. ; 2 Samuel i. ; 1 Chronicles xii. 20–22 ; Psalm xxxv.

WONDERFUL are the preparations of Providence for God's purposes. The preparations for the entrance of David on his reign were varied and wonderful. The high-priest, Saul by his own act had transferred to David. The disaffection of the people from Saul in his last days turned the latent thoughts of many in the tribe into an actual support of David at Ziklag. David was prevented from fighting against King Saul in his last battle by the Philistine lords. If he *had* fought among the victorious Philistines, he might have created a division among the people in respect to his fitness for the throne. If he had succeeded in deserting the Philistines at the crisis of Saul's death, and in rallying the Hebrew army to victory, he would have had to assume the responsibility amidst the uncertainties in respect to the death of all Saul's sons, and the possibilities of a disputed command. As it was, he was called to the throne afterwards by the free action of the people. It was by the divine foresight that three sons of Saul's house were slain. In the panic which swept over the land, at the rout of the Hebrew army, the next heir also to the throne in Saul's house—the first-born son of Saul's first-born, Mephibosheth, the son of Jonathan—

was so crippled that his physical vigor was forever broken, and it is probable his mental force impaired. The nurse who had the child in charge was probably at Gibeah when she fled, carrying him on her shoulder, according to the custom; in her haste she stumbled headlong with such force that the son of Jonathan lost the use of both his feet, and so was deprived of the power, if he had the disposition, to resist the new king. By an Amalekite's hands, too, the very crown and the bracelet (a golden "arm-band," a royal decoration) were now transferred to David. A prompt transfer, which shows where the thoughts of the people were.

Let us now turn southward to David. There could not have been more than a day's difference between the time when David discovered the smoking ruins of Ziklag and the night of Saul's terror at Endor. For it was on the third day after David left Aphek that he reached Ziklag; and it would not have taken more than two days for the Philistine army to reach Shunem from Aphek. David, too, was gone from Ziklag in pursuit of the Amalekites some two or three days; and, when he had been in Ziklag again two days and a part of the third, the messenger arrives with the crown and bracelet and the tidings of the king's death. We may think of David and his men, therefore, mourning over the loss of their families as they come to Ziklag, while Saul is trembling with terror on Mount Gilboa at the eve of battle, and of David plunging into the southern wilderness with utmost speed, or sweeping down on the Amalekite camp while the battle is raging in the plain of Jezreel.

Bitter were the outcries of David's men when they found the city of Ziklag taken, and their wives, sons, and daughters taken captive by the fierce rovers of the desert. Frantic and exasperated in their grief, they are ready to mutiny against David; for on him they lay the blame of compelling them to enter the Philistine army and leave the city defenceless. They speak of stoning him, although Ahinoam and Abigail, his wives, are captives, and David is in a frenzy of tears and grief like themselves. David, however, soon diverts them from rage and grief by directing their attention to the hope of recovering their wives and children. God is righteous. He will help them and pursue with them. "Bid the high-priest come forth with the ephod. Let us sacrifice and inquire of God whether we can overtake the marauders." "Pursue," is the divine answer: "for thou shalt surely overtake them, and free them all."

The nomadic tribes, which live by the plunder of each other, keep close watch of each other's movements. The Amalekites of the southern desert, therefore, knew that the whole Philistine strength was drawn off for their northern campaign, and that the south was left "uncovered." They may not have known at all that the Hebrew David occupied Ziklag; for, when David made his raid on the Geshurites and Gezrites and Amalekites towards Shur, they might have supposed it was a Philistine raid. It was an extensive raid which they had made, reaching from the south of Philistia across Judah to the south of Caleb, the neighborhood below Hebron; for they had taken "great spoil out of the land of the Philistines, and out of the land of Judah." They swept, therefore, completely around Ziklag. And they felt secure enough after a short stage of homeward march into the wilderness.

The pursuit of David and his six hundred was so eager in that hot and sandy district that when they came to the brook Besor—we do not know where the brook Besor was, but it must have been deep in the heart of the wilderness—two hundred were utterly faint and must be left behind. The four hundred press on till they find a famished, fever-stricken Egyptian near the road. He was too far gone to call even, "Water, water!" They gave him bread-cakes, which he ate; "they made him drink water; a piece of a cake of figs, and two clusters of dried grapes," they succeeded in making him take, and at length the poor body, which had been without food or drink for three days and three nights, began to show signs of animation. As they suspected, he was a slave belonging to the Amalekite troops, and soon told them the story of the Amalekite raid; and, on assurance of personal protection, was quite ready to lead the way to his oppressors. There were the Amalekite troops, eating and drinking and dancing, fully believing that no occasion could send back the warriors of Ziklag. When David surrounded them and came upon them, the surprise was complete. For a whole day, David fought them so skillfully that he recovered his own wives, the sons and daughters of his men, and their stolen goods and cattle, seized the flocks and herds of the enemy, and slaughtered their warriors. Four hundred young men who were alert, and who mounted their camels, escaped, and they only. This was the most complete success which David had yet had; and the revival of feeling from grief to joy gave them all a spirit of exultation as they drove the abundant herds homeward. David himself was wise to take a quick advantage of the occasion. It was time to teach the men who were ready to mutiny to be proud of their master. And this he did as the droves passed by, when he said, "*This* is *David's* spoil."

Another of those smaller crises, however, which test character, soon arose; and in which appeared the self-possession and decision of David's character. When the two hundred faint warriors at the brook Besor came out to meet the victorious return, David saluted them graciously; but the spirit of selfishness was yet rife in the more discontented of his men, and they said, "We will give them none of the spoil; they shall have nothing but their wives and children; they did not go with us to the battle." In this they selfishly claimed that their pursuit and victory were owing entirely to their own power, and that the faintness of the two hundred was owing to their disposition as well as their weakness. But David at once recognized God as the one who directed them in the pursuit, and who conquered the enemy by them; and said those who stayed behind had done their duty as much as those who went. And he maintained his position firmly by declaring that in his army the law should be, "He that stays to guard the stuff at home shall share equally with him that goes to battle." This decision, firmly and generously maintained on the very eve of David's promotion, made the rule an "ordinance" during the whole reign of David.

We assume now that, when David came back to Ziklag, he knew nothing as yet of the battle in the north. His heart had been torn by the recent struggles: Ziklag burned! Abigail and Ahinoam captives! his men in mutiny for grief! pursuit, rout, capture, slaughter, in the name of God! clamor and command! weary marching to, and triumph at smoking Ziklag! Towards those enemies of the south, what fiery oriental imprecation burst from his soul!

But what anxiety, too, in respect to Saul and the Philistines. Where will he next be driven when one of them or both turn back upon him,—suspected, slandered, and hated as he is of both.

The Thirty-fifth psalm may be considered as expressing both these attitudes of David's mind; in the first part, a demand for justice on God's enemies, and in the second part, outcry against unjust and slanderous persecution.

> Contend, O Lord, with them that contend with me;
> Fight against them that fight against me;
> Take hold of shield and buckler
> And stand up for my help.

Draw forth the spear and the axe against my persecutors.
Say unto my soul, " I am thy salvation."
Let them be confounded and put to shame that seek my life.
Let them be turned back with confusion that devise my hurt.
Let them be as chaff before the wind !
Let the angel of the Lord drive them !
Let their way be dark and slippery.
Let the angel of the Lord pursue them !
For without cause they have laid for me a snare,
Without cause they have digged for me a pit.
Let unforeseen destruction come upon them.
Let their snare which they have laid catch themselves.
Into that very destruction let them fall,
And my soul shall be joyful in the Lord !
It shall exult in his protection.
All my bones shall say, Who, O Lord, is like unto thee ?
Who doth rescue the afflicted from the oppressor ?
The afflicted and the destitute from the spoiler ?

False witnesses have risen up.
They charge me with things of which I know nothing.
They repay me evil for good,
Even unto the spoiling of my soul.
Yet I, when they were sick, was clothed with sack-cloth,
I humbled my soul with fasting !
And my prayer be turned into my bosom.
. . . .
How long, O Lord, wilt thou look on !
O rescue my life from their destruction,
My darling (life) from the young lions !
. . . .
Judge me according to thy righteousness, O Jehovah, my God !
Let them not triumph over me.
Let them not say in their hearts,
" Aha, we have our wish !"
Let them not say,
" We have swallowed him up !"

Let them be confounded and brought to shame
Who rejoice at my calamity.
Let them be clothed with shame and dishonor
Who exalt themselves against me.
Let *them* shout for joy, and be glad
Who favor my righteous course.
Yea, let them always say, " The Lord be praised
Who delighteth in the prosperity of his servant."
And my tongue shall speak of thy righteousness
And of thy praise all the day long.

David, however, foresaw the possible issue of every important battle in which Saul was a personal leader, and knew that Saul's death was divinely determined and could not long be deferred. His quick mind now saw the opportunity to strengthen his own power without opposing the king. He could send abroad to the people in the south the news of his triumph over their ancient enemies, and, at the same time, increase and create a feeling friendly to himself. A present of the spoil would indeed be only a grateful remembrance of the sympathy and the aid he had received from cities when he was less powerful than now. All through the breadth of Judah and Simeon, from Ziklag to the Salt Sea, and from Hebron southwards, he sent, therefore, his spoil of cattle and of garments to the elders at the city gates. Many a town through all that region—and there was hardly one not exposed to the attacks of the Amalekites—was most pleasantly affected towards David, as the "blessing" was brought to their officers. It was no selfish Nabal who had outwitted the Lord's enemies, but the generous grace and beauty of David and Abigail that embraced their friends in their joy and triumph. That two days' distribution at Ziklag proved both generous and discreet at a most opportune hour of his human destiny.

On the third day, a messenger came with all speed from the north. Earth was on his head, and his robes were rent. He enquired for David, and fell to the earth before him in profound salutations. In answer to David, he said that he came from the Hebrew army, escaping with his life; that the Hebrews were routed, and that the king and his son were killed. To the question, "How dost thou know that Saul and Jonathan are dead?" he told the story of Saul's overthrow, but he made prominent his own part in the death of the king. He said nothing of Saul falling on his own sword, but with evident satisfaction would have David believe that he himself made sure his death. He produced the crown and the royal bracelet to show that his story was true. For his discernment between a falling and a rising king, for his decision in transferring the kingdom when he saw so plausible an opportunity of disposing of the king at the king's own request, for the first tidings of the important event, and the prompt and safe delivery of the royal insignia, he was expecting some reward of wealth or honors from "King David." With only Amalekite ideas of feuds and dynasties, he little knew the spirit of David. To David, there was an awful calamity to the nation, little comporting with this indecent attention to private interests. He rent his clothes, he mourned and fasted with his men among his own spoils, till evening, over the king and Jonathan and Jehovah's people and nation. There had been nothing like this since the death of Eli! He called the young man before him again. He had heard him say he was an Amalekite. David was in no mood for Amalekites. "*Whence* art thou?" he said. He answered, "I am the son of a stranger, an Amalekite." "How didst thou take the responsibility of killing Jehovah's anointed king? Who knows how God might have preserved him? The story of thine own lips shows thee the murderer of the king. Thy blood upon thy head." As the proper avenger of blood—the king's son-in-law and privately anointed to the king's throne—David commanded him to be slain.

We catch here a clear illustration of the manner in which the psalms were probably composed. In all elevations and depressions of spirits, David's feeling ran freely into poetic and pious expression; and here, with his sensitive soul overwhelmed with grief at the personal and public loss, he pours out his pathetic elegy over Saul and Jonathan in an ode entitled

THE BOW.*

Published afterwards in the Book of Jasher:

The beauty of Israel is slain
Upon thy high places.

---

* "Not only because the bow is referred to, but because it is a martial ode, and the bow was one of the principal weapons used by the warriors of that age,

How are the mighty fallen !
Tell it not in Gath !
Publish it not in the streets of Askelon,
Lest the daughters of the Philistines rejoice.
Lest the daughters of the uncircumcised triumph.
Ye mountains of Gilboa,
No dew nor rain be upon you, nor fields of offerings,
For there the shield of the mighty is vilely cast away—
The shield of Saul, as if not anointed with oil.

From the blood of the slain,
From the fat of the mighty,
The bow of Jonathan turned not back,
And the sword of Saul returned not empty.

Saul and Jonathan were lovely and pleasant in their lives,
And in their death they were not divided.
They were swifter than eagles,
They were stronger than lions.

Ye daughters of Israel, weep over Saul,
Who clothed you in scarlet, with other delights,
Who put on ornaments of gold upon your apparel.

How are the mighty fallen in the midst of the battle !
O Jonathan, thou wast slain in thine high places !
I am distressed for thee, my brother Jonathan !
Very pleasant hast thou been unto me.
Thy love to me was wonderful,
Passing the love of women.
HOW ARE THE MIGHTY FALLEN,
AND THE WEAPONS OF WAR PERISHED !

---

and one in the use of which the Benjamites were particularly skillful. Other explanations are by no means so natural. It is beautifully significant that David required this ode to fallen Benjamites to be taught to the children of *Judah*."—*Keil and Delitzsch.*

Twenty-fifth Sunday.

DAVID, KING OF JUDAH.

LESSON.
2 Samuel ii. 1–7.

IT was time now for David to act. He knew that he had been annointed king to succeed Saul. But he did not presume upon even this knowledge, confirmed, as it was, by Samuel the Seer, and by so many providential intimations since the days of the anointment at Bethlehem. He had the high-priest and the ephod with him. There could certainly be no more important time than this to know the divine will. And it might be quite as important for him to know the method in which God would place him on the throne, as to know the fact itself that the time had come for him to be crowned. How was he to be crowned? Where was he to be crowned? Was his own tribe to act a leading part, or was it to be at the assembly of all the tribes? From love and loyalty to Judah shall he go into a city of his own tribe? or to avoid envy, shall he go outside Judah? Was the constitution of the kingdom by which he was to govern to be the same as that under which Saul reigned? With a solemn sense of the importance of his action, David, therefore, "inquired of God," as the Israelites did after Joshua's death, when his own tribe of Judah was the first directed to proceed with the conquest. There, at Ziklag, we see the humble-minded, valiant man. He has built an altar "apart," or returned to the altar at which he inquired of God whether he shall pursue the Amalekites. He has brought a goat for a sin-offering, "to make an atonement" for sin; and bullocks and sheep for a burnt-offering, to signify the dedication of himself to God; with a thank-offering of flour, oil, and wine for God's blessings and benefits. He stands in the midst of his people, while the fire and smoke ascend to the God of his fathers, as Abraham stood in the midst of his own people, teaching them through Abiathar's ministrations at the altar to conform to the law of Moses so far as the circumstances will permit. He communicates his prayer, "Shall I go up into *any* of the cities of Judah?" through the high-priest. He waits for the answer in the proper form, by lot, or voice, or dream, or vision, or prophetic insight.* His filial spirit has been nurtured through these ten years of persecution, his natural abilities strengthened and softened and unified, his faith and love for the Lord Jehovah made broad and deep, the poetry and the utility of his nature developed in praise and toil, his whole

---

* "We may represent to ourselves the process of seeking counsel ‘by Urim.’ The question was one affecting the well-being of the nation, or its army, or its king. The enquirer spoke in a low whisper, asking one question at a time. The high-priest, fixing his gaze on the ‘gems oracular’ that lay ‘on his heart,’ fixed his thoughts on the Light and Perfection which they symbolized, or the Holy Name inscribed on them. The act was itself a prayer, and, like other prayers, it might be answered. After a time, he passed into the new, mysterious, half-ecstatic state. All disturbing elements—selfishness, prejudice, the fear of man—were eliminated. He received the insight which he craved. Men trusted in his decisions as with us men trust the judgment which has been purified by prayer for the help of the Holy Spirit, more than that which grows only out of debate and policy and calculation."—*E. H. Plumtre, in Smith's Dictionary of the Bible.*

character mellowed and matured. The answer comes, "Go up." "Whither shall I go up?" Perhaps Bethlehem was in his thought. "To Hebron." At once preparation begins, the camels' and asses' loads are packed, the note and accent of high anticipations strike everywhere upon the ear, and with profound thoughts in the mind of the lordly sheikh who rides in the midst of his train, at early dawn the ascent begins.

Now that Saul is dead, and the fear of his cruel and stubborn temper is no more upon the people, the career and character of David present themselves vividly before the people of his tribe. Throughout all that southern part of Judah, and throughout Simeon, which, from Joshua's death, has been a brotherly part of Judah, there is a quick-flowing reverence and love for that native of Bethlehem whose gifts have already made room for him. The people flock towards the south where they know David is, their hearts divinely prepared to welcome him whom Samuel anointed, and whose loving and valiant character has been so thoroughly tested in their midst from Gath to Engedi, and from Gibeah to the wilderness.

To Hebron!—always the strong city of Judah, since Caleb took it, and changed its name from "the city of Arba," the giant, to Hebron, "the Friend," in memory, no doubt, of him, who from his tent near by went up the eastward hills to see the smoke of Sodom. Beautiful it was, too, "lying in deep repose along the vale of Mamre." Bethlehem was very likely at times its rival in the tribe. But Bethlehem was not so rich in historical associations. If Jacob came to Bethlehem after the vision in which he was named Prince of God, and in which he was told that a nation of kings should come from him, Abram came to Hebron after Lot chose the plain of Jordan and the garden of Gomorrah, and after God told him he would give the land to his seed forever—from here he pursued after the four kings and recaptured Lot, and was returning here when Melchizedek met him; here he saw that smoking furnace and that burning lamp that passed between the pieces of his offering; and here before Isaac was born he was called Father of a Multitude. If Bethlehem had the sepulchre of Rachel, Hebron has the field and cave of Machpelah, where were buried first Sarah, then Abraham himself by her side, then Isaac, and at last Jacob, when Joseph came up from Egypt in state to bury him. If Bethlehem had Boaz and Ruth, Hebron had Isaac and Rebekah. If Bethlehem was recovered by Salmon from the Canaanites, Hebron was recovered from the giants by Caleb the spy, who had helped to bear away the grapes of Eshcol from the valley near. Here, too, at "Mamre," sometimes so called from Abraham's Amorite friend and ally, the three angels came to Abraham's tent. And from Joshua's time, it had been a city of Levites and a city of refuge. There was no city in all the twelve states of United Israel which was so full of powerful associations. Let us look a little more closely at the town itself.

This city, to which David is now marching in dignity and power, and where he is to be crowned by the graves of his patriarchal fathers, is in a deep, narrow valley, entirely surrounded by high hills which are themselves the tops of the central mountain range. It was twenty miles from Jebus and twenty miles from Beersheba, and about half-way from the Salt Sea to the Philistine plain. The winter streams from Hebron flowed south-west to "the great sea westward," although down the eastward side of the next ridge they ran to the Salt Sea. The little valley in which Hebron is, is about three miles long, and runs from north-west to south-east, opening into the larger south-west ravine, which bears its waters to the Philistine plain. Here at the southern end of the little three-mile valley is the city, low down on the eastern slope, but reaching across to the western slope. The valley grows broad as you go north, and the rudely-paved road runs between stone walls of vineyards and olive-yards till it takes a northeast turn out of these hills on its rough and mountainous way to Bethlehem and Jebus. Vineyards cover the bottom of the plain, each with its walls and its stone lodge or tower in the corner, filled with the largest and best grapes in all Canaan. The slopes down to the valley are covered chiefly with olive-yards, terraced in many places; springs and wells are numerous; and the grove of terebinths or oaks is famous in David's time. Then the city was probably more populous than now, when it numbers eight or ten thousand souls. The houses were all of stone, no doubt, as now, and high-built, with windows and flat roofs. Perhaps small domes like those now there, were on the roofs. There are no walls now, although one or two streets have gates. Then, it may be, the surrounding hills and towers were thought a sufficient protection. And if the town, then as now, was built in three clusters, the business or bazaar part on the eastern slope, with a northern suburb and a western suburb on the western slope, the "cities of Hebron" may be one town, without including smaller villages on the circling hills and outward slopes beyond. At the large square reservoir of hewn stones between the bazaars and the western suburb and at the smaller pool—a stone parallelogram at the north end of the business part—both very ancient structures, doubtless in David's time, you might have seen men and women filling their large skin bottles, or bearing them away on their backs. In the bazaar were butchers' stalls, with beef and mutton, killed and dressed after the Hebrew manner, so as to leave no blood; raisins in abundance, and noted for their size; delicious large oranges from the Philistine Joppa in the tribe of Dan; pomegranates, figs, apricots, quinces, apples, pears, and plums from the hills around; syrup, called *dibs*, made from the juice of grapes; skin bottles, and perhaps glass armlets, and oriental lamps like those now manufactured at Hebron. Cooler and better watered than the rest of the "hill country," high above most of the "dry and withered valleys," the mountains, indeed four hundred feet higher than Jebus, Hebron was just now rising into its most glorious period. For just now David is on his way to make this his royal capital for the next seven years.

Behold the young sheikh as he comes yonder with his cavalcade up the south-west valley-road from Ziklag. The people have run forth to meet him, for the news has spread that he is coming. They are bringing him back with acclamation. People from Jattir and Aroer, and Eshtemoa, and Carmel, and Maon, and from the Kenite cities, are already in the town, or in yonder throng. The Ziphites tremble at the sight. He is now just thirty years of age. He is not large, but strong in frame and comely in form as he rides on yonder camel. His well-grown beard flows full from his handsome face, browned as it is with exposure, which his picturesque turban becomes not a little. His loose outer robes are wrought in high colors, and are perhaps rich garments from the spoil of his enemies. His wives and women-servants ride probably without a veil, since the use of the veil has increased in modern times. His captains and stout warriors, in various costume, mounted on camels or asses, ride with their "hundreds." Children appear here and there with the women or the men throughout the long procession. All Hebron is alive with joy and shouts as the cavalcade winds down the ridge into the gate. The acclamations are swelled by constant arrivals from all parts of the tribe. The jargon of voices is something wonderful, for the excited conversations of that oriental people are always vociferous and loud. Quickness, good sense, and grace characterize the movements and speech of David, and loving favor in the eyes of man and of God are the gracious gift of Jehovah to him. Beautiful is this sweet place in the eyes of the poet-warrior after the dry desert and the long tempest-tossed persecution. All the families of his warriors follow him—a thousand people or more in all—who fill every vacant space, and after the public ceremonies, are assigned a residence in houses or suburbs, or adjacent villages.

Without waiting to dispute the claims of Saul's house in the north, or to gain the assent of all the states of Israel, his own strong tribe is now ready to anoint David publicly to be king over their own territory. Simeon is included, as is evident from the region from which David came, and the help which had been extended to him there.

Priests and Levites from the priestly towns of Jattir and Eshtemoa and Debir and Juttah and Bethshemesh and Hebron, have now gathered around Abiathar. A flask or horn of new anointing oil has been sacredly compounded—the myrrh, the cinnamon, the sweet calamus, the cassia, the olive oil, quickly forthcoming from wealthy families or priestly houses. A day is set—the morrow; a place is appointed—the gate-court, or Abraham's oak outside the walls. Robes, brilliant in color and embroidery, woven, dyed, embroidered perhaps at Bethlehem, and preserved there in expectation of such a day as this, are assigned to the royal person. Arrayed in these, before the multitude, the handsome young man of thirty years—frankness and force beaming from his face—stands forth. Abiathar, the high-priest, pours on him the oil—the symbol of divine right, and the people shout the acclamations, "Live the king! Live the king!"

The king's first public act is an act of grace and of wise policy. "The men of Jabesh Gilead," he is told, "buried King Saul." Forthwith messengers are dispatched to that distant city, with blessings on them for their kindness to the dead, and invoking Jehovah's favor for the good thing which they have done. By their success, he appeals to them to be strong and valiant against the exulting Philistines; and bids them know that the nation is not left without government, for his own tribe—the leader in Israel—have anointed himself king over them.

Twenty-sixth Sunday.

KING ISH-BOSHETH.

LESSON.
2 Samuel ii.

THERE survived at least one resolute man of Saul's army—the son of Saul's uncle. This was Abner, the chief captain or general of Saul's army. He was a powerful and unprincipled man. He had been, no doubt, Saul's adviser during his persecution of David. We meet him now as the stout opponent of David's claim to royalty. He was quick to lay claim to the succession in the name of Saul's house. Although Ish-bosheth was forty years old, he seems to have had little ambition or energy himself. Abner acted for him in this crisis. And as the Philistines drove the Hebrew army from the towns up the valley of Jezreel and commanded the heights of the central mountains, Abner established the new king, Ish-bosheth, in the stronghold of the east country. Mahanaim was the place where he had him crowned, a place of which we know little, but which becomes a valuable point from its gathering historical associations. We suppose that it was in the neighborhood of Jabesh-gilead and about eighteen or twenty miles east of Beth-shan.* It was the place at

---

* Professor John A. Paine, of the American-Palestine Exploration Expedition, seems to have identified Mahanaim. He locates it " on the west side of Jebel-Ajlun, five miles directly down in an

which the angels of God met Jacob when he was on his way to his brother Esau, and which Jacob then named

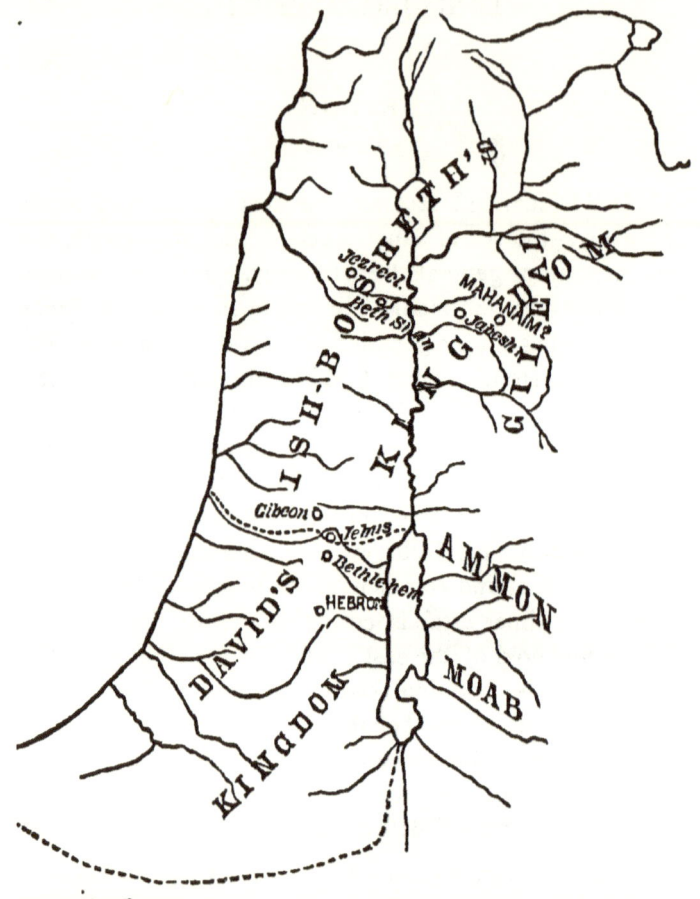

extremely rough, wild country. The forest is the wood of Ephraim as perfectly as could be, and too rough for cultivation, except in openings, while the locality is an exact retreat for a fugitive; whether David or Ish-bosheth. The site is a small one where two little valleys join and enter a third, on the end of the tongue of land of the two. The ruins are quite late and not extensive. There is a fountain in the third valley, just above where the two joined enter, and the bottoms of the valleys are

Two-Hosts, or Mahanaim.* This strong place in the mountains of Gilead was now designed to be the temporary royal residence, until the national forces could be rallied and possession of the country regained. There Ish-bosheth was crowned king " over Gilead," east of Jordan, "and the Ashurites"—we do not know who the Ashurites were, unless they were the Asherites of the tribe of Asher, on the great sea—"and over Jezreel," the strong city of the north, and over the two closely allied tribes of Ephraim and Benjamin, and over all Israel. As we shall see, Abner, in Ish-bosheth's name, attempted to gain possession of the royal tribe of Benjamin, and for two years of war he maintained Ish-bosheth's royal right to the whole realm of Israel.

David was king over Judah for seven and a half years. Ish-bosheth was king for two years. Was Ish-bosheth's two years during the first part or last part of David's reign in Hebron? Probably towards the last part; for the acceptance of David's reign by the twelve tribes evidently follows immediately the death of Abner and Ish-bosheth. Even allowing a year and a half after Ish-bosheth's death for all the tribes, one after the other, to give in their allegiance to David, we must still add four preceding years to the two years' reign at Mahanaim to make up the full seven and a half years. If David was crowned over all Israel *at once* after Ish-bosheth's death, then we must allow five and a half years to have transpired after Saul's death before Abner actually established Ish-bosheth across the Jordan. We may better distribute the time by placing about four years before Ish-bosheth, and a year and a half after him. During

---

still kept growing with fields of wheat. The present name is *Mahana*, as close to the old Mahanaim as anything could be." —*Manuscript Letter.* This is the site indicated more exactly in the map facing page 284.

* Genesis xxxii. 2.

these four years Abner may have been fully occupied in driving out the Philistines successively from the Gileadite towns, from the "Ashurites," from Jezreel and its plain, from Ephraim and Benjamin. This was the natural order, and if this order was preserved, then he advanced regularly from east to west, and from north to south, till all Israel was his to the boundary of Judah. When he came to the boundary of Judah the army of David met him.

In the north, we may suppose that the Philistines held possession of large and small towns during three or four years, but with a constant warfare from the tribes. Zebulun and Naphtali, "a people that jeoparded their lives in the high places of the field" in the day of Deborah, and Issachar, whose princes were with her against Sisera, could not have so utterly lost their ancient valor as to be content with the lordly Philistines in their towns. The middle and northern tribes at first hesitated whether to give in their allegiance at once to David. It is evident that Abner had influence over them and persuaded them to support Ish-bosheth's claims; for, when Abner went over from Ish-bosheth to David, he said to the elders, "Ye sought for David in times past"—"both yesterday and the third day," the Hebrew runs—"to be king over you." We suppose, therefore, that for the first three or four years Abner was occupied in arousing the people against the enemy, and in gaining over the consent of the elders and tribes to Ish-bosheth as their king. This at length they were not unwilling to do under the strong leadership of Abner himself; and the trans-Jordanic tribe, and the tribes from Benjamin and Ephraim northwards, accepted the proclamation of Ish-bosheth as king. Of course the region of Gilead, to the people of whom David sent his courteous message in hope that they would give allegiance to him, would naturally support Saul's house, not only from kinship and gratitude, but because the new capital was in their territory.

Another man of mark now comes into conspicuous notice on David's side; a man so strong that the success of David's kingdom has been attributed to him rather than to David. This is no less a person than David's nephew, Joab—a brave, fierce, decided, vindictive, ambitious man, who sometimes made his friends as well as his foes tremble by the tremendous impetuosity of his character. His brother Abishai, as we have seen, was with David at Adullam, and went at the price of his life to bring David a drink from the well at Bethlehem; but this is the first place at which Joab appears. He now appears, however, as the captain or general of the army, blowing the trumpet and commanding the men. It is a fair inference that he had already been some time in David's camp. We catch a glimpse of military excursions and raids against the Philistines, Amalekites or other enemies during these years, in the glimpse which we have of Joab at the head of David's servants as they "came in from pursuing a troop, and brought in a great spoil with them," just after Abner was gone. We may be sure that David gave the Philistines occupation and alarm enough at home to induce them to draw off some of their forces from the north and middle of the land. Abner on the one side, Joab on the other, we shall find to be two daring, passionate, and unscrupulous men, who each brought upon himself at last a violent death.

Sooner or later the two armies under the two captains were sure to meet. Perhaps in no district easier than in Gilead—the land of kindred, and where Saul's rescue of their city Jabesh from the cruel Nahash could never be forgotten—could Abner gather forces to maintain Saul's cause. Strong athletic men they were too, those hardy highlanders of the east country. With a considerable army, therefore, Abner had descended the hills of Gilead, crossed the Jordan ford, swept clear the valley of the ancient Kishon, and advanced down the central mountains. At last on a new campaign, his troop issued from his eastern capital, pushed down the Jordan gorge, climbed the passes of Ephraim or Benjamin, and sat down as in challenge, at Gibeon. Joab, out of the smiling valley of Hebron, led his troops over the familiar path northward past Bethlehem and the frowning Jebus towards the central plateau of the country. From between a northern and a southern army, the Philistines gradually withdrew.

Gibeon, where the armies met, was about six and a half miles north of Jebus. If the tabernacle was now at Gibeon, the place was important to each of them. Here in the "land of Benjamin" came the contest between the two determined men, the one set on the recovery of his own tribe and the re-establishment of the throne within the ancestral borders; the other, valiant for the divinely anointed king, and, we may be sure, not a little valiant for Judah and for Bethlehem. There is a pool at Gibeon to this very day, about one hundred and twenty feet long and one hundred feet broad, which may well be the pool on either side of which the armies encamped.

A challenge is sent across from Abner to Joab, half in pleasantry and half in earnest. "Let the young men arise, and play before us." This was a challenge to a friendly mock-battle as a trial of strength, as the word "play" may denote, or to decision of the contest by champions. Twelve Benjamites and twelve warriors of Bethlehem and the hill country of Judah meet in the open space between the opposing ranks. If they began in sport, they soon turned to earnest. Left-handed Benjamites and right-handed men of Judah, they caught each other by the head, wrestling with each other and thrusting their swords into each other's sides, neither party, as it would seem from the record, entirely mastering the other, until all or nearly all had fallen in a pretty equal contest upon an undecided field;

but the courage, strength, fortitude, and martial skill which were displayed were so heroic on either side that the place was named The Field of Strong Men.

The spectacle fired the battle-spirit. The day became a day of battle—in the first civil war since the time of the insurrection of Gibeah and Benjamin against the Theocracy. The army of Abner was driven before Joab towards the wilds between Gibeon and the Jordan. The fleet-footed Asahel chased Abner himself to capture or to slay him. More than a match for the defeated general in speed, Abner is more than a match for him in strength and skill. Well knowing that Joab would be a fierce avenger of blood, and moved, perhaps, with pity for the more gentle and more lovable Asahel, he bade him be content with the spoil of some other warrior than himself, and not compel him to turn upon him. And when the over-confident young man pressed too closely on his very person, with one powerful blow he struck the sharp hind end of his spear entirely through his body, and left him dying on the ground. The pursuers who came up gathered around the dead body, while Joab and Abishai took up Asahel's pursuit through the rough descent till the sun was going down. The scattered Benjamites, however, gathered themselves around their leader on the top of a rocky hill; and, when Joab and Abishai came up, Abner appealed to him to call off his men, and put a stop to this fraternal and civil conflict: "Command your people. Why permit them to slaughter their own brethren? Have you not victory enough without a bloody pursuit? Shall this thing go on for ever? Think of the bitter end."

This Joab accepts as a token of submission, but there is the very fire of heroic energy in his answer: "As God liveth, unless thou hadst spoken," and cried, Enough, "surely not until the morning light had the people ceased to follow every man his brother." On the instant, he blew the trumpet and sounded the retreat.

That very night both armies departed homewards, Abner and his men marching through the Jordan valley, and across the river, and through the Broken country (Bithron) probably of the ascent east of Jordan, until they came to Ish-bosheth's capital in the highlands of Gilead; Joab and his troops, with the body of Asahel, twelve or fifteen miles to Bethlehem, where they left the body of his brother, and then fourteen miles further to Hebron at the break of day.

The loss on David's side was twenty men, including Asahel, and on Ish-bosheth's side, three hundred and sixty dead, besides the wounded. There were, therefore, at least from four hundred to eight hundred men on a side in the two armies, and probably many more.

Twenty-seventh Sunday.

ABNER AND JOAB TRANSFER THE KINGDOM.

LESSON.
2 Samuel iii. iv.; 1 Kings i. 6; 2 Samuel xiii. 37, 38; 1 Chronicles iii. 1-4.

FIXING in mind, therefore, the time between Saul's death and Ish-bosheth's coronation as a period of about four years, let us see how the events in the north and south of the land harmonize with this distribution.

At Hebron, we now see David with six wives, according to the usage of polygamy. When he came up from Ziklag, he had but Abigail and Ahinoam. Whether his successive marriages were the result of policy by which he sought to strengthen his power by alliance with strong families, or was only from affection, some time must have transpired for the four marriages to take place. On the simplest supposition, four or five years do not seem too long a time. And if Eglah was the same person as Michal, Saul's daughter, as tradition has it, she was not welcomed back by David till near the end of his reign in Hebron, as we shall soon see.*

Abigail and Ahinoam, as we have already seen, were

---

* Eglah is for some reason called in this enumeration both in 2 Samuel iii. 5, and 1 Chronicles iii. 3, "David's wife." The birth of her son is also mentioned last of the six children born in Hebron, which harmonizes with the fact that she did not come back to Hebron till at least six of the seven years had passed.

from the lower part of Judah. If Eglah was Michal, she was from Benjamin and from Saul's house. Of Haggith's father and Abital's early home we know nothing. But we know that Absalom's mother, Maacah, was from Geshur, a city and perhaps a district belonging to the tribe of Manasseh, east of Jordan, the inhabitants of which continued to dwell among the Manassites.* Geshur was far north on the east side of Jordan, half-way from the Sea of Chinnereth to Damascus, and was considered as belonging to the general region of Syria. To his grandfather Talmai's distant home Absalom afterwards fled, when he had slain his own brother Amnon. There is a tradition that Maacah was taken by David in battle, and advanced to the position of his wife.

Six children were born to David during the seven and half years in Hebron, some of them, we may suppose, before the war with Saul's son. Three of these children were destined to wring with anguish their father's tender heart by their wilful ways and violent death. For Amnon the first-born was murdered by Absalom; and Absalom was slain for treason by this very Joab who now at Hebron saw the beautiful baby; and Adonijah, who, like Absalom, inherited his father's beauty, and who was a wilful and indulged child†, attempted to seize the throne in his father's old age, and was afterwards executed for treason by his younger brother King Solomon. Absalom's own daughter or granddaughter, who was wife of King Rehoboam and mother of King Abijah, was named Maacah, very likely for his mother Maacah. On the supposition that the mother Maacah was like her son Absalom and her descendants Rehoboam and Abijah, we may see in her the not unusual combination of beauty and a wilful temper. In this larger city of Hebron, in greater wealth and more

---

* Joshua xiii. 13; 1 Chronicles ii. 23. † 1 Kings i. 6.

imposing display, we now begin to see around David as a centre, the home-scene which we have pictured around Jesse at Bethlehem thirty-five years before.

The battle of Gibeon we place immediately after the act of crowning Ish-bosheth. The open act of crowning that weak man prince was of course considered by all the people as a challenge of David's supremacy. We consider this battle the opening of a two years' war between the rival houses. Frequent were the contests, now under David, now under Joab, on the one side, and under Abner on the other. The power of David steadily increased, and the weakness of Ish-bosheth became more and more evident.

The resolute Abner, however, considered himself, as he was, the real manager of Ish-bosheth's kingdom. He did, therefore, what in the ancient East was common in the successor of a king. The domestic household of a deceased king belonged to the one who took the throne. Abner, therefore, in a conscious independence of his subordinate, Ish-bosheth, took Rizpah, Saul's concubine, for his own, either in marriage or adultery—as Adonijah afterwards wished to take Abishag, the surviving wife of David, for his wife, and was condemned for treason.*

Weak as Ish-bosheth was, he could not brook an offence which was both the assumption of royal rights and an insult to himself. In answer to Ish-bosheth's indignation, Abner plainly told him that Saul's house was upheld by himself against David, and that *he* ought to be thankful that he had not delivered him up to David. After all his wisdom and energy, was he a dog's head, that he did not know his rights! Like Herod, when reproved by John the Baptist in this very region, Abner was in lofty and haughty

---

* 1 Kings ii. 22-25.

anger. He cowed the feeble king by threatening to take over to David the whole nation from Dan to Beersheba.

There was another motive now, no doubt, against Ish-bosheth in Abner's mind. The trans-Jordanic kingdom was failing, and he might be chief in a powerful government under David if he would bring to David these northern and eastern tribes. The very incident forced him to a new course of action; and he determined to make use of his occasion, to put his threat into execution. He sent messengers down to Hebron to make a league with David, offering to transfer the tribes. David was quite ready for such a league, but he was wise enough to insist on one condition first of all—the immediate restoration of his early wife, Michal. This was a matter of policy as well as of affection, for it transferred the only surviving member of Saul's family besides Ish-bosheth to himself. He, therefore, at once enforced his claim to Michal by sending messengers to *Ish-bosheth* demanding her restoration. It was also a test whether Abner would really surrender the interests of Saul's house to that of David. Ish-bosheth sent for her, of course with the consent or advice of Abner.

Gallim, the home of Phaltiel, was no doubt somewhere in Benjamin, although Phaltiel and Michal may both have been at Mahanaim. The husband followed the wife with whom he had lived from twelve to seventeen years with outcries and tears. The public necessities of her reunion with David, however, were imperative; and at last, at Bahurim, probably about three miles from Jebus on their way up along the Jericho road, Abner was imperative— "Go; return." It was death for Phaltiel to disobey. The league was, therefore, established; and Abner set himself about the reconciliation of the northern tribes to David. It was not a very difficult thing to do. He probably went to the prominent cites, like Jezreel and Beth-shan and Shechem and Gilgal and Mizpah and

Gibeah, and assembled the elders of the city or of the tribe. He reminded them that they had formerly wished to make David king.* He said, "The time has come. It is the will of God, for He had said, By the hand of David I will save my people from the Philistines and all enemies." He carried even Benjamin with him by his persuasions, and then went with an escort of twenty men to represent to David the attitude of the tribes. At an oriental feast David entertained Abner's company; the compact was concluded and confirmed by rites of hospitality, and King David dismissed his important guest to gather the proper civil and military representatives by which the submission should be made.

It is possible that this visit and feast of Abner were timed to take place when Joab was absent. David knew Joab from a child—his retaliatory and vindictive spirit; and had not Abner slain *God's creature*, the light-footed Asahel? Laden with spoil, Joab's troop returned to Hebron to learn the news that Abner and his escort had been there to make proposals to the king. Joab fired at once. He saw a dangerous rival. He remembered who was Saul's right arm in the persecutions. He saw the man that killed his brother. He suspected a spy—a subtle and acute foe. He saw the chance to extinguish the rival kingdom. He asked, Where is he? He quickly took his resolve. He plunged into David's presence, and upbraided him for receiving Abner. "Did he not know it was only to spy him out?" David did know the bloody fierceness of Joab, and read even Abner better than he. Forthwith, without a word to David, Joab sends messengers with words for the parting captain to return. And when Abner returned, in implicit reliance on David's good

---

* 1 Samuel xviii. 5; 1 Chronicles xi. 2. The numbers which had deserted to David before Saul's death showed the people's heart.

faith, he basely murdered him. He did it, too—for Abner knew the dangerous man—under the pretence of a private peaceful conference. Abashai was his accomplice in the crime.

There is no justification of this murder. Joab did not kill Abner as the avenger of blood, for the deed was done in the very gate of the city of refuge. Abner, too, tried to spare Asahel, and had at last slain him only in self-defence. The awful crime filled the soul of David with horror, and provoked from his lips a fierce oriental curse on Joab and his house. He has slain a guest in violation of customs of hospitality. He has treacherously pretended to be friendly. He has misrepresented the spirit of the king to his own kingdom, leaving the people to think David had conspired to entice Abner by a hospitable feast to his death. He had put in peril the recovery of the northern tribes by basely killing the man through whom it was to be brought about, and sending abroad the rumor that the new king was blood-thirsty, savage and treacherous. The very soul of David was rent with anguish, and to the very end of his life he remembered the awful crime of Joab as a crime that deserved by every human and divine law a just retribution. Joab, however, had taken him at a disadvantage. He was then too strong and too important to him for the young king to take the punishment into his own hands; but, with great energy, David declared himself and his kingdom free from complicity. He denounced Joab in the awful words of Moses's curses on those that break the divine commandments. He made Joab rend his clothes before the people, and wear sackcloth and mourn for Abner. The king himself followed the bier and made lamentation with the oriental wailers at a grave prepared in Hebron, and denounced over him again the horrid treachery by which Abner had lost his life, and the wicked men who took it. He would eat nothing till the sun went down. He eulogized Abner as a prince and a great man fallen. He said it was a weakness and a blot upon his kingdom. He confessed himself too tender for the hard hands of his sister's sons, but said the Lord himself shall execute justice one day upon this wickedness. A tremendous judgment it was to which his bold and bloody independence brought Joab at the end of his long and powerful life!

David acquitted himself in the eyes of the people from all this guilt. His deep and tender horror over Joab's murder, won their hearts everywhere. All things had, however, worked together to strengthen the throne at Hebron. Abner's death broke the power of the northern kingdom. While the fierceness of Joab's temper made the people at home tremble at his very name, his name struck terror to the Israelites under Ish-bosheth. King Ish-bosheth himself, without Abner, was utterly feeble. And as in all revolutions, so now there rose up men with private injuries to revenge on the heads of the falling.

How is it that these two captains, Baanah and Rechab, could so interpret David's disposition as to suppose that he would triumph over the head of Ish-bosheth? What was there so heathenish in *their* disposition as to venture on boasting of the assassination before him? A single glance will show us that they were descendants of Canaanites, and were probably animated by personal revenge against the house of Saul. They were "Beerothites."

The inhabitants of Gibeon, that in the days of Joshua "did work wilily" with old sacks, and rent wine-bottles, and clouted shoes, and mouldy bread, and that did by league become "hewers of wood and drawers of water," dwelt in *four* cities: Gibeon, Chephirah, *Beeroth*, and Kirjath-jearim.* They were a remnant of the Amorites. King

---

* Joshua ix. 17.

Saul, who was so easy with Agag, in a mad zeal to do something against the heathen, had broken the nation's solemn compact with them, and " sought to slay them."* It is evident that it was a bloody work which Saul did, for the Gibeonites exacted a bloody atonement afterwards. Beeroth was in Saul's own tribe, about ten miles north of Jebus; and it is very probable that it is this act of Saul's persecution and cruelty which is alluded to when it is said that " the Beerothites fled to Gittaim." Gittaim was probably either another city of Benjamin or a Philistine city; so that the Beerothites, like David, may have been compelled to go over to the Philistine country. At any rate, it seems likely that their Amorite fire was kindled at the first opportunity against the house of Saul. Trained under such a king in his own tribe, they retaliated with his own weapons.

Whether there was a remnant of Ish-bosheth's army in existence we are not informed. At any rate, these two captains knew something of the king's habits. Very likely they had belonged to the body-guard of the King, as Saul's body-guard were taken from the tribe of Benjamin.† They conceived the satisfaction of retaliating on Saul's house and of reward from David for extirpating the last hope of Saul's kingdom. In broad noon-day, they came to the king's house. It is the still and inactive part of the day, in the house of a quiet and irresolute man. "They entered the palace, as if to carry off the wheat which was piled up near the entrance. The female slave who, as usual in Eastern houses, kept the door, and was herself sifting the wheat, had in the heat of the day fallen asleep at her task. They stole in, and passed into the royal bed-chamber where Ish-bosheth was asleep on his couch. They stabbed him in the stomach or abdomen, cut off

---

* 2 Samuel xxi. 2. † 1 Chronicles xii. 29.

his head, made their escape—all that afternoon, all that night—down the valley of the Jordan ('through the plain,' that is, through the *arabah*, the Jordan valley), and presented the head to David as a welcome present."*

But David's policy was settled against all secret murders. He took the high position, so unlike oriental chiefs, that assassinations weakened his kingdom. Following on the heels of Abner's murder, he was in no heart for another murder plotted to help his cause. He was strong enough without it; and it was both a blot and a wickedness. When, then, the two captains held up the ghastly head of Ish-bosheth, as the achievement of their marauding boldness, David met them with stern indignation. By a solemn oath, he reminded them of what he had done six or seven years before to the Amalekite at Ziklag. And he solemnly told them their crime was even greater. In the quiet of their own home they had murdered an inoffensive person whom he himself held righteous. They should die the death for their dastardly crime. He ordered them to be executed. According to the usage of that rough time, he had their hands and feet cut off, and hung up over probably one of those reservoirs at Hebron which are still there, and every heathenish Beerothite and Gibeonite was taught that the King's sense of justice was loftier than his ambition. The head of Ish-bosheth was reverently buried with the body of his great kinsman and captain of his host, in the sepulchre where the king and his people wept over Abner.

---

* Stanley.

Twenty-eighth Sunday.

PSALMS IN HEBRON.

LESSON.

2 Samuel ii. 11; v. 5; Psalms lviii., xxvii., xxvi., lxxxvi., and cv.

WE are now on the eve of David's coronation over the whole kingdom. But how is it that we do not meet with any of David's psalms during this whole seven years at Hebron? Is Dr. Robinson right when he says, "In Hebron, too, he probably composed many of his psalms, which yet thrill through the soul and lift it up to God?" We have seen that some psalms were composed while he was driven before Saul. We know that some were composed shortly after Jebus was taken, and the ark of God brought home to that new capital. It does not seem at all likely that just between these two points of his life the young king's poetic soul was unstirred by the great events of the reign in Hebron. There, in Hebron, was now completed the peaceful establishment of his family and of the families of his men, who had so long been persecuted rovers. There his anointment over the powerful Judah at the direction of God. There was the gracious heroism of the men of Jabesh, who buried the Lord's anointed. There was the intrigue and manipulation of Abner in the north, in opposition to Samuel's prophetic declarations that the son of Jesse should be king. There was the lofty challenge and heroic struggle at the Field of Strong Men, and tragic fate of Asahel. There was the providential transfer of the unscrupulous Abner to the execution of the Lord's plan for the kingdom. There was the revenge of Joab and Abishai. All these were events on which a purely human imagination might have seized for lofty or pathetic expression. Indeed, over one of them David's soul did flow forth in rhythm and melody:

> "Died Abner as a fool dieth?
> Thy hands not bound,
> Thy feet not put into fetters,
> As man before the wicked, so fellest thou."

However frequent we may imagine the expression of poetic sentiment by David during this time, that portion of it which was preserved for sacred use conveyed general rather than local thought. We cannot certainly locate a single psalm at Hebron. There is no allusion to that city by name in any title or in any line of the psalms. There are, however, several psalms which may most appropriately have been written during this early period of the young king's rule. Let us look at five psalms, in respect to which we see no good reason why they should not be located just here. Let us take first the events over which we have just passed, and which ploughed David's very soul so deep—Joab's atrocity and the assassins' "retribution." At both these times the great fires in David burst forth in heat and flame of speech, cauterizing and consuming the crimes and the criminals. Even Joab must have quailed at the vehemence of the king's rebuke, and have been dismayed as the curses and vindictive predictions opened before him the thundering justice of Sinai itself. But David's solicitude was more for the people than for Joab. The impression made on their minds must have been much more powerful if he embodied his sense of retaliatory justice towards Joab or the assassins or both in an intense poetic expression like the Fifty-eighth psalm.

The psalm is but another expression of the law of Mosaic retribution, and justifies at its close its own terrible denunciatory appeals to God to suppress iniquity:

A PSALM OF DAVID

For the leader of music. To the tune of " Do not destroy."

Do ye indeed administer justice faithfully, ye mighty ones?
Do ye judge with uprightness, ye sons of men?
Nay, in your hearts ye contrive iniquity.
Your hands weigh out violence in the land.
The wicked are destroyed from their very birth.
Their lives go astray, as soon as they are born.
They have poison, like the poison of a serpent,
Like the deaf adder's, which stoppeth her ear,
Which listeneth not to the voice of the charmer,
And of the sorcerer, skillful in incantations.

Break their teeth, O God, in their mouths!
Break out the great teeth of the lions, O Lord!
May they melt away like a stream of water,
When they aim their arrows, may they be broken!
May they be like the snail, which melts away as it goes.
Like the abortion of a woman, that seek not the sun!
Before your pots feel the heat of the thorns,
Whether fresh or burning, may they be blown away!
The righteous shall rejoice when he seeth such vengeance.
He shall bathe his feet in the blood of the wicked.
Then shall men say, " Truly there is a reward for the righteous.
Truly there is a God who is judge on the earth!"
—*Noyes's Translation.*

When David is first peacefully established on the throne of his native tribe, we would naturally expect first some exultation of spirit, or at least some elevated satisfaction; and, therefore, first in order of time, we would look for a psalm expressive of satisfaction or of thanksgiving and praise to God. Such a psalm is the Twenty-seventh—the title of which in the Septuagint locates it before the anointing. Read it with a backward glance on David's long persecutions, with a forward glance to David's first public act after he gained the whole kingdom, the act of re-establishing the tabernacle-worship; read it with the conception of a growing desire for several past years in David's soul to reform Saul's abuses of the national religion, with the thought that David's aged parents, brought back from Mizpah of Moab, had at last died, and that there were enemies in the northern tribes who hated and maligned the young king, and we shall see how entirely appropriate it is to the circumstances of his early reign :

The Lord is my light and my salvation,
Whom shall I fear?
The Lord is the shield of my life,
Of whom shall I be afraid?
When the wicked came upon me to devour me,
Even my persecutors and enemies, they stumbled and fell.
Though a host should encamp against me, my heart shall not fear:
Though war should rise against me, yet will I be confident!
One thing have I desired of the Lord, that do I yet seek:
That I may dwell in the house of the Lord all the days of my life,
To behold the glory of the Lord,
And to gaze upon his temple.
For in the day of trouble he will hide me in his pavilion;
Yea, in the secret place of his tabernacle will he shelter me.
He will set me upon a rock;
Yea, already doth he lift my head above my enemies who are around me;
Therefore, in his tabernacle will I offer sacrifices with the sound of trumpets.
I will sing, yea, with instruments of music will I give praise unto God.

> Hear my voice, O Lord, when I cry unto thee!
> Have pity upon me, and answer me;
> When I think of thy precept, "Seek ye my face!"
> Thy face, Lord, do I seek.
> O hide not thou thy face from me,
> Cast not thy servant away in displeasure!
> Thou hast been my help, do not leave me!
> Do not forsake me, O God, my helper!
> For my father and my mother have forsaken me,
> But the Lord will take me up.
> Teach me thy way, O Lord,
> And lead me in the right path, because of my enemies;
> Give me not up to the will of my adversaries!
> For false witnesses have risen up against me,
> And such as breathe out injustice.

I trust that I shall see the goodness of the Lord
In the land of the living! Hope thou in the Lord!
Be of good courage; let thy heart be strong:
Hope thou in the Lord. —*Noyes's Translation.*

We trace in this psalm those alternations of devout courage and devout dependence which were one striking characteristic of David's piety.

We may expect at this time also some sentiments put into the lips of the people, which declare his own purpose as a Ruler. God has raised him up to re-erect the law of righteousness. The time had not yet come when he could re-establish the national worship, but no doubt he did construct, during those seven years in Hebron, some order of worship, where the people around the altar could render their devotions and receive instructions worthy of a priestly and royal city. In such a place, the young king's voice and example might have expressed the sentiment of a psalm which refers back to the general spirit of his past life, to his present convictions, and to his future purposes.

A PSALM OF DAVID.

Be thou my judge, O Lord, for I have walked in mine integrity.
I have trusted in the Lord, therefore I shall not fail.
Examine me, O Lord, and prove me,
Try my veins and my heart.
For thy loving-kindness is before my eyes.
And I have walked in thy truth.
I sit not with vain persons,
And go not in company with dissemblers.
I hate the assembly of evil-doers,
And do not sit with the wicked.
I will wash my hands in innocence,
So will I go around thine altar, O Lord,
To utter the voice of thanksgiving,
And tell of all thy wondrous works!
O Lord, I love the house of thine abode,
And the place where thy honor dwelleth!
Take not away my soul with sinners,
Nor my life with men of blood,
In whose hands is mischief
And whose right hands are full of bribes.
But as for me, I will walk in my integrity.
O redeem me and be merciful to me.
My foot standeth in a level place.
In the congregation I will bless the Lord.

—*Psalm* xxvi.

We may be sure that such expressions of sorrow for sin

as have been expressed in psalms already cited,* were in
Hebron repeated both in public and in private, for this is
necessary to reconcile the deception and duplicity of
which he had been guilty, with the divine favor which we
know approved his personal and kingly character. Here
was the king of broad and humble mind, in the midst of a
tribe and a nation of fierce, savage, fighting men, who
were ready to justify every retaliation and bitter reproach
and bloody revenge with all the intensity and narrowness
of an avenger of blood—a king, of just and pure mind in
an age of hacking swords, bloody passions, and physical
ambitions.

Sometimes during those seven years at Hebron his tender heart was no doubt depressed at the long-continued
resistance of Saul's house, the hostile power of Abner, and
the refusal of ten tribes to accept the Lord's anointed.
Seven years were a long time to wait patiently on the
Lord for the kingdom to which in his early youth he was
anointed. It was a discipline to make his soul humble
and mellow, as he thought of the sins into which he had
been betrayed during his persecutions. How many thoughts
passed through his mind at such an hour: the sins of
his youth up to Saul's death, his personal guilt in the cause
of this delay, the violent reproaches which reach his ears
from the jealous tribes of Benjamin and of Ephraim, the
rumors of Abner's strength, the danger to his tender offspring, the strange departure of the tribes from the divine
will, the prospect of civil war, and the miserable destruction of the whole land! In such a mood as this, perhaps
just as Joab is to lead forth his army for the first time
against Abner at Gibeon, we may suppose the Eighty-sixth
psalm—"a Prayer of David"—to have been composed.
Without quoting them in full—for its expressions are

---

* See Psalm xxv., on page 141, and Psalm xiii. on page 129.

general—we may notice such allusions as the following:

> Bow down thine ear, O Lord, and hear me,
> For I am poor and needy.
> Preserve my soul, for I am one thou favorest.
> Save, O thou my God, thy servant that trusteth in thee.
>
> . . . .
>
> Be merciful unto me, O Lord,
> For I cry unto thee daily.
>
> . . . .
>
> For thou, Lord, art good and ready to forgive,
> And plenteous in mercy unto all that call upon thee.
>
> . . . .
>
> Among the gods there is none like thee, O Lord!
> And there are no works like thy works.
> All the nations whom thou hast made
> Must come and worship before thee, O Lord!
> And shall glorify thy name.
>
> . . . .
>
> Teach me thy way, O Lord,
> I will walk in thy truth.
> Unite my heart to fear thy name.
> I will praise thee, O Lord my God, with my whole heart.
> And I will give glory to thy name for ever;
> For great is thy mercy towards me,
> And thou hast delivered my soul from the depths of hell.
> O God, the proud have risen against me,
> Bands of violent men have sought my life.
>
> Show me a token of thy favor,
> That my enemies may see it and be confounded,
> Because thou, O Lord, hast helped and comforted me.

The One Hundred and Fifth psalm is one which may have well been composed in Hebron, although the first of it was first published for public use at the entrance of the ark into Jerusalem, a year or two later.* Where more powerfully than at the very graves of the three patriarchs would the associations prompt David to call,—

> Talk ye of all his wondrous works,
>
> . . . .
>
> Remember his marvellous works which he hath done,
> His wonders and the judgments of his mouth.

---

* 1 Chronicles xvi. 7.

> O ye seed of Abraham his servant,
> Ye children of Jacob his chosen,

and to say,—

> He remembereth his covenant for ever,
> The word he commanded to a thousand generations.
> The covenant he made with Abraham,
> And his oath unto Isaac,
> Which he confirmed to Jacob for a decree,
> And to Israel for an everlasting covenant.
> "To thee," said he, "will I give the land of Canaan
> For the lot of your inheritance,
> When they were but a few men in number,
> Yea, very few, and strangers in it!"

After his defence of the Lord's anointed, how natural, too, are his words,—

> He suffered no man to do them wrong,
> Yea, he reproved kings for their sakes,
> Saying, *Touch not mine anointed*,
> And do my prophets no harm.

At no time could the rehearsal of the history of God among his people have been more opportune than in the early days of his reign, for the purpose of teaching the people,—.

> That they might observe his statutes
> And keep his laws.

Two things united to form here the beginning of that psalmody which under David advanced into so important a place in the New Tabernacle. David's long persecutions ripened his character early, and he was, therefore, likely to judge the outcry of his own heart in distress the outcry of others in their distresses. And that poetic genius which could not be suppressed, would be likely to preserve, collect, and make use of the psalms already composed.

Twenty-ninth Sunday.

THE CORONATION.

LESSON.

2 Samuel v. 1–5 ; 1 Chronicles xi. 1–3 ; **xii.** 23–40 ; Deuteronomy xvii. 14–20.

THE whole nation now was "knit together as one man" to accept and crown King David. Not a tribe was unrepresented. Every tribe was ready with numbers and with power. The wise elders that at Saul's death desired David for king, but were compelled to yield to Abner's power over the people or over other tribes, gladly turned to Hebron. The good everywhere were glad that Saul's miserable house had come to an end. They said it was the will of God that David should reign, that Samuel the Seer *had* truly and secretly anointed him king, and that God had been with him. They spoke of his valor against Goliath and against the enemies of the nation ; of his beautiful magnanimity towards King Saul. They believed David that it was no thought of his to slay Abner the son of Ner. Even the tribe of Benjamin was won over, and came with three thousand men to Hebron. Ephraim, from whom Joshua came, and within whose boundary was Shiloh, and that was so near of kin to Benjamin, yielded his jealousy and sent a great multitude— twenty-eight thousand eight hundred mighty men of valor, well established in reputation—to hail the young king. The seven years' waiting had not been in vain. All the tribes had learned the necessity of union. After being humbled by the tremendous victory of the Philistines over Saul, they had been perplexed and distracted, and at last further humiliated and made wise by the decline and death of Ish-bosheth. With one heart, therefore, they accepted the manifest will of God; and rallied not simply by representatives, but by armies. Manasseh on the west and Manasseh on the east sent her thousands. The eastern tribes across the Jordan, surrendering the temporary capital at Mahanaim, put on the march to Hebron, fully equipped, one hundred and twenty thousand men. Issachar, in the valley of Jezreel, whose men were intelligent and sagacious observers of the times, sent two hundred representatives, to place all their brethren at the command of King David. From Zebulun by the Sea of Chinneroth came a hearty fifty thousand; from Naphtali, still further north, thirty-seven thousand; from Dan in the farthest north and Dan on the borders of Philistia, twenty-eight thousand six hundred; and from Asher, on the great sea above Carmel, forty thousand experts. The peaceful house of Levi was not without its representatives. Jehoida, the leader of the priests,* brought thirty-seven hundred priests; and the Levites added, made up forty-six hundred. Among these was a young priest, Zadok, who became priest with Abiathar, who it appears now came over from Saul's house and who proved David's friend to the very end. The tribes of Judah and of Simeon were, of course, present in their fullest force, six thousand eight hundred from Judah that bore "shield and spear," and from Simeon seven thousand one hundred warriors. Three days this great multitude—over three hundred thousand people, a number which recent wars have taught us may be assembled in a small territory—were at Hebron in great convocation

---

* "The Aaronites;" *Hebrew*, [those] "of Aaron."

and festivity. To feed this mass of people their brethren made ready. The nearest tribes were all astir. The backs of asses and of oxen were piled with bread and meal, and cakes of fig and clusters of dried grapes, and skins of wine and oil. Droves of sheep and of oxen might have been seen all along the roads from "the south," and from the hill country north to Hebron. Even from Issachar, a tribe likened by Jacob to a strong ass crouching between two burdens, and from Zebulun and Naphtali, came loaded camels and mules bearing the same generous burdens, and teaching the people along their way that a new era had dawned. The nation was animated with a new life. "There was joy in Israel."

After that great assembly was fully gathered and arranged in hospitable order in the valley of Hebron, and had overflowed upon the outward slopes, the formal solemnities took place. The elders of the tribes and of the cities and the chief of the priests came to David in the city. They first expressed their national and loyal attachment: "Behold, we are thy bone and thy flesh." They next expressed their confidence in his abilities and their appreciation of his past services: "Even when Saul himself was king, it was thou that leddest out and broughtest in the nation." They said to him, thirdly, "that it was the will of God that he should reign, and that he had been already acting in Hebron by divine direction:" "The Lord thy God said unto thee, Thou shalt feed my people Israel, and thou shalt be ruler over my people Israel." Then David made his reply, himself presenting, the record intimates, the compact by which the king is bound to God and the people are bound to him and he to them.

What was this covenant or league? Probably the same in form as that laid down by Moses in Moab, and to which the people had bound themselves at Saul's anointment. That Mosaic law, providing for kings and a kingdom, contained, it will be remembered, the following conditions:

The king must be approved *both* by the *people* and by *God.*

The king must not be a foreigner, but a *native Hebrew.*

The king must not *multiply horses,* like a warrior for foreign conquest, nor for the purpose of importing horses, keep up a traffic with Egypt.

The king must not, in royal marriage, have *many wives.* His heart must not be turned away by many alliances, and so tempted to favoritism to his wives' relatives at home, or corrupted by royal houses abroad.

The king must not aim to make *himself rich.*

On the other hand:

The king must *study* and *understand* the *Mosaic law* on the *duties* of *kings,* and keep a special copy of it for his own use.

The king must be *loyal to the divine law,* and make it supreme above his own will and the will of the people.

We have already considered the application of these conditions of the kingly office of Saul. Let us now observe their application to David.

At the coronation at Hebron, we see now the sincerest union of the divine and human choice. Long since, the divine selection was signified by God's prophet. Years of persecution and years of tried abilities as a tribal king have tested David before the people, and at length have won their full consent and admiration.

As for his Hebrew blood, it was from the most honorable lineage, running back to Boaz of Bethlehem; to Salmon, captain at the fall of Jericho; to Nahshon, brother-in-law of Aaron the high-priest, and one of the twelve renowned of the congregation in the wilderness. Ruth was a Moabite, but she had freely become a proselyte of her own accord, and her pious devotion to the God of Israel was noted.

David, we shall find, did not create cavalry in his military operations. We shall soon see that when he captured a thousand chariots and their horses from Hadadezer, towards the *Euphrates*, he "houghed" or ham-strung the horses of nine hundred chariots. Although he reserved horses enough for a hundred chariots—that is, two hundred horses—yet he may be said to have kept within the scope of the reqirement: "He shall not *multiply* horses to himself, nor cause the people to return to *Egypt*, to the end that he should multiply horses."

But what shall be said of the divine condition, "Neither shall he multiply wives"? David at this very time has *six* wives. Saul's daughter was taken from him by force, and, probably without hope of seeing her again, he married Abigail and Ahinoam. One of his wives, Maacah, was of the house of a subordinate prince, the king of Geshur. Whether this number, in that age and land of polygamy—when often a large harem was kept—was a transgression of the condition, "*multiply*" or take *many* wives, we cannot tell. Whether the spirit of that rule was that, if the alliances were at home rather than abroad, we cannot tell. But David's wives were a small number compared with Solomon's seven hundred—a transgression of that wise king which brought idolatry and corruption and domestic misrule into the royal house.

The whole career of David shows that he did not appropriate the wealth of the nation avariciously to himself. His generous spirit was in the very spirit and letter of that part of the compact.

As to David's study and enforcement of the Mosaic law and his loyalty to the faith, his whole life is an open testimony to his general fidelity.

It was such a "covenant" or compact as this recorded in the Book of Deuteronomy, or such parts of this general outline as were there divinely appointed, to which

David and the people assented "in Hebron *before the Lord.*"

·Sacrifices were offered on an altar as at Saul's inauguration. The ark itself may have been transported in solemn procession to Hebron for the occasion, as the oft-recurring phrase, "before the *Lord*,"* here seems to imply solemn sanctions were received in answer by the ephod. Assent was given to the solemn declarations of the "covenant" on the one side by the elders, and on the other by King David. And then Abiathar, in the presence of a multitude of priests and of elders from hundreds of cities, poured the holy oil from the horn upon his head, saying, "I anoint thee king, in the name of the Lord." The young priest Zadok, who stood by, survived to do the like service thirty-three years later, at the coronation of King Solomon.

We have no record of the use of a crown. There can be hardly a doubt, however, that it was in use, and as Saul's crown and bracelet had been a royal badge to him, that the ceremonies were completed by placing the crown upon his head and hailing him king with the Hebrew acclamation : " Let the King live ! Let the King live ! "

Sacrifices and feasting in the city and through all the tents and assemblies of the tribes around, filled up the three days, till the joyful people departed, glad in the union of their nation and the reassured tokens of the divine favor.

---

* See Judges xi. 11; xx. 26 ; xxi. 2; Joshua xviii. 8; 1 Samuel xxi. 7 ; 2 Samuel vi. 21 ; vii. 18 ; Exodus xxxiv. 34 ; Leviticus i. 3, etc.

Thirtieth Sunday.

THE CAPTURE OF JEBUS.

LESSON.

2 Samuel v. 6-10; Joshua xv. 8, 63; Judges i. 8, 21; xix. 10-13; 1 Chronicles xi. 4-9; xxi. 18; 1 Kings ii. 10; viii. 1; Psalm cxliv.

THE kingdom was now consolidated, the members healthily articulated into one body politic. It was plain now to ordinary sagacity that the capital of the kingdom should be more central than Hebron. It would not be easy to build up a long, united reign, with a capital so partial in its location as Hebron. Where should the future capital be? Should David transfer the throne to Shechem, the old tabernacle town, in its central beautiful vale, and gather around him in that town of Ephraim his own tribal kinsman, Ephraim and Judah would be certain to vex each other with jealous suspicion and intrigue. Gibeah in Benjamin was in bad repute for its own sake and from Saul. There was one place, strong and central, harmonizing the interests of the tribes—the natural stronghold of centuries, just on the border of Benjamin and Judah. It was within the tribe of Benjamin, so that all the children of Joseph would be content with its position, and so near to all Judah that that strong tribe would be pleased. It had the advantage, too, of a fresh place, unembarrassed by past associations. If it could be taken from the enemy, the very triumph would give glory as well as unity to the national capital. That place was the frowning citadel of

Jebus, on which David had no doubt fixed his eye, as the natural center of power, from the time when he was anointed over Judah. Many a time since the days of Goliath, as he passed that rocky fortification, his thoughts mounted in holy challenge of the heathen Jebusite power. One day he would drive them off their throne!

The strength of Jebus at that time is shown in a single fact that for four hundred years, in the very heart of the land, it had defied the whole nation. Hebron and lesser mountain towns, and even Hazor of the north, were taken at the conquest. Indeed, the outside portion of Jebus seems to have been conquered, but the real fastness had never fallen. It looked down in defiance and in contempt on all the marches of Abner and of Joab.

Let us see if we cannot obtain some conception of Jebus as it was before it became Jerusalem. The city of Jerusalem now sits upon two hills, or two forks of a rocky peninsula jutting up between great gorges in the mountains. These two hills, or two forks like the prongs of a tooth, are divided by a narrow valley, which in the progress of twenty-six sieges during almost thirty centuries has been filling up.

One hill is the east hill on which the temple was after David's time built; and we know that on the west side of the east hill—the side, of course, sloping *towards* the west hill—are now massive and high walls, built up from the bottom of the separating valley. The east hill is a hundred feet lower than the west. We know that this east or temple-hill was bought by David near the close of his life from Araunah *the Jebusite*. From the time of David's capture of Jebus to the days of the purchase, therefore, it was a winnowing-floor. It must, therefore, have been free from *high* walls, which would have kept off the wind. Were this so, Araunah's hill was outside of the city. That it was either entirely outside of the city or surrounded by inferior walls, seems evident from the fact that "Araunah the king," "the *Jebusite*," retained possesion of it. That

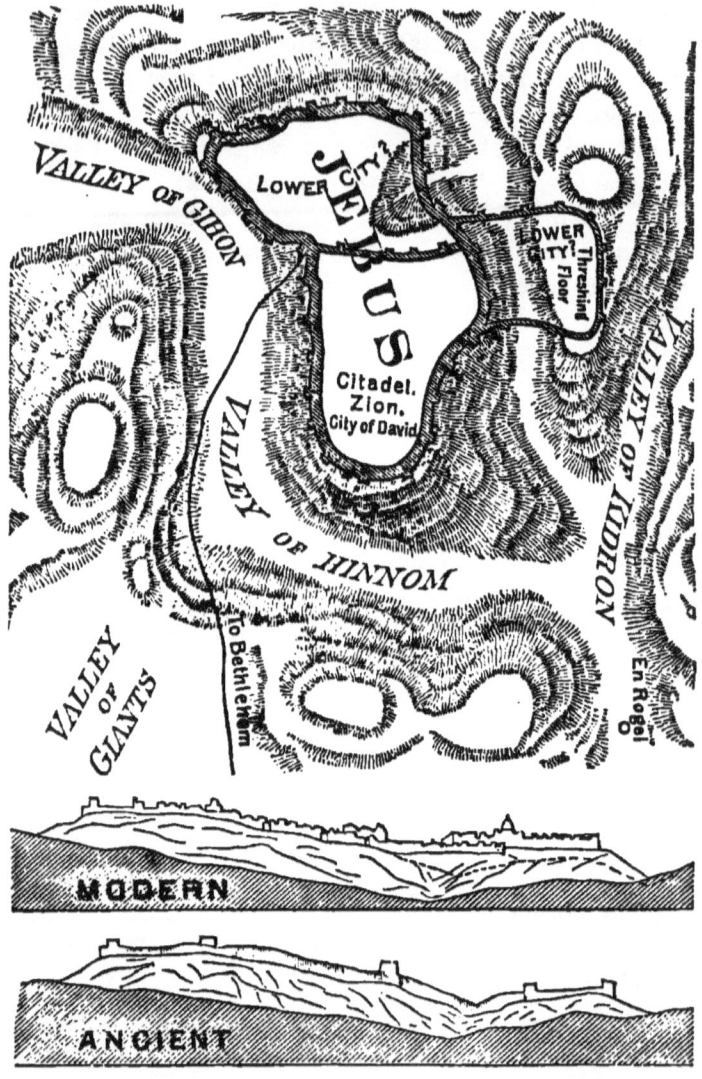

lower and outside suburb had once long since been taken by the Hebrews, and its inhabitants were in closer relations with the Hebrews than those of the upper city, as we shall presently see there is reason to conjecture. The real stronghold, then, was on the west and upper hill, two hundred feet or more higher than Araunah's threshing-floor.*

Whether the spies saw this towering height of rocks, with its strong walls above, and the abrupt, deep ravines around it, or only heard the fame of it, they brought back word forty years before the conquest of Canaan : " The cities are walled and very great," and " the Hittites and the *Jebusites* and the Amorites dwell in the mountains." After Joshua took Jericho and Ai, the next battle was with Adoni-zedek, the king of Jebus,† and his four confederates when he captured the five kings in the cave at Makkedah, and hung them on five trees, on that famous day when the sun stood still on Gibeon. But they could not carry Jebus all the years of Joshua's life. After Joshua's death, Judah and Simeon were ordered by the divine oracle at Shiloh or Shechem to lead the nation in completing the conquest. As they marched southward they had a battle and victory at Bezek, where they took prisoner and punished the fierce and cruel sheik, Adoni-bezek, and swept on to Jebus.‡ There they fought against the city, and took it, and put it to the edge of the sword, and set it on fire. Josephus says

---

* " The holy city is built upon a series of rocky spurs close to the water-shed or back-bone of Palestine, and it appears to be quite certain, from the nature of the surrounding country, that in early times the site of Jerusalem was a series of rocky slopes, the ledges covered here and there with a few feet of red earth. When, therefore, we get down to the surface of the rock, we get down to that surface which presented itself to view in olden times before the first inhabitants built their city."—*Recovery of Jerusalem*, p. 245. The dotted line in the MODERN elevation of the mountains and city, represents this rock surface. The other elevation may be taken to represent something of its ANCIENT appearance.

† Joshua x. 1-4.   ‡ Judges i. 1-8.

they besieged the city, and took "the *lower* city" after considerable time spent in the siege, but that "the upper city was not to be taken without great difficulty, through the strength of its walls and the nature of the place," and that for this reason they drew off their forces to Hebron. This explanation of Josephus may be taken as a reasonable explanation or conjecture in respect to that early capture of the city.

If it took considerable time to capture the lower city, and after taking it they could not take the upper city, there must have been an inferior wall outside the impregnable citadel and around the lower city. When it is said still later, therefore, that "the children of Benjamin did not drive out the Jebusites that inhabited Jerusalem, but the Jebusites *dwell with* the children of Benjamin* in Jerusalem unto" the day the Book of Judges was written, we see the rocky height still frowning as a foe, but the lower city in an intercourse more or less restrained with the surrounding people. The Levite journeying with his wife and servant from Bethlehem to Mount Ephraim could have entered into the city and lodged there had he not said, "No; it is the city of a stranger." There stood the defiant city that looked down on the civil war which raged over the Levite's wife and over Gibeah, and glad that a tribe was well-nigh extinguished; the city that had dared the bravest judges of the land, that smiled contemptuously at the craven spirit of Saul of Gibeah—the lofty, steep, rocky fortress of centuries.

When, therefore, David, at the head of all Israel, determined to assault the city, and two hundred thousand war-

---

* In Joshua xv. 63, the reading is: "The children of *Judah* could not drive them out, but the Jebusites dwell with the children of *Judah* at Jerusalem unto this day." Jebus was on the line of both tribes, and the two tribes very likely were mixed in their residence there.

riors from Hebron came swarming over the mountains on the south and up the ravines of Hinom, Gihon, and Kidron, the Jebusites laughed in derision. They barred their gates, and mounted their lame and blind on the walls, and rang out the challenge down the ravines, "The blind and lame are a match for you all!" David's whole soul was fired. It was like the challenge of Goliath again! "So he took the lower city by force," says Josephus, "but the citadel held out still." That is, he took either Araunah's lower city, or the lower part of the *northern* part of the western hill. We may imagine the haughty challenge renewed from day to day like the challenge of the Philistines' champion. The spirit of an insulted army rises with the spirit of the leader. "Behold the defiant enemies of God, who offer insult to Jehovah," says the king; "the impudent lame and blind, hated of the king's very soul. Their security and bravado shall be their weakness and ruin. Find out a place to scale the very precipice! Whoever climbeth the steep and dasheth them down the rocks, shall have the command!" The intrepid Joab is no man to have the command taken from him, if another should scale the wall before him. "All were ambitious to ascend," says Josephus; "but Joab prevented the rest, and, as soon as he was got up to the citadel, cried out to the king, and claimed the chief command." Fierce Bethlehemites and hardy Ephraimites and mountaineers from Gilead poured in, we may suppose, past Joab on the wall, driving down the astonished inhabitants, throwing open the lower gates, and admitting the triumphant Hebrew thousands. "It was the often-repeated story of the capture of fortresses through what appeared their strongest, 'and therefore became their weakest point. 'Steep, and therefore neglected.' Such was the fate of Sardis and of Rome, and such was the fate of Jebus."*

---

* Stanley. The explanation of the last part of 2 Samuel v. 8, "Wherefore they said, the blind and the lame shall not come into

Once in possession of the city, David immediately made his residence in the fort or castle, that is, in the stronghold or citadel of the town, the south-eastern part of the present city. It was the stronghold of Zion—Zion, the *sunny place* or the *dry place*, a name which now appears for the first time, given either before by the Jebusites or later by the Jews. This rocky citadel the king proclaimed to the nation "The City of David," and built it up from "The Ramparts" ("Millo") round about, a mound of defence somewhere towards the east hill.* The repair of the rest of the city, so far as it was broken down by the assault or had fallen into decay, was under the direction of Joab, famous for ever now as the Taker of Jebus and Commander of the Royal Army.

The fame of this wonderful victory went everywhere abroad. It filled Benjamin and Ephraim with admiration and delight. It was a victory of centuries. It solidified the government, and gave David at once a sure seat on his throne.† From Naphtali to Simeon, the mind of every

---

the house," appears to be this: Wherefore it grew to be a proverb in regard to any impregnable fortress, "The blind and lame are there: let him enter the place if he can."—*Fergusson, in Smith's Dictionary of the Bible.*

* "'*From Millo and inwards.*' The fortification 'inwards' must have consisted in the enclosure of Mount Zion with a strong wall upon the north side, where Jerusalem joins it *as a lower town,* so as to defend the place against hostile attacks on the north or town side. The 'Millo' was at any rate some kind of fortification, probably a large tower or castle. The definite article before *Millo* indicates that it was a well-known fortress, probably one that had been erected by Jebusites. With regard to the situation of Millo, we may infer from this passage and 1 Chronicles xi. 8, that the tower in question stood at one corner of the wall, either on the north-east or north-west, where the hill of Zion has the least elevation, and therefore needs the greatest strengthening from without."—*Keil and Delitzsch.*

† That the conquest of Jebus took place at once after the anoint-

Hebrew dilated, the heart of every Hebrew beat quick at the power and glory of their king. Even from distant Tyre soon came salutations from King Hiram, and offers of workmen to build a royal house suited to the royal capital.

It would have been quite in keeping with David's mind if after this unprecedented success, with his wives and children and the families of his brave warriors around him, his exultation had taken the form of the One Hundred and Forty-fourth psalm :

A PSALM OF DAVID.

Blessed be Jehovah, my rock,
Who teacheth my hands to war
And my fingers to fight !
My goodness ! and my fortress !
My high tower ! and my deliverer !
My shield ! and he in whom I trust !
Who subdueth the people under me !

Lord, what is man, that thou takest knowledge of him ?
Or the son of man, that thou makest account of him ?
Man is like to vanity,
His days are as a shadow that passeth way.

Bow thy heavens, O Lord, and come down.
Touch the mountains, and they shall smoke.
Cast forth lightnings and scatter them !
Shoot out thine arrows and destroy them.
Send thine hand from above.
Rid me and deliver me out of great waters
From the hands of aliens,
Whose mouth speaketh vanity,
And whose right hand is a right hand of falsehood.

I will sing a new song unto thee, O God,
Upon a ten-stringed psaltery will I sing praises unto thee
Who gives victory to kings
Who delivereth David, thy servant, from the hurtful sword.
Rid me and deliver me from the hand of aliens
Whose mouth speaketh vanity,
And whose right hand is a right hand of falsehood !

---

ment at Hebron " is apparent from the fact that according to verse 5, David reigned in Jerusalem just as many years as he was king over all Israel."—*Keil and Delitzsch.*

> That our sons may be as plants grown up in their youth,
> Our daughters as corner-stones,
> Polished after the similitude of a palace.
> That our garners may be full,
> Affording all manner of store.
> That our sheep may bring forth thousands
> And ten thousands in our streets,
> That our oxen may be strong to labour.
> That there may be no breaking in nor going out.
> That there be no outcry in our streets.
>
> Happy is that people that is in such a care,
> Yea, happy is that people whose God is Jehovah.

Did the name Jerusalem take the place of Jebus at this time, and become henceforth the name of the sacred capital? Jebus was the city of the Jebusites, and continued to be Jebus beyond all doubt from the conquest till the Jebusites were conquered. It was certainly Jebus in the time of the Judges, when the Levite refused to stop there over-night. It bears the name of Jerusalem from this time on. The name has been accounted for in various ways. The last part of the name, it is commonly argued, is the ancient name of Salem, and not without beauty and power is it supposed that it was the city of Melchizedek, "King of *Salem*, which is King of *Peace*." Some scholars conjecture that the name is the Hebrew words, *Jerush-shalem, Inheritance of Peace;* others, that it is *Jeru-shalem, Foundation of Peace.* On the supposition that the sacrifice of Isaac was on the hill of Araunah, or that Araunah's threshing-floor was the Mount Moriah of Abraham, some have supposed that a part of the divine message to Abraham, "The Lord will provide" (*Jehovah-jireh*), was prefixed to *salem* or *shalem*, and that *Jireh-shalem*, which became afterwards Jerusalem, means, "The Lord will provide Peace"; and it has even been supposed that, as the Lord Jehovah did provide a ram for Abraham's offering, so the full significance of the name now so celebrated was designed to be, "*Jehovah will provide peace by that Lamb of God that takes away the sins of the world."* The name is sometimes in the *dual* number in Hebrew. Jerusa*laim*, meaning the *double* Jerusalem, because it was on two hills or forks of rock. Still others suppose that the names Jebus and Salem were combined in one word, Jebusalem or Jerusalem, after this city became David's capital. Glorious are the associations of that powerful title! There is no name of earthly city that so sways men in all ages and all lands, from the time when Asaph sang,

"In Salem is his tabernacle,
And his dwelling-place in Zion,"

to the descent from heaven of the New Jerusalem, prepared and adorned as a bride for her husband.

Thirty-first Sunday.

DAVID'S GROWING FAME.

LESSON.

2 Samuel v. 11–25 ; 1 Chronicles xiv., xvii. 1 ; 1 Kings v. 1 ; Psalms xxx. and ci.

DAVID'S reputation and power were now at once and widely felt. In three directions there takes place a great advance, to which our attention is now called. The strongest enemy at home, the Philistines, is first put under. A warm friendship was formed with one of the strongest near neighbors—the kingdom of Tyre. An impression of admiration and of awe, such as widely prevails among kingdoms when a moderate State advances by one stride to the highest rank, rapidly grows in more distant nations like Egypt and Nineveh or Assyria.

First comes the contest with the Philistines, in which the Philistine power was broken. From this time onward through the reign of Solomon, their power wanes, and at no time recovers supremacy over any considerable portion of the Hebrew nation.

It had now been from fifteen to seventeen years since the boy-champion had met the giant-champion in the valley of Elah. The Philistines had learned to despise David, for had not this promising youth been hunted like a partridge for eight or ten long years by King Saul, unable to make headway against that stupid and blundering monarch? Had he not fled to Gath and played the madman? Had he not been a vassal to Achish, who gave him Ziklag?

Was not the double-minded rogue ready to go with themselves against his own Hebrew king? And had he not been unable for seven long years to take the throne of the nation with only King Ish-bosheth and his general Abner to hold out against him? But now that he had been made king of the whole land and captured Jebus, they thought it time to display their strength again. They would if possible unseat the treacherous young king before he fortified himself too strongly in Jebus. They therefore gather all their armies as they did before Saul's overthrow, and advanced perhaps in the hope of another such victory. Or if they were not so ambitious as this, they came up for the harvests for which the "plain" below Jerusalem was noted.

The hostile army boldly advanced, and encamped deep and wide in the valley of the giants (Rephaim)—a cultivated plain extending south-west from the very brow of the valley of Hinnom.* Gentle hills lie along the northwest side of it. Broad next the city, it slopes gradually, till at the north-western end it becomes a deepening and narrowing valley. Although the ground is stony and uneven, still it is a highly cultivated stretch of land. Extensive gardens of vegetables now grow in the valley, with olive-trees and vineyards stretching across the plain higher up. Women with loads of roses may be seen on their way to the city, where the roses are used for making rose-water, and from the fields of roses there cultivated, the name of the valley at the lower end, opening into the Giant's Valley, is "Valley of Roses." Wheat grew there in great abundance in ancient times,† and in David's day there were mulberry-trees. From the walls of the city the people could behold the Philistines encamped across the Hinnom ravine. David was ready to meet them; but not

---

* See map on page 208. † Isaiah xvii. 5.

till he had sought the direction of God. Occasions are frequent now, as we shall see, in which he consulted the high-priest to know the issue of his action, and to know from the Theocratic King himself, what his own action should be.

Having the assurance of victory, he led out his army. "When the battle was joined," says Josephus, "David came himself behind and fell upon the enemy on a sudden, and slew some of them, and put the rest to flight." So violent was the rout that it seemed as if a mighty dam had given way, and the overwhelming waters had swept every resisting obstacle before them. Such was the comparison in David's mind when he said, "Jehovah hath burst upon mine enemies before me as a burst of waters." Therefore, he named the place "The Place of the Burstings Forth." The idols thrown away or lost in the Philistines' haste were picked up, and by David's command burned, in accordance with law of Moses:—"Thus shall ye deal with them: ye shall destroy their altars, and break down their images, and cut down their groves, and burn their graven images with fire."

Recovering themselves, and probably reinforced, the Philistines return. Josephus says the reason why they were able to rally was that "all Syria and Phœnicia, with many other nations, came to their assistance and had a share in this war." But as Josephus says nothing whatever of Hiram, king of Tyre, whose city was of Phœnicia, we may either doubt his statement or consider the lower end of Phœnicia meant. In answer to his inquiry with respect to giving battle, Josephus says "the high-priest prophesied to him that he should keep his army in the groves called the Groves of Weeping, which were not far from the enemies' camp, and that he should not move nor begin to fight till the trees of the grove should be in motion without the winds blowing; but as soon as these trees moved and the time foretold to him by God was come, he should without delay go out to gain what was an already prepared and evident victory." From the phrase, " Thou shalt not go up, but *fetch a compass behind them*," and from the fact that David pursued and smote the Philistines from Gibeon or Geba, towns north-west of Jerusalem, down to Gazor on the very border of the Philistine plain, we infer that David cut off their retreat on the south, and that the sound of the going in the top of the mulberry-trees, from the south, was like the noise of the host in the ears of Benhadab when he afterwards besieged Samaria. They fled, therefore, panic-smitten before the Lord's excitement of their imagination, rushing to the north-west, turning to the left in the region of Gibeon, and chased with continued slaughter down to the great road to Egypt. It was a mighty and an effectual victory, and broke permanently the aggressive power of that rich and energetic and heathen nation.

The principal neighboring nations of the Hebrew kingdom in David's time were Ammon or Moab, the mountains of whose kingdom across the Salt Sea might always be seen from near Jerusalem, Edom in the south, Damascus of Syria, or "Syria of Damascus," in the north-west, and Tyre or "The Sidonians" in the north-east. There can be no question that Damascus and Tyre were the heads of kingdoms ancient in the days of David : Damascus commanding all the inland commerce between the vast east, from Nineveh and the Western Sea and the southern Canaan and Egypt, and exercising a controlling power over the petty sheikhs of surrounding Syria ; Tyre, an intelligent, enterprising people from before Joshua, skilled in the metallic arts, in wood-felling and stone-cutting, and spreading far and wide its coast-creeping commerce on the great sea.

We shall see how Moab or Ammon, Edom, and Damascus fell under David's assaults. With Tyre the Hebrews seem never to have had a war. A warm admiration sprang up in Hiram's mind for the young Hebrew king, and he became and remained "a lover of David." If Josephus is right with respect to the union of the *Syrians* with the Philistines against David, we must remember the Syria of those days was entirely distinct from the coast of the Sidonians. It was " Syria of Damascus" and " Syria of the two rivers," Euphrates and Tigris. No sooner, therefore, was David well established in Jebus, and had bearded the Philistine lion and given him a lasting wound, than Hiram sends him a courteous salutation, and proposed to erect for him a house worthy of the throne of Israel. So courteous and generous an offer must have touched the gracious and genial heart of David. The house was planned and erected. It was built of stone and of cedar. The trees were cut and perhaps hewn in the mountains above Tyre; they were no doubt floated to Joppa, as was the timber for the temple. The carpenters and stonecutters busy in the "city of David" among the interested and admiring Hebrews, were Tyrians. It was something elaborate for that time, we may be sure, worthy the name of a palace—not inferior to the growing fame of the king, who must by this time, have reached the twelfth year from his accession at Hebron. It must have had its numerous apartments for his numerous household and their servants. It was in the simple oriental style, with upper chambers leading to a flat roof,[*] with rooms for his body-guard or men-servants at the entrance to the court.[†] The adornment was rather internal than external. And when it was completed there was a dedication, in which the pious king lifted up his soul in thanks to God for his many deliverances and his prosperity. Such a dedication of a house

---

[*] xi. 2.   [†] xi. 9, 13.

was no uncommon thing, as we may infer from the direction to the officers of the army before a battle, who were to say, "What man is there that hath built a house and hath not dedicated it: let him go and return to his house, lest he die in the battle and another dedicate it."* For such an appointed time it was, when a review of his life would be both natural and appropriate, that was composed

A PSALM AND SONG AT THE DEDICATION OF THE HOUSE OF DAVID.

I will extol thee, O Jehovah, for thou hast lifted me up,
And hast not made my foes to rejoice over me.
O Jehovah, my God,
I cried unto thee, and thou hast healed me (or restored me):
O Jehovah, thou hast brought up my soul from the grave;
Thou hast kept me alive that I should not go down to the pit.

Sing unto Jehovah, O ye saints of his,
And give thanks at the remembrance of his holiness;
For his anger is for a moment,
But his favor is for life;
Weeping may lodge for the night,
But singing cometh in the morning.

And in my prosperity, I said, I shall never be moved:
Thou, O Jehovah, by thy favor hast made my mountain to stand strong.
Thou didst hide thy face, and I was troubled.
I cried unto thee, O Jehovah!
And unto Jehovah I made supplication:
"What will my blood profit thee when I go down unto the pit?
Shall the dust praise thee? shall it declare thy truth?
Hear, O Jehovah! and have mercy upon me.
O Jehovah, be thou my helper!"

Thou hast turned for me my mourning into dancing.
Thou hast put off my sackcloth and hast girded me with gladness
In order that my glory may sing praise to thee and not be silent.
O Jehovah, my God, I will give thanks unto thee for ever.
—*Psalm* xxx.

It may be the Tyrians were present at the dedication, and from it bore back to Tyre salutations to Hiram and generous gifts for themselves, and a knowledge of true piety and the one only God. For David had sagacity to per-

---

* Deuteronomy xx. 5.

ceive that the exaltation was for Jehovah's people in the earth and not for his personal honor. So began the warm love between kingly David and kingly Hiram, which glowed for twenty-five years, and which under Solomon brought the wisdom of Tyre to build for Jehovah a house "exceeding magnifical, of fame and of glory throughout all countries."

Within this house David removed the wives and children who were his at Hebron. Here at last was Saul's daughter in glorious estate. Here he introduced his other wives, preparing additional houses as his royal establishment increased. Here were born many sons, eminent among whom was Shammuah or Shimea, so named, no doubt, for David's older brother Shammah, whose growing son Jonathan, named perhaps for David's friend, slew afterward the six-fingered, six-toed giant of Gath, and preeminent among whom was Solomon the wise.

At such a time as this also, was an occasion which David would improve to set forth the character of a true Father and true Ruler to his people, such as we find described in the One Hundred and First psalm:

> I will sing of mercy and judgment
> Unto thee, O Lord, will I sing.
> I will behave myself wisely in a perfect way,
> O when wilt thou come unto me!
> I will walk within my house with an upright heart,
> I will set no wicked thing before my eyes,
> I hate the work of them that turn aside,
> It shall not cleave to me.
> A proud heart shall depart from me,
> I will not know a wicked person;
> Him who secretly slanders his neighbor,
> I will cut off.
> Him that hath a high look and a proud heart
> I will not suffer,
> Mine eyes shall be upon the faithful of the Lord,
> That they may dwell with me.
> He that walketh in an upright way shall serve me;
> He that practiceth deceit shall not dwell in my house;
> He that telleth lies shall not tarry in my sight.
> I will early destroy all the wicked out of the land,
> That I may cut off all evil doers from the city of Jehovah.

Beyond Lebanon, beyond the wilderness, beyond the river of Egypt, the fame of the mighty Hebrew king began to extend. It "went out into all lands, and the fear of him upon all nations." For, walking in the fear of the Lord, the king had arisen to whom was promised empire from the wilderness and Euphrates and Lebanon to the uttermost sea, and to whom was being fulfilled the promise, "I will lay the fear of you and the dread of you upon the nations that are under the whole heaven, who shall hear report of thee and tremble." *

---

* Deuteronomy ii. 25 ; xi. 24, 25.

Thirty-second Sunday.

THE NEW TABERNACLE FOR THE ARK.

LESSON.

2 Samuel vi. 1-19; 1 Chronicles xiii., xv., xvi.; 2 Chronicles i. 3; Psalms xxiv., cv., xcvi., cvi.

THE piety of David is seen in his exaltation of religious worship before the nation, just at this very time of his growing fame and certain prosperity. It is easy to say that the reformation of religion was a sagacious movement to consolidate his power; for all kings have been compelled to recognize the religious instinct in their people, and to provide or recognize religious observances. But it is plain that David's *whole heart* was in the honor which he now rendered to God. He did not dismiss the matter to the priests or to a deputy. He taught the priests themselves piety by the noble devotion of his personal example. He exhibited the most sincere personal reverence and fear of the only living God, and the most unaffected personal joy in his favor. His psalms on bringing the ark to Jerusalem, as well as for the tabernacle service afterwards, are the breath of the pious of all ages.

We have already seen that the tabernacle worship was broken up in the times of King Saul. After the ark was returned by the Philistines to Beth-shemesh, it remained for twenty years in Kirjath-jearim. This twenty years must have ended about the time of David's birth. Whether the ark continued at Kirjath-jearim all the days of Saul, or was carried from place to place during those rough times, and brought back again, we do not know. At any rate, some twelve years after David's accession at Hebron —for we assume that he had now been in Jerusalem about five years—and when David was therefore forty-two years old, it was still at that place.

What had now become of the tabernacle at Shiloh from which the ark was taken? We cannot follow it year by year. But we know that when David fled from Saul's court, when he was about twenty or twenty-two years of age, the table of shew-bread, the ephod, the high-priest Ahimelech, and eighty-five priests wearing the linen ephod, were at Nob, about six miles north-west of Jebus. The tabernacle was, therefore, there *then*. We know, too, that now, when David brought up the ark from Kirjath-jearim, the tabernacle of Moses was at Gibeon, six and a half miles north of Jerusalem,* and that it continued there throughout David's life, till the temple was built by Solomon.† The ark was, therefore, separate from the tabernacle,‡ and worship to God by all pious families and pious persons, had probably gone back largely to the patriarchal form of personal or family altars. David took, therefore, the first opportunity to honor the law given to Moses : " Take heed to thyself that thou offer not thy burnt-offerings in every place that thou seest, but in the place which

---

* 1 Chronicles xvi. 39. † 1 Kings iii. 4 ; 2 Chronicles i. 3.

‡ "One of the principal motives for allowing the existing separation of the ark from the tabernacle to continue, may have been that, during the time the two sanctuaries had been separated, two high-priests had arisen, one of whom officiated at the tabernacle at Gibeon, whilst the other, namely, Abiathar, who fled to David, had been the channel of all divine communications, at the time of his persecution by Saul, and also officiated as high-priest in his camp. He could depose neither."—*Keil and Delitzsch.*

the Lord shall choose in one of thy tribes; there thou shalt offer thy burnt-offerings, and there thou shalt do all that I command thee." The time had come at last when that "place" should be established, and when the true ceremonial should be re-established.

The first thing, therefore, which David did, was to build a new tabernacle. For some reason, he did not remove the old Mosaic tabernacle that was at Gibeon, only six miles and a half away, to Jerusalem. Perhaps it had fallen into decay. The materials of which it was built were very old. It must have been many times repaired during four hundred years. The boards and curtains and other materials were, of course, retained as long as possible. With the neglect even of the *ark* by Saul, with the distraction in the minds of the people on account of the separation of the ark from the tabernacle, and with the long time that had elapsed since Eli's death, the old tabernacle was well worn out. If removed to Jerusalem, it would have had to be entirely reconstructed. Perhaps it continued to be reverenced for association's sake, as we shall see, till the temple was built. God, therefore, honored David's plan of building a new tabernacle in the city of David.

It is evident that this new tabernacle was something more than a tent. For there was a place for the ark, and a place for the altar of burnt-offerings, and priests and Levites were sanctified, and a "due order" established, and singers and musicians and porters appointed. Kingly plans had been made for the king's house, and workmen from Tyre had drawn public attention to the building of the royal palace. Certainly we should infer that royal attention and skillful labor honored the new tabernacle as much in the public estimation as they did the palace. The new tabernacle was probably at no great distance from the "king's house."

When all was ready, David gathered the first choice of

the nation—thirty thousand picked men from the tribes—to bring in the ark of God. He consulted with the leaders in reference to the matter, asking them if it seemed to be "of the Lord our God." He sent abroad invitations to the priests and Levites in their cities, and to the people from Egypt to Hamath. All the people were pleased. A great multitude assembled. With harps, psalteries, timbrels, cornets, cymbals, trumpets, and what they supposed to be full preparation, they went to Kirjath-jearim—or "Baalah of Judah," as it was sometimes called—nine or ten miles north-west from Jerusalem, on the boundary of the tribes of Judah and Benjamin.* The road was the road to Joppa, a barren and uninteresting path; but the town itself—the town which modern scholars agree to have been Kirjath-jearim — was "prettily situated in a basin, on the north side of a spur jutting out from the western hill." The ark was not in the town itself, but on a hill near by.† When it came back from Philistine Ekron, Abinadab's son Eleazar had been sanctified as its keeper. Eleazar had probably died, for his younger brothers Uzzah and Ahio now had care of it. They had prepared—perhaps by David's direction—a new cart for the removal, in which the ark was now placed. Ahio went before, guiding the oxen, and leading the king and his rejoicing thousands. Music and songs filled the air as the procession moved towards Jerusalem, and as they all hailed the speedy reunion of ark and tabernacle in their mountain capital. But "at this point—perhaps slipping over the smooth rock—the oxen stumbled." Uzzah put forth his hand to steady the holy ark, and met with a sudden and

---

* See Map on p. 16.

† The word "Gibeah," in 2 Samuel vi. 3, means literally *a hill*, and is so rendered in our English version in 1 Samuel vii. 1. These two passages refer to the same place.

awful death, from the anger of the Lord. Silence and awe and fear fall upon king and people. Whether the threshing-floor of Nahshon was nearer Kirjath jearim or Jerusalem, we cannot tell, although Josephus intimates that it was near Jerusalem.

Four reasons may be given why this dreadful punishment was inflicted on Uzzah: First, that he put forth his hand in an ambitious, officious, rash way, when there really was no need of his doing so. Secondly, That not being the priest, he touched the ark and was slain for it, as thousands were slain years before at Beth-shemesh for looking into the ark. Thirdly, That the ark was being carried in *a cart*, just as the heathen Philistines had sent it home, and not on the shoulders of the priests, as the law directed, and that, therefore, it was subjected to accidents just such as this of stumbling oxen and an overturning cart.* David himself said, after he thought over the cause of it, "The Lord our God made a breach upon us, because we sought him not *after the due order.*" Fourthly, As now the time for reforming the ceremonial had come, God would signify to David himself and to all the nation the transcendent importance which he placed on every requirement designed to maintain his sacredness or holiness. He would make David himself afraid of disregarding the order of the ceremonial. Another subordinate reason may have been to direct the nation's attention to the ark, and to hold the attention profoundly for three months, as a preparation for a lasting veneration when it should be taken to Zion.

David *was* afraid. He called the place "The Breaking-Forth on Uzzah." "How shall I bring this ark near to my house?" he said. One man was not afraid to receive it —Obed-edom, whose house was not far away.† For his

---

* The Septuagint says the oxen "overturned the cart."

† "He is called the Githite or Gathite, from his birth-place

confidence in the benefits for which the ark of God was designed, we may suppose, he and his family and all that he had were blessed for three months. Then the king saw that the Lord intended blessings and not judgments by his ark. The ancient glory, long separated from the nation, was returning. God was honoring the design of removal to the tabernacle. Forthwith, with gladness he called the people again. He said, " None must carry the ark of God but the Levites; and they in the appointed manner." He assembled the priests and Levites, and selected a proper number from their families. He called the high-priests, Zadok and Abiathar, and six heads of the Levites, and bade them sanctify themselves and their brethren in accordance with the law. He directed the Levites to select from their number singers and musicians, under whose appointment Heman, Asaph, and Ethan come now into view. Porters and door-keepers for the ark were also appointed, of whom Obed-edom was one. The king himself aspired to the highest priestly service. He relished the spiritual meaning of the sacred order. He clothed himself with a robe of fine linen and an ephod of linen, and provided robes for the Levites that bore the ark and for the singers. So David and the elders of Israel and the captains over thousands went to the house of Obed-edom with joy. Everything was now conducted in order and with solemn reverence. The Levites took the ark upon their shoulders, by the staves, "as Moses commanded." When they had advanced six paces and met with the divine approval, the priests offered seven bullocks and seven rams for the purpose of inaugurating or consecrating the procession. The trumpeters proceeded, and did blow with trumpets before the ark of God. A vast multitude followed. King David, before the majesty of the divine

---

the Levitical city of Gath-rimmon in the tribe of Dan."—*Keil and Delitzsch.*

resting-place, and in holy spiritual joy, leaped and danced with all his might. In solemn jubilation, amid the mighty chanting and the sounding instruments, the procession wound through the gates, up the hill of the citadel, to the tabernacle prepared on Zion, the swelling voices of the white-robed singers, sending upward that psalm which—by common consent of modern writers—the king had exquisitely fitted to this occasion.

A PSALM OF DAVID.

First Choir.

The earth is the Lord's, and the fulness thereof;
The world, and they that dwell therein.
For he hath founded it above the seas,
And established it above the floods.
Who shall ascend into the hill of the Lord?
Or who shall stand in his holy place?

Second Choir.

He that hath clean hands and a pure heart;
Who hath not lifted up his soul unto vanity nor sworn deceitfully,
He shall receive the blessing from the LORD,
And righteousness from the God of his salvation.
This is the generation of them that seek him,
That seek his face, O Jacob! Selah.

First Choir.

Lift up your heads, O ye gates:
And be ye lifted up, ye everlasting doors;
And the King of glory shall come in.

Second Choir.

Who is this King of glory?

First Choir.

The LORD strong and mighty,
The LORD mighty in battle!
Lift up your heads, O ye gates!
Even lift them up, ye everlasting doors,
And the King of glory shall come in.

Second Choir.

Who is this King of glory?

First Choir.

The Lord of Hosts, he is the King of glory. Selah.
—*Tholuck's Arrangement.*

Great must have been the power of such a chant, which the king's poetic mind devised, and which, no doubt, the king's outstretched hand led, his voice at the head of the choirs, and his dilated form in step to the solemn rhythm of the music, as they delivered this Holy Casket containing the law-tables, the golden pot, and Aaron's rod into the Most Holy Place of the new tabernacle.* There they placed the ark in its resting-place, and amid burnt-offerings of dedication and peace-offerings of thanks, new psalms of the royal singer were borne up on the voices of Asaph and his brethren:

> Give thanks unto the Lord; call upon his name;
> Make known his deeds among the people, etc.
>
> *Psalm* cv. 1-15.
>
> Sing unto the Lord, all the earth;
> Show forth his salvation from day to day.
> . . . .
> Give unto the Lord the glory due unto his name;
> Bring an offering, and come before him;
> Worship the Lord in the beauty of holiness.
> Let the heavens be glad and let the earth rejoice,
> And let men say among the nations, Jehovah reigneth.
> Let the sea roar and the fulness thereof:
> Let the fields rejoice, and all that is therein.
> Then shall all the trees of the wood sing out at the presence
> of Jehovah,
> Because he cometh to judge the earth.
>
> —*Psalm* xcvi.

---

* The "everlasting doors" may be the city gates, ancient as the times of Abraham, old as the everlasting hills, or interior gates of massive citadel walls; or the spiritual gates of God's habitation, symbolized by the frail curtains of the tabernacle; or city gates, citadel gates, tabernacle doors, and the everlasting spiritual doors of the divine residence associated together. "The hoary gray castle-gates, through which many a worldly king of the Jebusites had entered, are too low to receive the King of heaven; they are, therefore, called upon to raise their heads. As yet, they know him not in his dignity. A mighty echo returns the question, 'Who is the King of Glory?' It is the Lord, strong and mighty. How many victories have been won by his ark! The gates must not deny admission to him. But the question re-echoes once more, as if to furnish the occasion for a louder and more confident declaration of glory."—*Tholuck.*

> O give thanks unto the Lord, for he is good!
> For his mercy endureth for ever.
> And say ye, Save us, O God of our salvation,
> And deliver us from the heathen,
> That we may give thanks to thy holy name,
> And glory in thy praise!
> Blessed be Jehovah, the God of Israel, for ever and ever.
>
> *Psalm* cvi.

The people responded with loud amens. They were in heart with the jubilant heart of their leader, the priestly king.

But before they depart to their houses, the royal bounty is ready for their bodily wants. For man and woman are ready a cake of bread, a piece of flesh—from the sacrifice, no doubt—and a flagon of wine. So were God and the king exalted before the nation.

Thirty-third Sunday.

MICHAL AND DAVID.

LESSON.

2 Samuel vi. 20-23; 1 Chronicles xv. 16-24, 29; xvi. 4-7, 37-43; xxi. 29; 1 Kings iii. 4; 2 Chronicles i. 3-6; Exodus xxix. 38-42; Numbers xxviii. 3-8; 1 Chronicles vi. 31-48; Psalm cxxxvi.

ONE person highly disapproved of the king's mode of showing his joy at the incoming ark; and that was Michal, his wife. The ark was made little of in her father's day; and she had *inherited* no love nor reverence for its solemn rites. We are right, therefore, probably, in supposing that she had slight sympathy with the warm piety of Jesse's house. The re-establishment of the ancestral worship was all very well; but why should the king be in such a heat over it? why go himself? why dance like a minstrel at a wedding? So she thought as the procession came into the city of David and filed past her latticed window. How much, too, of envy and jealousy in the harem may be revealed by this cynical complaint, we cannot say; but when Michal, on her return to David's house, found Abigail and Ahinoam and other wives, she was not like other oriental wives, she was least of all like Saul's daughter, if she was free from the miserable, petty jealousy which is the curse of all polygamous households. Instead, therefore, of mounting to the height of the occasion, animated by that lofty spirit which bears one away on a generous and self-forgetful enthusiasm for a great and signal event in honor of God, she was far down on the low level of finical proprieties, and despised David in her heart. She thought nothing of the people's joy at the removal from Kirjath-jearim three months before, and of the blessings on Obed-edom's house. She forgot, or chose to forget, the exultant dance of Miriam and her women, when the horse and his rider were mightily overthrown in the Red Sea. She forgot, or chose to forget, the self-forgetful dance of Jephthah's daughter, when twenty cities testified to her father's triumph over Ammon. While the psalms and sacrifices were celebrated in the new tabernacle and the people were edified at the joyful spectacle, her temper was ruffled at home with a Saul-like pettishness at her lord's demeanor. And when David, full of the spirit of the great event, returned to bless his house, she met him with ridicule and satire: "Glorious indeed for the king! the king of all Israel to-day! to uncover himself before the very servants—the very maidens—as a foolish fellow uncovers himself in the dance!"

It mattered little to David that he had thrown off his outer robes and uncovered himself in public—as kings do not often do.* He was in a condition of mind altogether too elevated to be affected by her petty satire. "There is reason for forgetting self," he said sharply, "and honoring Him who put me in the place of your father, and made me ruler! I *will* play before the Lord indeed, and debase myself, that He may be honored. If this be vile, I will be more vile. If this be base, I am willing to humiliate myself in my own esteem to exalt Jehovah. And as to the servants and maidens, they are wise enough to honor it and to honor me"—a fit vindica-

---

* "The proud daughter of Saul was offended at the fact that the king had set himself down to the level of the people. She availed herself of the shortness of the priest's shoulder-dress to make a contemptuous remark concerning David's dancing, as an impropriety that was unbecoming in a king."—*Keil and Delitzsch.*

tion of the God of the covenant, and a fit answer to a most untimely ridicule. For her contempt and derision Michal received a divine punishment: she was condemned to be childless. It may have been a providential design to prevent the perpetuation of Saul's house in any form, and yet as a purely personal punishment, most severe to a Hebrew woman.*

But David's zeal was not confined to the new tabernacle. He had not neglected the old Mosaic tabernacle at Gibeon. A sacred respect was maintained for the time-honored Tent, now vacant of its holiest treasure. That venerable tent still enclosed the brazen altar of burnt-offering made for Moses by "Bezaleel, the son of Uri, the son of Hur, of the tribe of Judah." The priests were, therefore, instructed by David to include that in their arrangements for orderly worship. As we find that tabernacle and its altar still at Gibeon at the time of the temple dedication under Solomon, and great offerings made there at that time, we infer that a regular sacrifice was there kept up, although all the great and holy festivals centered from this time in Jerusalem.

Let us gather now from what hints we have, some idea of the service and ceremonial as King David re-established it.

1. *The Sacrifices.* The regular morning and evening sacrifice was revived, a lamb and meat-offering of flour and oil, a drink-offering of wine at morning, and a lamb and a meat-offering and a drink-offering at evening. These were offered in the holy place, and were the "continual burnt-offering which was ordained on Mount Sinai," to be "throughout your generations at the door of the taber-

---

* She is three times called "daughter of Saul." "Michal is intentionally designated the daughter of Saul here, instead of the wife of David, because on this occasion she manifested her father's disposition rather than her husband's."—*Keil and Delitzsch.*

nacle." Where there was attention to the daily offerings, the Sabbath would also be respected with its two lambs and double-sized meat-offering and drink-offering. The monthly offerings at the new moon followed next in the Mosaic ritual, of two young bullocks and a ram and seven lambs and multiplied meat-offerings and drink-offerings, according to the dignity of the animal slain. The three great festivals—seven days each—the feast of the Passover in the month of April, the feast of Pentecost fifty days afterward, and the feast of Tabernacles after the harvest of the corn and the wine, these certainly were not neglected when all the tribes thronged their new and glorious city, now more richly glorious with the feet of God.

2. *The Priests.* There were two high-priests, or two priests at the head of the priestly tribe, Zadok and Abiathar. We have noticed that David appointed them to bring in the ark.* Abiathar was the great-great-grandson of Eli. He belonged to the Ithamar line of Aaron's family, and he had first come to David at the time when his priestly father Ahimelech was slain at Nob. It would be natural, therefore, that he should be mentioned first, and that we should read "Abiathar and Zadok," and not "Zadok and Abiathar," as we find the record. But Zadok was of the Eleazar line—the line of the older son of Aaron's house. Both these priests proved true to David through Absalom's rebellion, but Abiathar supported Adonijah for David's successor, while Zadok supported Solomon. Zadok's name is, therefore, mentioned first. Now, however, at the first, to Zadok and his line of priests was assigned the tabernacle at Gibeon. Zadok very likely under Saul had charge of the tabernacle at Gibeon. Abiathar and his line, therefore, had charge of Jerusalem.

---

* 1 Chronicles xv. 11.

We shall find hereafter that Zadok and his line superseded the line of Abiathar. Of David's twenty-four courses, arranged now or afterwards, sixteen chief men were from the house of Eleazar and only eight from the house of Ithamar. We shall see that Abiathar, who did much to reclaim the fallen reputation of Eli's house, at last died under the curse pronounced on Eli's posterity.

3. *The Levites.* Two classes of the Levites are here specially mentioned, the musicians and the porters. The full order and service of the Levites we will consider hereafter. Worthily, Obed-edom, whom God had blessed, was placed at the head of the porters.* Another Obed-edom, a son of Jeduthun, with Hosah, were with them. There were thirty-eight in all. We shall hereafter find, as the tabernacle arrangements are amplified, that the station of Obed-edom and his company was at the south gate and Hosah at a west gate. As by the permanent location of the tabernacle a large part of the duties of the Levites were ended—" for David said the Lord God of Israel hath given rest unto his people, that they may dwell in Jerusalem forever; and also unto the Levites, they shall no more carry the tabernacle, nor any vessels of it for the service thereof."†—their offices were then confined to the courts and offerings and protection of the holy sanctuary. The service of a doorkeeper naturally included the care of the interior courts, as now the doorkeeper or sexton of a church has the care of the interior building, in the lighting and warming and cleanly keeping of the house. We shall notice the "orders" and particular arrangements when we come to the more complete establishment under David.

4. *The Musicians.* David's poetic and musical genius vas full of suggestions for the musical praise of Jehovah in

---

* Compare 1 Chronicles xvi. 38 with xv. 18 and xxvi. 4, 5, 8.

† 1 Chronicles xxiii. 25.

his sanctuary. There must already have been expended no little instruction and skill when the Levites "appointed for song" could chant and accompany with instruments the psalm which their king composed for the reception of the ark. David himself invented instruments of music.* And after the tabernacle and ark were established on Zion, he began that grand order of musical service which he enriched from time to time with his psalms, until it was ready for Solomon's grander introduction into his temple. The leader of this musical service was a grandson of Samuel the Seer,† under whose pious nurture, at Naioth in Ramah, David's genius itself was kindled with holy fire. Very likely the grandfather, when he found his sons corrupt, secured his little grandson and educated him in minstrelsy, theology, and piety at Naioth. This was Heman, "a singer" of the Kohathite order, the Levite family who had been the ark-and-altar-carrier on the ancient journeys. Asaph was his associate, of the Gershouite order, the family who had been the tent-and-curtain-carriers of the tabernacle; and Ethan or Jeduthun, who were no doubt the same person, was the third leader, of the Merarite order, the Levites who had been the board-and-pillar-carriers. By this orderly appointment of the Levites, at the suggestion of David, the foundation was laid for the growth of musical families and musical training which long endured, as well as for the harmony and consolidation of the Levites themselves. These three leaders had themselves the cymbals for their instrument, no doubt to keep the time. Under them, at the first, were eight men with psalteries, a guitar-shaped instrument made by David of fir or cypress, and six with harps, and Cheneniah, the chief instructor in the voice and the chant. In har-

---

* Amos vi. 5; 1 Chron. xxiii. 5; 2 Chron. xxix. 27.

† Compare 1 Chronicles vi. 33 with 1 Samuel viii. 2.

mony with these, seven priests, on grand occasions, sounded the trumpet in pulse-like notes of solemn bass.

With this arrangement of the "musical instruments of God" and of trained voices, the singers were "to give thanks to the Lord, because his mercy endureth for ever." Here, therefore, or shortly following this time, we may place the One Hundred and Thirty-sixth psalm, with its refrain and chorus and its joyful recital of the history of God's favored people.

O give thanks unto the Lord, for he is good,
    For his mercy endureth for ever.
O give thanks unto the God of gods,
    For his mercy endureth for ever.
O give thanks to the Lord of lords,
    For his mercy endureth for ever.

To him alone who doeth great wonders,
    For mercy his endureth for ever.
To him that by wisdom made the heavens,
    For his mercy endureth for ever.
To him that stretcheth out the earth above the waters,
    For his mercy endureth for ever.
To him that made great lights,
    For his mercy endureth for ever.
The sun to rule by day,
    For his mercy endureth for ever.
The moon and stars to rule by night,
    For his mercy endureth for ever.

To him that smote Egypt in their first-born,
    For his mercy endureth for ever.
And brought out Israel among them,
    For his mercy endureth for ever.
With a strong hand and with a stretched-out-arm,
    For his mercy endureth for ever.
To him who divided the Red Sea into parts,
    For his mercy endureth for ever.
And made Israel to pass through the midst of it,
    For his mercy endureth for ever.
But overthrew Pharaoh and his hosts in the Red Sea,
    For his mercy endureth for ever.

To him which led his people through the wilderness,
    For his mercy endureth for ever.
To him who smote great kings,
    For his mercy endureth for ever.

And slew famous kings,
>For his mercy endureth for ever.
Sihon, king of the Amonites,
>For his mercy endureth for ever.
And Og, king of Bashan,
>For his mercy endureth for ever.
And gave their land for a heritage,
>For his mercy endureth for ever.
Even an heritage unto Israel his servant,
>For his mercy endureth for ever.
Who remembered us in our low estate,
>For his mercy endureth for ever.

And hath redeemed us from our enemies,
>For his mercy endureth for ever.
Who giveth food to all flesh,
>For his mercy endureth for ever.
O give thanks unto the God of heaven,
>For his mercy endureth for ever.

Thirty-fourth Sunday.

PSALMS FOR THE TABERNACLE.

LESSON.

Psalms xcviii., xcv., xcix., xxxvi., xv., lxv., lxvii., v., cxxxviii., viii.

WE now enter upon the palmy years of King David's reign, the high level of his renown and power at home and abroad. We have seen him at thirty years of age anointed at ·Hebron ; at thirty-seven years of age, the conqueror of Jebus and king on Zion ; and in order to make up a probable chronological order of his life, we assume that the introduction of the ark into the new tabernacle took place in the fifth year at Jerusalem. Let us suppose that the battles with the Philistines were during the first and second years in Jerusalem, and that the king's palace was being built by the Tyrians during the third year and finished in the beginning of the fourth year. Then we may suppose that the king·went to Kirjath-jearim for the ark near the end of the fourth year, that the three months at the house of Obed-edom carried the arrival of the ark over into the fifth year at Jerusalem, which was the twelfth year of David's reign and the forty-second year of his life. Between this time of David's full establishment as king and the great and notorious crimes which defiled and weakened his royal dignity, was a period of nine or ten years, reaching to the fifty-first or fifty-second year of his age. These nine or ten years we will find compacted full of events exalting and expanding the material and spiritual strength of the kingdom.

Just here, at the beginning of this period, we may be sure that other psalms of the tabernacle service were composed. The evidence of this is, that David had already been absorbed with preparations of tabernacle and ceremonial, priest and Levites, music and psalms, up to this time, and his thoughts are immediately after this time turned to building a permanent house for Jehovah. The death of Uzzah, the blessing of Obed-edom for three months, the ark, Zion, and the new tabernacle, were the talk of the tribes from Gilead to Carmel, and from Dan to Beersheba. Just in these high days of religious devotion, therefore, we may safely locate the composition of some of the more spiritual psalms. It is not so easy, however, to tell which psalms were composed then. Not one of the titles locates a psalm at that time. We have, at least, two things to help us in making our selection: first, the resemblance of certain psalms to that psalm which, from the sixteenth chapter of first Chronicles, seventh verse, we know *was* composed at the introduction of the ark into the tabernacle; and, secondly, the internal sentiment and structure of the psalms themselves. With these helps, let us notice the beautiful adaptation of certain psalms to this period of David's life.

We have already seen that the One Hundred and Fifth and the Ninety-sixth psalms were parts of the psalm on that great day of religious inauguration, "first delivered into the hand of Asaph and his brethren." The Ninety-eighth psalm is so like to these that it may well have been written soon after, or "adapted" from the Ninety-sixth to celebrate more pointedly the Victorious God who had established the Hebrew nation on their heights of power:

> O sing unto the Lord a new song,
> For he hath done marvellous things;
> His right hand and his holy arm have gotten him the victory.
> The Lord hath made known his salvation;

> His righteousness hath he openly showed in the sight of the nations,
> He hath remembered his mercy and truth towards the house of Israel.
> And all the ends of the earth have seen the salvation of our God.
>> Shout unto the Lord, all the earth!
>> Break forth into joy, and exult and sing!
>> Sing to the Lord with the harp,
>> With the harp and the voice of song!
>> With trumpets and the sound of cornet,
>> Make a joyful noise before the Lord the King;
>> Let the sea roar, and the fulness thereof;
>> The world, and they that dwell therein.
>> Let the rivers clap their hands,
>> And the mountains be joyful together
>> Before the Lord! for he cometh to judge the earth.
>> With righteousness will he judge the world,
>> And the nations with equity.

With the same sentiment and the same reference to history, the Ninety-fifth psalm may have been written. We are to think of Jerusalem on her heights, looking down upon the deep Jordan chasm, and off upon the Salt Sea and the Great Sea, both of which could be seen from the heights near the city.

> O come, let us sing unto the Lord,
> Let us make a joyful noise to the rock of our salvation.
> Let us come before his presence with thanksgiving,
> And make a joyful noise unto him with psalms.
> For Jehovah is a great God!
> And a great king above all gods!
> In his hands are the deep places of the earth.
> The strength of the hills is his also!
> The sea is his, and he made it.
> And his hand formed the dry land.
> O come, let us worship and bow down!
> Let us kneel before Jehovah our maker!
> For he is our God,
> And we the people of his pasture,
> And the sheep of his hand.
>
> O that to-day ye would hear his voice!
> "Harden not your hearts," etc.

No person knew better than David, that the worship of God is designed to quicken our hope and delight in an Admirable, Glorious, and Powerful Ruler, as well as to humiliate the pride of our sin. He could, therefore, represent from the history of the nation, Jehovah's love for the loving as well as his hardness toward the hardhearted.

> Jehovah reigneth : let the nations tremble !
> He sitteth between the cherubim : let the earth quake !
> Great is Jehovah upon Zion ;
> He is exalted over all the nations !
> Let men praise thy great and terrible name !
> It is holy.
> Let them declare the glory of the King who loveth justice !
> Thou hast established equity ;
> Thou dost execute justice in Jacob !
>
> *Response.*
>
> Exalt ye Jehovah, our God,
> And bow yourself at his footstool !
> He is holy.
>
> Moses, and Aaron, with his priests,
> And Samuel, who called upon his name,
> They called upon Jehovah, and he answered them.
> He spoke to them in the cloudy pillar,
> They kept his commandments
> And the ordinances which he gave them.
> Thou, O Jehovah, our God, didst answer them :
> Thou wast to them a forgiving God,
> Though thou didst punish their transgressions.
>
> *Response.*
>
> Exalt Jehovah, our God,
> And worship at his holy mountain,
> For Jehovah, our God, is holy !
>
> PSALM xcix.—*Substance of Noyes's Translation.*

From reflection upon the rewards of those who, with him, have attempted to serve God and the folly of the wicked who despise God, arose the Thirty-sixth psalm, dedicated to the chief-musician as "A Psalm of David, the Servant of God," beginning :

> .... "The transgression of the wicked saith within my heart."

Or, as it has been rendered :

> "To speak of the guilt of the wicked is in my heart."

It is appropriate here as the natural thoughts of a ruler watching to administer his government at a prosperous time, so as to repress wickedness and encourage righteousness.

After the terrible death of Uzzah, and after the blessing on Obed-edom, and the successful removal of the ark to Zion, nothing could be more natural in thinking of the divine sanctuary and worship than for the king to ask who is fit to enter the courts of God's house; nor anything more natural than for him to express that thought in a psalm of instruction for the *individual* worshipper. In this temper of mind was, no doubt, composed the Fifteenth psalm, the first two questions of which we may imagine chanted by a male voice in a bass solo, and the answer returned in a chorus.

> Lord, who shall abide in thy tabernacle?
> Who shall dwell in thy holy hill?
>
> He that walketh uprightly and worketh righteousness,
> And speaketh the truth in his heart.
> He that backbiteth not with his tongue,
> Nor doeth evil to his neighbor,
> Nor taketh up a reproach against his neighbor,
> In whose eyes a vile person is contemned.
> But he honoreth them that fear the Lord,
> He that sweareth to his own hurt and changeth not.
> He that putteth not out his money to usury,
> Nor taketh reward against the innocent,
> He that doeth these things shall never be moved.

And now, as a year rolls around, we should consider the regular feasts of all the tribes joyfully celebrated in Jerusalem. The first joyful convocation of the tribes at the incoming ark would make the re-establishment of the three great festivals the outspring of popular patriotic and religious enthusiasm. David's piety would secure their observance, and his kingly wisdom would welcome them as a strong bond of the tribes in the one nation. We may, therefore, imagine the scene and apply to it the psalm which naturally associates itself with the service.

After the sheaf of the first-fruits was offered on the second day of the Passover, which was in the spring, while the flocks, released from winter keeping, clothed the pastures, and hill and valley were covered with the grain, the Sixty-fifth psalm may have been sung; or it may have been the song of praise for the year's blessings at the Feast of Tabernacles, the thanksgiving day of the nation. We can see the families of the holy city and of all the tribes encamped in green booths on housetops, and in open spaces, and on hill and in valley outside, the multitude overflowing the city, while in the temple the thank-offering and lofty chant of thanks went on under the chief-musician.

A PSALM AND SONG OF DAVID.

Praise waiteth for thee, O God, in Zion,
And unto thee shall the vow be performed!
O thou that hearest prayer,
Unto thee shall all flesh come!
Iniquities prevail against me.
Our transgressions thou shalt purge them away!
Blessed is the man whom thou choosest
And causest to approach unto thee
That he may dwell in thy courts!
We shall be satisfied with the goodness of thy house,
Even of thy holy temple.
By terrible things in righteousness wilt thou answer us,
O God of our salvation!
Who art the confidence of all ends of the earth,
And of them that are afar off upon the sea.

. . . .

Thou visitest the earth and waterest it!
Thou greatly enrichest it with the river of God, which is full of water.
Thou preparest them (the people of the earth) corn when thou hast so provided it.
Thou waterest the ridges thereof abundantly.
Thou settest the furrows thereof.
Thou makest it soft with showers,
Thou blessest the springing of it.
Thou crownest the year with thy goodness,
And thy paths drop fatness.
They drop upon the pastures of the wilderness,

And the little hills rejoice on every side.
The pastures are clothed with flocks,
The valleys also are covered over with corn,
They shout for joy, they also sing.

On such a grand festival, too, with a grand chorus accompaniment of stringed instruments, the Sixty-seventh psalm may have been sung, which begins, it may be observed, with the blessing of Moses and Aaron on the people: (Numbers vi. 24.)

A PSALM OR SONG: FOR THE CHIEF-MUSICIAN ON STRINGED INSTRUMENTS.

God be merciful unto us and bless us,
And cause his face to shine upon us. Selah.
That thy way may be known on earth.
Thy saving health among all nations.
Let the people praise thee, O God,
Let all the people praise thee!
O let the nations be glad and sing for joy:
For thou shalt judge the people righteously,
And govern the nations up earth. Selah.
Let the people praise thee, O God!
Let all the people praise thee.
Then shall the earth yield her increase,
And God, even our own God, shall bless us!
God shall bless us!
And all the ends of the earth shall fear him.

In the spirit in which these psalms magnify the nation, and yet lifts God high above the nation's head and king, we suppose two other psalms were composed, which are the personal praise of the king of Israel, himself the humble subject of the King Eternal. These are the Fifth and One Hundred and Thirty-eighth psalms, the first of which seems to be a morning song of praise, and is dedicated

TO THE LEADER OF THE MUSIC: UPON WIND INSTRUMENTS:
A PSALM OF DAVID.

Give ear to my words, O Lord!
Consider my meditation.
Hearken unto the voice of my cry, my King and my God!

For unto thee will I pray.
My voice shalt thou hear in the morning, O Lord!
In the morning will I direct my prayer unto thee and will look up.
For thou art not a God that hast pleasure in wickedness,
Neither shall evil dwell with thee.

. . . .

But as for me, I will come unto thy house in the multitude of thy mercy,
And in thy fear will I worship toward thy holy temple.*
Lead me, O Lord, in thy righteousness, because of mine enemies [*margin*, those which observe me].
Make thy way straight before my face.
For there is no faithfulness in their mouth ;
Their inward part is very wickedness,
Their throat is an open sepulchre,
They flatter with their tongue.
Destroy thou them, O God!
Let them fall by their own counsels :
Cast them out in the multitude of their transgressions!
But let all those that put their trust in thee rejoice.
Let them ever shout for joy, because thou defendest them!
Let them also that love thy name be joyful in thee,
For thou, Lord, wilt bless the righteous,
With favor wilt thou compass him as with a shield.

In the morning or evening or Sabbath service of the tabernacle, the king's voice itself may have borne upwards these psalms. How noble is he as we hear this majestic chant before the people and unto God!

I will praise thee with my whole heart.
Before the gods will I sing praise unto thee.

. . . . . .

All the kings of the earth shall praise thee, O Lord,
When they hear the words of thy mouth!
Yea, they shall sing in the ways of the Lord,
For great is the glory of the Lord.

. . . .

The Lord will perfect that which concerneth me.
Thy mercy, O Lord, endureth for ever.
Forsake not the works of thine own hands.

—*Psalm* cxxxviii.

---

* The "temple" in David's psalms does not necessarily mean, even by anticipation, the temple of Solomon, for the same word is used of the tabernacle in the days of Eli. See 1 Samuel i. 9, iii. 3.

One other psalm we may locate here, or soon after this time. David was now a father. His little children born at Hebron were growing about him. Amnon, the oldest, ten to twelve years of age; Absalom the fair, the third child, from eight to nine; Shimea and Shobab and Nathan, the first three of his nine children in Jerusalem, must have been born not far from this time. No father was more fond of his little children than this loving David. No pious father would be surer to think of the religious instruction of children than he. No good king would be more certain to teach the nation the importance of such instruction by example and precept. We may, therefore, suppose the Eighth psalm composed for some such occasion as the circumcision of a royal child, or as the presentation after circumcision of his own or of other children in the tabernacle. With thoughts of the dignity of a little child in God's kingdom, of the strength of his kingdom on earth by pious generations, in godly families, and of the dominion of man over creation, he brings the lamb, the pigeon and turtledove to this tabernacle; and as the smoke of the burnt-offering ascends,* this psalm arises under the leadership of Asaph or Heman or his own kingly voice:

TO THE LEADER OF THE MUSIC: UPON THE GITTITH:
A PSALM OF DAVID.

O Jehovah, our Lord!
How excellent is thy name in all the earth!
Thou hast set thy glory above the heavens!
Out of the mouth of babes and sucklings hast thou ordained praise;
Because of thine enemies,
To silence the enemy and the avenger.

When I consider thy heavens, the work of thy fingers,
The moon and the stars which thou hast ordained,
What is man, that thou art mindful of him?
And the son of man, that thou carest for him?
Yet thou hast made him little lower than the angels;
Thou hast crowned him with glory and honor.

---

* See Leviticus xii. 6–8; Luke ii. 23.

Thou hast given him dominion over the works of thy hands ;
Thou hast put all things under his feet ;
All sheep and oxen, yea, and the beasts of the forest,
The birds of the air, and the fishes of the sea,
And whatever passeth through the paths of the deep.
O Jehovah, our Lord,
How excellent is thy name in all the earth !

And if composed for such an occasion, how beautifully does it heighten our Lord's quotation from it, in the temple itself, against the unchildlike rulers.*

---

* Matthew xxi. 16.

Thirty-fifth Sunday.

A HOLY HOUSE OF CEDAR.

LESSON.

2 Samuel vii.; 1 Chronicles xvii. 1–15; xxii. 7, 8; xxviii. 2, 3; 1 Kings v. 3; viii. 17, 18; Psalms cxxxii., xvi., cx., cxxxi.

DAVID is now at the height of prosperity. There is enough in his thriving kingdom to busy the thoughts of a mind so fertile as his, and enough to occupy the hands of his executive and administrative energy. But in the midst of civil affairs the heart of David takes strongest hold of God's law and God's honor. The psalms, as well as his great acts towards the tabernacle and a house of cedar, show this, whether the selection and location of psalms here made is precisely correct or not. It is no mere desire for personal aggrandizement which now suggests a new plan for the glory and power of the sanctuary. The nation, the king sees, is no longer a nation living in tents, but in walled houses and fenced cities. The surrounding nations are subdued; and there is no longer need to bear the ark before the army to victory. The king himself has a palace of cedar, built by foreign hands and adorned with luxury. Why, then, shall the ark of God remain any longer in a tent? Surely it is painfully unbecoming for the royal palace to be more imposing than the Holy Palace of the Divine King. So runs the reasoning of the king's piety.

A new person here comes into notice whose appearance

gives new character to the royal establishment and to the royal piety. This is " Nathan the prophet." He appears at once as a full-grown man and as established in the prophetic office. But he is not, like Samuel, venerable in years and dignities and imposing influence. He is younger than David, for he remains some years as prophet in Solomon's kingdom after David is dead.* The three occasions in which he is conspicuous show that he was both intimate and influential with the king. These three occasions are when Nathan reproves the king for his crimes against Uriah, when the infant Solomon receives his name probably at his circumcision,† and when Solomon is proclaimed king. The fact, too, that he wrote a life of David and a life of Solomon shows that he was, like Samuel—from whose school at Naioth of Ramah he, no doubt, came—a man of affairs and held in high consideration.‡ The tone and bearing of the consultation to which we now come, introduce him to us as already David's friend and adviser. We may imagine the two together in the court of the king's new palace. Beams of cedar of Lebanon project above them. The close-grained, light-colored boards worked with dark knots and veins, ceil the polished walls, the court itself spacious and luxurious for that time. David, in the full prime of his years, sitting on a divan in the corner of the court, his feet folded under his loose and ample robes, his head folded in a brilliant turban, his dark Hebrew eye flashing with animation, his flowing beard and mustache perhaps already touched with gray, his hand stretched out in eager gesture. Nathan, younger, less solid and compact, but not less marked in feature and

---

* 2 Chronicles ix. 29.   † Luke i. 59–63; ii. 21.

‡ "The biography of David by Nathan is, of all the losses which antiquity, sacred and profane, has sustained, the most deplorable."—*Grove.*

attitude, standing in plainer turban and robe, to consider his royal friend and master's communication. With a gravity suited to the subject, and an animated eagerness which flows from an active and sprightly mind, the king opens his plans. Or we see them as, mounted to the housetop, overlooking Zion and the city, they confer. "See this luxurious abode," says the king, "built by the Tyrians, its ceilings and spacious apartments, and broad roofs which look off upon the city, and even down upon the tabernacle of our God. The ark of God is within the tent cloth !" And he proceeds to unfold his plans of a splendid temple worthy of the King of all the earth.

"Do all that is in thine heart," is his friend's answer. "God is surely with thee in this thing." This is the prophet's private opinion, derived from the manifest past co-operation of God with David and the excellence of the suggestion itself; for the prophet assumes that David will execute his plans only in consultation with the divine oracle.

But at night a divine vision interposes. God speaks to Nathan, as to Samuel in the tabernacle. He honors the thought of David's heart, but forbids the execution of his plan.

At early morning we see the young prophet with serene, calm face, and close-wrapped girdle, entering the private apartment of the king. He unfolds a divine communication:

1. 'Thou art forbidden to build the house. (Verses 4 and 5 in both chapters.)

2. To this day thy God has chosen a Tent, and aspired not to a House of cedar. Yet the proposal is honorable to thee. (2 Samuel vii. 5–7 ; 1 Chronicles xvii. 5 ; and compare 1 Kings viii. 18.)

3. The reason why thou art forbidden, is that thou hast been a man of war and of blood. It is not suitable that

the great house of Jehovah should be associated in the eyes of all nations with the cruelties of war, lest the true God be esteemed blood-thirsty and cruel. (1 Chronicles xxii. 8 ; xxviii. 2, 3.)

4. God has exalted thee, that he might establish his people in an immovable place against all enemies. (2 Samuel vii. 8–11 ; and 1 Chronicles xvii. 7–10.)

5. For thy pious and honorable purpose, Jehovah solemnly telleth thee that *He* will build *thee,* a *house*(11 and 10).

6. Thy son, and not thyself, shall build the house for me in a kingdom which I will confirm (12 and 11, 12).

7. Thy son shall introduce a royal house ! and a royal kingdom shall be established *forever*—thy throne, *forever !* (13–16 and 13, 14).

Marvellous is this sublime revelation, limiting the broad purposes of the historic nation to the King's family.

The answer of David to this great personal revelation is the answer of an humble and thankful mind awake to recognize the infinite magnitude of the favor bestowed on him. How comprehensive, and profound, and full of harmony with God is his prayer of praise and thanks and submission, in which he—

1. Magnifies the exalted, humble condescension of God towards himself and his house ; and the more marvellous wisdom which speaks of that house "for a good while to come" (18–20).

2. Exalts the fidelity and devotion which fulfills the long-pledged word of God (21, 22).

3. Magnifies the divine Founder of the nation, the nation which he has founded, and the nation's mission now confirmed again for the long future (23, 24).

4. Accepts with blessings, and grateful supplication of blessings, the divine plans for himself and his family, as the plans of "God over Israel," and with prayers that his royal line may dwell " before God" always.

If David had had thoughts of personal glory in his conception of a holy house, they were utterly lost in the broader conceptions of the Lord of Hosts. The palace and its glory were lost in the Perpetual Support of the Divine Honor in the Earth. In David's mind this could include nothing less than that Great Anointed One who was one day to come in wisdom, and righteousness, and glory.

We do not, therefore, merely suppose, but we know that just here psalms were written which breathe the sentiments of this prayer. The One Hundred and Thirty-second psalm, is closely connected with this personal revelation made to David.

O Lord, remember David
And all his affliction!
How he sware unto Jehovah,
And vowed to the Mighty One of Jacob:
"I will not go into my house
Nor lie down on my bed,
I will not give sleep to my eyes,
Nor slumber to my eyelids,
Until I find a place for Jehovah.
Behold we heard of it at Ephratah (at Bethlehem we heard of it).
We found it in the fields of the wood (Kirjath-jearim, that is, Town of the Woods.)
We will go into his tabernacles,
We will worship at his footstool.

Arise, O Jehovah, into thy rest,
Thou and the ark of thy strength.
Let thy priests be clothed with righteousness,
And let thy saints shout for joy.
For the sake of David thy servant,
Turn not away the face of thine anointed.
Jehovah hath sworn in truth unto David,
He will not turn from it:
"Of the fruit of thy body, will I set upon thy throne,
If *thy* children will keep my covenant
And my testimony which I teach them;
Their children also throughout all ages
Shall sit upon thy throne."
For Jehovah hath chosen Zion,
He hath desired it for his habitation.

> "This is my rest for ever!
> Here will I dwell, for I have desired it.
> I will abundantly bless her provision;
> I will satisfy her poor with bread.
> I will also clothe her priests with salvation,
> And her saints shall shout aloud for joy.
> There will I make the horn of David to bud.
> I have ordained a lamp for my anointed.
> His enemies will I clothe with shame,
> But upon himself shall his crown glitter."

"I will not go into my house" may refer to some vow which David took not to enter the house built by Hiram's workmen, until the ark was established in honor and rest.

Here are connected the celebration of the removal of the Ark, the exaltation of Jehovah's permanent Rest, the recognition of his Anointed and his Spiritual Line and the prophecy of the Permanent Abode of Jehovah.

That the Sixteenth psalm contains a lofty spiritual recognition of the Coming One, we have very definite assurance. For St. Peter at Jerusalem, at Pentecost declares in his argument, that David "being a prophet and knowing that God had sworn with an oath to him, that of the fruit of his loins, according to the flesh, he would raise up the Messiah to sit on his throne—seeing this before, spake of the resurrection of Christ," etc.* In an hour of highest inspiration, then borne on in vision to the future fulfilment of God's ancient promises, and elevated in thought at a just appreciation of his own important relation to the lineage, his thoughts take form in

A GOLDEN PSALM OF DAVID.

> Preserve me, O God, for in thee do I put my trust,
> O my soul, thou hast said unto Jehovah
> Thou art my Lord!
> My goodness extendeth not to thee,
> But to the holy that are in the earth,
> And to the excellent in whom is my delight.

---

* Acts ii. 25, etc.

Their sorrows shall be multiplied
Who hasten after other gods.
Their drink-offerings of blood will I not offer,
Nor will I take their names unto my lips.
Jehovah is the portion of my inheritance, and of my cup.
Thou dost maintain my lot!
The lines have fallen to me in pleasant places,
Yea, I have a goodly heritage,
I will bless the Lord, who hath given me counsel,
My reins (heart), also instructs me in the night seasons.
I have set the Lord always before me,
Because he is at my right hand, I shall not be moved!
Therefore my heart is glad, and my glory rejoiceth,
My flesh also shall rest in hope,
For thou wilt not leave my soul in hades;
Nor wilt thou suffer thy Holy One to see corruption.
Thou wilt show me the path of life;
In thy presence is fullness of joy;
At thy right hand are pleasures for evermore.

It is in an exalted state like this, also, that he affirms his priestly office outside the Mosaic line, claims the office by commission extraordinary, like Melchizedek's, and asserts the spiritual lordship of the Great Anointed, over himself and all kings, in a psalm also cited by St. Peter at Pentecost,* in that notable expression of prophetic insight, quoted by our Lord in the climax of his contest with the apostate rulers.†

A PSALM OF DAVID.

The Lord said to my Lord,
Sit thou at my right hand,
Until I make thy foes thy footstool.
The Lord shall send the rod (sceptre) of thy strength (power) out of Zion.
Rule thou in the midst of thine enemies.
Thy people shall be willing in the day of thy power,
In the beauty of holiness, from the womb of the morning
Thou hast the dew of thy youth.
The Lord hath sworn and will not repent,
" Thou art a priest for ever
After the order of Melchizedek."
The Lord at thy right hand
Shall strike through kings in the day of his wrath.

---

* Acts ii. 34, 35.   † Matthew xxii. 43-45.

> He shall judge among the heathen,
> He shall fill the places with dead bodies ;
> He shall wound the heads over many enemies.
> He shall drink of the brook in the way ;
> Therefore he shall lift up the head.
>
> —*Psalm* cx.

As to those moods in which he felt the personal disappointment of not being permitted to build the temple—a disappointment which, at times, David did, no doubt, feel keenly—this was the spirit of his ascent to the tabernacle :

A SONG OF DEGREES OF DAVID.

> Lord, my heart is not haughty, nor mine eyes lofty ;
> Neither do I exercise myself in great matters,
> Or in things too high for me.
> Surely I have believed and quieted myself,
> As a child that is weaned of his mother :
> My soul is even as a weaned child.
> Let Israel hope in the Lord,
> From henceforth and for ever.
>
> —*Psalm* cxxxi.

Thirty-sixth Sunday

FULL CONQUEST.

LESSON.

2 Samuel viii. 1–8 ; 1 Chronicles xviii. 1–8 ; Deuteronomy xi. 24, 25 ; Joshua i. 1–4 ; 1 Samuel xiv. 47 ; Psalms xx., xix., xxxiii., lxxvi.

DELIGHTFUL as the work of ordering the divine worship on Zion was, there was a more severe work for David to do. The sweet exercise of devotion, the profound contemplation of God's great purposes, the glow and effusion in songs and praises to Jehovah, the arrangement of the national festivals, the peaceful convocation of the tribes—these were pleasing, useful, and of divine appointment; but there was another service which the nation had long been slack in completing. The whole territory predetermined by God for the Hebrew people was to be possessed. David was born and raised in the Lord's school to be the Lord's *warrior.* He was to understand, as he studied the sacred rolls and sought their interpretation with Nathan, Abiathar, and Zadok, that it was not for the people's righteousness nor for his own excellence that conquest was given him. He was to fix it firmly in mind that, "for the wickedness of these nations, the Lord thy God doth drive them out." In the same roll in which he read the prediction and assurance of a permanent place of worship in the land, he read also that the land given to the Hebrews was "from the wilderness and this Lebanon, and from the river Euphrates,

even to the uttermost sea." In the more ancient rolls, he pondered God's promise to Abraham, Isaac, and Jacob: "Thy seed shall be as the dust of the earth, and thou shalt spread abroad to the west and the east, and to the north and to the south; and in thee and in thy seed shall all the families of the earth be blessed." Still more, in explicit directions to Moses and to Joshua, he saw the boundaries of the land particularly defined.*
Just in proportion, therefore, as the pious king examined the divine law on which to build anew the ceremonial and the worship, and by which to guide the divinely-appointed career of the nation, just as he perceived the spiritual grandeur of the nation's destiny, did he feel the powerful obligation to subdue the wicked tribes, and to develop the full growth of the kingdom which God had planned. He remembered, too, that his predecessor was dethroned, when in the height of power, for his leniency to these wicked tribes. God took the responsibility of their punishment, and would take the responsibility of removing *him* from *his* throne if he failed to execute his just sentence on people ripe for execution. After, therefore, sufficient time had elapsed to consolidate the tribes in their religious institutions, and give the tabernacle service new impulse by psalms of praise—from two to four years, we will suppose—the king's undivided attention is given to the full possession of the land. The poet is dismissed; the priestly office is laid aside; the warrior is summoned; but whether poet, priest, or warrior, in the fear and name of God!

Three nations occupied his plans, either at once in the beginning, or one after the other—the broken Philistines below, the Moabites across from Jerusalem, and those distant dominions towards Damascus to the Euphrates

---

* Numbers xxxiv. 1-12; Joshua xiii. 1-14.

FULL CONQUEST.

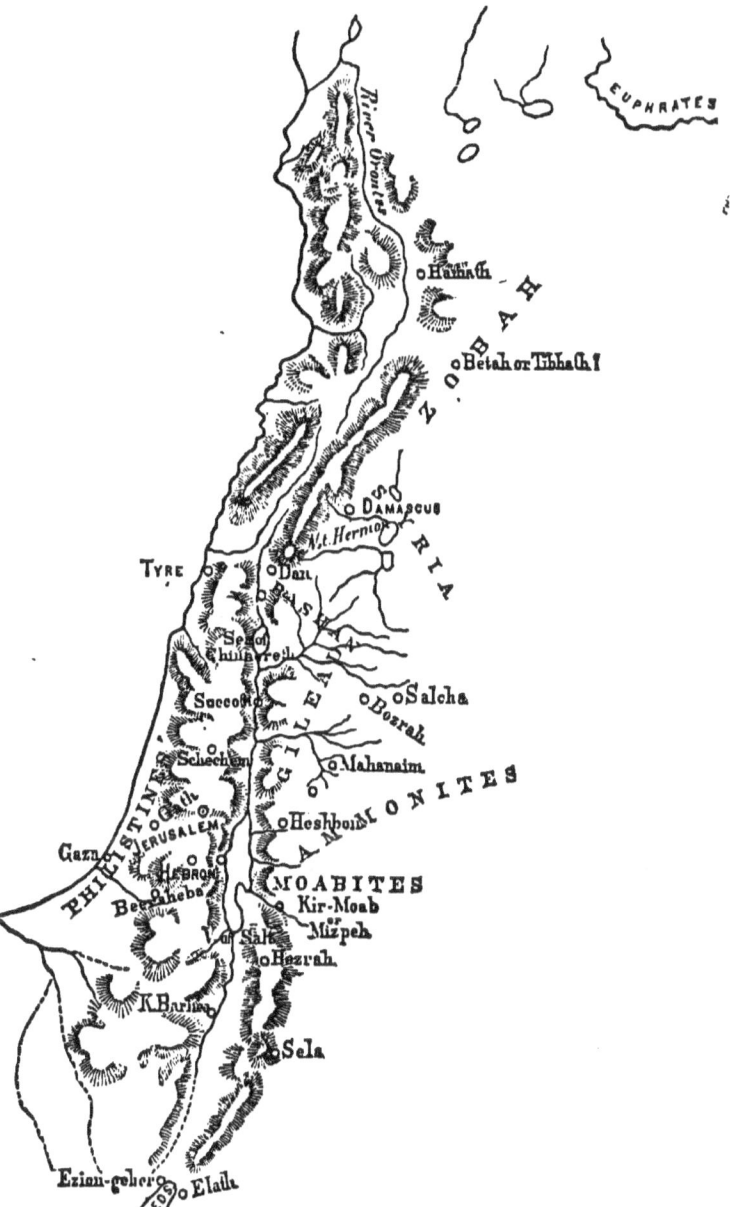

which King Saul partly conquered, but weakly lost. And at length the fourth nation of the Edomites became involved in the conquest.

The army was, therefore, summoned from the tribes, first, probably, in smaller force. The Hebrews descended to the low country, upon that bitter and haughty nation which waited only an opportunity to torment and overthrow the Hebrew people. And this time—Jebus now frowning a *Hebrew* defiance — they *utterly* subdued the Philistines, or *bowed their knees*, as the word might be rendered. They accomplished this by taking "Methegammah," or the Bridle of Ammah, out of the hand of the Philistines. The parallel in the Chronicles reads, "Took Gath and her towns out of the hand of the Philistines." Ammah means mother, and the Bridle of Ammah may mean the bridle of the mother-city.* And if this be the meaning, then "Gath and her towns" signify Gath, the mother-city, and her daughter towns. And the two records clearly support each other. As Gath was the Philistine city nearest the actual Hebrew possessions, as Gath had been the foremost leader in assault on the Israelites, as Gath was the city where David was compelled to humble himself as if idiotic or mad, as David himself in adversity had been vassal to King Achish of Gath, when King Achish himself led the five lords of the Philistines against King Saul, to bring that mother city to her knees was to capture the strategic key to both the nations, or to wrest the bridle from the hand of the careering horseman. The reins of that metropolis came into David's hand.†
Thus ended for all future time the Philistine hope of

---

* See 2 Samuel xx. 19 : " Thou seekest to destroy a city, even a mother-city" (Hebrew *Am*, Greek and English, metropolis, mother-city) " in Israel."

† " An Arabic idiom, in which giving up one's bridle to another is equivalent to submitting to him."

ascendancy. Henceforth the kingdoms of David and of Solomon sweep down to the gates of Gaza.

The army ordered by the king to the Moabite country was probably larger. That ancient enemy across the sea would have been more terrible had not the awful chasm intervened. The ancient hostility had continued to the height of Saul's power, when Saul drove all before him on every side, from Philistia through Edom, Moab, Hermon, around to Zobah in the north. David and Jesse and his wife were harbored in Mizpah of Moab; but more out of hostility to Saul, it may be believed, than from friendly feeling to the grandson of Ruth, more to help a rebel than to serve a future king.

David's war with the Moabites was a fierce and terrible one—little short of an exterminating war. Two-thirds of the people taken were put to death, the other third to service and to tribute. The captured fighting-men were made to lie on the ground. They were then measured with a line :—two lines to death, one line to life—a savage punishment, but thoroughly oriental and consonant with all ideas of warfare known in those days. Even this was mild compared with the English act in India of blowing Sepoys from the cannon's mouth. Spoils from cities, sanctuaries, and people were taken and kept for the cedar-house to Jehovah. Some special act of insult or perfidy may have been the occasion of this terrible vengeance —like the insult of the Ammonites afterwards; or, as has been conjectured, the King of Moab may have killed David's parents, or may have surrendered them to Saul during David's persecutions. Neither conjecture is necessary. David's zeal was divinely aroused to purge his nation from contamination, and to put those nations far off from the Hebrew confidence and approach. In the book of the law he read: "An Ammonite or Moabite shall not enter into the congregation of the Lord, even to the tenth generation, because they met thee not with bread and water in the way, and because they hired Balaam to curse thee. Thou shalt not seek their peace nor their prosperity all thy days for-ever." And in the compulsive prophecy of Balaam, in which he predicted a star of Jacob and a sceptre out of Israel, who shall smite the corners (or chieftains, who sit in the divan-corners of Moab),* David undoubtedly recognized a rising royal power which he was himself to wield. Many a great man, oriental and occidental, who has had small reason compared with David, has considered himself commissioned of God to fulfil a purely *fanciful* prediction. The war with Moab was really a war of God, punitive and retributive. Jehovah alone took the responsibility. He who condemned Saul for sparing Agog, approved David for exterminating the Moabites. It was the only style of punishment against a thoroughly base and an incorrigible people, which at all comported with the level to which human civilization had come.

It is quite likely that in this campaign Benaiah—promoted, perhaps, for the achievement, to be the captain of David's body-guard—distinguished himself by slaying two lion-like warriors of the enemy, an acceptance of challenge, and a triumph likely to turn the scale of victory.†

The next campaign to the Euphrates must have required still more formal preparation. Some months may have elapsed, or David may have quickly massed his forces, and followed up the spreading fear and fame of the Moabite victory. Hadadezer seems to have massed an army at the Euphrates to attack the Hebrews; for the words "to recover his border," mean strictly "to return his hand;" that is, to stretch it out again to recover his power. To David it was as truly a religious campaign as the first conquest of the Canaanites. When, then, the

---

* Numbers xxiv. 17. † 1 Chronicles xi. 22.

army is marshalled at Jerusalem for its northward march, the king and captains and warriors are animated by sacrifices and lofty hymns of praise and supplication. They were going against a nation of chariots and horses, not for external conquest, but to recover the land given by God to Abraham, Isaac, and Jacob. They were to fight under a king who observed the condition of his office, not to multiply horses. As they pass the Jordan by the well-known fords, or by the Sea of Chinerath, and cross the stretching plains towards Damascus and beyond, we may imagine the march resounding with the Hebrew chant which David before their start set in order at the tabernacle for their battle-hymn:

TO THE CHIEF MUSICIAN: A PSALM OF DAVID.

The Levite singers.

The Lord hear thee in the day of trouble;
The name of the God of Jacob defend thee;
Send thee help from the sanctuary,
And strengthen thee out of Zion;
Remember all thy offerings,
And accept thy burnt sacrifice. Selah.
Grant thee according to thine own heart,
And fulfil all thy counsel.
We will rejoice in thy salvation,
And in the name of our God we will set up our banners.
The Lord fulfil all thy petitions.

David sings.

Now know I that the Lord saveth his anointed.
He will hear him from his holy heaven,
With the saving strength of his right hand.
Some trust in chariots and some in horses:
But we will remember the name of the Lord our God.
They are brought down and fallen,
But we are risen and stand upright.

The Levites sing.

Save, Lord, the king.
He [the Lord] will hear us when we call.

—*Tholuck's arrangement of the Twentieth Psalm.*

Two battles were fought in the general region of Damascus: the first with the forces of King Hadadezer, who marshalled a great array of warriors and of chariots from his country of Zobah; the second with the allied forces of Zobah and Damascus. The number of prisoners taken in each battle by David—in the first battle, 1,000 chariots, 700 horses, 20,000 infantry; in the second battle, 22,000 footmen—show that the armies on both sides were large, and the sweep and shock of oriental battle on those high plains tremendous.

Where, now, was Zobah? For we cannot mistake Syria of Damascus, which must have been the thirty-mile fertile circle of which Damascus was the centre and head. Zobah was probably that region of *Aram* or Syria which lies between the kingdom of Damascus and the Euphrates —not eastward into dry desert, but north-eastward from Damascus, on the skirts of the mountain-ranges. A straight line from Jerusalem *through* Damascus strikes the Euphrates near its most westward bend and about east of Antioch. Projected across the Euphrates, it strikes into Padan-Aram in Mesopotamia. Zobah, it is supposed, lay alongside this line between Damascus and the Euphrates. David's army on the march were on the path of Abraham's servant and his ten camels from Beersheba to the city of Nahor. The high crests of Lebanon looked down from the west; the great Arabian desert stretched away to the south; the Euphrates brought down its volume of waters from the north and ebbed away to the east. The shields of gold, "by which we are probably to understand iron or wooden frames overlaid with plates of the precious metal," and the abundance of fine brass which David took, show the wealth of the country. Possibly Zobah stretched over Lebanon to the sea, for the city Berothai which David captured has by some geographers been thought to be the modern Beirut, one of the seaports of Damascus. And the other city, Betah, or

Tibhath, may have been the modern Taibeh, half-way from Damascus to "the river." In King Saul's time, there was more than one king in Zobah, very likely a number of petty, independent chieftains, for "he vexed the kings of Zobah." But now, in David's day, these chieftains were united under their one sheikh, Hadadezer*, who ruled from Euphrates to Syria of Damascus, had friendly relations with Damascus, and had had wars with the neighboring King of Hamath on the Orontes, towards Antioch. Wherever the battle was, however many kings there were under Hadadezer, David had the victory, and in it "lifted up the name of his God." Faithful to his coronation vows, he houghed (hamstrung) the horses, reserving not enough for ambition or conquest. The hundred preserved were certainly within the condition, " He shall not *multiply* horses," and we do not hear of horsemen under David.

The Syrians of Damascus rallied to Hadadezer, and the reinforced army met the Hebrew army again. But the result was another great victory for David—twenty-two thousand Syrians were slain; the Syrian cities were garrisoned by Hebrew soldiers; Damascus itself, of course, was occupied—here first mentioned since Abraham's day; and all Syria was subject to David. The gold and the large bulk of brass were sent to Jerusalem for the future holy house, and were afterwards used by Solomon.

On the homeward march, moving silently by night beneath the deep illimitable heavens, over those broad eastern plains of sand or more verdant table-lands, or awake on his pillow, his mind clear and free as the hemisphere above him, his courageous spirit submissive to the perfection of God's majestic rule in nature and in grace, let us place the origin of the sublime Nineteenth psalm, perfected, perhaps, on his house-top in Jerusalem :

---

* 2 Samuel x. 19.

The heavens declare the glory of God,
And the firmament sheweth his handy-work.
Day uttereth speech unto day,
And night showeth knowledge unto night.
No speech ! no language !
Their voice is not heard !
Their rule is gone out through the earth,
And their words to the end of the world.
In them hath he set a tent for the Sun
Which is like a bridegroom coming from his chamber,
And rejoiceth like a strong man, to run a race.
His going forth is *from* the end of the heaven,
And his circuit *unto* the end of it.
And there is nothing hid from his heat.
The law of the Lord is perfect, converting the soul.
The testimony of the Lord is sure, making wise the simple.
The statutes of the Lord are right, rejoicing the heart, etc.

Thirty-seventh Sunday.

THE CONQUEST COMPLETE.

LESSON.

2 Samuel viii. 9–14 ; 1 Chronicles xviii. 9–13 ; 1 Kings xi. 15, 16 ; Psalms lx. cviii. xxi. ix. ii.

THESE two great victories made a profound impression on all that northern country. The prowess of the great warrior of the south went on the wind to all the sovereign rulers. Toi, of Hamath, whose city and country controlled the Orontes valley northward down to Antioch, and the southward valley between the two Lebanon ranges, to which "entering in of Hamath" the Hebrew kingdom was to extend, thought it politic rather to court David's friendship than to offer resistance. Possibly communications with his neighboring king of Tyre may have given him esteem for David. He sent his son, therefore, to salute King David, with gold and silver and brazen vessels for gifts, which David dedicated to the future holy house.

God did not now permit David's ambitious pride to corrupt him when his dominion thus swept from Hamath and Euphrates to Mizpeh of Moab and Gaza, from the great eastern desert to the great sea westward. For he wounded any rising ambition which he might have felt by another short campaign, which humbled him, while it confirmed the whole broad territory under him. The record in

Samuel says that after David returned from Syria (Aram) he "got him a name in the Valley of Salt," where eighteen thousand men were slain. The record in Chronicles assigns the command of this expedition to Abishai. The title of the Sixtieth psalm and the allusion in Kings, which evidently refer to the same campaign, assign the command to Joab. Such a supposition as the following will harmonize the different records. While the strength of the Hebrew army is with David under Joab, in the conquest of Syria of Zobah (Aram-zobah), the Syrians assisted very likely by help across the river,* couriers come with the news that the Edomites in force threaten the south. The few troops left in Judah and Ephraim cannot stand before the array, and have probably been already driven northward, if not defeated. "Two short days more would suffice to bring the Edomites to Hebron, and seven hours from Hebron to Jerusalem." The southern tribes are trembling. With all haste, David despatches Joab and Abishai with troops to strengthen and command the reserve at home, and advance couriers fly to announce help at hand. From the psalm, if we rightly locate it here, it is evident that the Edomites had pressed back the Hebrews, and perhaps defeated them in a skirmish or pitched fight. But the news from the north now supports the Israelites, and they hold the Edomites at bay till on Joab's approach, they retreat from the mountains about Hebron down the ravines to the remarkable Valley of Salt, at the southern end of the Salt Sea, on the borders of their own country. Thither Joab pushes on to battle, Abishai in advance, who perhaps has already been in command of the southern army, so that Abishai has the chief place in the battle, which is under the general command of Joab; and there in tumultuous and irresistible assault, and with a slaughter of from twelve thousand to

---

* From Syria across the Euphrates, that is, Syria of the two rivers—Hebrew, *Aram-naharaim ;* Greek, *Mesopotamia.*

eighteen thousand,† they utterly shatter the Edomite power. Meanwhile David is full of solicitude. He has Berothai, Tibhath, Damascus, and perhaps other towns to secure with garrisons, lest new Syrian troops sweep down through Manasseh and Gilead, on Jacob's path from Padan-aram to Succoth and Shechem.

The army of the kingdom seems scattered and broken and subject to great perils, a part in the north, part in the south, and part on the way between ; his home-defenders deserted. Ephraim and Judah are the nation's bulwark ; but Moab, Edom, and Philistia taunt and exult over the absent and foolhardy monarch. In this state of mind David pours out his song of complaint, solicitude, and confidence to God.

TO THE CHIEF MUSICIAN, TO THE TUNE, "THE LILY OF THE TESTIMONY," A GOLDEN PSALM OF DAVID, TO BE LEARNT BY HEART.

When he was at strife with Aram-naharaim and Aram-zobah, when Joab returned and smote of Edom in the Valley of Salt twelve thousand.

O God, thou hast cast us off ; thou hast scattered us ;
Thou hast been displeased ; oh ! turn thyself to us again !
Thou hast made the land tremble ; thou hast broken it.
Oh ! heal the breaches thereof ; for it shaketh.
Thou hast made thy people to see hard things.
Thou hast made us drink the wine of reeling.
Thou hast given a banner to those that fear thee,
To be lifted up before thy truth ! Selah !
That thy beloved may be delivered !
Save with thy right hand, and hear me !

God hath spoken in his holiness.
I will triumph ; I will divide Shechem,
And measure out the valley of Succoth.
Gilead is mine, and Manasseh is mine,
And Ephraim my helmet, Judah my sceptre,

---

† Reckoned in the title of the Sixtieth psalm at 12,000, but by the authors of the historical books at 18,000, and in either case probably intended only as round numbers. Nothing is more common than a difference of reckoning in respect to the dead on the field of battle.

Moab my wash-pot (*for the feet*), to Edom (*as a slave*) I will throw my shoe.
O Philistia, triumph over me ! (*ironical.*)

Who will bring me to the strong city (*Sela or Petra ?*)
Who will lead me into Edom ?
Wilt not thou, O God ! who didst cast us off,
And didst not go forth with our armies?
Give us help from trouble.
For vain is the help of man.
Through God we will do valiantly,
For he will tread down our enemies.

—*Psalms* lx. *and* cviii.

Animated and active, the Syrian garrisons secured, David comes on with the rest of the forces; with the genius of a military master, he pushes past Jerusalem and Hebron, perhaps by way of Jericho and Engedi, to follow up Joab's victory, and penetrate through the very depth of the land, securing every stronghold of Edom. The persecutions of Saul have made him familiar with those gorges and rocks and their people. But gorges and rocks make the campaign obstinate. For six months did the war continue under David or Joab as personal commanders, until every man was slain or driven out of the Edomite country. Hodad, the Edomite king's son, a little child, fled to Egypt, whence as a full-grown man he came back to annoy King Solomon. David's success was complete. "Throughout all Edom he put garrisons, and all they of Edom became subject to him." He must, therefore, have occupied the principal capital towns of the Edomite country. The fertile and strong part of Edom lay straight south of Moab to the Red Sea, while its waste pasture and wilderness stretched westward on the south of Simeon; and the capital towns at that time were probably Bozrah and Sela (Hebrew, *Sela;* Greek, *Petra;* English, *The Rock*) and Maon, all of which were directly south of Mizpeh of Moab on the same high, fertile, broken, rocky plateau, along the gorge between the Salt Sea, and the Red Sea, and Elath and Ezion-geber at the head of the Red Sea. These towns were no doubt held firmly through David's life, for Solomon equipped his navy at Ezion-geber. And thus was fulfilled another portion of that marvellous prophecy spoken from the tops of the rocks of Moab, when that gifted seer who had come from Syria* looked off on the Hebrew tents on the east, their future land on the west, and the Edomite heights on the south :

> And Edom shall be a possession,
> Seir also shall be a possession for his enemies
> And Israel shall do valiantly.
> Out of Jacob shall come he
> That shall have dominion.
> And shall destroy him that remaineth of the city.
> —*Numbers* xxiv. 18, 19.

This grand sweep of victories, from Philistia to Moab, from Zobah to Edom and the Red Sea, was the lofty confirmation of God's promise and of David's power. Well might the victorious son of Jesse, as he turned his retinue homeward, as he thought of these marvellous conquests as he rode past Ziph and Carmel, Hebron and Bethlehem, repeat to himself those other words of Balaam :

> According to this time it shall be said of Jacob and of Israel,
> *What hath God wrought ?*
> —*Numbers* xxiii. 23.

The nations were compelled to bow before Jehovah's nation, and to acknowledge the powers of Jehovah in His king. The king's fame, as it went abroad, was the fame of his God. The stories of his youthful exploits and his manly achievements were repeated by his own soldiers, as deeds achieved in the name of Jehovah, in garrison-camps, and in tents and towns of his enemies, from the Red Sea and the river of Egypt to the Euphrates. Great must have been the rejoicing as the victorious king came to Jerusalem, as the fact of the preservation of the Sixtieth psalm shows. He was now in the full beauty of his physi-

---

* Aram, Numbers xxiii. 7 ; Mesopotamia, Deut. xxiii. 4.

cal manhood—a beauty and power enhanced so much by the brilliant costume of the Orient, and his power filled his people with admiring awe. God's mode of discipline has prevented in him the petty conceit of vanity, and developed a noble dependence on his divine Lord. With a piety mature and stalwart as his power, we may behold him taking his way soon, in a mingled concourse of warriors and people, to the holy hill of Zion, the tabernacle, where, while the thank-offerings smoke on the altars, the choir and the king lift up new songs of praise like these:

TO THE CHIEF MUSICIAN: A PSALM OF DAVID.

The King sings.

The king shall joy in thy strength, O Jehovah!
And in thy salvation, how greatly shall he rejoice!
Thou hast given him his heart's desire.
And hast not withholden the request of his lips. Selah.
For thou overwhelmest him with the blessings of goodness!
Thou settest a crown of pure gold upon his head.
He asked life of thee, and thou gavest to him
Length of days, for ever and ever.*
His glory is great in thy salvation.
Honor and majesty hast thou laid upon him.
For thou hast made him most blessed for ever.
Thou hast made him exceeding glad with thy countenance.
For the king trusteth in Jehovah.
And through the mercy of the Most High he shall not be moved.

The Levites sing.

Thy hands shall find out all thine enemies.
Thy right hand shall find out those that hate thee.
Thou shalt make them as a fiery oven in the time of thy anger.
Jehovah shall swallow them up in his wrath.
And the fire shall devour them,
Their fruit shalt thou destroy from the earth,
And their seed from among the children of men.
For they intended evil against thee.
They imagined a mischievous device
Which they were not able to perform.
Therefore shalt thou make them turn their back.
When thou shalt make ready thine arrows upon thy strings against the face of them.
Be thou exalted, Jehovah, in thine own strength!
We will sing and praise thy power.
—*Tholuck's Twenty-first Psalm.*

---

* A reference to the prediction of his kingdom and his house forever.

TO THE CHIEF MUSICIAN, TO THE TUNE, "DEATH TO THE
SON": A PSALM OF DAVID.

I will praise thee, O Jehovah, with my whole heart.
I will show forth all thy marvellous works.
I will be glad and rejoice in thee.
I will sing praise to thy name, O thou Most High!
Because mine enemies are turned back,
And did fall and perish at thy presence.
For thou hast maintained my right and my cause.
    Thou satest in the throne, judging right.
    Thou hast rebuked the heathen.
    Thou hast put out their name for ever and ever.
    The destructions of the enemy are come to a perpetual end.
    And thou hast destroyed their cities;
    Their memorial is perished with them.
But Jehovah shall endure for ever.
He hath prepa ed his throne for judgment;
And he shall judge the world in righteousness.
He shall minister judgment to the people in uprightness.
Jehovah also will be a high-place for the oppressed,
A high-place in times of trouble.
And they that know thy name will put their trust in thee.
For thou, Jehovah, hath not forsaken them that seek thee.
    Sing praises to Jehovah, to Jehovah who dwelleth in Zion.
    Declare among the people his doings.
    When he maketh enquiry for blood, he remembereth them.
    He forgetteth not the cry of the humble.
Have mercy upon me, O Jehovah!
Consider my trouble from those that hate me,
Thou that liftest me up from the gates of death,
That I may show forth thy praise in the gates of the daughter of Zion:
I will rejoice in thy salvation.

The heathen are sunk down in the pit that they made,
In the net which they hid is their own foot taken.
Jehovah is known by the judgment which he executeth.
The wicked is snared in the work of his own hands. Meditation. Selah.
The wicked shall be turned into hell,
And all the nations that forget God!
For the needy shall not always be forgotten.
The expectation of the poor shall not perish for ever.

    Arise, O Jehovah! let not man prevail;
    Let the heathen be judged in thy sight;
    Put them in fear, O Jehovah!
    That the nations may know themselves to be but men. Selah.
—*Psalm* ix.

As he retires once more to the tranquil contemplations of the holy city, and the power of Jehovah's great personal promise breaks again on him in its fulness of meaning, he is again caught up into high and inspired utterance. At some such time of triumph over heathen foes, and of the prospective completion of the victory of God's kingdom over all enemies, and with some faint intimation of Him of whom he was speaking, and whom he himself represented, was the Second psalm—that grand Messianic hymn —composed.*

>Why do the heathen rage
>And the people imagine a vain thing?
>The kings of the earth set themselves,
>And the rulers take counsel together
>Against the Lord, and against his Anointed, saying
>
>Let us break their bonds asunder,
>And cast away their cords from us.
>
>He that sitteth in the heavens shall laugh!
>The Lord shall have them in derision.
>Then shall he speak unto them in his wrath,
>And vex them in his sore displeasure.
>
>Yet have I set (or *anointed*) my king
>Upon my holy hill of Zion.

---

* See Acts iv. 25, where David is called the author. See also Acts xiii. 33; Hebrews i. 5, and v. 5. Professor Stowe considers this psalm an inspired vision of the Messiah, entirely independent of David's reign—" in form and spirit strictly dramatic." " In prophetic ecstasy, he beholds the events actually occurring, he sees the multitudes assembling, he hears what they say, he sees God quietly seated on his throne, etc., and he writes down the whole scene." " When these dramatic psalms were sung in the temple-worship, the different persons were easily represented by different parts of the choir responding to each other." In the Second psalm, the whole choir might chant the first stanza as the words of the Psalmist, a portion of the choir chant the next couplet as the words of " the Rebels," the whole choir the next stanza as the psalmist vision of God's easy contempt for the rebels, a solo voice next represents Jehovah's anointment, another solo voice Messiah's decree, and then the whole chorus the psalmist admonition to all Kings and Rulers.—*Bibliotheca Sacra*, 1850.

> I will declare the decree:
> The Lord hath said unto me,
> Thou art my son,
> This day have I begotten thee.
> Ask of me, and I will give thee the heathen for thine inheritance,
> And the uttermost parts of the earth for my possession.
> Thou shalt break them with a rod of iron,
> Thou shalt dash them in pieces like a potter's vessel.
>
> Be wise now therefore, O ye kings!
> Be instructed, ye judges of the earth!
> Serve the Lord with fear,
> And rejoice with trembling.
> Kiss the son, lest he be angry,
> And ye perish from the way;
> When his wrath is kindled but a little.
> Blessed are all they who put their trust in him.

It is not necessary to suppose that David had an explicit conception of the Messiah. It is enough to suppose that he identified both himself and the Future Anointed with that "house," in respect to which God had spoken both to himself and to the Greatest Son of the line, THOU ART MY SON, THIS DAY HAVE I BEGOTTEN THEE.

In these great days of the kingdom, may have been sent to the Levite musicians by the king, and with his approval, psalms of Asaph such as those beginning:

> The mighty God, even the Lord hath spoken
> And called the earth, from the rising to the setting sun,
> Out of Zion, the perfection of beauty
> God hath shined.
>
> —*Psalm* l.
>
> Truly God is good to Israel,
> Even to such as are of a clean heart.
>
> —*Psalm* lxxiii.
>
> In Judah is God known.
> His name is great in Israel.
>
> —*Psalm* lxxvi.

Thirty-eighth Sunday.

EAST OF JORDAN.

LESSON.

2 Samuel viii. 15 ; 1 Chronicles xviii. 14 ; xii. 8-15 ; xxvi. 31, 32 ; vi. 78-81 ;
2 Samuel xvii. 24, 27-29 ; Psalms cxxxiii. cxxviii.

WITH the subjugation of Zobah, Damascus, Moab, and Edom, David's eastern boundary ran along the great Arabian desert from the Euphrates to the Red Sea. Some strong cities, or a single strong district like the Ammonite country, clung to independence, but the fear of the Hebrew king was upon all. Henceforward, we see gradually maturing that tribal order and national union which bore ripest fruit in the forty years' peaceful reign of Solomon. We cannot make out the full details of government ; but let us take such hints as we can find on a visit to some of these tribes in these palmy days of David's rule.

Let us first cross the Jordan to the eastern pastoral tribes. From "the wide table-land, tossed about in wild confusion of undulating downs," you may look westward across the Jordan chasm upon the more barren hills of Ephraim and Benjamin, the softer perspective of the plain of Jezreel and the faint blue cliffs of Carmel. Face about now to the sun-rising, and climb to the very highest of those highlands of the east. You stand on the mountains of Gilead, among the families of Gad. The shepherds whom you see everywhere are hardy and adventurous, more wild and daring than those who play the pipe among the flocks and feeding-troughs of Reuben. Eleven of them, swift as the gazelles down the mountains, braved the over-

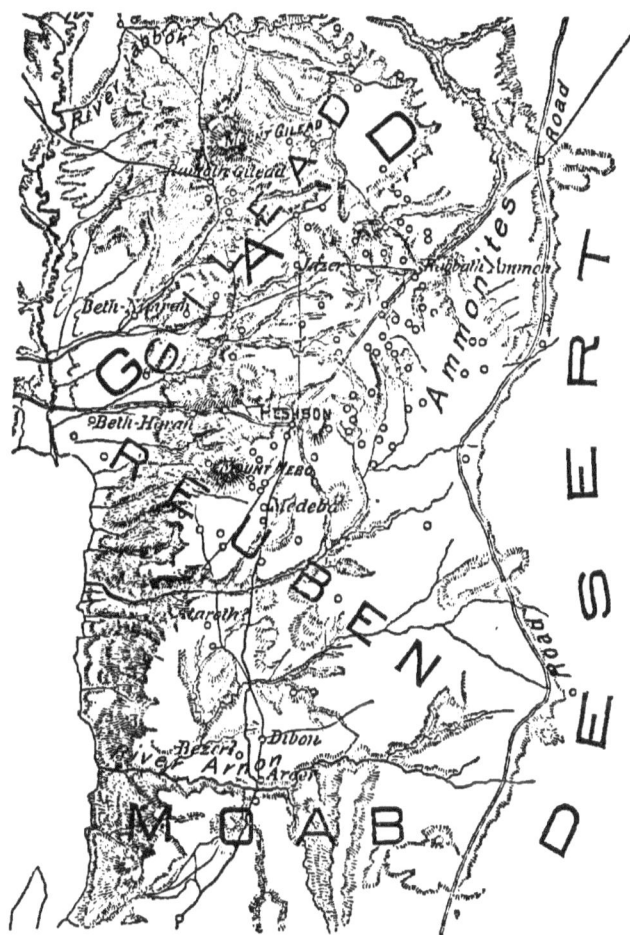

flowing Jordan to join the persecuted David in the rocks of Judah, and, with faces like lions, drove all before them. Towards the sun, beyond yonder glowing horizon, the shelving highland slope gradually away to the Ishmaelites' desert. To your right, the scattered herds of cattle look over the edge of Reuben's pastures down into the Salt Sea, and roam the ample swards eastward. To the left, your eye runs across the ragged fissure of Jabbok, the more distant line of the wide-branching Jarmuk, trips past the edge of Chinnereth far up the snow-helmeted Hermon, and sweeps back by Damascus, the rough basalt of Argob, and the doubly-broad fields of Bashan. That is the land of Manasseh, far beyond which are the outlying Zobah and the border of Euphrates. Here and there eastward you may catch the white glint of a tent where the flock edges on the desert, but solid towns and walls all through this region are the defence of the tribe. Ramoth-gilead is the central city. Let us descend to the lower mountains and enter it. We pass the little villages which lie near its walls. We salute the elders who sit at the gates, not only for the town and its suburbs, but for the whole Jordan valley, and for all the broad highlands from the Salt Sea to even beyond the Jabbok,—for this is the central city of refuge for the eastern tribes. It holds a high and commanding position, or it would not have been chosen for the purpose. Many of the people whom we meet are Levites on their way to or from the gates, revered by the people; for this is a Levitical city also. Here come two rough-clad shepherds accompanied by a score of long-limbed, resolute Gileadites, bow and pike in hand, who are off with them against a band of prowling robbers who threatened, yesterday, the flocks on the frontier; for to this place the score of shepherd villages and the thousand shepherds look for protection when roving Amalekites or Ammonites sweep in upon them from the sand. Here at the chief house of the place we find some such sheikh as Geber,* whose son

---

* 1 Kings iv. 13.

becomes one of Solomon's twelve officers over his kingdom twenty-five years later. Full of vigor, with a rude and stalwart beauty, he holds, we suppose, substantially the same power which his son will hold at that later day, ruling the small towns which Jair originally took under Moses,* if not the sixty great cities with walls and brazen bars in the land of Bashan.

Across the Jabbok to the north in forests of oak and a wild country, we find that other Levitical city of consequence, Mahanaim, where King Ishbosheth attempted a capital. We enter either of its two western gates under a chambered wall or tower, and find it large enough to contain some hundreds and thousands besides its regular population.† It is revered for its age as well as for its power, for here the angels met Jacob; and now, since David at Hebron slew Ishbosheth's assassins and hung up the hands and feet that did the deed and brought the tidings, no city is more loyal to the rising king. What is this subordinate town under the shadow of its power? It must be Rogelim. The gray-bearded Barzillai, a very great man, is the patriarch of the place, seventy years old. Pottery and household wares are sold in the streets. Wheat, barley, and lentiles grow in the fields around. Bees hum in the woods and blossoming herbs. Butter, cheese, and honey, sheep and kine, are abundant. Festivals are made glad by singing men and women, and oriental luxury abounds under Berzillai's wise and generous sway, whom David afterwards so learns to love as to invite him to his court at Jerusalem.

And yonder town, what is that? That is Lodebar, where lives "the principal man of Gilead,"‡ Machir, who has under his roof, unknown to the king, a lame prince of Saul's house, about twenty-three years of age.

---

* Numbers xxxii. 41. † 2 Samuel xviii. 4. ‡ Josephus.

It is that son of Jonathan, whose stumbling nurse crippled him for life in the panic after his father was slain.

Down at the boundary of Reuben is Heshbon, with massive walls and double reservoirs like two eyes at the gate,* the first conquered city where Sihon held his capital.

This side of it is Jazer, at the head of which waters in the old conquest run to meet the Jordan near Jericho. Her "daughter-towns" are around her, and she herself is of high consequence as the home of Jerijah, under whom are twenty-seven hundred Merarite Levites, distributed through all three of the eastern tribes. Diligent is his labor and diligent their study after the oriental type, to be skilled in the appointments and sacrifices of the tabernacle, and to provide instruction in these laws to all these people of flocks and herds. Some of the fathers and sons, and perhaps himself, are now absent at Jerusalem. Dignified in his office, powerful with the royal court, revered for his religious mission, exalted over his twenty-seven hundred brethren, the visits of Jerijah and his company of scribes and assistants command profound respect from Damascus to Bozrah.

Along that border, where herdsmen of Gad and herdsmen of Reuben mingle, are Atroth-shophan, and Jogebah, with walled folds for sheep, at hand. Dibon and Ataroth are far toward Moab near the Arnon and its branches. Low down in the Jordan valley are Beth-haran and Beth-nimrah—all "fenced cities," long ago built by the people of Gad, and Succoth and Zaphon are yonder up the Jordan valley towards Chinnereth.

Beyond the oak-forests which clothe the upper banks of the Jabbok, half-way from that torrent to Chinnereth, is *Jabesh*-gilead, whose elders still gratefully preserve the

---

* Song of Solomon vii. 4.

bones of Saul under a tree near the city, in remembrance of his rescue of their town from Nahash.

Let us go northward into Manasseh. Our mules take easy pace across these high downs, for we go far enough east to avoid the lower broken steeps of the Jabbok, and not far enough east to feel the desert sand. Past scores of flocks we go, down the little upper ravines, threading them and climbing them again, past herds of Manasseh, startling here a bevy of partridges and there a herd of gazelles or a fox, till we come to the broad waters of the stream Jarmuk.* We are now more distant from Chinnereth on the east than the Carmel headland is distant from Chinnereth on the west. We can see as we travel on, what are the natural boundaries of the eastern half-tribe of Manasseh. It sweeps a circuit around the head rivulets of this one stream, whose branches stretch far and wide, almost like the radii of a semicircle, and which is the largest tributary to the Jordan. Damascus, which is north of the centre of the tribe, is an outlying territory of the kingdom. Here at the extreme east we are in Bashan, with desert on the south and east and north-west. The men are warriors, resolute against Syrians or Ishmaelites. The cities are massive stone cities, at the entrance to which we see massive stone gates hung on great stone swivels. We will turn our steps only to Bozrah. Here we enter a city a mile and a half in diameter, with lofty walls and higher turrets, with a population of tens of thousands. The thriving sons of the desert are attracted here, for it is near at hand to them, and has plenty of fountains and provisions. They lurk near the smaller towns for desperate adventures, or boldly mingle for barter in these streets and traders' stalls. Everything is stone

---

* We do not know the name of this stream at that time. It was at a later time called Jarmuk.

—its thick walls, the roofs and doors and window-shutters of houses, built irregularly along its straight streets, its great gates, its simple, primitive dwellings. The din of a busy oriental population greets you. Wayfarers, travelers from Damascus, or Sidon, or Succoth, or Ramoth-gilead, farmers with asses' loads or camel loads of harvest-products, throng the highways. The rich soil teems with grains and plants, and the turbaned citizens chaffer and salute each other on the streets. Sheikh Iddo rules here over all these strong cities to the rivers of Damascus. He will entertain you with the hospitality of a patriarch. At evening he will gather all the elders of the town into the court or the reception chamber of his house. You occupy the seat of honor on the raised divan next the corner at his side. Salaam after salaam bend to you as the principal men come in. Rings of turbans in concentric circle surround you. The divan is full, and the rest fold their legs under them on a thin mattress on the floor. An Abyssinian or Syrian slave brings in the fragrant mead or the "wine of Hebron," while you are questioned for news from Jerusalem, or Hebron, or the whole company talk of Hebrew politics, of war and prowess under King David, of the ancient poetry of Job, the stirring new psalms of the royal singer, or the wits of the company run up a graphic and rhythmic description of the hero of Zobah and of Elah.

Next morning, from the citadel, a large square tower overlooking all the battlements, he will point out to you the whole plain of Bashan and of distant Moab. Standing here, you see diverging in straight lines a series of highways to the leading cities of Bashan, Arabia, and Syria. One runs straight east twelve miles to Salcah on a conical hill, a small town, but important, as the villages near it and the companies on the road to it show. Another runs northward, and then bends north-west to Edrei; two others north east up the

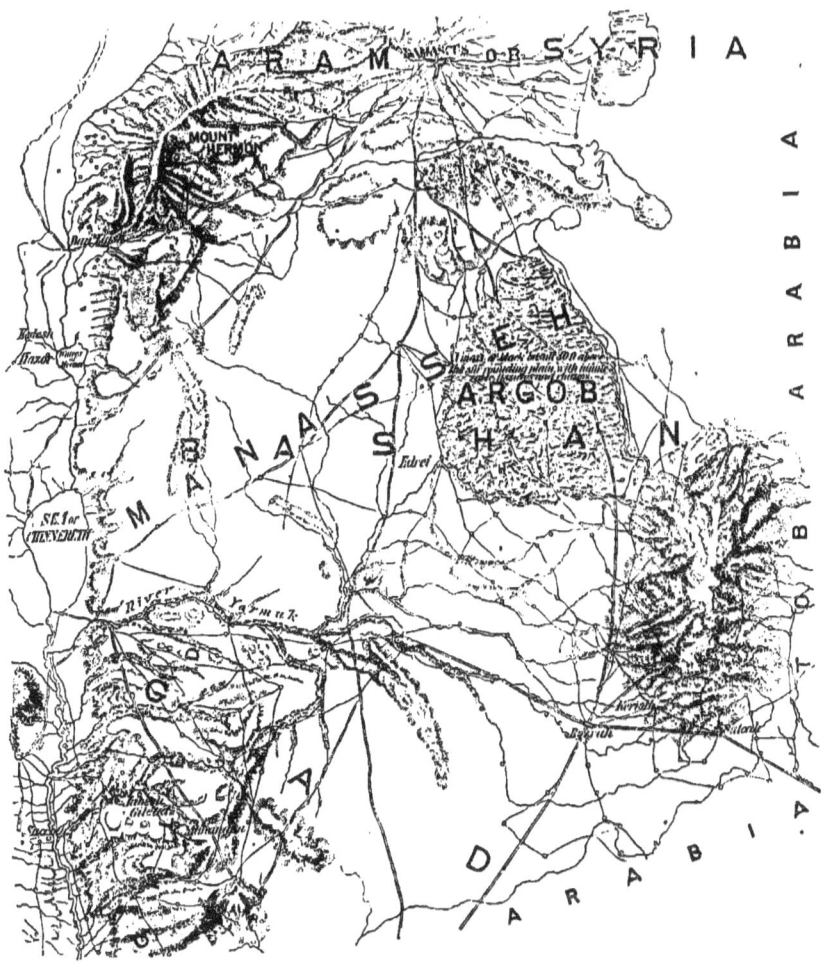

Face page 284.

mountains of Bashan ; and to Kerioth ; and another north to far-off Damascus. In the plain around you see a black loamy soil, luxuriant with grass and grain, with little hills, like islands, and towns on them or beside them, and everywhere dotted with settlements, and rich with terraces, or fig-trees, or noble woods of oak. Shepherds leading out their lines of sheep go with bow and arrow, and sling, or knife, or battle-axe, or pike, for protection from skulking robber or prowling hyena and wolf. Sheikh Iddo, splendidly dressed in scarlet robe, and silken sash, and graceful turban, armed with a silver-hilted sword of Damascus and a dagger, stands in brilliant contrast with his humble brethren at the head of the sheep, with their coarse cotton shirts, leathern girdles, goat's-hair robes, and head-kerchief fastened with a camel's-hair fillet. We must not accept his invitation to take with him his circuit of cities. We will accept only this well-mounted guide, and return the parting salaams of the crowd around. Leaving him to gather his tax of sheep and oxen, grain and figs, wine and oil, labor and shekels—which are to be in part delivered to Jerijah for his Levites, and in part rendered to the government at Jerusalem—to bear the orders of Joab for levies of men, and to distribute all the details of judicial and military and financial administration, we must press northward. As we behold the quiet and harmony of towns and tribes, we repeat with admiration and delight, the psalm which a returning Levite has brought from Jerusalem :

> Behold how good and how pleasant it is
> For brethren to dwell together in unity,
> Like the precious ointment (perfumed) up the head,
> That ran down upon the beard, even Aaron's beard.
> That went down to the skirts of his garments,
> Like the dew of Hermon.
> Like the dew that descended upon the mountains of Zion—
> For there the Lord commanded the blessing.
> Even for evermore. —*Psalm* cxxxiii.

Or as we see the young families in their fresh health and

power, we recall the psalm which the king has set to its chant for marriage festivities or for the "presentation" of children in the tabernacle:

> Blessed is every one that feareth the Lord.
> That walketh in his ways,
> For thou shalt eat the labor of thine hands.
> Happy shalt thou be and it shall be well with thee.
> Thy wife shall be as a fruitful vine by the sides of thine house.
> Thy children like olive-plants round about thy table!
> Behold, that thus shall the man be blessed
> That feareth the Lord.
> The Lord shall bless thee out of Zion
> And thou shalt see the good of Jerusalem,
> All the days of thy life.
> Yea, thou shalt see thy children's children.
> And peace upon Israel. —*Psalm* cxxviii.

Straight before us on our way to Edrei, cutting the horizon between us and Damascus, is Argob, whose rocky boundary rises like a line of cliffs out of this stoneless soil. For from this splendid plateau of fine mould, which stretches almost without a stone from Chinnereth to the desert, the rocky oval of Argob, twenty-one miles long and fourteen broad, stands up like a rocky island in the sea. The boundary is so distinct that it is called the "rope"—a black strong line from a distance. Within you find an ocean of basaltic rocks and boulders tossed about in the wildest confusion, and intermingled with fissures and crevices in every direction. Scores of solid cities are here, which we cannot now take time to visit. Hither refugees run from all regions and easily conceal themselves. This is the region which Machir, Jair, and Nobah, conquered in the days of Moses. Brave warriors they were; and their descendants are loyal hearts, for Manasseh sent at least 40,000 to Hebron when David was crowned. The district of Geshur lies somewhere here in Argob, or near it. The daughter of Sheikh Talmai is wife of King David. It is suspected he took her to secure this Cyclopean, rock-ribbed, dangerous refuge, as well as for her beauty. Some say that Maachar was actually captured in battle or on a raid. It is wild blood, as Talmai's handsome grandson at Jerusalem is proving. Wild blood, indeed, to mingle with the pious stock of Jesse, and it will drive the mischievous and stubborn youth to fly to the protection of those heights of Geshur, as we shall see.

Thirty-ninth Sunday.

ORDER, RENOWN, AND POWER.

LESSON.

2 Samuel viii. 15-18; 1 Chronicles xviii. 14-17; v. 9-11, 18; vii. 1-5; xiii. 1;
1 Chronicles xxvii.; Psalms cxxii., civ.

HAD the Hebrews only put into thorough execution the divine design for the Hebrew state, they would have taken rank at the very conquest with the strongest nations the world has since seen. David aimed to complete the divine plan of order and of power. The union of federated tribes was consolidated under him, and each tribe made strong by an internal order and government. With all their intellectual power the Greeks were never 'able to do what David did—to compact twelve States into a mutually sustaining and mutually sustained civil power.

We have already seen something of this tribal order in the eastern pastoral tribes of Gad and Manasseh. Let us go on our way to some of the other tribes.

Quickening the pace of our mules from Edrei and the Argob, and leaving the wide pastures, we may join a troop of horsemen, with their tall spears and glittering scabbards, on their way straight north to their garrisons at Damascus or Tibhath, but we cannot journey in their company to the distant garrisoned towns of Aram-Zobah. Turning to the left, we near the great Hermon, till we strike the road as it descends from Damascus southwards to the westward side of Merom and Chinnereth. Dan-laish, "quiet and secure," we pass at the head of the marshes of Merom. Meeting here another "thousand" of Joab's footmen on

their way to their military posts in the outlying territory, and meeting there a footman or a traveler from Hiram and the stirring Tyre on our right, we follow the road down to Kedesh of Naphtali. It is not a large town, we see, but on a fine site, looking down upon a small green vale, and the whole surrounded by fertile fields, where Sheikh Jerimoth rules over his tribe. We have come into a more compact country. These mountains are smaller and more even than the wild heights of Gilead. The scenery is quiet and beautiful, the forests rich, the prospects noble and varying; the soil so fruitful as to invite the very sluggard to labor; the trees of all sorts. Here you see the burdened asses on their way to Hammoth-dor; there lies Kartan; yonder as you cross into Zebulun you catch a glimpse of a fishing-boat crossing the full breadth of Chinnereth.

In these smaller States the population becomes more dense, and the people both seem and are more active. From the days of Deborah, the Zebulunites have handled the pen of the scribe. Fisheries of Chinnereth; "outgoings" of commerce at the great westward sea; figs, grapes, wine, oil, grains, more abundant than sheep and oxen; profits of merchandise with traders from Damascus and Phœnicia and even Egypt—all these, as well as those valiant warriors not of double heart, who can "set the battle in array," and some of whom we met in yonder "thousand"—must be cared for by Ishmaiah, the tribal ruler who, from Rimmon or from Chisloth-tabor, details his assistants, and goes to render account of his stewardship at Jerusalem.

Issachar is a still more attractive community—a little State nestling in its gentle valleys. You may count nearly a score of towns as you look down into this charming lap of country: Jezreel is the centre, with Mount Gilboa to the east, Shunem on the west beyond Little Hermon, Chesulloth on the north-west of Tabor, Endor between Hermon and Tabor, Taanach and Megiddo on the eastern end of Carmel's northward slope, Beth-shan down by the Jordan. North-east the hill-country screens off the waters of Chinnereth, and north-west a high parallel crest "trends away to the hump of Carmel." Omri here keeps wisdom and justice and authority over a tribe of men who have understanding of the times, and who know what Israel ought to do. His people are of one heart, as they are compelled to be, for their valley is the high-road of nations and of battle—the funnel through which wide streams of people pour or rush—and full of fruits and crops and beauty to allure the robbers up the gateway of the Jordan at Beth-shan or the Philistines over the notches of Carmel. Here comes Sheikh Omri out of Jezreel. His lively mule, sleek and fat with barley, bears his manly form, more broad and stately from his ample turban and flowing robes. His bright-faced son, whose downy cheek betokens the coming beard, rides by his side, bearing spear and fierce, free glance like his father. Milk in a lordly dish, bread-cakes fresh from the oven, chickens and a calf steaming under the napkins, he turns back to offer you, a Hebrew traveler from Gilead. Free in gesture, independent in bearing, he will honor your visit by a ride to the chief places in this valley, already so remarkable. Up and over the undulating table-land, park-like with clumps of tree and vistas of green turf, he takes you by a zigzag path through the dwarf-oak and prickly shrubs to the top of Tabor, where he pictures to you the battle-scene when Sisera lighted down from his chariot and fled away on his feet, and points out the opening in the mountains through which Barak chased him to the house of Heber. Another day he will take you over to Mount Gilboa to show you where the Philistines stripped King Saul; and thence onwards, not stopping to return the salaams of his people, through wide-spread meadows and vineyards, through shadows of fig-trees and palms and terebinths, past gardens and olive-yards where men, women, and children are gathering the first-fruits for the Feast of the Tabernacles—discoursing of Gideon and his dream and the Midianite plunderers—he brings you to the gates of Beth-shan, past which Gideon's host plunged after the enemy, and from which the men of Jabesh-gilead took the bodies of the king and his sons. "Those days," he says, "were before our good King David. Against him the Midianites and Philistines do not dare lift a spear." "Down the valley yonder is Succoth, where our father Jacob made booths for his cattle. After two Sabbaths is the Feast of Booths. To-morrow we proclaim the new-moon at Jezreel; and after one Sabbath, this year the caravan goes this away down the valley up to Jerusalem. Ishmaiah, son of Obadiah, brings our brother Zebulun with us, and we make up the caravan here at Beth-shan. Asher and Naphtali go together over the mountains."

If we should meet the caravan on its way, we would hear, perhaps, the voices from the train chanting the king's psalms, or dwelling with long reiteration on a song of ascent to the sacred and joyful feasts of the Lord, recently composed, as

A SONG OF DEGREES OF DAVID.

I was glad when they said unto me:
Let us go into the house of the Lord;
Our feet shall stand within thy gates, O Jerusalem!
Jerusalem is builded as a city that is compact together,
Whither the tribes go up—the tribes of the Lord—
Unto the testimony of Israel,
To give thanks unto the name of the Lord.
For there are set thrones of judgment—
The thrones of the house of David.
Pray ye for the praise of Jerusalem:
They shall prosper that love thee.
Peace be within thy walls,
And prosperity within thy palaces!
For my brethren and companions' sake will I now say:
Peace be within thee.

Because of the house of the Lord our God,
I will seek thy good ! —*Psalm* cxxii.

We must not linger in every tribe and at every city, as the people are everywhere now in the comfortable assurance of peace and prosperity. Not that they are free from the presence of their old enemies, for the faces of the Amorite and Hivite and Canaanite are here and there mixed with the people of the towns, and here and there they hold a town of their own. But they are subdued. There is a subtle power all abroad in the land. Joab by the king's direction has a military officer for every month in the year; and twenty-four thousand warriors in turn are constantly ready against the foe. They dare not move against the orderly administration of this God-fearing king, for there is a God who is with him as his shield and his mighty strength. Everywhere, therefore, you see the peaceful administration of elders at the town gates—each city with its own municipal administration; each tribe with its own tribal head and tribal arrangements; every tribe bound to every other by a common education, a common religion, a common ancestry. Levites instruct; priests interpret the sacrifices; scribes unfold with reverent care the parchments of Mosaic law, the histories of Samuel, the king's Psalms, the ancestral traditions—and all this is alike through all the tribes, for priests or Levites from every tribe meet at Jerusalem, and compare and correct their teachings. The fields are filled with husbandmen. Smiths forge the rude tools of husbandry. The spindle and the distaff take hold of the wool and the flax. Skillful maidens and housewives elaborate and embroider robes and girdles which will be heir-looms for generations. City walls are repaired or rebuilt. Fields are bought. Wells are dug. Terraces are laid along the hill-sides. Vineyards are planted. Convocations of tribes assemble. Marriages are happy in pious union. Burials have the assurance that the sepulchre will not be defiled by hostile foes. Births and wealth are the increase of the nation.

Look into the valley of Sharon—a very garden, beautiful and large. In pastures amid oranges, lemons, plums, quinces, apricots, and bananas, you may see the royal herds. Each herd has its keeper. But over the keepers, as Doeg was in Saul's day, is Shitrai of the Sharon plain, responsible to the king's officers at Jerusalem for his trust, as he is for tribal rule to Hosea of Ephraim, or Joel of Manasseh under whichever he may lead his flock. Others have other trusts directly under the king: Shaphat over herds in valleys and plains outside Sharon; the Ishmaelite Obil over the lines of tethered camels from pasture to pasture; Jehdeiah over the asses, "the riding and breeding stock of the king;" and the Hagerite Jaziz, overseer of the royal sheep and his flocks. The royal vineyards located in the tribes are cared for by Shimei of Ramah, but the grapes themselves and wines are stored in cellars under Zabdi of Siphmoth in Judah.* The nurture of the king's olive-trees and sycamores in the low country by the sea is under the horticultural skill of Baal-hanan of Geder; the olive-oil stored in cellars by Joash. All royal fields for tillage are cared for by Ezri-ben-Chelub. And Jehonathan is the general superintendent of all store-houses in open fields, walled cities, small villages, and strong castles. And thus, every portion of the king's provisions, located at a distance, has a supervisor under the king's council and government clerks at Jerusalem, while each tribe its efficient order. But the two greatest and most powerful tribes at the head of affairs, historically and politically, are Ephraim and Judah. Judah is now in the ascendant. The warriors of each have always swarmed at

---

* 1 Samuel xxx. 28.

the first alarm of the trumpet. Benjamin and Manasseh have long allied themselves to Ephraim, and Simeon to Judah ; and the wise and able elders of Ephraim or Judah have borne sway over the less conspicuous tribes from the day when the two tribes had the first lots in the distribution of the land. It was a master-stroke of David—a providential disposition of boundaries and of history— to place the capital at Jerusalem, where he was actually in Benjamin, while he was next to Judah ; virtually conceding to Ephraim the location, while he made his brother Eliab tribal ruler of Judah, and his nephew Joab general-in-chief of the army. During Saul's reign, the tribe of Judah had been much alienated by his cruel persecution of one of her sons. Now, however, the very towns made conspicuous by the persecutions—Ziph, Maon, Carmel, Ziklag, Hebron, Bethlehem—appear in honor and are intense in their attachment to the royal outlaw.* Benjamin is gratified that the stronghold of Jebus is at last captured and is the seat of all the royal accessories. The consummate address and tact of David make the jealous Ephraim content. Two of the twelve monthly military captains are from Ephraim. As more than half the tribes must usually pass through that tribe thrice a year to the great national festivals, and thus increase her internal trade and activity, as with Manasseh and Benjamin she is in the very centre of position and power, she still may consider herself the chief of all the tribes. She has not the coldness of the north ; she has not the dry heat of the south.

---

* Jashobeam, who joined him at Ziklag (compare 1 Chronicles xii. 6 with xxvii. 2); Benaiah from Rabzeel in the extreme south (xxvii. 5, 6, with xi. 22) ; Ira from Tekoa (xi. 28, with xxvii. 9); Hezrai of Southern Carmel (xi. 37, with 2 Samuel xxiii. 35) ; and Uriah the Hittite, or Hethite (1 Chronicles xi. 41, with 2 Samuel xxiii. 39), from Hebron, or from near Hebron.

She has a moist, vapory atmosphere and a various climate. Dipping her plain of Sharon into the great sea, and her eastward valley into the fords of Jordan, her wide, high plains and running streams and hundred villages and towns are in the heart of the central mountains. Shechem, with Ebal and Gerizim, Shiloh, Gilgal, Beth-haran, with their orchards, vine-terraces, olive-valleys, pastures, and prospects—these, with a great highway from north to south in the Sharon valley, a great highway on the mountains, and her inaccessible mountains themselves, give her a glory which her energetic population nourish and praise.

The king himself goes out at times to survey his realms. Full of an instinctive admiration of the grand mountains of the north and of the immeasurable sea on the west, with an eye for the beautiful and the sublime in grass, rills, birds, fruits, fishes, storms, oriental thunder, the sun, the moon, the darkness, the mystery of food and of life, the marvelous variety of climate and surface and production of that wonderful little land, his heart wells up in lively emotion towards the Giver and Creator. From such a survey of nature in his own kingdom, does he pour forth to his lyre, the noble One Hundred and Fourth psalm :

> Bless the Lord, O my soul,
> O Lord, my God ! Thou art very great !
> Thou art clothed with honour and majesty !
> Who coverest thyself with light or with a garment !
> Who stretchest out the heavens like a curtain ! etc.
>
> . . . . .
>
> He causeth the grass to grow for the cattle,
> And the herb for the service of man,
> That he may bring forth food out of the earth.
>
> . . . . .
>
> The trees of the Lord are full of sap,
> The cedars of Lebanon which he hath planted
> Where the birds make their nests ;
> The stork ! the fir-trees are her house !
> The high hills, a refuge for the wild goats !
> The rocks for the conies !
>
> . . . . .
>
> O Lord, how manifold are thy works !
> In wisdom hast thou made them all, etc.

Fortieth Sunday.

THE ROYAL COURT AND FAMILY.

LESSON.

2 Samuel viii. 16-18 ; xx. 23-26 ; xxiii. 20-23, 37-38 ; 1 Chronicles xviii. 15-17 ; xxvii. 5, 6, 25, 32-34 ; 2 Samuel iii. 2-5 ; 1 Chronicles iii. 1-9 ; Psalm ciii.

THE very ambition which enticed the Hebrew nation to seek a king was the ambition for kingly display. David therefore was surrounded with royal circumstance, and on State occasions with Oriental pomp. To conduct the business of the realm, there was a cabinet composed of men made illustrious by their deeds or their character. The Minister of War was Joab, whose achievement in taking Jebus could never be forgotten, and whose personal fierceness made him a terror alike to rebel and to foreign foe. He commanded in person except when the king commanded. As an armor-bearer, he had a valiant man, Nahari, of a town, Beeroth, ten miles north of Jerusalem. He had his own house in the wilderness, that is, the wilderness of Judah. He had a strong bodyguard when he went out to war.* He had lands in his own right not far from Jerusalem. Benaiah was captain of the king's body-guard, who came from Kabzeel, in the south of Simeon, whom David undoubtedly found there in his humiliation. Benaiah inherited valor from a valiant father. Although not literally one of the three mightiest men, he was so rich in deeds that he was reck-

---

* 2 Samuel xviii. 15.

(297)

oned as belonging to the three, and as ranking higher for personal bravery than the thirty mighty, of whom Joab's armor-bearer, Nahari, was one. Among his mighty deeds, he had braved a lion in his den, on a cold, slippery, snowy day;* killed two lion-like warriors in the war with the Moabites; and, in his native borders, had met an Egyptian brave, wrenched his spear from him, and had slain him with his own weapon. He had under him the Cherethites and Pelethites, *executioners and runners*,† and he commanded the army in the third month. He lived to the days of Solomon, was Joab's executioner, and was advanced to the supreme command of the army after Joab's death.‡ The Minister of Finance was Adoram. He must have had a singular aptitude for his difficult duties of assessment and collection; for he continued financial minister throughout the whole reign of Solomon, and met his death under King Rehoboam, in the faithful discharge of his duties.§ His position, if not now established, became established five or six years later. The Recorder or Chancellor was Jehoshaphat, who keeps the chronicles as they were kept in the Persian court in the times of Esther, Ezra, and Daniel—an office of great

---

* "Apparently in a severe winter, a lion had come up from his usual haunts to some village in search of food, and had taken possession of the tank or cistern to the terror of the inhabitants."—*Speaker's Commentary*.

† The meaning of Cherethites and Pelethites is not clear. From the fact that Cherethites are mentioned in 1 Samuel xxx. 14, in close connection with Philistines (16), or as apparently synonymous with Philistines, it has been thought that the Cherethites and Pelethites were foreign mercenaries, a thing not uncommon in Oriental monarchies. But is it probable that David, who had such personal power over his own people in the beginning of his pious zeal, would have surrounded his person with heathen soldiers?

‡ 1 Kings ii. 34, 35.   § 1 Kings xii. 18; 2 Chronicles x. 18.

importance. He probably had under him scribes, made record of the decrees of the king, of the signal services of any subject, catalogues of troops, statements of revenue administration, and produced at the king's desire, the record of all events in the kingdom — in short, he kept the annals of political, judicial, and military events.* Sheva or Seraiah, we suppose, was the king's private secretary, or keeper of the king's personal journal of the king's own acts or words. It was his duty to answer letters, to reply to petitions, to write despatches, to draw up proclamations and edicts. The Chief Ministers of Religion were Zadok and Abiathar, over the two lines or houses of priests; and Azmaveth was the Royal Treasurer, or custodian of the public moneys.

While this was the arrangement for the grand departments of state, we catch a glimpse also of the royal household. The children of David were now growing to be young men and young women. Amnon, the oldest, born shortly after David was crowned at Hebron, could not have been less than nineteen years of age; and Chiliab, or Daniel, the beautiful Abigail's son, might have been only a few months younger. Adonijah, the fourth child, as well as Absalom, the third, was very fair; and the indulgent

---

* For the mode in which events were noted by a Recorder, —see Esther ii. 23; vi. 1; iii. 12; viii. 9; Ezra v. 17, vi. 1, 2 and iv. 15, 19.

"Jehoshaphat was Chancellor, not merely the national annalist, according to the Septuagint and Vulgate, *i. e.*, the recorder of the most important incidents and affairs of the nation, but an officer resembling the *magister memoriæ* of the later Romans, or the *waka nuvis* of the Persian court, who keeps a record of everything that takes place around the king, furnishes him with an account of all that occurs in the kingdom, places his *vise* upon all the king's commands, and keeps a special protocol of all these things."—*Keil and Delitzsch.*

father could never deny him anything.* Absalom's young sister Tamar, a mere girl, had a Jewish beauty like her brother's, and was quite dear in his affection, selfish youth though he was. Shephatiah and Ithream must have been between fifteen and eleven years of age. Ibhar and Elishama and Eliphelet were probably at that time the only children in childhood and infancy born in Jerusalem. As David, like the patriarchs Abraham and Jacob, took concubines in addition to wives, there were other children not admitted to royal rights, but holding a subordinate relation to the family. So that we see the propriety with which David himself is called "patriarch" in the book of the Acts. The sons, for instruction or for care, we suppose, were "under Jehiel, the son of Hachmoni," or "the Hachmonite." They acted either, young as they were, in some way as priests, or in some way as assistants about the court.

There was a strong affection in the king's heart towards his children. This we know in respect of Absalom and Adonijah. The child Adonijah, we are expressly told, he did not like to displease. The king's recall of Absalom, and his kiss, about nine years after this time, after his murder of Amnon, his pitiful sorrow over that beautiful traitor's death, as well as his grief over Amnon, show his deep, tender heart. We need no proof that the heart out of which flowed all the tender effusions of the Psalms, and the generous grief over Abner and Saul and Jonathan, was full of a quick sensibility towards children. We may be sure there was animation and sparkle in eye and face and bearded lip and gesture, as the king made sport with his little ones, or gave zest and quickening to their now ripening minds. We are not likely to be wrong if we think of him taking some of them with him on an

---

* 1 Kings i. 6.

excursion to Rachel's tomb and Bethlehem, and there telling over the stories of his father Jesse; or giving more advanced instruction in the history and principles of religion to the older sons on important visits to Sharon, Shiloh, or Jericho, through Manasseh to Gilboa and Jezreel, or through Judah and Simeon to Hebron and Kabzeel or Hormah. For the children of his house, as well as for the children of the nation, perhaps after some one of his own house had been sick, or he had seen the children of other houses cut off as flowers beneath the feverish south wind, he may have written that most pathetic and most noble psalm, the One Hundred and Third. Who can fail to see that this is indeed

A PSALM OF DAVID.

Bless the Lord, O my soul,
And all that is within me, bless his holy name.
Bless the Lord, O my soul! and forget not all his benefits,
Who forgiveth all thine iniquities,
Who healeth all thy diseases, etc.

. . . .

The Lord is merciful and gracious,
Slow to anger, and plenteous in mercy;
He hath not dealt with us after our sins,
Nor rewarded us according to our iniquities.

. . . .

Like as a father pitieth his children,
So the Lord pitieth them that fear him.
For he knoweth our frame,
He remembereth that we are dust!
As for man, his days are as grass!
As a flower of the field so he flourisheth!
For the wind passeth over it, and it is gone,
And the place thereof knoweth it no more.
But the mercy of the Lord is from everlasting to everlasting,
Upon them that fear him,
And his righteousness unto children's children.
To such as keep his covenant;
And to those who remember his commandments to do them.
The Lord hath prepared his throne in the heavens,
And his kingdom ruleth over all,
Bless the Lord, ye, his angels, etc.

—*Psalm* ciii.

There were other persons, like Jehiel, who held positions around and near the king's family, but whose specific duties, like Jehiel's, are not clearly defined. Ira the Jairite (perhaps from the Jattir of David's persecution) was a prince or chief man about David. Some person must have been appointed of course to make daily provision for the royal family; to supervise the retinue of servants, and be responsible for the accumulating service of brass and silver and gold, as Ahishar was over the king's household in Solomon's time.* An uncle or nephew (the word may mean either) of the king, Jonathan, in high repute for wisdom, and a scribe, was a counsellor to the king, very likely in an office of *friendship;* for Ahithophel, from the little town of Giloh, south of Hebron, and whose wisdom was beginning to be reckoned almost divine,† was the official counsellor. And Hushai, the A·chite, was the king's private companion and confidant, and was in the end more than a match for Ahithophel. Gad and Nathan, to be sure, stood in less demonstration of power towards David, on account of his general piety, than Samuel stood towards Saul. Gad we have already seen with David in the "hold" of Moab, and Nathan we have seen in the palace of Jerusalem, considering with the king the cedar house unto the Lord; Gad the older, Nathan the younger. They were connected with the royal court, for each wrote a book of the Acts of David,‡ and Nathan lived to write a book of the Acts of Solomon. Both gained a long celebrity in assisting King David to perfect the musical arrangements of the worship.§

These all, with the multitude of servants necessary to the details of Oriental life, allied as they all were to the double lines of priestly families and to that ceremonial

---

* 1 Kings iv. 6.   † 2 Samuel xvi. 23.
‡ 1 Chronicles xxix. 29, 30.   § 2 Chronicles xxiv. 25.

which the king was developing into great impressiveness, and to the musicians, constituted a great, powerful, and imposing establishment. Everything had largely expanded since the day's of Saul's court, twenty years before. Indeed, all things considered, there had *never* been anything like this in the world. And the youthful David, the friend of Jonathan, who played the minstrel at Saul's court, was now the inspiring head of all. Skilful with his simple lute or lyre when a youth, he was now at the head of majestic choruses, which sent his own pious verse and song down to every lowliest home of a pious nation. Expert in daring when a youth, he was now the head of the army ; pious in youthful life, he was now at the head of grand religious institutions. " More remarkable still, though not himself a priest, he wore the priestly dress of white linen, offered the sacrifices, gave the priestly benediction, and, as if to include his whole court within the same sacerdotal sanctity, Benaiah, the captain of his guard, was a priest by descent and joined in the sacred music. David himself and the ' captains of his host' arranged the prophetical duties, and his sons are actually called priests,* as well as Ira of Manasseh. Such a union was never seen before or since in the Jewish

---

* The Hebrew in 2 Samuel viii. 18 reads, "and David's sons were priests." Of course they could not act in the office of priest till thirty years of age, even if extraordinary, divine appointment assigned them like their father to the office. But David may have intended that some of them should grow up as it were in the tabernacle, like Samuel. It is possible that they may have assisted as young Levites or in the singing, or as attendants on the priests on some occasions. The parallel passage in 1 Chronicles xviii. 17, reads in the Hebrew, "were chief at the board of the king, which may be taken as explaining 'priests.'" They may have been advisers admitted to the king's confidence. The same Hebrew word in 1 Kings iv. 5, is used of one called the king's friend.

history. Even Solomon fell below it in some points. But from this time the idea took possession of the Jewish mind and was never lost. What the heathen historian Justin antedates by referring it back to Aaron, is a just description of the *effect* of the reign of David: 'The priest soon is made the king; and always thereafter, this was the custom among the Jews, to make the same persons kings and priests, whose justice and religion being mixed, it is incredible how strong they grew.'"*

We need now only to bring before us the adornment of the capital city, and we shall see the advancing dignity of their king before the people. Joab had undertaken the rebuilding of the city, on the capture of Jebus. King David's palace had gone up under Tyrian workmen. Soon we find separate houses for separate sons. The new tabernacle had been skilfully wrought and pitched in its elaborate compartments near the palace. The Ark brought with it revival of ceremonious care. The whole ceremonial must have been carefully revived. The festivals and Sabbaths were restored and made glad by David's kingly and priestly presence in the courts of the Lord's house. Ministers of State and of Religion, whose homes were in distant towns of the tribes, had their apartments near palace and tabernacle, and worshipped before the altars. Victory, triumph, deliverance, on every side, with the advancing power of Jehovah were in the choruses of thanksgiving and praise which ascended with the smoke of the altar.

---

* Stanley.

Forty-first Sunday.

A GENEROUS AND ADORING HEART.

LESSON.
2 Samuel ix. ; 1 Samuel xx. 11-17, 23 ; xxiii. 16, 17 ; Psalms xxiii., cxlv., xcii., xxix., xc., cxxxiv.

WITH all this grand regal power and a pomp which could at any hour be displayed to awe the people, we find the king as natural and simple in the benevolent impulses of his heart as when a child at Bethlehem, a minstrel at the court of Saul, or a persecuted outlaw in the mountains of Judah and Simeon.

An illustrious example of his simplicity and generosity now occurs. The king recalled, one day, his loving covenant with Jonathan. He had been this score of years absorbed in the multifarious details of establishing and arranging the kingdom. Nothing had occurred to prove any descendant of Jonathan alive, but he had given his promise perhaps too little thought. The promise had reference, however, to the time when his enemies should be put down and his kingdom established ; and as he now was fully confirmed on his throne, he should take leisure to make detailed inquiry. That day had truly come which Jonathan had predicted, when the Lord had cut off the enemies of David, every one from the face of the earth. "Beautiful prince of a miserable king!" must the king have thought, "so magnanimous and so pious! would that I *could* fulfil the covenant! Alas! He cannot even be next to me. I cannot even show kindness to his house. Is there no way to return his loving magnanimity and piety? It may be that some child in all Saul's house lies hid away from the divinely powerful king. For Jonathan's sake, it must not be so." Forthwith he bids inquiry be made. A man named Ziba, who had been a servant in Saul's family, is brought to the king. Josephus says that he was a freedman. If so, then he was undoubtedly set free by the ruin of Saul's house. At any rate, during the twenty years, he has acquired considerable estate, having secured twenty servants of his own and a large family of fifteen sons. David examines him, and compels him to tell what he knows of the house of Saul, whether any one is left—a fearful question to be asked by an oriental monarch. "*Jonathan* has a *lame son*, living." "*Jonathan!* a *son! Where?*" "Across the Jordan, in Lo-debar, near Mahanaim, in the house of Machir, the son of Ammiel." Forthwith royal messengers—of the Pelethites probably—are despatched with friendly and assuring words to Mephibosheth. There they find him, a married man of twenty-five years, himself the father of a young child, Micha. The family are brought to Jerusalem. A fear and a humility, such as is natural to persons in his physical condition, mark his presentation to the king; but the generous and tender interest of a father towards an unfortunate child marks the bearing of the king. Plausible pretexts were neither wanting nor unfamiliar to such an oriental court as David's for preventing that succession which was here in danger of being perpetuated, and which *was* afterwards perpetuated for generations through Mephibosheth and Micha.* This was not David's mind. He at once restores to Jonathan's son all the personal estate of Saul. Ziba is summoned, who probably has made his success by occupying some part of the king's

---

* 1 Chronicles viii. 34, 40; ix. 40–44.

possessions on Saul's death. He is notified that Saul's lands are Mephibosheth's, and that he and his family and servants are appointed to the care of the lands under Mephibosheth's orders—an appointment which, perhaps, took from Ziba his absolute freedom, but which yet gave him an honorable connection with the king's court and palace.* As for Mephibosheth, King David provided his family a dwelling near his palace, or an apartment in it, and gave him a place with his own sons at the royal table —a beautiful fulfilment of his covenant with Jonathan; for it was when David was compelled to absent himself from his seat at Saul's table, that Jonathan and David had pledged their loving faith. What a touching example now is this to the growing children in the king's house of nobility of soul and lofty truth of character, silently repeated at every daily meal! Michal herself, who had no children, must have taken pleasure at the presence of her noble brother's son and the little grandson—the only survivor of her father's house.

Happy must have been the king's heart—more happy in its satisfaction over such an act than in all the contemplation of his power and renown. Happy the sweet adoration and gratitude which went up to God in private devotion and open worship. Glad the psalms of praise springing out of this joyous domestic life, and out of the consciousness of a generous respect of his people, but still more out of a heart divinely moved to godlike impulses and purposes—psalms of instruction alike to the children of his house and the people of his nation.

Here, therefore, in this happy and pious state of mind,

---

* "The difference this would make in Ziba's portion would only be that instead of paying in the fruits of the confiscated land to David, he would have to pay them in to Mephibosheth."—*Speaker's Commentary.*

we like to find the spring of some of those rippling and melodious psalms which are like the gentle, sunlit, deep waters in their quiet and constant trust in God.

After some such excursion with family or children, as we have imagined to his brother Eliab's house-ruler of Judah, at Bethlehem, when every memory of the old home-life and of the old pastures would be awakened, and be powerfully associated with the power and fidelity of God, at such a time, we think of the king expressing his own repose on God, and seeking to teach his children and his people the excellence of such a reliance, in

THE TWENTY-THIRD PSALM.

The Lord is my Shepherd;
I shall not want.
He maketh me to lie down in green pastures;
He leadeth me beside the still waters;
He restoreth my soul.
He leadeth me in the paths of righteousness,
For his name's sake:
Yea, though I walk through the valley of the shadow of death,
I will fear no evil.
For thou art with me;
Thy crook and thy staff they comfort me;
Thou preparest a table before me in the presence of my enemies:
Thou anointest my head with oil;
My cup runneth over.
Surely goodness and mercy shall follow me all the days of my life,
And I shall dwell in the house of the Lord for ever.*

Who can admire enough the lowliness of a king so exalted, who makes himself but one of a flock under God the Shepherd, or the beautiful mode in which meekness, dependence, confidence and absolute repose of soul are here transfused into the hearts of the people.

In such a spirit as this, too, it was both natural and honorable in David to confess and teach that he, in his height of power, was but an humble subject under *God*

---

* The psalm may have been substantially composed in his youthful shepherd life, but retouched and sent, with additions, to the tabernacle on some such occasion as this.

his King. Precisely such a psalm is the One Hundred and Forty-fifth, of which the ancient Jews held so high an opinion that they said that "he is a son of the world to come who is able to pray this psalm three times a day from his heart."

A PSALM OF PRAISE OF DAVID.

I will extol thee, my God, O King,
And I will bless thy name for ever and ever;
Every day will I bless thee.
And I will praise thy name for ever and ever.
Great is Jehovah, and greatly to be praised,
And his greatness is unsearchable;
One generation shall praise thy works to another,
And shall declare thy mighty acts;
I will speak of the glorious honor of thy majesty,
And of thy wondrous works.
And men shall speak of the might of thy terrible acts,
And I will declare thy greatness;
They shall abundantly utter the memory of thy great goodness,
And shall sing of thy righteousness.
Jehovah is gracious, and full of compassion,
Slow to anger, and of great mercy;
Jehovah is good to all;
And his tender mercies are over all his works.
All thy saints shall praise thee, O Jehovah,
And thy saints shall bless thee;
They shall speak of the glory of thy kingdom,
And talk of thy power.
To make known to the sons of men his mighty acts,
And the glorious majesty of his kingdom;
Thy kingdom is an everlasting kingdom,
And thy dominion endureth throughout all generations.
Jehovah upholdeth all that fall,
And raiseth up all that be bowed down.
The eyes of all wait upon thee,
And thou givest them their meat in due season;
Thou openest thine hand,
And satisfiest the desire of every living thing.
Jehovah is righteous in all ways,
And holy in all his works;
Jehovah is nigh unto all that call upon him,
To all that call upon him in truth.
He will fulfil the desire of them that fear him;
He also will hear their cry, and will save them;
Jehovah preserveth all them that love him,
But all the wicked he will destroy.
My mouth shall speak the praise of Jehovah:
And let all flesh bless his holy name, for ever and ever.

We are to consider now that among the revised and established institutions of the land the Sabbath was honored by king and people. For the tabernacle worship, then, we have

A PSALM OR SONG FOR THE SABBATH-DAY.

It is a good thing to give thanks unto the Lord,
And to sing praises unto thy name, O most High;
To show forth thy loving-kindness in the morning,
And thy faithfulness every night.
Upon the ten-stringed instrument and the lute,
Upon the harp with a solemn sound;
For thou, Lord, hast made me glad by thy doings.
In the works of thy hands I greatly rejoice.

How great are thy works, O Lord,
How deep thy purposes!
But the unwise man knoweth not this,
And the fool understandeth it not.

When the wicked spring up like grass,
And all who practice iniquity flourish,
It is but to be destroyed for ever!
Thou, O Lord, art for ever exalted.
For, lo! thine enemies, O Lord.
For, lo! thine enemies perish,
And dispersed are all who do iniquity!
But my horn thou exaltest, like the buffalo's,
I am anointed with fresh oil;
Mine eye has gazed with joy upon mine enemies,
Mine ears have heard with joy of my wicked adversaries.

The righteous shall flourish like the palm-tree,
They shall grow up like the cedars of Lebanon;
Planted in the house of the Lord,
They shall flourish in the courts of our God.

Even in old age they shall bring forth fruit;
They are green and full of sap;
To show that the Lord, my rock, is upright;
That there is no unrighteousness in him.

—*Noyes's Translation of the Ninety-second Psalm.*

So also does a heart in this temper find spiritual refreshment in every aspect of nature as well as of grace. No eye was quicker than David's, no intellect at that time more perceptive, no tongue flowed more sweetly, no soul more impassioned with lofty sentiments, when all caught up the theme of the works of God, and the glorious attributes of God in them.

The Twenty-ninth psalm undoubtedly describes the glory of God in the thunder-storm. If we give the poem both a geographic and poetic structure, we enhance its spiritual power. From his place on Mount Zion, the poet-king had watched the coming storm rising over the Mediterranean; driving with flashing lightnings against Lebanon and Hermon; gradually wrapping the nearer north and the mountains of Ephraim in its thundering power; bursting in oriental tempest on Jerusalem, sweeping south-eastwards down the mountains, as flood and earthquake, to the wilderness of Kadesh.* Far higher than its high poetic beauty is the moral sublimity of its calm trust in that God who sits upon the flood and the sweet peace under his voice.

A PSALM OF DAVID.

Give unto Jehovah, O ye sons of God,
Give unto Jehovah glory and strength :
Give unto Jehovah the glory due unto his name,
Worship Jehovah in the beauty of holiness.
The voice of Jehovah (*the thunderer*) is upon the waters,
The God of glory thundereth :
Jehovah is above the great waters.
The voice of Jehovah is powerful ;
The voice of Jehovah is full of majesty ;
The voice of Jehovah breaketh the cedars.
Yea, Jehovah breaketh the cedars of Lebanon,†
He maketh them to skip like a calf.

---

* "One ought to realize an oriental storm, especially in the mountainous regions of Palestine, which, accompanied by the terrific echoes of the encircling mountains, by torrents of rain like waterspouts, often scatters terror on man and beast, destruction on cities and fields. Wilson, the traveler, describes such a tempest in the neighborhood of Baalbek : 'I was over-

† "A large branch of one of the oldest trees of the cedar grove had recently been broken by the tempest, and in its fall, had partly destroyed a younger tree. There it lay before my eyes, amid the ruin it had caused, as if to show the power of the storm, and to illustrate the words of the Psalmist."—*Porter*.

Lebanon and Sirion (*Hermon*), like a young unicorn (*buffalo*);
The voice of Jehovah divideth the flames of fire (*the lightnings*);
The voice of Jehovah shaketh the wilderness;
Jehovah shaketh the wilderness of Kadesh;
The voice of Jehovah maketh the hinds (*for terror*) to calve,
And layeth bare the forests:
And in his temple every one speaks of his glory.

Jehovah sitteth upon the storm,
Yea, Jehovah sitteth King for ever.
Jehovah will give strength unto his people;
("And now," says Hamilton, "the sun shines out again ")
Jehovah will bless his people with peace.*

Did David introduce or revive the use of the psalm ascribed to Moses? If it had been in use by Levites in the service at Shiloh, or Nob, or Gibeon, he would certainly have brought it forward into prominence in the enlarged service. If it simply existed amid the parchments of the Scribes, David would surely have known of its existence, and the death of the aged—especially of the honored, ripe in years and wisdom, whose loss was universally mourned—would suggest the introduction of that expression of human mortality and divine eternity which is instinct with the grandeur of Sinai and of Moses' life.

A PRAYER OF MOSES, THE MAN OF GOD.†

" Lord, thou hast been our dwelling-place in all generations;
Before the mountains were brought forth,
Or ever thou hadst formed the earth and the world,
Even from everlasting to everlasting,
Thou art God."
Thou turnest man to destruction,
And sayest, Return, ye children of men,

taken by a storm, as if the flood-gates of heaven had burst; it came on in a moment, and raged with a power which suggested the end of the world. Solemn darkness covered the earth; the rain descended in torrents, and, sweeping down the mountainside, became, by the fearful power of the storm, transmuted into thick clouds of fog.' "—*Theluck.*

---

* See also Psalm xcvii.

† This psalm, by one writer, has been attributed to a younger Moses of David's time, but it is instinct with the very spirit of the great Lawgiver.

> For a thousand years in thy sight
> Are but as yesterday when it is past.
> And as a watch in the night
> Thou carriest them away as a flood, etc.

The tabernacle, now in a great city, as it had never been before, and associated with the palace of him who was both priest and king, was now subject to greater watchfulness and care. In Solomon's day, and probably in David's, there were porters and watchmen *by night* as well as by day.* For them there was a psalm, chanted by the sentinel as he looks up to the firmament, or pursues his solitary beat along the courts of Jehovah's house. One sentinel from one court may have answered to another, or one departing chanted to another coming at the relief of guard, or the psalm may have been employed in turn in each and all of these ways. And because there was a change or *ascent* in the watches of the night, or in the advance of the sentinel to take his place, it might have been called

A PSALM OF STEPS OR DEGREES.

The coming Temple-guard.
Behold, bless ye the Lord,
All ye servants of the Lord ;
Which by night stand in the house of the Lord ;
Lift up your hands to the sanctuary,
And bless the Lord.

O   *The retiring Temple-guard.*
The Lord that made heaven and earth,
Bless thee out of Zion.

—*Tholuck's Arrangement of Psalm* cxxxiv.

---

* Compare 1 Chron. ix. 33 with 22.

Forty-second Sunday.

THE HEATHEN AND THEIR INSULT.

LESSON.

2 Samuel x.; 1 Chronicles xix.; Psalms cxxi., cxxiv., cxx.

SUCH a spirit as this in King David naturally diffused itself abroad through the nation. A Sabbath peace and love beamed like the gentle sun on this high level of the Hebrew kingdom. And the influence of such a spirit flowed naturally back also upon David, to elevate his zeal for God's worship and service. We may suppose, therefore, that here in the central period of his life the religious institutions of Moses had their very best historical expression. The three great national festivals were therefore celebrated in the full power of their meaning. The gathered throngs from every tribe in Israel filled the tabernacle courts on Zion, and breathed the devotion with which the triumphant and happy choirs of David rendered to God the new songs of the royal singer. Could you as a Gentile have looked in from the outer court, you might have heard some such psalm as this:

A SONG OF DEGREES OF DAVID.

I will lift up mine eyes unto the hills
Whence cometh my help.
My help cometh from the Lord,
Which made heaven and earth.
He will not suffer thy foot to be moved.

> He that keepeth thee will not slumber.
> Behold, he that keepeth Israel will not slumber nor sleep.
> The Lord is thy keeper.
> The Lord is thy shade upon thy right hand.
> The sun shall not smite thee by day,
> Nor the moon by night.
> The Lord shall preserve thee from all evil.
> He shall preserve thy soul.
> The Lord shall preserve thy going out and thy coming in
> From this time forth for evermore.
>
> *—Psalm* cxxi.

Or, as the victorious advance of the nation, and God's mighty power over past enemies, filled their adoring minds, this was their psalm:

> A SONG OF DEGREES OF DAVID.
>
> If it had not been the Lord who was on our side,
> Now may Israel say,
> If it had not been the Lord who was on our side,
> When men rose up against us,
> Then they had swallowed us up quick,
> When their wrath was kindled against us.
> Then the waters had overwhelmed us,
> The stream had gone over our soul,
> Then the proud waters had gone over our soul.
> Blessed be the Lord,
> Who hath not given us a prey to their teeth.
> Our soul is escaped
> As a bird out of the snare of the fowlers
> The snare is broken,
> And we are escaped.
> Our help is in the name of the Lord,
> Who made heaven and earth.
>
> *—Psalm* cxxiv.

Caught up on the hearts of the multitudes, swelling high in chorus or simple harmony, touching tenderly, powerfully, every patriotic and religious instinct and memory, bearing their minds swiftly backwards into the past, all abroad through the present, into the future, the joyful strains were borne homeward by the retiring caravan-trains in every direction, to tribe, and town, and hamlet, till the ascent again to the next solemn festival fired anew their songs, and poured their converging chants into the great praises of Jerusalem.

Into this joyous and pious harmony of ruler and people and sanctuary now came a coarse affront, like a rude insult into a wedding feast. Full of lofty, generous spirit, forgetful that jealousy of his intentions could exist, David was touched by the death of a king who had showed him kindness in his days of trial. He said, "*I* will show kindness to his son." Fierce as had been David's battles with Moab, the Ammonites still existed as a kingdom. What the kindness was which Hanun's father showed to David, we do not know. The Ammonites, in their hostility to Saul, would have sympathized naturally with David. Nahash himself defeated in battle by Saul at Jabesh-gilead, would have been in a temper to send aid and comfort to any outlaw who was powerful enough to disquiet King Saul.*

Death touches every true heart with tenderness. And for the hour, the real spirit of the heathen tribes was entirely absent from his mind—a spirit of low grudging and suspicion everywhere. Forthwith he starts off his messengers with words of sympathy, and very likely with customary presents, to King Hanun, the son. But no sooner is their approach known than King Hanun's attendants inflame his mind. "Comfort! Honor to thy father! The cunning dog! He wants the city!" Hanun needs little to instigate his temper. He remembers David's treatment of Moab. He is young and buoyant and considers himself strong. The messengers of comfort are caught as if they were spies. They are gloried over with

---

* "The Jewish traditions affirm that the kindness of Nahash consisted in his having afforded protection to David's brothers, who escaped alone when his family was massacred by the traitorous King of Moab, and who found an asylum with Nahash," —*Grote*.

every indignity to their persons and message, as if superior sagacity had seen through their Hebrew plot. Their Oriental robes are cut off at the girdle, leaving them literally half-naked; and their long beard—that sacred part of the person—is shaved in half to make them still more ridiculous. The laughing-stock of the heathen, they are driven off with hooting and derision. Ashamed enough, they make their way back to Reuben's borders, the laughing-stock of their brethren and their grief. Clothing their brethren can furnish, but not beards. The news runs faster than the messengers. King David is mightily aroused. It is a public insult to him, his nation, and his God. The very appearance of the men brings the nation into contempt. He sends word, "Tarry at Jericho till your beards be grown." The sincerity and goodness of his intention make the mean suspicion far more base and sordid. The pious temper of his mind which his career has excited in him, both makes this heathen suspicion the more horrible, and inspires in him contempt for the contemptible Ammonites. Their time will come; God will avenge his own honor.

But King Hanun is not at ease. He begins to see that his people have offered a low and cruel insult to a high-minded and powerful king. The very nobility of his nature and the rage of his people will sweep them all away; and both are certain to be aroused. They make haste, therefore, to prepare, and their preparation proved the provocation which they should have avoided. They made an alliance of such proportions and with such tribes that David was compelled to take prompt notice of it. Messengers with a thousand talents of silver were despatched to David's conquered vassals in the north. The Syrians of those parts—of Zobah, of Rehob, of Tob, and of Maacah —were enticed to break with the Hebrew king. The double lure of money and independence was too strong.

Speedily they gather forces, and soon are pitched, thirty-three thousand strong, in the fields about Medeba. To Medeba—one of their impregnable cities, four miles south of Heshbon, and near the heights of Nebo—the Ammonites come in force.

Here we may place another psalm, as if originally pointed at Hanun, and reduced afterwards to a "song of ascent." Just when his whole kingdom would be at peace with all the earth, war must be thrust in by these vile heathen! The north and the south are confederate, threatening both treason and aggressive war; David is taken back to his old distresses in the wilderness of Paran, where he dwelt among the fierce Bedouins of Amalek and Edom, and when he kindled his fires with the juniper-roots. Woe is it that he must still live among these northern and southern pagans.*

> In my distress, I cry unto the Lord,
> And he answereth me!
> O Lord, deliver me from lying lips,
> From the deceitful tongue.
> What profit to thee!
> Or what advantage to thee is thy false tongue
> It is like the sharp arrows of the mighty!
> Like coals of the juniper!
> Alas for me, that I sojourn in Mesech,
> That I dwell in Kedar!
> Too long have I dwelt
> With them that hate peace.
> I am for peace, but when I speak for it,
> They are for war!
>
> *—Noyes's Translation.*

---

* Mesech was a son of Japheth, and stands for his descendants in the regions beyond the sources of the Euphrates (modern Caucasia). The Muscovites perhaps descend from Mesech. In the days of Ezekiel these people were slave-traders (Ezekiel xxvii. 13). With David, Mesech stands undoubtedly for the horde of northern savages and barbarians, while Kedar, who was a son of Ishmael, represents the Arabs. The juniper-root coal in that desert now makes the hottest kind of fire.

David loses no time. He sends at once the might of his army, headed by Joab.

What the allied kingdoms intended to be their strength became their weakness. They divided their armies—the Syrians on this side, the Ammonites on that—to crush Joab between the mill-stones. Joab was too expert and too daring not to retaliate by conquering in detail. The strength of the young Hebrews he took for his own command against the thirty-three thousand of the north, and the rest of the army he put under Abishai against the more familiar Ammonites. They were to support each other, as either might be hard pushed; and under the appeal to right and to Jehovah, they rushed to battle. The Syrians gave way before assault. The Syrians' flight struck dismay to the Ammonites. They made good their retreat to their own city—probably the city of Rabbah—in which they were besieged the next year. This seemed to Joab sufficient for the present. The Ammonites were shut up to their old defences. It is probable the campaign season was over, for "at the return of the year" the siege was resumed.

The fleeing Syrians did not, however, relinquish their hostility. They gathered the Syrians beyond the Euphrates, and proposed to recontest the ground at home on which the Hebrews had once subdued them. The once powerful King Hadarezer, himself the head of kings, whose golden shields hung as trophies at Jerusalem, and whom David had driven beyond the river, sent his captain and army to the help of his countrymen of Zobah and Maacah.

This is another matter much more formidable to David than the Ammonites. Hadarezer's success threatened his dominion from the whole east. King David, therefore, puts *himself* at the head of the grand army of the nation, and crossed the Jordan for the north. One decisive battle was fought at Helam—probably not far from the Euphrates. It was a great battle of great armies, as is evident from the numbers slain. David came forth, as always up to this time, the master of victory in the name of God. Hadarezer's general, Shobach, was slain on the field; four thousand cavalry were disabled or slain; seven hundred chariots were taken, and all the vassal kings over whom Hadarezer sought eminence were effectually subdued. A wide awe and fear, deeper and stronger than before, fell on all those outlaying borders. Euphrates became a tide over which they dared not pass.

Forty-third Sunday.

PSALMS OF VICTORY AND PRAISE.

LESSON.

2 Samuel xi. 1 ; 1 Chronicles xx. 1 ; Psalms xlvii., lxxvi., lxvi., lxxxi., c., xcvii.

THE progress of the nation now under David has been one constant ascent of power. The nations on every side have felt the Hebrew authority and prowess. Although almost every tribe in turn rises up to shake it off, the Hebrew grasp is too firm to be unloosed. Ammon, still the strongest of them all, excites no fear. The God of battles goes before the Hebrew armies. Still David needs all his wisdom to keep those surrounding tribes subdued. In every one of them are forces which may bring trouble and destruction. The people have need to know that it is not the skill of man which has subjugated their enemies and kept them under the yoke, but the power of Jehovah. In advance of the thousands of Israel, a subtle, spiritual force from God has penetrated the hearts of those savage and revengeful foes. To Him, therefore, do we find directed psalms which recount *His* prowess and victory. They are addressed to that God of the Hebrews who claims His absolute right to all lands, and to the holy life of all the tribes of men who have fought for them. It is Jehovah, King of all the earth, who has asserted His authority.

These triumphant psalms were written at times when

signal victories had been achieved or when the people had been summoned to victorious battle in the name of God, or at a time of the enjoyment of the wide results of success. In either case, this class of psalms had been accumulating up to this time in David's life. We may safely conclude that they had their place before the beginning of David's downfall.

Here is one, the imagery in which seems to be taken from the king's outward march in confident expectation of victory, or from the king's exultant assault at the head of his column, or from the king's triumphant return to his city with the acclamations of victory. Or, still better, it may have been that when David himself returned from such a victorious expedition, amid clapping of hands from the crowds, and had "gone up with a shout" and a trumpet into the city of David, he found his people might make too much of himself; and by a true stroke of poetic genius, as spiritual as it was happy, transferred the object of exultation from the human to the Divine King.

TO THE CHIEF MUSICIAN: A PSALM FOR THE SONS OF KORAH.

O clap your hands, all ye people,
Shout unto God, with the voice of triumph.
For the Lord most high is terrible;
A great King over all the earth!
He shall subdue the people under us,
And the nations under our feet.
He shall choose our inheritance for us.
The excellence of Jacob whom he loved. Selah.

God is gone up with a shout!
The Lord with the sound of a trumpet!
Sing praises to God, sing praises!
Sing praises unto our King, sing praises!
For God is the king of all the earth.
Sing ye praises with understanding!

God reigneth over the heathen!
God sitteth upon his holy throne!
The princes of the people are gathered together,
The people of the God of Abraham!

For the shields of the earth belong unto God!
He is greatly exalted!
—*Psalm* xlvii.

We must bear in mind that David was to be the Instructor of his people, and that the mass of the people were on a lower level than himself. His pious impulses and inspired utterances in the psalms were designed to correct and confirm and guide them in respect to divine doctrines and right spiritual habits. The same purpose would have been served by the approval of psalms written by Asaph or Heman or others. Hence, after victory over the insulting king of Rabbah and the slaughtered confederates on the eastern highlands, such a psalm as this, recounting the security of God's abode, as the abode of his people :

TO THE CHIEF MUSICIAN ON STRINGED INSRUMENTS.*
A psalm or song for Asaph or *of* Asaph.

In Judah is God known : his name is great in Israel.
In Salem also is his tabernacle, and his dwelling-place Zion.
There break he the arrows of the bow,
The shield and the sword and the battle! Selah.
Thou art more glorious and excellent than the mountains of prey.
The stout-hearted are spoiled : they have slept their sleep.
And none of the men of might have found their hands.
At thy rebuke, O God of Jacob,
Both the chariot and horse are cast into a dead sleep.
Thou, thou art to be feared!
And who may stand in thy sight when once thou art angry.
Thou didst cause judgment to be heard from heaven.
The earth feared and was still,
When God arose to judgment,
To save all the meek of the earth. Selah.
Surely the wrath of man shall praise thee :
The remainder of wrath shalt thou restrain.

Vow and pray unto the Lord your God.
Let all that be round about him bring presents
Unto Him that ought to be feared!
He shall cut off the spirit of princes.
Terrible to the kings of the earth!
—*Psalm* lxxvi.

---
* The harp, psaltery or vial, sackbut, instrument of three strings and instrument of ten strings.

As Salem means Peace, if this psalm refers to the triumphs at Medeba and at Helam, then the use of Salem may be an allusion to his previous psalm, in which he says, "I am for peace, but when I speak first they are for war."

In the same spirit is the Sixty-sixth psalm, but based on a longer view of the nation's history:

Make a joyful noise unto God, all ye lands.
Sing forth the honor of his name.
Make his praise glorious.
Say unto God, How terrible art thou in thy works.
Through the greatness of thy power shall thine enemies submit themselves
  unto thee.
  All the earth shall worship thee and shall sing unto thee.
  They shall sing unto thy name.
  Come and see the works of God,
  Terrible in his doing towards the children of men.
  He turned the sea into dry land.
  They went through the flood on foot.
  There did we rejoice in him.

. . . .

For thou, O God, hast proved us.
Thou hast tried us as silver is tried.
Thou broughtest us into the net.
Thou laidst affliction upon our loins.
Thou hast caused men to ride over our heads,
We went through fire and through water,
But thou broughtest us out into a wealthy place.
  I will go unto thy house with burnt-offerings.
  I will pay thee my vows which my lips have uttered.
  And my mouth hath spoken when I was in trouble.
  I will offer unto thee burnt sacrifices of fatlings,
  With the incense of rams.
  I will offer bullocks with goats. Selah, etc.

The Eighty-first psalm has the same historic retrospect, but is adapted evidently to a "new moon" or "feast day," and from the high standpoint of complete conquest, laments the previous faint-heartedness of Israel in respect to conquest:

TO THE CHIEF MUSICIAN UPON THE GITTITH.
A psalm for Asaph or of Asaph.

Sing aloud unto God our strength!
Make a joyful noise unto the God of Jacob.

Take a psalm and bring hither the timbrel,
The pleasant harp with the psaltery.
Blow up the trumpet in the new moon,
In the time appointed, on our solemn feast-day.

> For this was a statute for Israel,
> A law of the God of Jacob.
> This he ordained in Joseph for a testimony,
> When he went out through the land of Egypt :
> Where I heard a language which I understood not.

I removed his shoulder from the burden :
His hands were delivered from the pots.
Thou calledst in trouble and I delivered thee ;
I answered thee in the secret-place of thunder.
I proved thee at the waters of Meribah. Selah.
. . . .
> Oh that my people had hearkened unto me,
> And Israel had walked in my ways !
> I should soon have subdued their enemies,
> And turned my hand against their adversaries.
> The haters of the Lord should have submitted themselves unto him, etc.

The spirit of triumph is not the only spirit in these triumphant psalms ; the spirit of commendation of Jehovah, the King and Deliverer, as worthy the admiration and praise and service of all the earth, breathes through them also. This is directly and intensely expressed in the One Hundredth psalm, entitled

A PSALM OF PRAISE.

> Make a joyful noise unto the Lord, all ye lands.
> Serve the Lord with gladness.
> Come before his presence with thanksgiving.
> Know ye that the Lord, he is God.
> It is he that hath made us, and not we ourselves.
> We are his people and the sheep of his pasture.
> Enter into his gates with thanksgiving and into his courts with praise.
> Be thankful unto him and bless his name.
> For the Lord is good ; his mercy is everlasting ;
> And his truth endureth to all generations.

In a loftier spirit than all these, is the tone of another class of psalms, which represent the majesty and righteousness of Jehovah, and the joy of God's people at the execution of justice at last on the incorrigibly wicked. The profound sympathy expressed with the noble stability of God's holiness and with the proper overthrow and destruction of the persistively guilty, is like that thunderous joy of the mighty multitude over the fall of Apostate Babylon, when they cry, "Alleuia, for the Lord God omnipotent reigneth."

> The Lord reigneth ; let the earth rejoice,
> Let the multitude of isles be glad thereof.
> Clouds and darkness are round about him :
> Righteousness and judgment are the establishment of his throne.
> A fire goeth before him,
> And burneth up his enemies round about.
> His lightnings enlightened the world :
> The earth saw, and trembled.
> The hills melted like wax at the presence of the Lord,
> At the presence of the Lord of the whole earth.
> The heavens declare his righteousness,
> And all the people *see* his glory.
>> Confounded be all they that serve graven images,
>> That boast themselves of idols :
>> Worship Him, all ye gods!
>> Zion heard, and was glad ;
>> And the daughters of Judah rejoiced
>> Because of thy judgments, O God.
>> For thou, Lord, art high above all the earth,
>> Thou art exalted far above all gods, etc.   —*Psalm* xcvii.*

---

* The Ninety-third and the Ninety-ninth psalms are similar, but neither of them so majestic and powerful.

Forty-fourth Sunday.

CRIME IN THE KING.

LESSON.

2 Samuel xi.; xii. 1-25; Psalms li., xxxii., and vi.

WE now come to the crimes which have been for ever a stain on David's character. They introduced the decline of his power. From the very hour of his sin, step by step he goes down to trouble, calamity, weakness, to domestic distraction, civil faction, treason, and revolt. We shall see, however, that these very sins were the *occasion* which really tested the beautiful piety of a veritable man of God.

When the campaign season came the next year, a strong army was despatched under Joab beyond Heshbon to Rabbah. The people felt the insult as well as the king; and the *nation* was summoned. Alas for David that he did not command in person!

For his own purposes, God left him at home to be tempted to adultery. Forgetful of his position as acting priest and real leader of religion, forgetful of kingly office and kingly example, forgetful of his family—as all sin hastens to the forgetfulness of good—he yielded to the selfish passion. One horrible sin committed—a crime towards man, a tenfold darker crime towards God—David was like every other deluded victim of Satanic craft. Temptations to other crimes to conceal the first were as quickly accepted by that great man, as ever a little child quickly lied to hide a theft. The next thing he did was to prevaricate and play a base cunning with the brave soldier whom he had wronged, who was one of his thirty commanders, and who was just then avenging an insult to God and the king. What a miserable and withering revulsion at once took place in David's inward devotional life, as when a dry desert wind shrivels the outbursting life of a vineyard! But as David failed in his low falsehood, his next plan was to murder Uriah by a formal order to Joab to expose him on the field. Next he adopted the spirit of indifference to right and wrong prevalent among oriental tyrants, and stopped at nothing to gain his end. He enticed Joab to wanton wickedness, and virtually, if he did not actually, as Josephus says, accused Uriah of crime. The next thing when the messenger came with the news, was the horrible pretence that Uriah's death was the fortune of war. Thus driven by fear of exposure—miserably planning to have his own child appear Uriah's child—before he was aware that he had lost his spirit of devotion, and did not know of it, he was a liar, a hypocrite, an adulterer, and a murderer.

Probably he was not at times without a stern sense of wrong, but it is evident that concealment was still his delusion. For, whether his act of bringing Bathsheba home as his wife, after a short mourning, was an act of justice to her, as it is more charitable to suppose, or was a further part of his design to hide his sin from public view, he still continued without any adequate sense of wrong, even after the birth of the child, when Nathan came. We cannot have an adequate sense of David's guilt, without considering that for nearly a whole year—from his adultery to Nathan's rebuke—he had no real sense of the magnitude of his guilt—and that for nearly a whole year he was planning crime after crime to conceal his guilt. It must have been nearly a month that he consumed in sending for Uriah, contriving with him, and sending him back to Joab with his own death-warrant in his hand. Some time must have been spent by Joab before the fitting opportunity occurred when Uriah could be exposed without indecent haste. Then, after the returning message reached the king, some months still of mourning passed. Then, after Bathsheba became his wife, it was not till after the child was born—probably not till some time after that—that Nathan appears. During all this time, a mind like David's could not have been utterly insensible to its wickedness. Neither will the historical account permit us to think his heart keenly alive and stinging under the reproaches of conscience. The truth probably is, that his thoughts were now in tumults and agitations, now in a false calm and hard insensibility, now accusing him with terrible reproaches and deep agonies, now excusing him by paliating the character of Uriah's death, the honor which Bathsheba had attained, or by other blandishments so readily suggested in kingly courts. During all this time he kept up, no doubt, the outward show of piety at the tabernacle—now with a hollow, impenitent heart, now with a self-conscious guilt which seemed too great to be forgiven. He fancied his guilt was known to few. The messengers of his house did not know his purpose—no one knew his object in sending for Uriah. Joab could be trusted with the secret order. His marriage to Bathsheba might appear even an honorable provision for a noble warrior's widow. His sense of sin and shame began perhaps to wear off, and he was in danger of remaining a confirmed hypocrite—another royal murderer and liar before God and man.

God had other plans. He saw with other eyes, and determined by terrible punishment to vindicate his own honor and his nation's purity. The real truth was, that

David's crimes *were* known. There had been too many conversant with so long a course of sin for it to be kept secret. The shame and reproach of it were everywhere extending among the people. Everywhere the infidel and the impure caught up the miserable story with greedy satisfaction. Benjamite enemies and all the sensual heathen of the land, the profane and the idle, soon handed the shameful deeds, one after the other, with ridicule and leering, from one low haunt to another—some of them repeating with blasphemous exultation what the infidels ever since have been so ready to say, "Aha! *This* is the man after God's own heart!" Religion and the church were wounded in the very heart of their life. Pious men hung their heads; the priests blushed and grieved; the nation itself was degraded by this hypocritical denial of law, this conspicious, godless example of lawlessness and license. But while families see blasting and mildew on all neighborly and moral virtues, and good men see rottenness undermining the church of God, David himself seemed wrapped in the very delusions of hypocrisy. If he repents at all, it is a repentance which reckons his crimes light, and to be pardoned for slight and private regrets. If he does not repent, his crimes are more appalling than King Saul's. How shall the king's self-disguise be broken. How shall he be made to see his appalling guilt? God has his way.

The king's friend, Nathan the prophet, comes to the palace. He has an important errand. The king bids him to the house-top. He follows Nathan's picture of the rich man and the poor man, depicting to his own lively mind, we may suppose, now this city, now that, as the place of the scene, as Nathan goes on, so lifelike is Nathan's story of Oriental greed and injustice. It was too much like Nabal, of Carmel, for David not to feel keenly its power. Had Nathan come to him immediately after the commission of his crimes, the king would have detected the prophet's purpose; but so long a time had elapsed that he was thrown off his guard, and cried in a righteous and passionate indignation, "As God lives, the man ought to die! The poor man shall have the rich man's lambs fourfold! Where is he? Who is the man that did this?"—a righteous outcry against the petty loss of a pet lamb; the contemptible injustice of some wretched lordling. Nathan turned back the king's sentence upon himself with lofty calmness and courageous eye. His form dilating with holy inspiration and outstretched gesture, we see him answer: "THOU *art the man.*" What does God say to thee, Jehovah of Israel? Hear his message! "I anointed thee king! I rescued thee from Saul! I gave thee his royal family! I united under thee the nation! I established thee in royal wealth of wives and children in Hebron and Jerusalem! I gave thee awful forewarning of Saul's failure! I had ready abundance to add to thee, that thou mightest reign in holiness in my holy house and before the nation! And what hast thou done? Thou hast *murdered* Uriah! Thou hast *committed adultery* with his wife! Thou hast *lied* to Joab and to the army! Thou hast *played the hypocrite* before the people! Thou hast in everything *despised* ME and *left* ME! Therefore, thy punishment shall be terrible, like thy sin. The sword of war shall strike through thine own house. It shall *be* struck *by* thine own house! Thy neighbor shall commit adultery with *thy* wives! It shall not be secret, as thou hast planned crimes in secret. It shall be in light of this sun, proclaimed from this housetop. The nation shall know it!"

David is borne down beneath these crushing strokes. He has grace to break out in sobs of confession. "It is all true. It is all just. I have sinned against Jehovah. I know it. Privately I have tried to acknowledge it, but it is not enough. I confess it openly. I have robbed and killed, and ruined men and all God's house. Let me die! I deserve the sentence! Have mercy, O God!"

There was in the thoroughness of David's confession the germ which would grow into all possible private and public reparation to man and to God; and, therefore, Nathan was divinely moved to answer: "Jehovah puts aside thy sin. Thou deservedst not to live—thou shalt not die. But because by this deed thou hast given God's enemies great occasion to revile God and his worship, the child born shall certainly die."

The prophet left him. And David, broken and crushed under the greatness of his sin, cries unto God. Although all the individual sins which he had committed were *sins against man*, yet his agony of confession is a confession of sin *against God*. Alone in Jehovah's presence, the crimson blush upon his face at the thought of God seeing him, his cry is, "Against thee, thee only, haved I sinned. Thou art just in thy sentence! My soul is corrupt from my birth! Purge me, wash me! Hide thy face from my sins! Blot them out, O God! Create a clean heart in me! Renew me! Cast me not away! Restore to me the joys of salvation! Strengthen me! I will yet teach transgressors thy ways, and they shall be converted! O God! deliver me from the guilt of blood, and my tongue will sing of thy righteous law and punishment. What are *sacrifices* to thee, O God! or *burnt-offerings*—hypocrisy! O God! thy sacrifice is a broken spirit. O God! do thou not despite *my* broken and contrite heart. Remember thy Zion! Build her walls which I have broken down. Then will sacrifices and burnt-offerings and bullocks proclaim again thy holy justice and saving mercy!" With such a tumult of broken agonies and petitions, David lays open his soul to God. With the confidence of one who has known a past union to God, he hopes for forgiveness. And with the honesty of real penitence, he at once sets about the only reparation now in his power—a public acknowledgment of his wickedness before the nation. It is a little thing now, to him, to be sorry privately. He will be as careful of *God's honor and purity* as he would wish a subject to be towards himself, a King. In the very sanctuary on which he had poured such contempt, he will make public confession. Thither the tender-hearted penitent sends his written acknowledgment. Gathering up his own broken feeling, his approval of God's just sentence against him, his lowly petitions and hopes for forgiveness, he puts upon perpetual record against himself his bitter condemnation of his own sin. There, divinely directed to be the outpouring of all contrite hearts, overtaken by sin, in all generations, he sends

TO THE CHIEF MUSICIAN, A PSALM OF DAVID,
When Nathan, the prophet, came unto him, after he had gone into Bathsheba.

Have mercy upon me, O God!
According to thy loving-kindness,
According unto the multitude of thy tender mercies,
Blot out my transgressions,
Wash me thoroughly from my iniquity,
And cleanse me from my sin.
For I acknowledge my transgressions,
And my sin is ever before me.
Against thee, thee only, have I sinned,
And done this evil in thy sight;
So that thou art just in thy sentence
And upright in thy judgment.

Behold, I was shapen in iniquity,
And in sin did my mother conceive me.
Behold, thou desirest truth in the inward parts,
And in the hidden part shalt thou make me to know wisdom.
Purge me with hyssop, and I shall be clean.
Wash me, and I shall be whiter than snow.
Make me to hear joy and gladness,
That the bones which thou hast broken may rejoice!
Hide thy face from my sins,
And blot out all my iniquities.
Create in me a clean heart, O God!
And renew a right spirit within me!
Cast me not away from thy presence,
And take not thy Holy Spirit from me!

> Restore unto me the joy of thy salvation,
> And uphold me with thy free spirit.
>
> Then will I teach transgressors thy ways,
> And sinners shall be converted unto thee.
> Deliver me from blood-guiltiness,
> O God! the God of my salvation,
> And my tongue shall sing aloud of thy righteousness.
> O Lord! open thou my lips!
> And my mouth shall show forth thy praise!
> For thou desirest not sacrifice, else would I give it.
> Thou delightest not in burnt-offerings.
> The sacrifices of God are a broken spirit—
> A broken and a contrite heart, O God! thou wilt not despise.
>
> In thy good pleasure, do good to Zion:
> Build thou the walls of Jerusalem,
> Then shalt thou be pleased with the sacrifices of righteousness,
> With burnt-offering and whole burnt-offering:
> Then shall they offer bullocks upon thine altar.

Search all the history of kings, and find, if you can, another example like this of public confession of personal shame and cruelty by a king, in the height of his power! Where is the example in Darius, or Cambyses, or Xerxes, or Alexander, or the Cæsars, or the Napoleons, or the Henrys? Yet this great warrior, king, poet, and priest, admired and loved by his people, with a thousand royal excuses for justifying or ignoring his sin, openly proclaims the enormous wrong of his *sin against God*, and his deep mortification and sorrow before Jehovah. How god-like, honorable, and even beautiful is his acknowledgment and renunciation of personal guilt!

But this is not all. The child, for whom now a strong affection had sprung up in David's heart, is stricken with sickness. With the dawn of forgiveness for his sin arises the hope in David that God may spare the child's life. In his penitence and grief, therefore, he prayed and wept and fasted and lay on the ground all night, night after night, beseeching God for his child. His servants stood in awe of his woeful grief. He would eat nothing day after day. He *would* not be lifted up by the elders of his house. There was more than love for the child apparent in his sorrow. A deep, sober grief for sin overspread all his demeanor. Unutterable emotions of humiliation before God affected his soul, as he cried bitterly for his infant son's life. The child died after six days. The servants feared that the king would actually do himself harm if they should tell him of it. When he himself perceived the truth, he accepted at once the will of God. He arose, washed himself, anointed himself, and changed his whole behavior, to signify his entire submission to Jehovah's will. Forthwith he went openly to the house of God, appearing in humiliation, perhaps with the psalm which he had written—and with a sense of God's pardon. Then, with relief and with submission to God, he came back to his house and ordered meat to break his fast. His servants were astonished at his conduct. But the words which come from his lips have great power : " I submit to God. He has done right. I had hoped that he might so forgive that the child would live. But no ; I cannot bring him back. But since forgiveness is mine, I shall go to him, though he will not return to me." This is evident by the meaning of his words, which are more significant than at first appears. Beautiful example—the more beautiful because in a king's house—both of behavior under affliction and of assurance of God's forgiveness under severe chastisement for sin. In this humble and submissive state David regains the sense of God's favor ; and out of his low depths rises into a subdued and happy confidence in God. Then, by blessed contrast with his former misery, he could set forth the joy of forgiveness to every sinner, in

A PSALM OF DAVID, GIVING INSTRUCTION.
Blessed is he whose transgression is forgiven,
Whose sin is pardoned !
Blessed is the man to whom Jehovah imputeth not iniquity,
And in whose spirit is no guile !

>   While I kept silence (refused to confess) my bones were wasted,
>   By reason of my groaning all the day long.
>   For day and night thy hand was heavy upon me,
>   My moisture dried up as in summer's drought.
>   At length I acknowledged to thee my sin,
>   And did not hide my iniquity.
>   I said, I will confess my transgression to the Lord,
>   And thou forgavest the iniquity of my sin!
>   Therefore shall every pious man pray to thee while thou may'st be found.
>   Surely the floods of great waters shall not come near him.
>   Thou art my hiding-place: thou preservest me from trouble:
>   Thou compassest me about with songs of deliverance.
>
>   I will instruct thee and show thee the way thou shouldst go:
>   I will give thee counsel and keep mine eye upon thee:
>   Be ye not like the horse or mule, which have no understanding;
>   Whose mouths must be pressed with the bridle and curb,
>   Because they will not come near thee.
>
>   The wicked hath many sorrows,
>   But he that trusteth in the Lord is encompassed with mercies.
>   Rejoice in the Lord and be glad, ye righteous,
>   Shout for joy, all ye that are upright in heart!
>   —*Noyes's Translation.*

It could have been, however, no misery of an hour, which, alleviated by a confession and a psalm returned no more, which David felt. Though conscious of forgiveness, his heart was so sensitive, his mind so clear, that more than once he went down into the tumultuous depths and cried in broken agonies to God. Such a time the Sixth psalm represents, dedicated afterwards, for some personal or musical reason,

> **TO THE LEADER OF THE STRINGED INSTRUMENTS.**
>   On the Eighth.
>
>   O Lord, rebuke me not in thine anger,
>   Neither chasten me in thy hot displeasure!
>   Have mercy upon me, O Lord, for I am weak!
>   O Lord, heal me, for my bones are vexed!
>   My soul is also sore vexed,
>   But thou, O Lord, how long!
>   Return, O Lord! deliver my soul.
>   O save me for thy mercies' sake,
>   For in death there is no remembrance of thee.
>   In the grave, who shall give thee thanks!
>   I am weary with my groaning,

> All the night make I my bed to swim,
> I water my couch with my tears!
> Mine eye is consumed because of grief!
> It waxeth old because of all mine enemies.
>
> Depart from me, all ye workers of iniquity,
> For the Lord hath heard the voice of my weeping!
> The Lord hath heard my supplication;
> The Lord will receive my prayer.
> Let all my enemies be ashamed and sore vexed,
> Let them return and be ashamed suddenly.

There can be no doubt of the pleasure which God took in David's true penitence. A sorrow so broken and sincere was a signal mark of David's true piety. There is no surer mark of a godless man than his refusal to make acknowledgment for sin. Bathsheba no doubt shared his sorrow, for God afterwards blessed them both. David took her tenderly as his wife. It was the only honorable course for him to pursue. God gave them, a few years later, a son,* whom David named the Peaceable (Solomon), whom it is supposed his mother called, Dedicated to God,† and whom the faithful prophet named Beloved of the Lord (Jedid-jah), or, perhaps, in allusion to David's own name, The Darling of the Lord.

---

* Plumptre thinks Solomon, the child of David's old age, "the last born of all his sons." He says: "The narrative of 2 Samuel xii., gives, it is true, a different impression. On the other hand, the order of the names in 1 Chronicles iii. 5, is otherwise unaccountable. Josephus distinctly states it." But if born later than this time, he must have been younger than twenty years when he took the throne.

† Lemuel, Proverbs xxxi. 1.

Forty-fifth Sunday.

THE CURSE OF SINS AT HOME.

LESSON.

2 Samuel xii. 26-31 ; xiii. ; 1 Chronicles xx. 1-3 ; Psalms xxxviii., lxix., xxviii.

JOAB had meanwhile during the year ravaged the Ammonite territory, and the seige of Rabbah was sufficiently advanced to ensure success. The siege must have lasted nearly or quite two years long, and the fall of the city would be no mean glory for the kingdom. Like a true servant and general of his royal master, Joab sends for David to come and command the final assault and surrender. With a good humor which might easily pass into good earnest, he rallies the king ; " Now, therefore, come, take it, lest *I* take it, and it be called after my name."* It may be that, with that keen insight which was one of his marked character-

---

* "'The royal city' is the city with the exception of the acropolis, as verse twenty-seven clearly shows, where the captured city is called the water-city. 'The northern height is crowned by the castle, the ancient acropolis, which stands on the north-western side of the city and commands the whole city, (*Burckhardt and Ritter.*) After taking the water-city, Joab sent messengers to David to inform him of the result of the siege, and say to him, 'Gather the rest of the people together and besiege the city (*i. e.*, the acropolis); take it that I may not take the acropolis also and the glory of the conquest be given to me."—*Keil and Delitzsch.*

istics, he foresaw the result of David's crimes. Joab was worldly wise, a politician and strategist in state affairs. And to ward off the inevitable effect of the king's weakness, he determined to make for the king an occasion. The pomp and glory of a really great victory should avert defection, and, so far as the civil administration was concerned, make his faults the mere incidents of a long and glorious campaign. At Joab's suggestion, therefore, the people were summoned. A multitude from the tribes go over, the king at the head, to swell the army. With what a heart did David himself go, probably to the very town where Uriah fell? But the city of waters, under his orders and inspiration, was taken by storm. King Hanun is taken in his own city, from which he made David's messengers of comfort the laughing-stock of his nation, in bitter and hateful violation of Oriental custom, and where he planned revolt and treason for David's provinces. Punishment for such offences was savage in those days of savage warfare. How many we do not know, but some— probably not a few—were cut with saws, harrows, and "made to pass through the brick kiln." Some form of torture was undoubtedly employed as punishment, as a tremendous revenge, a tremendous fulfilment of the divine orders against Ammon and Moab. Cruel and intense was the execution of that law which read, "An eye for an eye, and a tooth for a tooth." A fierce and bitter retaliation for a fierce and bitter insult, aggravated by sedition and treason. This was the oriental law. The very law of Moses was a law of retaliatory *justice*. King Nahash demanded the savage exaction of the *right eyes* of all the inhabitants of Jabesh-Gilead. Their warfare was no doubt in that shameless and cruel spirit. David avenged them in the only way in which such monsters could be punished in his age, even under the Mosaic law. "According to Josephus, the seige of Jabesh in Saul's day, was but the climax of a long career of ferocity on the east of Jordan." With the fall of the royal city, all the cities fell. The jubilant army divided among themselves abundant spoil, and the army and people went in great triumph back to Jerusalem—David with King Hanun's golden crown,* and the people laden with treasures.

However the prowess of David might keep alive his military power, the curse of his personal sins could not be shaken off. They lingered with deadliest influence in just the place where their power never should have been known. In his own home, outward pomp could not conceal the father's horrid example of license. The misery of his sin multiplied its miseries in the king's sons. Polygamy begins to show its evils. Better had he kept strictly to the constitutional restriction, "The king is not to multiply wives," and guarded his own household. The sons were left much to the discipline and care of their different mothers. The Ruler in affairs abroad was lenient at home.

His first-born son, born in Hebron when David was first proclaimed, and therefore dear to him, and now from twenty-two to twenty-four years of age, copies now his father's sins, and dies by his brother's hand, when merry with wine. Amnon had his own house, and, therefore, probably, his own wife, but is infatuated by a frantic passion for his half-sister Tamar. Fatally advised by his cousin Jonadab—a "subtle man," "one of those characters who, in the midst of great and royal families, pride

---

* The one word rendered "their king's crown" may be rendered Malcham's crown, the crown of the Ammonite god. The weight of a talent was nearly or quite a hundred pounds—too heavy for the strongest man's head. The Hebrew traditions has it as *Malcham's* or *Moloch's* crown and that Ithai the Gittite tore it off and brought it to David.

themselves and are renowned for being acquainted with the secrets of the whole circle in which they move"*— his miserable self-will released from self-control by his father's horrible example, he ensnares Tamar, commits adultery with her against her will, and then with brutal hatred, drives her from his house.†

Tamar—the palm-tree—stands forth in the narrative in the beauty and integrity of her character. Daughter of Maacha, King of Geshur, as she was, she was of noble and pure mind. She held the crime a dishonor to Israel as well as to herself, which none but a fool would commit. She saw, probably, the shame would be the more opprobrious on account of her father's sin. She made at once an outcry, though Amnon was the king's first-born; she tore her royal robes, the symbol of her lineage and of her virginity; with ashes, she laid her hand on her head, and went on crying. Her brother Absalom received her into his own house, learned the story, bid her hold her peace, and himself maintained a terrible silence.

The king was enraged, but he did not punish Amnon, the Septuagint says, because he loved him as his first-born, although the crime was by law a capital offence. But how could he punish him? He was compelled to feel the misery of his own crime, and the painful inconsistency of punishing with death his oldest son and of letting himself go free when guilty of an equal and similar capital offence.

But Absalom considered himself, as he was, the natural avenger of his own sister's rights. He watched his opportu-

---

* Stanley.

† "When thy father cometh to see thee," verse five. "An incidental proof of David's known affection and kindness to his children—in spite of the demoralizing influence of polygamy."— *Speaker's Commentary.*

nity. For two years he brooded over it, and planned how to punish the criminal. It would seem as if he at once openly declared that he would kill Amnon, for Jonadab afterwards said, "By the *mouth* of Absalom (*see margin*) this hath been determined from the day," etc. And if he made the threat to him but once, Amnon would naturally be wary of his handsome and wilful brother. But Absalom was subtle as well as Jonadab; and he found means to outwit Amnon, and to get him into his power. He planned at sheep-shearing a family festival on his estate at Baal-hazor, a town either in Benjamin, near the boundary of the tribe of Ephraim, or a town near the town of Ephraim, now unknown. He invited, first of all, the king and his victim; well knowing, perhaps, that the king could not or would not go. As the king declined, he begged the honor of Amnon, the prince-royal. It may be the king discerned danger—for he did not let Amnon go without his four brothers, thinking them, no doubt, a protection. And Amnon, thrown off his guard by the appearance of a family festival to which the king had been invited, thinking the invitation to himself as perhaps an indication that Absalom wished now to forget the past and be friendly, and knowing that Chileab, Adonijah, Shephatiah, and Ithream would be there, accepted the invitation in all simplicity. He entered freely into the hospitalities of his brother. Wine flowed freely. It was for him in special honor, as firstborn, and he grew as merry as his treacherous brother would have him. Absalom was no man to fear venture. Quite likely, we may judge from his subsequent life, he thought it a good thing to have the heir-apparent out of the way, for was not he himself a prince by descent from mother as well as by father? His order to his servants, then, was to strike sure and quick when the wine was in.

Dismay and horror seized the princes, who, like the people, evidently thought the death of *all* planned; for at

THE CURSE OF SINS AT HOME. 343

once the rumor came to Jerusalem that Absalom had murdered all the king's sons. The alert Jonadab, however, assures his uncle, the king, that only Amnon has fallen for his crime against Tamar—an assurance quickly confirmed by the watchman's announcement of the princes' approach. Mourning filled the palace over the first-born's death—a death which providentially made the way to the throne for the infant Solomon.

Absalom, although he might have had a shadow of right on his side, dared not brave the storm at Jerusalem. He fled to Geshur, to his grandfather, King Talmai, where he could gain a ready sympathy as the avenger of Maacha's daughter's shame. There, very likely, in the impenetrable defences of the Argob, he concealed himself, not venturing for three years to take one step towards Jerusalem. As the sharp edge of David's grief over his first-born wore off, and he saw, as he must have done, that Absalom had at least a plausible plea for his act, his heart relented. But he could not bring him home.

The iron had already entered David's soul, sharp and deep. God's retribution was on him. His own sins had produced their just fruit at home. His fair Tamar was dishonored. His first-born, the prince-royal, was dead—justly dead, for crime in imitation of his father. His beautiful Absalom was little better than a murderer, treacherous and malicious—alas! with sufficient provocation and legal sanction to justify his offence. His whole family were thrown into distraction, hatred, and woe. God was turning his own sins, like a heavy flood of fire, back upon his own heart.

The keenest anguish filled his soul at the renewed sense of his own guilt. His enemies everywhere had new occasion for leer and low triumph. His own friends were overpowered anew at this new result of the king's crimes; and his perception was too quick not to see that now the crimes of his children also were weakening the kingdom. Tossed anew by these miseries, perhaps from a sick-bed to which his cares and agitations have driven him, he cries out in penitence to God, in

A PSALM OF DAVID TO BRING TO REMEMBRANCE.

O Lord, rebuke me not in thy wrath,
Neither chasten me in thy hot displeasure ;
For thine arrows stick fast in me,
And thy hand presseth me sore.
There is no soundness in my flesh
Because of thy anger :
Neither is there rest in my bones
Because of my sin.
For mine iniquities are gone over mine head ;
As an heavy burden they are too heavy for me.
My wounds stink, and are corrupt
Because of my folly.
I am troubled ; I am bowed down greatly.
I go mourning all the day long ;
For my loins are filled with burning,
And there is no soundness in my flesh.
I am feeble and sore broken.
I have roared by reason of the disquietude of my heart.
Lord, all my desire is before thee,
And my groaning is not hid from thee.
My heart panteth ; my strength faileth me :
As for the light of mine eyes, it also is gone from me.
My lovers and my friends stand aloof from my stroke,
And my kinsmen stand afar off.

. . . .

Thou wilt hear, O Lord my God,
For I said, Hear me,
Lest otherwise they should rejoice over me !
Lest when my foot slippeth, they magnify themselves against me.
For I am ready to halt,
And my sorrow is continually before me ;
For I declare my iniquity,
I am sorry for my sin.

. . . .

Forsake me not, O Lord.
O my God, be not far from me.
Make haste to help me,
O Lord, my salvation.

—*Psalm* xxxviii.

Pitiful are the expressions of some of the other psalms,

which are nowhere more appropriate than when assigned to this time of trouble—those pitiful exclamations which remind us of suffering Job in his troubles; such as in the Sixty-ninth psalm, in which he not only utters his anguish, but appeals to God that he has tried to set *His* honor right in the holy places.

> Save me, O God, for the waters are come unto my soul.
> I sink in deep mire, where there is no standing.
> I am come into deep waters where the floods overflow me.
> I am weary of my crying;
> My throat is dried; my eyes fail,
> While I wait for my end.
> . . . .
> O God, thou knowest my foolishness,
> And my sins are not hid from thee.
> Let not them that wait on thee, O Lord of lords,
> Be ashamed for my sake.
> Let not them that seek thee, O God of Israel,
> Be confounded for my sake:
> Because for thy sake, I have borne reproach.
> Shame hath covered my face.
> I am become a stranger unto my brethren,
> And an alien to my mother's children.
> For the zeal of thine house hath eaten me up,
> And the reproaches of them that reproached thee, fell on me.
> When I wept and chastened my soul with fasting
> That was to my reproach.
> I made sackcloth also my garment
> And I became a proverb to them.
> They that sit in the gate speak against me,
> And I was the song of the drunkards.
> . . . .
> Thou hast known my reproach and my shame and my dishonor.
> Mine adversaries are all before thee.
> Reproach hath broken my heart,
> And I am full of heaviness,
> And I looked for some to take pity
> But there was none,
> And for comforters,
> But I found none.
> They gave me also gall for my meat,
> And in my thirst they gave me vinegar to drink, etc., etc.

Or, as in the Twenty-eighth psalm:

> Unto thee will I cry, O Lord, my rock.
> Be not silent to me, lest if thou be silent to me,
> I become like them that go down into the pit, etc.

Forty-sixth Sunday.

CONSPIRACY BY ABSALOM.

LESSON.

2 Samuel xiv.; xv. 1-12; xix. 10; Psalms xxxix., cxxxix., xl.

ABSALOM, in self-exile in Geshur, must have been at least twenty-five years of age, David himself being from fifty-eight to sixty years old. He was remarkably handsome in form and feature, with luxuriant hair and a full, soft, luxuriant beard, his father's features, graceful and agile like his father, sagacious and daring, and with the very charm of personal address. He was universally admired. He was probably the heir-apparent to the throne; for he was the third son of David, the first of whom, Amnon, was dead, and the second of whom, Chileab or Daniel,*

---

* David had at least twenty-one children. We read only of four —Solomon and Adonijah, Shimei and Rei, who were living in his old age. There were probably others. But in so large a family some must have died besides those who died by violence. To make the picture of domestic life complete, we must imagine an oriental funeral occasion, in which the mourning is so much more public than with us—with loud cries or screaming by the wives or the hired mourners, with rending of garments, with songs of lamentation, with sack-cloth worn by some or by all the members of the family, with the body embalmed and borne on a bier with august procession and wailing, to the place of burial in the city of David. The Thirty-ninth psalm may 'have been written when David's heart was bruised with such a

(346)

was probably dead, since neither at this time nor when
Adonijah afterwards aimed at the throne, is he mentioned.
He had his own house and home at Jerusalem, with his wife
and two or three children ; for about three years later he
had had three sons and one daughter. The daughter, a
beautiful child, the affectionate brother named for his fair
sister Tamar, who was, no doubt, still dwelling in his family. In the full vigor of his beauty and manhood, Absalom stood ready to make use of his royal opportunities to
secure his personal fortune. His very protection and revenge of his sister Tamar would have many admirers, and
few would deny that the villainous Amnon had met his
just fate.

If Chileab was dead, there is a special reason why
David should have set his heart on Absalom's return.
Now that the deed was done, the handsome, sagacious,
active young prince was the actual heir to the throne.
David *might* have come to think better of Absalom's

---

grief—perhaps for Chileab, whose name signifies in Hebrew *like
his father*—and when he could hardly *believe* that God would
take from him a lovely and promising child.

>I said, I will take heed to my ways.
>. . . . . . .
>I was dumb with silence, I held my peace even from good,
>And my sorrow was stirred.
>. . . . . . .
>Lord, make me to know mine end,
>And the measure of my days, what it is,
>That I may know how frail I am.
>Behold thou hast made my days as a handbreadth,
>And my age is as nothing before thee ;
>Verily every man at his best estate is altogether vanity.
>. . . . . . .
>I was dumb, I opened not my mouth,
>Because thou didst it.
>When thou with rebukes dost correct man for iniquity,
>Thou makest his beauty to consume away like a moth ;
>Surely every man is vanity.
>. . . . . . .
>O spare me that I may recover strength
>Before I go hence to be no more.

revenge than he did at first. At any rate, in the desolation of his afflictions, he yearned to have him home again under his own care rather than familiarized with the rough heathen life of the Geshurites. And yet he wavers, as if swayed by an ocean-tide. How *could* he bring himself to summon home and give kingly protection against the blood-avenger, to one who had taken his brother's life, the life of the first-born, the prince-royal. Terrible as Amnon's offence was, to protect Absalom might be to protect malice which aimed at his brother's inheritance.

Joab perceived what was the real desire of the king's heart. He saw quite likely in Absalom's succession a way in which to protect himself from punishment as a murderer, and from David's fearful curses on him. He devised a way to meet both his own wish and the king's desire. He sent for a wise woman at Tekoa, six miles beyond Bethlehem, a place from which the warrior Ira came. Ira may have given his commander information of this woman, or Joab, ever watchful for persons for public use, may have observed her and her reputation. When she came, he instructed her in this manner: " Here is Absalom. He has killed the heir-apparent. He is now himself heir-apparent, and himself exposed to the blood-avenger. The king is in a personal dilemma. One of his sons has slain another of his sons. Grief overpowers him for the loss, and justice seems to him to require the death of the offending son also. There is danger of internal and exterminating feud in the royal house if Absalom come home without the king's express authority; and danger of complication, faction, and endless trouble if he stay away. Both public security and the king's peace of heart require that Absalom be brought openly home, his revenge of Tamar tacitly accepted, and he set forth as the king's restored son before the nation." Such is evidently Joab's view of the situation, and he constructs for the woman a parable which embodies these facts. Expert in speech and wit and prudence, the woman goes to the king as a widow with a story of two sons, one of whom has killed the other, and the survivor of whom is in danger of being slain by the blood-avenger, so that her family shall be extinguished. When the king, touched by the widow's weeds and the pitiful story, has yielded the general principal that such a case ought surely to be an exception to the law of blood-revenge, she immediately presses boldly and delicately the instance of the king's sons, and his obligation to protect and "bring home his banished." She even presses on him his inconsistency. By an ingenious and subtle twining of the imaginary story and the actual facts, she holds the king now to the pitiful case of the two sons and now to his own two sons, as she watches his varying mood. The king at once detects the true actor behind the parable, and says, gravely: "Is not this Joab's device?" But his sagacity saw in it the proof of Joab's intense devotion to his house and of his practical judgment in public affairs.

The woman is dismissed. Joab is sent for. "I have done this thing," David says. "Go bring the young man Absalom." Joab evidently considered a delicate point in the public policy gained. He thanked the king, and congratulated himself on his success. To give power and significance to Absalom's return, as the king intended, and as if assuming before the people the responsibility himself, he sets off in person to Geshur. In the name of the king, he brings Absalom home to the capital. But the king cannot yet see his son. He has had his eyes opened to the greatness of the crime of murder, and he is not sure what was Absalom's intention in the crime. He will signify the greatness of his personal displeasure at the offence even while he gives public protection to the offender. So great is his jealousy of truth and right, that for two full years Absalom watches in vain for an audience with the king. He is evidently offended that he is suspected and not received into full favor. "Better be in Geshur than here!" At length he sends for Joab. Joab, thinking that the father and son will make their way to each other, takes no notice of Absalom's first nor second summons. Offended and enraged, Absalom compels Joab to attend. He can play at artifice as well as Joab. He sends off orders to his servants on his estate to set Joab's barley-field afire. Then Joab comes promptly enough to complain of Absalom's servants. But Absalom let him know quickly that it is a device to secure his presence. "Why did you bring me home from Geshur? If I am to be suspected and shut out, better to be in Geshur still. Bring me to the king. Tell him, if I deserve death, I am willing to die." Joab at once puts the matter properly before the king. And when David knew Absalom's attitude of mind, he sent for him. Absalom abases himself, and the king gives him the kiss of reconciliation.

We might think that there was a certain honesty in Absalom's mind up to this point, were it not that soon after, by open hypocrisy, he began to mature a conspiracy against his father, and were it not that the culmination of his conspiracy is by means of an awful falsehood, amounting to both perjury and plasphemy. This falsehood runs back to a resolve taken at Geshur more than two years before. We have seen that Absalom was capable of self-control, and could hold self-contained a deliberate, well-formed purpose for two full years against Amnon. That he held a secret purpose against his father's government, nourishing and revolving it till the time should come to strike, seems evident from his reference to his vow in Geshur. Just as he goes to Hebron to raise the standard of revolution against his own father, he can say in a hideous hypocrisy, "I pray thee, let me go and pay *my vow* in Hebron, which I have vowed unto Jehovah. For thy servant *vowed a vow* while I abode at Geshur in Syria, saying, If Jehovah shall bring me again to Jerusalem, then I will serve Jehovah." If there be here a reference to a purpose formed at Geshur to seize the throne, the bitter hypocritical irony of these words reveals a malice consistent with his cruel wickedness afterwards.

The secret spring which was the fountain of conspiracy in Absalom's heart was undoubtedly, first of all, his inordinate conceit of himself. This conceit the flattery of the people inflamed. The old man was in his dotage! He would reënact his father's early life, and prove the hero! The success of his punishment of Amnon, its plausible justification, and his successful escape, exalted still more his importance in his own eyes, while the cover of the blood-revenge concealed from the people his deep satisfaction that Amnon was dead, if it did not conceal a jealousy which prompted the crime. His own wild independence, indulged at home probably as Adonijah was indulged, would be intensified by his two years in Geshur. The aspiration of the king's wives for their sons—Bathsheba for Solomon, Haggith for Adonijah, Maacah for Absalom—may have fired him. His father's refusal to see him was misinterpreted. It irritated and alienated him from the king and from Joab till his secret purpose was fixed. And thus the stream was full-formed which rushed on to the precipice.

There can be no doubt, too, that King David, absorbed by overwhelming afflictions and a sense of deserved punishment, was abstracted from public affairs. He was conscious, too, of a weakened hold on the nation, and did not meet the people with the same self-confidence as formerly. This Absalom saw. He took advantage of it. He professed a willingness to die for his crime, but he knew it was too late now for the king to execute him. He wanted the kiss of reconciliation, and he no sooner gained it than he began to plot. He prepared himself a retinue of chariots and riders and attendants, and boldly assumed a degree of pomp before the nation—such a pomp as no one but the heir-expectant could assume. He took advantage of the king's laxness—personal attention to persons in controversy being a feature of Oriental rule—and stood by the king's gate, at once complimenting the city and tribe from which every complainant came, and complaining himself of the king's injustice in neglecting the injured and oppressed. He insinuated his own deep desire for justice. If *he* had only had power to decide and administer. And a kiss from the handsome, graceful prince was always ready for leaders who would do him reverence.* So he fairly stole the hearts of the people.

At length the period of forty years from David's anointment by Samuel is ended, and the hypocrite and conspirator deems it time to strike. He cloaks his treason under the pretence of devotion to God. Like some hypocrites, he may have been deluded into the belief that his wickedness *was* devotion to God. He professes a vow to God made in Geshur—a vow indeed! a profane oath that he would himself be king in Hebron as his father had been. The king gave his blessing to him and to his vow. But Absalom's spies were abroad through the tribes notifying the trusted that his trumpet of coronation would soon sound. He had a strong hold on the people, for when the trumpeters stationed in the tribes sounded, the people responded. Two hundred men from Jerusalem were beguiled into the plot, and induced to go to Hebron with the prince to pay his *vow!* He succeeded in carrying with him, by artifice and policy, even David's privy

---

* "It was by conduct of this kind that Agamemnon is said to have secured the command of the Grecian army."—*Keil and Delitzsch.*

counsellor, whose advice was an oracle. Ahithophel, the counsellor, was sacrificing in Giloh, just south of Hebron. When summoned, and when he saw how the tide was running with the prince, he made the miserable mistake of casting in his fortunes with Absalom; or possibly disaffected from David for his weaknesses, he had retired from court life to his private home. And there at Hebron, his own birthplace, which the traditionary memories of his father filled with enthusiasm, in a tribe flattered at the thought of a second king, among a people gathered from the tribes, like the assembly which crowned David, the beautiful young prince, enrobed in the splendor of Oriental dress, and false at heart as any Oriental conspirator, was anointed and crowned king of Israel. The people shouted, and sent abroad the cry from Ziklag to Geshur, "King Absalom reigneth in Hebron."

If David's attention had been instinct at the time with public more than with personal affairs, he would at once have discovered the extent and progress of the conspiracy. But it is reasonable to suppose that he was lying sorebroken by the blows of God's righteous rebukes and punishment. We may believe that his spirit was tenderly alive to the divine honor and to the quality of his own repentance before God, and seeking rather to avert impending judgments in this way than by the powers of his right arm. While, therefore, Absalom was plotting in Jerusalem and committing treason in Hebron, we may suppose the king occupied with such thoughts as these :

TO THE CHIEF MUSICIAN: A PSALM OF DAVID.

O Lord, thou hast searched me and know me.
Thou knowest my down sitting and uprising.
Thou understandest my thought afar off.
Thou compassest my path, and my lying down,
And art acquainted with all my ways.
. . . .
Whither shall I go from thy Spirit,

Or whither shall I flee from thy presence?
If I ascend up to heaven, thou art there, etc.

. . . .

Surely thou wilt slay the wicked, O God!
Depart from me, therefore, ye bloody men.

. . . .

Search me, O God, and know my heart.
Try me and know my thoughts.
And see if there be any wicked way in me.
And lead me in the way everlasting.

—*Psalm* cxxxix.

TO THE CHIEF MUSICIAN: A PSALM OF DAVID.

I waited patiently for the Lord,
And he inclined unto me, and heard my cry.
He brought me up also out of a horrible pit, out of the miry clay,
And set my feet upon a rock, and established my goings.

. . . .

I have preached righteousness in the great congregation.
Lo! I have not refrained my lips, O Lord, thou knowest.
I have not hid thy righteousness within my heart.
I have declared thy faithfulness and thy salvation.
I have not concealed thy loving-kindness and thy truth
From the great congregation, etc.

—*Psalm* xl.

Forty-seventh Sunday.

THE KING'S ESCAPE.

LESSON.

2 Samuel xv. 13-37 ; xvi. 1-15 ; Psalms vii., iii., lxiii., iv.

THE king only needed his attention aroused. A messenger announced the conspiracy and its public success. Once awake, his quickened mind took in the situation. Absalom! Hebron! Judah! The tribes! He saw at a glance Absalom's arts, his perfidy, his attractions of beauty, pomp, and display; his own neglect of Absalom's temper, the defection of the people from their guilty king, the sword of God's predicted punishment. The thrones of all early Oriental empires, as well as the terrible slaughters of the northern Hebrew kingdom after Solomon, tell us what David expected from a wilful and treacherous son. No parley would be admitted by such a temper as Absalom's. What would be the fate of even the impregnable Jerusalem, when God had bidden the sword of his own house strike! Flight would save the city from siege and blood, and might gain delay till the infatuation of the people should pass by, or until God would show his own will.

The king's word went out, "We must leave the city!" to which there was a large and quick response. We may assume that, in the capital itself, the sincerity and nobility of David's repentance were better appreciated than in more distant parts of the land. A loyal people in the city answered the word of loyal officers, and resolved to share the fate of the royal household. Forthwith at the departure of the king's family, the army and people throng forth from the gates down over the Kidron valley. The Septuagint says that David stood under an olive-tree.* There he took in a quick review of the people and army, their forces and their affection, as they hastened past: he sharing their peril, as they shared his calamity.

The plan of flight seems to have designed two things. One was to put the Jordan chasm between him and his pursuers. He could not venture on his old retreats in the south. The other was, to put himself among the tribes least affected by Absalom, and which had also been recently delivered by himself from the Ammonites. The critical thing was to reach the rocky descent to Jericho, past dangers from the Bethlehem and Hebron road.

Six incidents occur now in rapid succession, which, like such incidents in hours and days of revolution, are significant of the temper of the people, and of the ability and disposition of their ruler. They give us especially evidence of the quickness, the wit, the sagacity of David's mind when sharpened to action in an emergency. One after the other he turns events to his own use, or leaves them untouched by a wise abstinence.

The first incident has to do with his "old guard." As the people, with their outcries of lamentation, and the officers, and the Cherethites and Pelethites, pass by, his faithful six hundred come up. These we suppose to be a regiment whom David had honored from the time when

---

* "Tarried in a place that was far off," verse 17. The Hebrew may be rendered "at the far-house"—perhaps the last suburban house before crossing the Kidron.

the six hundred with him left the service of King Achish of Gath, rescued Ziklag, and went up to his first coronation at Hebron. They were his original army, the original number kept full, and the " band " honored for their devotion to the king. Either because their fortunes became fully identified first with David's when he was at Gath or in subjection to Gath, or because a good number of them came from Gath itself, they were called Gittites. Their present leader was Ittai, who was not one of the original band, and was himself a proselyte. He had had, therefore, only the experience of prosperity, and knew nothing of adversity with David. This, we suppose, was what struck David's mind when he saw Ittai and the old six hundred approach, and thought that the days of future adversity might be as great and as numerous as the days of past adversity. Forthwith he thrust in a test to try the devotion of Ittai. "Why go with us? Go back to King Absalom. You have been here but a little time. Why take the risks with us? Take back your company, and serve the new king. My blessing shall be with thee." But the loyal Ittai endured the test. " Thy life or death, O King, shall be life or death to me. Where thou art, there am I." A noble devotion in a Philistine proselyte, and a noble proof of David's personal magnetism over a "stranger" and an "exile." "Pass on — hasten the march," said the king; and the next time we meet Ittai, it is as one of the three division-commanders of the army.

The next incident springs out of the appearance of the priests and Levites. Zadok and Abiathar, the high-priests, with the Levites in service at Jerusalem, come down the slope, bringing the ark. They set down the ark, and the same Abiathar who, nearly forty years before, fled from Nob to Keilah, bringing the ephod, stood and watched till the last of the people had passed out the gate. They would have the ark sanction the Anointed of God and protect his true subjects. A beautiful endorsement is this of David's penitence! "Carry back the ark," is David's order to them so soon as he discovers their purpose. "I shall come back to the ark if God wills; and, if not, let him do what seemeth him good. If God wills my return, what is the Seer's office but to discern the interest of the kingdom? And the high-priest's sons can carry me word. I will wait your word in the wilderness of Jericho." Nothing breaks David's spirit more than separation from the ark and God's worship. While Levites and priests and ark go back, the people and king with bitter cries climb Olivet, the king with head and face covered and feet sandalless, the king in tears, the people in tears, at the abandonment of the beautiful city and sacred tabernacle, made glorious for a quarter of a century under God's warrior, poet, and priest.

A third incident breaks in upon their grief. "Ahithophel is among the conspirators!" Ahithophel—acquainted with David's private counsels and the nation's affairs— clear-headed and strong; a tower of strength to Absalom, wisdom for his folly, and stability for his fickleness— a solid cause of alarm to David. If Ahithophel was the grandfather of Bathsheba, as there is some reason for supposing,* David's crimes may have been the occasion of his defection from the king. He may have foreseen the inevitable decay of the nation after hypocrisy and crime so gross as that of David. And his desertion to Absalom was a sure proof that to his prudent mind the rebellion is strong. Ahithophel! *brother of foolishness!* "If he can be baffled, Absalom is as good as routed, and the head of the conspiracy cut of."† But what can David do? Nothing but pray to God, and watch to outdo his strategy. "O Lord, turn the counsel of this Brother

---

* Compare xi. 3 with xxiii. 34. † Henry.

of Foolishness *into* foolishness!" is the deep outcry of David's heart to God. It seems as if while he was speaking he was answered in the opportunity to outvie Ahithophel's advice. For in the next verse we read that David, when he came to the top of the hill, worshipped; and while he prayed or prostrated himself in bitterness and agony of soul before God, the fourth important incident occurred.

The "king's friend," Hushai, with robe rent and earth on his head, met him. David is quick to see what Hushai can do, as a trusty and prudent man. "With your tender heart you will be nothing but a burden to me in the wilderness. Go make yourself Absalom's servant. Tell him you are his friend, as you have been his father's friend, and defeat by all means the counsels of Ahithophel. Zadok and Abiathar are there. Tell them your messages. Jonathan and Ahimaaz will bring me word." He will put a counselor against Absalom's counselor, and will commend him to God and to his priests.

The fifth incident is that, over the top of Olivet, Ziba, the well-known servant of *Saul's grandson*, comes up. He has saddled asses for the king's family, bread-cakes, dried grapes, fruits, and a skin of wine, figs, dates, etc. David's first question seeks out Saul's descendant and *his* attitude in the revolution. "What is the meaning of this?" The answer is, that these things are not at all the present of Mephibosheth, but of Ziba himself. "And where is Mephibosheth?" "At Jerusalem," says the ingratiating and lying servant. "He says Saul's kingdom will be restored." Plausible indeed it seems. "Thine is all that is Mephibosheth's," said the too hasty king, as he pushed on. "I humbly thank thee," said the fawning hypocrite. Cheap indeed to buy Mephibosheth's estate with a present of Mephibosheth's asses and fruits!

One incident more—the sixth—occurs in this turbulent

and crowded day, as he goes over the rough ridges at the top of the Jericho road. Another person of Saul's house—a real and bitter Benjamite—is on the watch for him—one of those men who never relinquish a petty party or clan feeling even if their opponent has turned night into day for the universal good. This is Shimei, son of Gera,* who strides along high on the opposite ridge to show himself a bitter zealot for Saul's fortunes, a snarling cynic against David's successes. He has heard of David's downfall, and his time has come ; but he takes care to keep the other side of the gorge. Out he comes, exulting, cursing, reviling, with slang and fierce abuse. "Aha! thou bloody man, thou son of the devil. Aha! the blood of Saul's sons is on thee! Thou bloody man, Uriah's blood is on thee! Out with you! Out on you! Down now! Go down! I knew it. The Lord is against thee. Aha! thine own son will take the kingdom from thee. Taken in thy mischief at last, thou son of Belial and man of blood!" He runs along the crest opposite, just out of reach, flinging stones and dust with his curses at the king's party. Abishai, with the spirit of his mother, asks nothing better than to go over and take off his head. But David estimates the fellow and his curses at their worth. He will not honor him by giving any one occasion to say, Shimei was right, for David shed Shimei's blood. "Besides, if God permits my own son to seek my life, he may have good ends in this Benjamite's curses. Let him tell my faults. I will suffer all God's will for his own sake."

And so the king, and his mighty men and all his people, press down the narrow and tortuous road, out of the reach of Absalom. It has been a long and weary day. At last,

---

* Gera was an ancient name at the head of old families in Benjamin. (See 1 Chronicles viii. 3 ; Genesis xlvi. 21 ; Judges iii. 15.)

at the foot of the steep hills, they are where they can defend themselves for the night, and at the first alarm put the Jordan behind them. They are in the upper end of the "wilderness of Judah," as it extends upwards from the Salt Sea along the Jordan. Here the fleeing king is in the upper end of that same desolate wilderness, the lower parts of which he so well knew as a fugitive from Saul. They are not far from an easy ford of the river. Here they set up their camp, and station their trusty men at the narrow approaches.

The incidents of David's flight show in striking relief the versatility, sagacity, and generosity of David's mind.

As to Ittai, he made sure of his devotion. As to Zadok and Abiathar, he put them where they could modify Absalom's government, if it had proved God's will that Absalom should succeed, and where they could help himself, if God's will required his restoration. As to Ahithophel, he has commended his counsels to God's overruling mind. With respect to Hushai, he has bidden him be Absalom's true friend should Absalom prevail, and Ahithophel's antagonist to test the Lord's disposition of his Anointed. We must remember, in respect of David's advice to Hushai, that David in either alternative did not look at all for the death of Absalom, and in either event was seeking the true interest of Absalom. As to Ziba, the treachery of Mephibosheth, if real, of itself confiscated his estate. And as to Shimei, David's magnanimity is the magnanimity in the cave and the night-encampment against Saul. It is the quick-witted David still driven anew by persecution and affliction. The result will show how wise were his dispositions for the true interest of God's earthly kingdom.

What a tossing sea of conflicting thoughts filled the king's mind in his tent that night! The first thing to be settled is, how wide does the disaffection extend? How far has Absalom charmed the people, and how much secret disaffection is there, ready to burst out enraged, like the wrath of Shimei? How far do the tribes of Benjamin and Ephraim hold himself guilty of slaying Saul's house, and how far are they ready to avenge the fancied crime by making joint cause with Absalom? Shimei's bloody words overwhelm him with horror. He is innocent of the crimes he charges, or forgiven of God. He would have been a *savage, black at heart* like Shimei, to have slain the house of God's anointed. If we consider that the "Cush the Benjamite," mentioned in the title to the Seventh psalm, is Shimei, called the Cushite or Ethiopian, on account of his treachery and godless affront to the Lord's anointed, we may consider the Seventh psalm as the expression of David's mind that night on the plains of Jordan.

A SONG OF DAVID WHICH HE SANG UNTO THE LORD CONCERNING THE WORDS OF CUSH THE BENJAMITE.

O Lord my God, in thee do I put my trust:
Save me from all them that persecute me, and deliver me;
Lest he tear my soul like a lion,
Rending it in pieces, while there is none to deliver.

O Lord my God, if I have done this;
If there be iniquity in my hands:
If I have rewarded evil unto him that was at peace with me
(Yea, I have delivered him that without cause is mine enemy);
Let the enemy persecute my soul, and take it;
Yea, let him tread down my life upon the earth,
And lay my honor in the dust.
. . . .
The Lord shall judge the people:
Judge me, O Lord, according to my righteousness,
And according to mine integrity that is in me.
Oh! let the wickedness of the wicked come to an end;
But establish the just:
For the righteous God trieth the heart and reins.
. . . .
His mischief shall return upon his own head,
And his violent dealing shall come down on his own pate.

I will praise the Lord according to his righteousness,
And will sing praise to the name of the Lord most high.

These we may suppose the thoughts of David in that

private hour which he was accustomed to have with God before his sleep, composing himself under God's protection. But the morning brings the same conflicts, as he still waits to hear from Zadok and Abiathar. If Benjamin and Ephraim are ready to revenge Saul, how far will Judah, for kindred's sake, follow the false son of the tribe? In this mind, the king breathes in prayer to God

A PSALM OF DAVID WHEN HE FLED FROM ABSALOM HIS SON.

Lord, how are they increased that trouble me!
Many are they that rise up against me.
Many there be which say of my soul,
" There is no help for him in God!"
    But thou, O Lord, art a shield for me;
My glory, and the lifter up of my head.
I cried unto the Lord with my voice,
And he heard me out of his holy hill.
    I laid me down and slept;
I awaked; for the Lord sustained me.
I will not be afraid of ten thousands of people,
That have set themselves against me round about.
    Arise, O Lord! Save me, O my God!
For thou hast smitten (*hitherto*) all my enemies upon the cheek-bone;
Thou hast broken the teeth of the ungodly.
Salvation belongeth unto the Lord:
Thy blessing is upon thy people!   —*Psalm* iii.

Many are the events which transpire in a single day at such a time. A few minutes seem an hour. The heart is turbulent with feeling; during the suspense, expectation and excitement prolong the day. Little incidents seem to decide now this way, now that. Had not bad advisers helped his son, no trouble could have arisen. To calm his own heart and to derive strength from his divine helper, as we may suppose, David composed his turbulent thoughts into the substance of that psalm afterwards known as

"A PSALM OF DAVID WHEN HE WAS IN THE WILDERNESS OF JUDAH."

O God, thou art my God: Early will I seek thee.
My soul thirsteth for thee, my flesh longeth for thee,

In a dry and thirsty land, where no water is,
To see thy power and glory,
As I have seen thee in the sanctuary.
Because thy loving-kindness is better than life,
My lips shall praise thee.
Thus will I bless thee while I live.
I will lift up my hands in thy name,
My soul shall be satisfied as with marrow and fatness,
And my mouth shall praise thee with joyful lips.
When I remember thee upon my bed,
I meditate on thee in the night-watches.
Because thou *hast* been my help,
Therefore in the shadow of thy wings *will* I rejoice.
My soul followeth hard after thee,
Thy right hand upholdeth me.
But those that seek my soul to destroy it,
Shall go down into the lower parts of the earth.
They shall fall by the sword.
They shall be a portion for jackals,
But the king shall rejoice in God.
Every one that sweareth by him shall glory.
But the mouth of liars shall be stopped. —*Psalm* lxiii.

How naturally the Fourth psalm, as a psalm at night, follows the Third, which we have placed in the morning. For at night, probably *in* the night, they broke up the camp, hastened across the Jordan, and not till the later watches were encamped again on the other side. The cry of need and the cry of trust, exclamations of defence and exhortations to trust, alternate here and show the same conflict of feeling which pervades the two preceding psalms.

TO THE LEADER OF MUSIC: WITH STRINGED INSTRUMENTS.
A Psalm of David.

Hear me when I call, O God of my righteousness.
Thou hast made room for me in my straits.
Have mercy on me and hear my prayer.
O ye son of men, how long will you turn my majesty into shame?
How long will you love vanity and seek falsehood?
But know that the Lord hath chosen his holy one.
The Lord will hear when I call upon him.
Stand in awe, and sin not.
Commune with your own hearts upon your bed,
And be still.
Offer righteous sacrifices,
And put your trust in the Lord!

> There are many that say, "Who will show us any good?"
> Lord, lift thou the light of thy countenance upon us:
> Thou hast put gladness in my heart,
> Greater than theirs when their corn and wine have increased.
> I will both lay me down in peace and sleep,
> For thou only, O Lord, makest me dwell in safety.

Happy king, bruised and mellowed by affliction, who, harp in hand, can thus charm away his own distress, by seeking the comforting presence of his God!

Forty-eighth Sunday.

THE REBELLION AND THE REBELS.

LESSON.

2 Samuel xvi. 15-23; xvii., xviii.; Psalms xlii., xliii., lxiv., xvii., xli., lv.

THE rebellion under Absalom probably lasted two or three months. For there was time for Absalom to gather and organize a great army from all the tribes. There was time for David to number and grade and officer his broken followers, and to put them under division commanders. There was time to transfer Absalom's army across the Jordan, and for the two armies to pitch in camp in the land of Gilead. Let us look at the details of policy and of warfare on either side.

Hardly are David and his army well down the Jericho road before the triumphant line of Absalom comes coursing into Jerusalem; some thousands of footmen, gathering numbers as they come, headed by the handsome prince and his leading men on mules, with trumpets sounding the new reign, and with Ahithophel to crown the revolution with power and *éclat*.

Hushai and Zadok and Abiathar are there in Jerusalem to meet them. Jonathan and Ahimaaz are outside the gate in the Kidron valley at Enrogel, so that no hindrance may block their way to David. Hushai at once puts himself in position to support whomsoever God appoints king. He can say in all sincerity, "God save the king!

God save the king!" for it is David's wish and will, as his own, that, whether father or son, God's Anointed may rule. And he inspires Absalom's confidence in his honest adherence to the fortunes of the royal house. He is immediately called to meet Ahithophel.

Ahithophel advises two things, both thoroughly wise according to the wisdom of an unscrupulous worldly policy: the first to make an irreconcilable breach between the old government and the new; second, to overwhelm with a sudden destruction the royal house. His counsel is, therefore, first, that Absalom, after the manner of Oriental kings, take to himself the king's wives left in Jerusalem, and that by tent-life on the house-top he so openly enter the harem that the people will see that father and son can never be one again; and, secondly, that with twelve thousand select warriors, he push on after David and crush him at a blow, before he has time to rally. "Strike *David only*, and the whole people will come back to thee!" The first recommendation Absalom at once accepts. He sees that it will compel his supporters to an irreconcilable hostility to David. He, therefore, fulfills Nathan's prediction to David: that adultery shall punish adultery in his own house. The second recommendation he sets aside for Hushai's advice; for Hushai's magniloquent advice appeals to his own vanity. There is something magnificent in deliberately gathering the whole nation and going out in pomp to overpower the old warrior in his flight. But this policy Ahithophel saw to be fatal. He well knew that all that David needed was *time*. Chagrined, therefore, to find his years and authority and wisdom put aside at the start by the petty vanity of this upstart prince, foreseeing David's certain success over the weakness of Absalom, over whom he himself would hold no stable power, finding too, perhaps, that he had misinterpreted the strength of attachment to Jerusalem in David, mortified that he had, by his own counsel to Absalom, put himself beyond the hope of restoration to David's favor for this weak and silly conspiracy, he mounted his mule, pushed back to Hebron, on to Giloh, gave directions to his house, and hung himself.

Hushai, however, without waiting to see the result of the counsel on Absalom's mind, and fearing Ahithophel's advice, at once communicates to Zadok and Abiathar the two opposite lines of policy advised, and bids them to lose no time in telling David. They inform Jonathan and Ahimaaz outside at Enrogel. *They* hasten over the hill toward Jericho, but are suspected and followed. At Bahurim, where Shimei lived,* they hide in a well or running fountain, on the mouth of which a woman spreads her pounded grits. She tells her pursuers who inquire for the two young men, with wit and a double-tongue, "They have gone over the brook of water," meaning the well, but which the pursuers understood to mean the Jordan, or a ravine towards Jericho. David gets the message—his haste has been none too great—and by morning light he and his people are safe across the Jordan. All this may have happened on the same day on which David left Jerusalem, but it may have been after a day had intervened.

There is leisure now for him to proceed to Ish-bosheth's old capital. David's summary punishment of Ish-bosheth's murderers and his tender treatment of Mephibosheth had long since knit that town to him.

Once there, the princely men of the adjacent towns sent him abundant supplies. The servants and families and retainers of Shobi† of Rabbah; and of Machir of

---

* "They were not all Shimeis at Bahurim!"

† Very likely appointed tributary governor of Rabbah.

Lodebar, from whose house David had taken Mephibosheth; and of Barzillai of Rogelim, came with loads of good things for the unfortunate king. It was no forced act of fear. They said, " The people are in the wilderness, hungry, thirsty, and weary;" and sheep, honey, beans, lentiles, wheat and barley, flour, butter, cheese, and roasted wheat, mats and quilts, cups and pots and earthenware come plentifully in to supply their wants. It is a touching return of kindness to a kind-hearted king.

During the two or three months spent here—in the midst of these steep ravines and deep forests outside the town and among Ish-bosheth's old adherents within the city—several psalms also must have been written. For there are psalms which express the condition of a matured worship in Jerusalem, and which are written evidently when David was driven from the tabernacle; and this is the only time when he was driven away, after both the kingdom and the worship were established. The Forty-second and Forty-third are such psalms. There are other psalms which appeal to God for the defence of the right, to defeat the wicked usurpers and to use his power to promote a fear of God. The Sixty-fourth and Seventeenth are such psalms. There are other psalms which lament with profound disappointment the treachery and apostasy of familiar friends, such a treachery as he has just now discovered in his own people of Hebron, such a painful apostasy as he now found in Ahithophel. Such psalms are the Forty-first and Fifty-fifth. We must suppose that a spirit so keenly sensitive as David's, was during this time full of alternations of feeling, now despondent and now hopeful. We shall find him, however, always returning in some form to the expression of his trust in God.

Shut out from the sanctuary which he had built, from the services in which God had satisfied his want, lamenting over his son's wickedness and over his own iniquities, and tormented by the taunts of the infidels and the abandoned, he breathes in his chamber at Mahanaim, the very soul of poetry and of pity in that psalm which, so long as the world shall last, penetrates and comforts the heart of the despondent.*

> As the hart panteth after the water-brook,
> So panteth my soul after thee, O God.
> My soul thirsteth for God, the living God.
> When shall I come and appear before God?
>   My tears have been my meat day and night,
> While they say to me continually, "Where is thy God?"
> When I remember these things, I pour out my soul in woe;
> For I went with the multitude, I went with them to the house of God,
> With the voice of joy and praise,
> With a multitude that kept holyday.
>
> Why art thou cast down, O my soul,
> And why art thou disquieted in me?
> Hope thou in God, for I shall yet praise him,
> For the help of his countenance.
>
> O my God, my soul *is* cast down within me
> While I remember thee from the land of Jordan and of the Hermonites,
> From the little hill.
> Deep calleth unto deep: as the noise of thy cataracts.†
> All thy waves and billows have gone over me;
> Yet the Lord will command his loving-kindness in the day-time,
> And in the night his song shall be with me,
> My prayer unto the God of my life.
> I will say unto God my rock, Why hast thou forgotten me?
> Why go I mourning because of the oppression of the enemy!
> As with a sword in my hands, mine enemies reproach me,
> While they say daily unto me, "Where is thy God?"
> Why *art* thou cast down, O my soul, etc.   —*Psalm* xlii.

These thoughts, so powerful and so tender, pulsate through his whole being. They are, for the time, like his

---

* We know that David at this time longed for the sanctuary, because when Zadok and the Levites brought the ark with them ready to flee with David, David said, "Carry back the ark of God into the city. If I shall find favor in the eyes of the Lord, he will bring me again and show me both it and his habitation." See 2 Samuel xv. 25.

† The poetical reference may be to the storm-torrents down the steep wady on which Mahanaim was situated.

life-blood. He cannot throw them off. The cruel ingratitude of the nation, and cruel deceit of the powerful Ahithophel—without whom Absalom would have been a mere child—fills him with acute pain. But God is a reality to him, and to him he appeals.

> Judge me, O God, and plead my cause
> Against an unmerciful nation.
> O deliver me from a man of deceit and iniquity,
> For thou *art* the God of my strength.
> Why dost thou cast me off?
> Why go I mourning because of the oppression of the enemy?
> O send out thy light and thy truth:
> Let them lead me: let them bring me
> Unto thy holy hill, and to thy tabernacles;
> Then will I go unto the altar of God;
> Unto God, the gladness of my joy.
> Yea, upon the harp will I praise *thee*,
> O God, my God.
>
> Why *art* thou cast down, O my soul, etc. —*Psalm* xliii.

David probably did not know at this time the miserable death of Ahithophel, but he must have been brooding over what Jonathan and Ahimaaz had told him of Ahithophel's plots in Jerusalem, and praying for Hushai's success, when he cried,—

> Hear my voice, O God, in my prayer;
> Preserve my life from fear of the enemy.
> Hide me from the secret counsel of the wicked;
> From the insurrection of the workers of iniquity,
> Who sharpen their tongue like a sword,
> And bend their bows to shoot their arrows, bitter words,
> That they may shoot in secret at the upright.
> Suddenly *do* they shoot at him, and do not fear.
> They encourage themselves in evil speech;
> They commune to hide snares;
> They say, "Who shall see them?
> . . . .
> But God shall *shoot* at *them*.
> Suddenly shall they be wounded.
> . . . .
> And all men shall fear,
> And shall declare the work of God.
> . . . .
> And all the upright in heart shall glory. —*Psalm* lxiv.

In the same spirit is this " Prayer of David " :

Hear the *right*, O Lord: attend unto my cry ;
Give ear unto my prayer that goeth not out of lips of deceit.
Let my sentence (the sentence of a judge in the impending controversy) come
    forth from thy presence.
Let thine eyes behold the things that are equal, etc.   *—Psalm* xvii.

Read now the Forty-first psalm; consider it written when tossed by this same tumult of soul, excited and distracted even unto sickness after his calamities; or consider it as referring to some recent occasion when he had been seriously sick in Jerusalem, and how wonderfully is it apposite to this time.

" Blessed is he that considereth the weak (or the sick);
  The Lord will deliver *him* in time of trouble.
. . . .
The Lord will strengthen him on a bed of languishing.
Thou wilt make all his bed in his sickness.
I said, Lord, be merciful unto me,
Heal my soul! for I have sinned against thee;
Mine enemies speak evil of me :
" When shall he die and his name perish ? "
. . . .
" An evil disease cleaveth fast unto him;
And now that he lieth, he shall rise up no more."
Yea, mine own familiar friend, in whom I trusted,
Who did eat of my bread, hath lifted up his heel against me, etc.

Even more desolate is the Fifty-fifth psalm :

. . . .
Destroy, O Lord, and divide their tongues,
For I have seen violence and strife in the city ;
Day and night they go about upon its walls,
Mischief and sorrow are in the midst of it.
Wickedness is in the midst thereof ;
Deceit and guile depart not from her streets.
For it was not an enemy that reproached me ;
Then I could have borne it.
Neither was it he that hated me,
That did magnify himself against me.
Then I would have hid myself from him ;
But it was thou, a man mine equal (or according to my rank).
My guide and mine acquaintance.
We took sweet counsel together,
And walked unto the house of God in company.
. . . .

THE REBELLION AND THE REBELS. 373

> The words of his mouth were smoother than butter,
> But war was in his heart.
> His words were softer than oil ;
> Yet were they drawn swords.
> Cast thy burden on the Lord, He shall sustain thee.
> He shall never suffer the righteous to be moved ;
> But thou, O God, shall bring *them* down into the pit of destruction.
> Bloody and deceitful men shall not live out half their days ;
> But I will trust in *thee*.

Here during this time in Mahanaim, the king set himself to the reorganization of his army into companies and regiments, and into three divisions under Joab and Abishai and Ittai the Gittite. Probably these energetic men do the real work.

Absalom gathered the army of the tribes—a large army —for there were slain afterwards twenty thousand. From the facts that the battle which was fought was near Mahanaim ("that thou succor us out of the city"), and, therefore, on the east side of Jordan, and that the forest is called the forest of Ephraim, a tribe all whose possessions were west of the Jordan, it has been conjectured that the forest was so called from the battle itself, and from the numbers of the Ephraimites in Absalom's army. Whether this be so or not, it is otherwise probable that the powerful tribe of Ephraim constituted a large part of Absalom's strength. At any rate, a great army ascended the Jericho road, crossed the Jordan fords, pitched in Gilead high up from the Jordan gorge, and now come to battle in the forest.

David is ready to go to the battle at the head of his divisions, but his devoted people earnestly remonstrate on the value of his life, and compel him to stay with the reserve. With a solemn charge to his commanders and to the people to be tender to Absalom personally—thinking doubtless that Absalom's faults were the results of his own neglect—he reviewed the army at the gate, and sent it to battle.

The rough country compelled scattered and wide-spread fighting. Many were destroyed by the tangled woods, ravines, and precipices. And Absalom himself was caught by the head in the oak branches. Joab caught at the news brought him. He upbraided the man that saw the prince hanging for not killing him on the spot. Although he had restored Absalom to favor, he evidently counted his conspiracy a weak attempt at the throne. " The traitor! The hypocrite! Why did you not kill him!" He had no sympathy with the king towards his atrocious son. By every law the wretch ought to die! By every dictate of policy the sooner the better! With his body-guard he hunted out the place. He fell upon Absalom and despatched him, blew the trumpet for halt and return, and in the presence of the people cast the ignominious body into a pit, and heaped a great pile of stones upon it. The people, astounded at his fierceness and boldness, fled from the spot to their tents, as if fearful the king would detect them each one in the slaughter. Joab was no man to play at war. He saw the stern necessity of Absalom's death. He was ready to strike the moment he could do so, and sagacity and fierceness were, in his eyes, the virtues of the Lord's avenger.

Ahimaaz, who had brought the news from Hushai, was present, and wished to carry this news to David. Joab preferred a blunter Cushite or Ethiopian slave, but after he had gone, he permitted Ahimaaz to follow. Ahimaaz either knew the country better than the Ethiopian or could run faster, and was, therefore, first spied by David's watchman at the gate of Mahanaim; but he had no heart to tell David more than that victory was his. The king evidently suspected the truth, and put Ahimaaz aside for the more blunt Cushite. A single sentence from him broke the fearful tidings.

The king was overpowered. What a terrible review of

his past life swept through his soul! His beautiful child! His neglect of his wilful temper! His own example! And his crimes before his family and the nation! Amnon and Tamar! Absalom's murder! and restoration! and rebellion! Nathan's prediction of the sword! The terrible chastisements of his own house! His Absalom! The beautiful, corrupt, and treacherous instrument of punishment, lost forever in his own sins! With the very ecstasy of anguish, he cried, as he walked the chamber over the gate, "O my son Absalom! my son, my son Absalom! would God I had died for thee! O Absalom, my son, my son!"

Forty-ninth Sunday.

TUMULT AND RESTORATION.

LESSON.

2 Samuel xix. 1–23, 31–40; Psalm cxliii.

THE armies were thrown into a tumult of excitement by the horrid death of the handsome Absalom. David's army was horrified by Joab's savage disobedience, as well as by Absalom's awful end. Absalom's army was panic-stricken by the sudden ruin of Absalom's kingdom, and a punishment threatening them like that from a bear robbed of her whelps.

In David's army, there was a worse demoralization in progress than that arising from horror. There was a justice in Absalom's death palpable to the common sense of all. But the king on whom they expected to lean in commotion, and whom they expected to assert the majesty and authority of government at this very hour, was himself overpowered. It began soon to appear that he was retiring out of sight, wailing and lamenting for the wretch who would have struck his father in an instant to the earth. The army, therefore, instead of daring to rejoice that so dangerous and so vile a traitor had met his reward, were ashamed of their victory, and were in imminent danger of a sympathetic sorrow over Absalom's just doom, and of a prevailing regret that his life had not been spared.

The panic in Absalom's army was likely to extend to the

whole nation. The hour had come when long and bloody factions between rival tribes or rival houses might spring into being—an evil scarcely less than anarchy itself.

Joab saw the crisis. It was no time for sentiment over such a wretch and fool. He hastened up to the city and to the king's headquarters. "Thou hast made thy brave defenders all ashamed," he said. "Thou carest more for Absalom than for all the loyal and true. I solemnly swear, if thou dost not play the man, they will all soon leave thee. If thou dost desert them, they will desert thee; they will be gone to-night: and thou wilt be worse off than since the days of Saul's madness in thy youth."

The king saw the tremendous necessity. He would judge Joab's crime another time.* Certainly now Joab was right in urging him to secure his throne. Absalom *was* a rebel against God and man. At once the king went to the gate and let it be known that he was at the station of judgment and command. At once the people rallied to him out of their tents, to which they had scattered, broken loose from all authority.

The western tribes were confounded at the news of Absalom's death. They were amazed at the unexpected, rapid stride of events. David fled, on the instant of Absalom's revolt! Absalom in Jerusalem! Ahithophel's suicide! Absalom's horrors in his crimes! Absalom dead! King David slow to come back! They were perplexed and troubled; and stood wondering and irresolute that no tribe moved to bring back the king.

David was sagacious enough to see that to go back to his own people by force had its dangers, and that to wait long for a universal invitation had equal dangers. His own tribe ought to be foremost in welcoming him home, but

---

* Observe that when David charged Solomon to execute the law upon Joab for the murder of Abner and Amasa, he does not charge him with the murder of Absalom. 1 Kings ii. 5.

they had rebelled with Absalom. He resolved at once to reassure them of his favor; and, inasmuch as the weakness of the kingdom was partly his own fault, even to make some concession to them. He sent, therefore, his messengers to the high-priests, and through them told his own tribe they should be quick to heal the present distractions. Overlooking their anointment of Absalom at Hebron, he appeals to their blood and tribal pride, and sends word to Amasa, whom he has just defeated in battle : "Joab must be removed. Thou art of my kindred : thou shalt be captain of the host." This master-stroke of policy and of magnanimity was successful. The hearts of the people melted as one heart. It was the old David of Engedi and Ziklag. They sent a prompt invitation to him. They flocked down to Gilgal as a tribe, and led other tribes down there, to escort him back to Jerusalem.

And now behold the weakness and hollow wickedness of human nature ! The first men of the tribe of *Benjamin* to trim their sails to the returning wind were the miserable Shimei and the hypocrite Ziba. While the men of Judah were preparing and sailing across their ferry-boat on the Jordan as a suitable conveyance for the royal household— it may have been the time of year when the Jordan overflowed its banks, or rains may have swollen the fords— Shimei was in a mortal terror, and was preparing himself with professions of sorrow and loyalty. In David's mind, he knew there was no greater crime than to curse the Lord's anointed. By law, divine and human, his sentence was death. His only hope is to be among the first to return to loyalty, and, on the flood of the king's return, to ride into favor sufficient to gain a pardon.

Ziba, too, hastened to be beforehand with the king. He would do good offices enough to carry him past the king's discovery of Mephibosheth's loyalty. With his whole retinue of fifteen sons and twenty servants, he was early *across* the Jordan, offering his welcome and assistance with the regiment of Benjamites—a service which could not fail to be pleasing to one whose eye, like the king's, quickly discerned the tribe and family from which every returning adherent came.

What varied feeling now as the royal army approaches down the east bank of the Jordan! How different from every triumph of David before! Sixty-five years now sprinkled his beard and hair! The more venerable. Barzillai and his attendants are in close company with the king and his guard; but no one among all has passed through such personal suffering and trouble as the king himself. Shouts rend the air as the ferry-boat with the royal family cross to the multitude of Judah and as the army of footmen take to the ford; but the shouts are subdued by a tender compassion for the domestic afflictions of him who now begins to be an old man.

Once safe across—himself on the territory of his own tribe—one of the first things the king does is to invite the aged sheikh, who has so befriended him, to make his future home in Jerusalem. He offers him a home and honors in his old age at the capital, and all the attentions of courtly life. It is evident that there was a congeniality of disposition and thought in the two—a noble generosity and sense of truth in each responding to the other. But Barzillai wisely pleads his old age and failing life, and wish for death and burial at his old home, as a reason for declining the more courtly and more animated life of the capital. Not to seem insensible, however, to the king's noble heart, he assigns his faithful servant Chimham to receive something of the king's bounty. Chimham is accepted,* and the king, as the Lord's anointed, kisses and blesses the gray-bearded sheikh, and dismisses him, full of honors and benevolence, to his own home.

During this beautiful and affecting separation, or even

---

* Chimham had his place near Bethlehem, which continued Chimham-place down to the captivity. See Jeremiah xli. 17.

before it took place, Shimei can hardly keep from pressing himself before the king. We can hardly think David much surprised to see before him the fawning hypocrite, bewailing his blasphemous tongue and protesting himself the first of all the rebels in Benjamin and Ephraim to hail him back again. Abishai is not slow to point out his crime. He cursed the Lord's anointed. But David is now erect in conscious majesty and strength. Does not this very trembling Benjamite show the curse that is upon his tribe? The king will inaugurate now no vindictive slaughter of his foes. "Will I begin to put to death?" he says. "Does not God show that I am king again? You sons of Zeruiah are always fierce for blood, and would provoke hostility just when conciliation is needed." He therefore signalized Shimei's appearance before him, by showing his disposition to pardon the rebellious party, in a solemn act of pardoning this traitor. He solemnly swore to Shimei he should not die by his own hand for his offence. This protected the double-tongued rebel while David's life should last.

Meanwhile the people of other tribes stream down to Jericho and Gilgal; Dan and Benjamin, down the Bahurim pass; Ephraim and Manasseh, down the Michmash ravine; Issachar and Zebulun and Gad, down the river roads, until half the people of the remaining tribes have joined the multitude from Judah and Simeon.

Together they bring the king up the hills, with a sober satisfaction rather than a tumultuous joy; for they begin to see what they have escaped in escaping the reign of a weak and heartless tyrant. Nor is the satisfaction free from discord, for already the tribes, like the Lord's disciples afterwards, ascending this very road, have begun to wrangle about precedence in honor and power. David's distractions are not yet over, for this envious wrangle is but the muttering before another rebellion.

It is with a "spirit overwhelmed" and "a heart within him desolate," that he enters Jerusalem. His beautiful, foolish, ungrateful, wicked son, who had wrung his heart in life and death, forever gone, his home dishonored, his sceptre enfeebled, and with a work still before him in his advancing years of reuniting a divided people. Alas! how have his own sins brought it all on him! But it is a king subdued by his God, penitent and with a lowly and unswerving confidence in Jehovah, that comes back to the tabernacle with a petition like this :

> Hear my prayer, O Lord! give ear to my supplications!
> In thy faithfulness answer me, and in thy righteousness.
> And enter not into judgment with thy servant,
> For in thy sight shall no man living be justified,
> For the enemy hath persecuted my soul.
> He hath smitten my life down to the ground!
> He hath made me to dwell in darkness,
> As those that have been long dead.
> Therefore is my spirit overwhelmed within me.
> My heart within me is desolate.
> > I remember the days of old.
> > I meditate on all thy works,
> > I muse on the works of thy hands.
> > I stretch forth my hands unto thee.
> > My soul thirsteth after thee, as a thirsty land. Selah!
> > Hear me speedily, O Lord, my spirith faileth!
> > Hide not thy face from me,
> > > Lest I be like unto them that go down into the pit.
> > > Cause me to hear thy loving-kindness in the morning,
> > > For in thee do I trust.
> > > Cause me to know the way wherein I should walk,
> > > For I lift up my soul unto thee.
> > Deliver me, O Lord, from mine enemies!
> > I flee unto thee to hide me.
> > Teach me to do thy will, for thou art my God.
> > Thy Spirit is good! lead me into the land of uprightness.
> > Quicken me, O Lord, for thy name's sake!
> > For thy righteousness' sake bring my soul out of trouble.
> > And of thy mercy cut off my mine enemies
> > And destroy all them that afflict my soul,
> > For I am thy servant. —*Psalm* cxliii.

For there were enemies still resolute and vindictive, against whom he must vindicate himself as the Anointed servant of his God.

Fiftieth Sunday.

THE REBELLION OF SHEBA.

LESSON.

2 Samuel xix. 24–30, 41–43 ; xx. 1–23.

THE quickness and the success of the Judahites in bringing back the king, provoked the other tribes. The northern people were irritated and their princes and leaders were jealous. The wrangle began either at the camp on the plain, or as the cavalcade started to defile up the rough steep (xx. 2). Representatives of Ephraim, Benjamin, and the tribes north, came to King David's tent, where men of Judah constituted the guard of honor. They complained that the tribe of Judah had been stealthy and sly. Without a word of public notice, they had hastened down before the other tribes, had escorted his royal person across the river, and were ready to take possession of the king as their own. Miserable complaint it was, as the men of Judah taught them. . " Well, is not the king our kinsman ? Why are you in a rage ? Do you think that we came down to get the king to feed us ? Where are the gifts and honors which we have been looking after." " But why did ye not take *our* advice also ? Ten tribes have ten parts : more right than you." It is easy to imagine the reply of Judah : " Why, then, were you so slow to hasten down ? You lay nearer than we. If you were so hot to have the king back, why were you not at Jordan in time to consult? You know well enough that hesitation was putting all Israel in peril. Now that all goes well, it is easy indeed to find fault." And thus they laid on in a fierce oriental clamor. But the southern people were too fierce for the northern, and too obviously in the right. But though the northerners were beaten, their discontent continued, and soon after flamed out into insurrection. Many of them left the cavalcade before it reached Jericho or the mountains (xx. 2).

No sooner had king David reached Jerusalem, than another important incident occurred. The most important man, in many respects, in the whole north, at this critical time, hastened to pay him honor. This was the lame Mephibosheth—impotent enough as a personal leader, but with an admirable title for a hostile rallying cry. Where had he been hidden? Certainly he could not have ventured into the public under Absalom. With uncombed beard, his clothes unwashed, his crippled feet undressed, he sought the king. "Why did not *you* go with me?" is the king's piercing question. "My lord, I was basely betrayed. I was prepared, even with gifts. Ziba played false. He took my ass, and what could a lame man do in the tumult? Behold, my beard and my dress do show how I have mourned over thy sorrow, and over my own betrayal. I do come to submit the case to thee. As an angel of God, is thy heart; when my father's house was dead, thou didst lift me up to thy table. I have no right but thy good pleasure, my lord, O king." Thus the humble, true-hearted man went on, knowing that Ziba's story was plausible, and that the nation would approve, if the king bids his servants to thrust him through. At length the king said, "Say no more. I cannot now go back on Ziba. This is ordered. Divide the estate between you." "It matters little if he have it all, since thou art restored," said the devoted, grateful man. David's brusque manner to him may have been provoked by the critical attitude of the Benjamites and Ephraimites, for hardly had there been time for this significant event to take place, and for David to signify, by a public act, his abhorrence of Absalom's adultery, than a new and alarming turn is given to affiairs. A bold man rises up, willing to risk the championship of the northern discontent. This is Sheba, not only from Saul's tribe, but from Saul's branch of the tribe, for both Saul and Sheba were Bichrites or sons of Bicher, and Mephibosheth and Sheba were of the same stock. Sheba must have been a man of some power, as he was certainly a man of some resolution, for the people followed him, and one of the most prudent cities of the north fortified itself for him. He divined that the time had come to bring back the power of government to Benjamin or Ephraim. One word he believed would now concentrate and direct the flood of passion; so he blew the signal of revolt: "Judah claims the son of Jesse. We have no part! To your tents, O Israel"—not only a cry for the dispersion of the army and a rally to their reserved rights and original judgment, but also a summons to Sheba's standard. The ten tribes did rally to him, and nearly accomplished that which Jeroboam accomplished after Solomon's death.

Now came the time to try the mettle of the new general. Promptness and power, and a stroke, were all-important. "Assemble the full force of Judah; lose no time. Be back in three days," is the king's order to Amasa. But Amasa lacked rallying power in his own tribe, or he did not appreciate the occasion. Neither orientals then, nor occidentals now, like to accept, in a day, the summons of a defeated general. Annoyed by the delay, the king said to Abishai, "If Sheba gather strength, he will be stronger than Absalom. Take the royal guard and our soldiers here, and go. Let him not gain a fortified city." It was the flower of the army. Joab and his men, the Cherethites, the Pelethites, and all the mighty men. They pushed towards Gibeon. They were soon enough to drive Sheba; but they were not too soon for Amasa. More alert than they supposed, he had already crossed from Judah to Benjamin; passing Jerusalem in haste, to make up for delay. There, across the stony ridges, just by "the great stone" at Gibeon, was Amasa's army. There, where thirty years before the young men of Abner and of Joab had played on "the field of strong men," they met. A raging fire of passion is Joab's heart, to see his rival above him, and ahead of him in the pursuit, and the very place is suggestive of challenge and triumph. But the challenge even of passion and hate would have been honor itself compared to Joab's horrid treachery. With malicious disregard of oriental honor, he went forward to salute his cousin. The kissing of the beard is not an every-day compliment. With stately ceremony, therefore Joab raised the beard of his superior to kiss it. The very posture would conceal the sword in his left hand. With one terrible girdling stroke he disemboweled his rival, bespattering himself from girdle to sandals with the blood.* At this, Joab vaults over Abishai into his old place. One of his body-guard cries out, as the people came up to the ghastly body, "He that likes Joab for general and David for king, go after Joab." With that, he removed the bloody body out of the road, and covered it with a cloth, and sent on the men. They drove Sheba to the very north. They gave him no chance to secure a city till they came to Abel, which was even beyond Dan. By pushing on, he had adroitly gained sufficient time to secure the ear of a people famed for good judgment; and he so repre-

---

* See 1 Kings ii. 5.

sented the posture of the tribes that the citizens gave him their city.

At what cities might Sheba have made a stand? At Bethel in Benjamin, which Jeroboam afterwards made one of his capitals—had it not been so near Jerusalem. At beautiful Shechem in Ephraim, queen of the vale, dignified with mountains of blessings and cursing, where Rehoboam was in the anointed king. At Jezreel, afterwards Ahab's capital. But Amasa's army was too sharp in pursuit for him to stop even there. He thought best to put the Esdrælan valley between himself and the royal army. Hazor, which had been twice the head of kings, to the terror of all Israel, was probably stripped of defences. Kedesh in Naphtali was so far to the north, that Abel, the prudent, but little beyond, was preferred as stronger, and more commanding in reputation. The position once secured there, he will gradually advance southwards. Everywhere along the way his outrunners gather the disaffected. From Benjamin and Ephraim, and Manasseh, and Issacher, and Zebulun, and Naphtali, as he went north, and from "all the Beerites"— whoever that unknown people of the north were — he gathered a motley army, which, to the multitude, seemed to have elements of strength. With the people of Abel, Sheba could use plausible arguments. He rehearsed, no doubt, the rebellion of Absalom, the dissatisfaction and discontent, the crimes and shame of David, the success of Absalom, the real weakness of the king, the claim of Judah that David was their king, the exclusion of the ten tribes from the royal counsels, so that they had been compelled to take up arms. It was the old story—repeated so often since—of the disaffected arrayed against the acknowledged faults of a generally good government. But it was plausible enough, and Sheba, at the head of representatives from so many tribes, seemed powerful enough to deserve sup-

THE REBELLION OF SHEBA. 387

port. Especially would it be so, if the tribes should flow in in a few days, and signify that the revolt had large proportions. So it seemed to the Abelites.

But behold, in a day or two, the forces which appeared were not the gathering forces of northern tribes, but the royal forces. At once a siege rampart was thrown up around the city; trees were felled, approaches to the walls were made, battering rams were swung, and tower and wall began to tremble at the blows. There was a tremendous energy and prompt despatch against the city, which struck terror to the multitude within, and confirmed the suspicions of the wise that all Sheba's wisdom was not right. The people found out that it was the terrible Joab and not Amasa at their gates.

Forthwith a wise woman appeared on the wall and called for the commander of the outside forces. On his appearance, she wished to know if he were indeed Joab. And having made sure that she was addressing his sagacious mind, she said (1.) The city of Abel had always had the reputation of being a wise town. (2.) That the people —certainly no one more than herself—were disposed to be peaceful and faithful. (3.) That Joab was about to destroy a mother-town—the Lord's inheritance for his people. To which Joab replied that neither he nor his royal Master wished to destroy any town or people in the kingdom. It was simply a matter of treason. Sheba was exciting revolt. If he were delivered, he himself would leave the city at once. The woman comprehended the truth. There was no large disaffection. Sheba was a mere disturber. Confident of her power with the rulers, she said, "His head shall be flung to thee over the wall." She went to the elders and the people. In good words and chosen reasons, she set the matter in its true light before them, showing the wickedness of Sheba, and the just danger in which they had placed the city. The city were of one mind with her. They flung Sheba's head over the wall.

And Joab, disdaining to follow or to reorganize the paltry army, sounded his trumpet, drew back to his encampment, and took up his leisurely march for the capital, leaving the miserable defeated to sneak back to their tribes and towns.

Joab again, vindictive as he was, the astute Joab had killed the rebellion at its birth. Commander he was born to be, commander he would be, and commander he continued to be over all the host of Israel.

Fifty-first Sunday.

SONGS OF FAITH IN TROUBLE.

LESSON.

2 Samuel xx. 1, 2, 4-6, 23-26; Psalms xl., lxx., xiv., liii., xxii., xxviii., lxi., cix.

WHAT a ceaseless sea of afflictions and of cares had now beaten on David for more than forty years, for he is now more than three-score of age. But these last afflictions are the most terrible of all. The schemes of an ambition early awakened in him by God's prophet, conducted by God himself in marvelous directions, and culminating in a united kingdom and in a sublime display of the divine glory, seem now either thwarted or weakened. Sin, crime, shame, punishment, family shame, treachery, rebellion, cruel, hopeless death, all these now followed by general national destruction, bow down his head and heart. While the new rebellion of Sheba is in progress, and even before the king has time to discern the real situation of Jerusalem, what fears and temptations assail him ! Is God to break up his kingdom, as he did King Saul's ? Are his sins to bring on him his just deserts ? Is his own example to lead bad men to wicked success ? Is God to avert his favor, by sending him down to his grave miserable and dishonored, even though he raise up a son afterwards to keep the succession ? Some such thoughts as these in all probability agitated the king's heart, as he at first watched the attitude of

Mephibosheth, or as afterwards he saw the royal guard go northwards, leaving him defenceless—to take the place of the tardy Amasa—or as he heard of Joab's new malice over the bloody body at Gibeon. He must have been some other person than David not to have had at this time such commotions within himself. But the course of feeling in many a psalm of David shows that lofty courage takes finally the place of disheartenment, and high faith in God at length the place of doubt. To this confidence in God we know that he did return—the confidence of faith, of obedience, of penitence, of indignant denunciation of the wicked and their wickedness.

Several psalms which may be classed together, and which obviously belong to this general period of his life, we may locate here. They are the expression of a mature inward life which rests now deep down on the very attributes of God—on his promises; on the predictions of his kingdom; on his just anger and overthrow against the wicked; on assurance of God's favor to himself generally, and which rises at times into a priestly identification of himself with that Seed of his line in whom all nations should be blessed.

Of these psalms, take up first *the Fortieth*. In this psalm the expressions are deeply spiritual—the mature expressions of a person who has a profound sense of sinfulness, and who has a profound sense of the value of pardon:

> I waited patiently for the Lord,
> And he inclined unto me and heard my cry.
> He brought me up also out of a horrible pit, out of the miry clay,
> And set my feet upon a rock, and established my goings.
> And he hath put a new song into my mouth, praise unto our God!
> Many shall see it and fear, and shall trust in the Lord.

These words have special significance if they represent David's personal sins, his personal wretchedness, the effort which it cost him to confess in public, the sweetness of God's recognized pardon, and the effect of such an example of forgiveness on others.

The great Seer's awful rebuke to King Saul, " Hath the Lord as great delight in burnt-offerings and sacrifices as in obeying the voice of the Lord ?" he has laid to heart; and such is his true acceptance of God's will for himself as prophet, priest and king, his profound recognition that the spirit is above the ceremonial,* that his spirit is at one with that Greater One who said on coming into the world†—

> Sacrifice and offering thou didst not desire,
> Mine ears hast thou opened.
> Burnt-offering and sin-offering hast thou not required,
> Then said I, Lo ! I come : in the volume of the book it is written of me,‡
> I delight to do thy will, O God !
> Yea, thy law is written in my heart.

What power is given to the meaning, when we consider that David has vindicated the righteousness of God's law against himself and all his sins, confessing and abasing himself before the nation, and exalting the pure truth of God's law, even in spite of the jeers of scoffers and infidels and vile men, when we read,—

> I have preached righteousness in the great congregation,
> Lo, I have not refrained my lips, O Lord, thou knowest,
> I have not hid my righteousness within my heart ;
> I have *declared* thy faithfulness and thy salvation,
> I have not concealed thy loving-kindness and thy truth
> From the great congregation.

What an appeal for God's mercy, and God's preservation in consistence with truth, does he base on the unre-

---

* How much more significant is this when we remember what David himself had done for the ceremonial.

† Hebrews x. 3–7.

‡ In the volume of God's promises, it was written that such a Seed should come to set up a kingdom for God.

served acknowledgment of his troubles and of his sins as the cause of his troubles:

> *For* innumerable evils have compassed me about,
> Mine iniquities have taken hold upon me,
> So that I am not able to look up;
> They are more than the hairs of my head,
> *Therefore* my heart faileth me;
> Be pleased, O Lord, to deliver me, etc.

The rest of this psalm constitutes the Seventieth psalm also, and is there declared to be

> A psalm, *to bring to remembrance.*

If it was designed to bring to his own remembrance the time when he was driven out of his throne and subjected to Shimei's malice; to bring to remembrance publicly the crime and shame of reviling the Lord's Anointed; to bring to Shimei's remembrance his offence and his dependence on the king's clemency; to bring to the remembrance of all revilers of God, their certain defeat before God; if it was designed to bring to remembrance David's distraction when he came back to Jerusalem, it would serve a powerful purpose as the conclusion of one psalm and as a separate psalm reiterated:

> Be pleased, O Lord, to deliver me,
> Make haste to my help, O Lord!
> Let them be ashamed and confounded that seek after my soul to destroy it,
> Let them be driven backward and put to confusion that wish me evil,
> Let them be desolate for a reward of their shame,
> That say unto me, Aha! Aha!
> Let all those that seek thee rejoice and be glad in thee!
> Let such as love thy salvation, say continually,
> "The Lord be magnified."
> But I am poor and needy,
> Yet the Lord thinketh on me;
> Thou art my help and my deliverer,
> Make no tarrying, O my God!

The Fourteenth and the Fifty-third psalms are substantially one. They represent, as the closing verse signifies, a time when people were in *captivity;* but that the "captivity" does not necessarily refer to the exile to Babylon, is plain from Deborah's description of a captivity at Israel in her time (Judges v. 12), and from the fact that the people in the Judges' time were sold into the hands of oppressors. To be sold into the hands of Absalom and Ahithophel was a captivity. And at no time more than in such a captivity, would bad men rise up to make capital of David's offences, to declare religion a craft, the existence of God a delusion, and to throw off all moral obligation. None of them could shake David's confidence in God, nor deceive him with respect to that condition of the heart which endeavored to shake off God and his obligations.

A PSALM OF DAVID.

To the leader of Music on *Mahalath*.

The fool hath said in his heart, " No God !"
Corrupt are they, and have done abominable iniquity.
There is none that doeth good !
God looked down from heaven upon the children of men,
To see if there were any that did understand,
That did seek God, etc.
. . . .
Oh that the salvation of Israel were come out of Zion,
When God bringeth back the captivity of his people.
Jacob shall rejoice,
And Israel shall be glad.

In strong confidence that the God who promised, "I will make thee a house," will fulfill his promise to him and his seed, even though all men have forsaken him, the Twenty-second psalm was composed. His kingly and priestly place make him in this a type of Messiah, who was forsaken of all, even of God. David may or may not have had a consciousness that in describing his own person and sorrow, he was describing his own Great Son when denied his right seat at the head of the nation and reviled by the multitude.

A PSALM OF DAVID.

To the Leader of Music : on " the Hind of the Morning."

My God, my God, why hast thou forsaken me.
Why art thou so far from helping me,
And from the words of my roaring.
. . . .
All they that see me laugh me to scorn.
They shoot out the lips, they shake the head !
" He trusted in the Lord, that he would deliver him.
Let him deliver him, seeing he delighted in him."
But thou art he that took me out of the womb,
That didst make me hope upon my mother's breast.
. . . .
My strength is dried up like a potsherd,
And my tongue cleaveth to my jaws,
And thou hast brought me into the dust of death.
For the dogs have compassed me.
The assembly of the wicked have enclosed me.
They pierced my hands and my feet.
I may tell all my bones.
They look and stare upon me.
They part my garments among them,
And cast lots upon my vestments.
But be not thou, O Lord, far from me.
O my strength, haste thee to help me.
. . . .
All the ends of the world shall remember,
And shall return unto God.
And all the kindreds of the nations shall worship before thee,
For the kingdom is the Lord's,
And *He* is the Governor among the nations.
. . . .
A seed shall serve him,
It shall be accounted to the Lord for a generation, etc.

Against the temptation which comes from disappointment and from the prevalence of specious bad men, at some such time as this, David prays in the Twenty-eighth psalm :

Unto thee will I cry, O Lord, my rock,
Be not silent to me, lest if thou be silent to me
I become like them that go down into the pit.
Hear the voice of my supplication, when I cry unto thee,
When I lift up my hands towards thy holy oracle.
Draw me not away with the wicked and with the workers of iniquity,
Which speak peace to their neighbors,
But mischief is in their heart, etc.

So, too, does he express his personal confidence that his own kingly life will certainly be spared, and that his reign shall flow on in the long succession of generations.

A PSALM OF DAVID

(Afterwards dedicated to the Chief Musician upon the Stringed Instruments).

> Hear my cry, O God!
> Attend unto my prayer.
> From the end of the earth will I cry unto thee,
> When my heart is overwhelmed:
> Lead to the rock that is higher than I.
> For thou *hast* been a shelter for me,
> And a strong tower from the enemy.
> I will abide in thy tabernacle for ever:
> I will trust in the covert of thy wings.
>> For thou, O God, hast heard my vows;
> Thou hast given me the heritage of those that fear thy name.
> Thou wilt prolong the king's life;
> And his years as many generations.
> He shall abide before God for ever.
> Oh! prepare mercy and truth, which may preserve him.
> So will I sing praise unto thy name for ever,
> That I may daily perform my vows. —*Psalm* lxi.

Of quite another kind is the One Hundred and Ninth psalm, in which he invokes the divine punishment on the wicked. The vindictive appeals are appeals to *God.* In David's conception such has been the incorrigible wickedness of these men, that God is no longer to hold his peace. They have abused both right and love. They have persisted in giving malice in return for kindness, and they presume upon forbearance and mercy. They assail with lies and curses the Lord's Anointed—pulling down the divine constitution of his kingdom set up for the benefit of all mankind—revelling in the downfall of the king's shame and calamity, and refusing to see the jealous care which his confession and penitence have for purity and holiness and God's law. They are fit, therefore, only for the place of the incorrigible pagans of the earth—to be cast out under the fearful curses of the law of Moses. If their sins are to go unpunished, then all government and all justice and all love must suffer. For his Anointed's sake, who is set for righteous rule, for his kingdom's sake, God should arise against them. And if David would make them feel the power of his just indignation against their horror of sin, then must he utter his sense of their deserts, in the oriental form, as he did over Joab's horrid treachery, at the slaughter of Abner at Hebron.* This strong imprecatory psalm is therefore just and right. It is just what every good man will instinctively feel, when war rises up in his own government and the absolutely malicious element comes boldly forth, with devilish persistence and perversion, to distort the good and to practice evil. In such a situation undoubtedly arose this famous imprecatory psalm, dedicated, for the support of justice and authority, to the tabernacle service and delivered to the chief musician.

A PSALM OF DAVID.

Hold not thy peace, O God of my praise,
For the mouth of the wicked and mouth of deceit
Are opened against me.
They have spoken against me with a lying tongue.
They compassed me about with words of hatred,
And fought against me without a cause.
For my love they are my adversaries,
But I give myself unto prayer.
And they have rewarded me evil for good
And hatred for my love.
Set thou a wicked man *over him*,
And let Satan (or an adversary) stand at *his* right hand.
When he shall be judged, let him be condemned.
And let his prayer become sin.
Let his days be few ; and let another take his office.
Let his children be fatherless and his wife a widow.
Let his children be continually vagabonds and beg.
Let them seek their bread also out of their desolate places.
Let the extortioner catch all that he hath,
And let the strangers spoil his labor.
Let there be none to extend mercy unto him;
Neither let there be any to favor his fatherless children,

---

* 2 Samuel iii. 28, 29.

> Let his posterity be cut off.
> In the generation following let their name be blotted out.
> Let the iniquity of his fathers be remembered with the Lord,
> And let not the sin of his mother be blotted out.
> Let them be before the Lord continually,
> That he may cut off the memory of them from the earth.
> Because that he remembered not to shew mercy,
> But persecuted the poor and needy man,
> That he might even slay the broken in heart, etc.

Whatever may be the spirit of this psalm, it is but the spirit of curses denounced against the disobedient by the law of Moses, in which every evil to body, mind and estate, person, family and nation, is declared.* That which by divine revelation was deemed necessary in order to make an impression upon the coarse civilization and gross tendencies of the age, is here specifically applied to those who despise God's Anointed Ruler, and that great realm of truth and holiness impersonated in his official character. On the supposition that the psalm is addressed by David as God's Anointed, to God to no longer hold his peace against the incorrigible, from whose advance His kingdom is in danger, the law of Moses—the *law* in its terrible justness—would seem to be here properly applied. If revelation of such a thing to Moses in law was right, then revelation of such a thing to David in psalms was right also.

---

* Read Deuteronomy xxviii. 15–68. It is wonderful to note the things specified: consumption, fever and inflammation, botob, scab and itch, madness and blindness, cursing; vexation and rebuke, sword, blasting and mildew, drought and blight, spoiling and captivity, hunger, thirst and nakedness, siege and famine, "every sickness and every plague;" dispersion and weariness of life, etc.

Fifty-second Sunday.

THREE YEARS' FAMINE.

LESSON.

2 Samuel xxi. 1-14; Joshua ix. 3-21: Numbers xxxv. 31-33; Psalm lxviii.

WE come now to a terrible event, which shows the wide contrast between David's times and our own. Notwithstanding the amiable graces of David's reign, the spirit of ancient Eastern society was hard and fierce. Joab is a truer type of that life than David. Fierce, vindictive, and wilful, had Joab been king he would have been a royal brother to Cambyses and Darius and Smerdis, to Pharaoh, and to the later Assyrians, if he had not been an ignoble example to Ahab himself. The general rule of all the East was absolute tyranny. The king's *will* must show its authority in acts of *power*. Cruelty and blood were swift and easy ways to vindicate authority. Severe as was Moses' law of retaliation, it was a lenient law compared with the cruel exactions outside the Hebrew nation. It was a law of justice in place of a habit of caprice. "Blood for blood; limb for limb; tooth for tooth;"—it was often terrible, but still it was a powerful modification of mere wilful vengeance, royal or private. So, too, the right of the blood-avenger was a merciful right—although it descended from father to son, and doubtless often perpetuated or generated vindictiveness. It was of the utmost importance to the kingdom under God, and to the honor of the Mosaic law, that these two laws should be maintained.

Now in Saul's reign, a terrible wrong had been committed. For it, neither pardon had been bestowed nor had justice been rendered. It had broken not only the plighted public honor of the nation, but the plighted honor of the Divine Sovereign. The crime had been committed by the king himself before all the nation against a people taken solemnly under the protection of the nation, and unable by their humble station to defend himself. That Jehovah, therefore, who rose up in jealousy for His own humiliated people in Egypt, arose now against his own people in Canaan for their Egyptian outrage on the humiliated and outraged Gibeonites.

Let us take the story in order.

1. A famine appeared in the land. The rain probably ceased, and for three or even four or five years, the crops failed, until there were three full years of famine.

2. David recognized this famine as a divine infliction, and sought by sacrifice and priests the reason for it. The answer from the divine oracle gave as the reason, "Blood defileth the land." It was a punishment of the nation for not exacting justice between Saul's house and the Gibeonites. It may be that punishment was inflicted *at that time* for the additional reason that the refractory nation needed to be subdued by a divine hand.

3. The crime was this: At some time during Saul's reign—very likely after his leniency to Agag, and his terrible loss of favor—Saul awoke to a spasmodic zeal against the heathen nations of the land. But, instead of royally fighting with the really formidable heathen, he fell on the innocent Gibeonites. The Gibeonites were neither rebels nor heathen. They had submitted—there were four cities of them*—at the very beginning of the conquest—their

---
* Gibeon, Chephirah, Beeroth, and Kirjath-Jearim (Joshua ix. 17.)

very artifice having been but a dexterous acknowledgment of Jehovah's power and of the Hebrew triumph. This was a bold stroke for them, and it brought on them the kings of Jebus, Hebron, Jarmuth, Lachish and Eglon in that famous battle when Joshua said, "Sun, stand thou still on *Gibeon.*" They obtained a solemn league with the nation, confirmed by an oath taken by the princes of the congregation. The agreement was that the Gibeonites would be hewers of wood and drawers of water to the nation, and that the nation would preserve and protect *them.* And so thoroughly had they incorporated themselves with the Israelites that the historian of the Second Book of Samuel stops to explain that they were "not of the children of Israel, but a remnant of the Amorites." This solemn league and formal oath, the conditions of which had been observed by the Gibeonites for long years, Saul ruthlessly broke. Whether Saul sought to exterminate them, or waged only a battle or two against them, he had committed a great crime, disastrous to the very foundations of holiness.

4. David at once acknowledged the wrong, and the right of the Gibeonites to demand justice according to the law, by calling to himself the representatives of the city or cities, and asking what atonement the nation should make.

5. The Gibeonites claimed their right. They would take no silver or gold—a compensation so common among nations that the Hebrew law presupposed its general practice (Numbers xxxv. 31.) They said that the house which committed the wrong should pay the penalty, and they demanded the blood-avengement of the law. As "satisfaction," according to law, for their slaughtered kinsmen, and their attempted extermination, they said, "Deliver us seven—a round number—of Saul's house, and their lives shall pay the penalty. We will show the Lord that justice has been rendered."

THREE YEARS' FAMINE. 401

6. No choice remained to David but to yield to this legal requisition. God had taken the wrong into His own hands, to avenge by His own power, and famine was perhaps destroying far more than blood-revenge required. He therefore did not simply consent, but approved this fulfillment of the law, and at once proceeded to meet the demand.

7. Who now should the seven be? His oath to Jonathan would not permit Mephibosheth to be a victim, and there was no other son of Saul by the male line. There were, however, two sons of a concubine of Saul, Rizpah, in respect to whom Abner had the fatal rupture with Ishbosheth (iii. 7). And there were also five sons either of Michal or Merab.* These seven men, full grown, were taken and delivered. Whether their character deserved the punishment we do not know.

8. The same persons delivered to the Gibeonites, were, by the Gibeonites, hung up on a stake † "before the Lord," just on the very spot where the Ark of God was once consulted by Saul (1 Samuel xiv. 16–18). The *mode* of death was probably the Gibeonites' choice; and the

---

* 2 Samuel xxi. 8, says, "Five sons of Michal whom she brought up for Adriel." 1 Samuel xviii. 19 says that "Merab, Saul's daughter, was given unto Adriel." We may solve the discrepancy by this supposition: Merab died before the coronation of David, having been Adriel's wife ten or twelve years. After Merab's death Michal adopted the children of her sister at the request of Adriel, her brother-in-law. When Abner brought back Michal to David, the children left behind across the Jordan were from seven to fifteen years old; and now when taken as victims they were men from thirty-three to forty-two years old.

† The Hebrew word translated "hanged" means crucified, or rather hung up and dislocated—not on a cross, a later Roman punishment, but on a stake. Perhaps they were put to death first and hung up afterwards as a public exhibition of punishment.

hanging them up "before the Lord," may have been connected in their minds with the fact that Jehovah had, by the famine, called public attention to the crime. This strange sacrifice or execution was not in Gibeon, but in *Gibeah*, so that the retaliation might be manifest to all.

9. This was done at the beginning of the barley-harvest, and yet the famine was not stayed. In the face of the blazing summer sun the bodies hung, as were hung up on the plains of Moab those heads of the people of Israel who sacrificed in sensual worship with the Moabites.*

Rizpah, in one of the most pitiful pastoral spectacles of all history, sat down before the victims. With a pitiful horror of that which Asaph afterwards described when the heathen conquered Jerusalem,—

> "The dead bodies of thy servants have they given
> To be meat unto the fowls of heaven.
> The flesh of thy saints
> Unto the beasts of the earth,—"

an end most abhorrent to the Hebrew,—" she spread on the rocky floor the thick mourning cloth of black sackcloth, which as a widow she wore, and crouching there she watched that neither vulture nor jackal should molest the bodies.† That she did not seek to take them down, that no one, moved by her devotion, offered to help her, seems to show that all acquiesced in the execution of the approved law. That she waited for water to drop out of heaven, signifies that she waited for the token of the cessation of the wrath of heaven in the falling rain in October."

10. At length the attention of the king was directed to Rizpah's constancy and her prolonged devotion. The picture of the old woman crouching before the dead bodies stirred anew his pity. The Gibeonites, through ignorance

---

* See Numbers xxv. 4. † Grove.

or otherwise, might not have observed the law of Moses. "The body hung upon a tree shall not remain all night, that the land shall not be defiled."* David might also have been moved by the apparent breach of the Mosaic Law. For this neglect the divine reconciliation might be stayed.

At once, therefore, the king ordered the bones of Saul and of Jonathan to be gathered from the oak at Jabesh-Gilead, and the dried bodies of the seven to be taken down. Then all together were honorably buried by the king's commandment in the family sepulchre at Zelah, a few miles from Gibeah. Thus mercy and justice were expressed; and the prayers at the tabernacle and throughout the land for relief from famine were at last heard.

It has been supposed, that after the abundant rain had refreshed the land, and all the people were rejoicing in the restoration of God's favor, the people themselves subdued and united under God's chastisement, David gave utterance to the joyful sense of His wise and just rule, in the sublime Sixty-eighth psalm:

A PSALM OR SONG OF DAVID.

TO THE CHIEF MUSICIAN.

Let God arise: let his enemies be scattered,
Let them also that hate him flee from his face.
As smoke is driven away, so drive them away.
As wax melteth before the fire, so let the wicked perish at the presence of God.
But let the righteous be glad.
Let them rejoice before God; yea, let them rejoice with gladness.
Sing unto God, sing praises to his name.
Extol him that rideth upon the heavens by his name JAH,
And rejoice before him.
A father of the fatherless and a judge of widows
Is God in his holy habitation.
God setteth the solitary in families,
He bringeth out those which are bound in chains;
But the rebellious dwell in a dry land.
O God, when thou wentest forth before thy people,

---

* Deuteronomy xxi. 22, 23.

When thou didst march through the wilderness. Selah !
The earth shook, the heavens also dropped at the presence of God.
Sinai itself was moved at the presence of God, the God of Israel.

Thou, O God, didst shake out a plentiful rain.
Whereby thou didst confirm thine inheritance when it was weary.
Thy congregation hath dwelt therein.
Thou, O God, hath prepared of thy goodness for the poor.

. . . .

Blessed be the Lord, who daily loadeth us with benefits.
Even the God of our salvation. Selah !
Our God is the God of salvation,
And unto God the Lord belong the issues from death ;
But God shall wound the head of his enemies,
The hairy scalp of such a one as goeth on still in his trespasses.

The Lord said, I will bring again from Bashan.
I will bring my people again from the depths of the sea.

. . . .

Bless ye God in the congregations,
The Lord from the fountain of Israel.
There is little Benjamin with their ruler.
The princes of Judah and their council,
The princes of Zebulon, and the princes of Naphtali.
Thy God hath commanded thy strength.
Strengthen, O God, that which thou hast wrought in us.
Because of thy temple at Jerusalem shall kings bring presents unto thee.

. . . .

Ascribe ye strength unto God.
His excellency is over Israel and his strength is in the clouds.
O God, thou art terrible out of thy holy places.
The God of Israel is he
That giveth strength and power unto his people. Blessed be God !

Fifty-third Sunday.

SONGS IN OLD AGE.

LESSON.

2 Samuel xxi. 15-22 ; xxii. ; 1 Chronicles xx. 4-8 ; xxvii. 11 ; Psalms xviii, lxxi., xxxvii.

DAVID was about sixty-seven years of age, at the beginning of the famine ; and now at the end of the famine, he was about sixty-four. There was one more battle to be fought against the Philistines,— a mere fight — a parting salute to those old haters, and then his wars will be over.* But it was quite another thing to fight as a grey-beard than to fight as a lively youth. For when David went down to the old region of Gezer and Gath, his old age so failed him that one of the Rephaim, Ishbi-benōb, a gigantic fellow with a brass or bronze spear-point, weighing eight pounds, thought he had him in his power. But for the fierce Abishai, who could not have been much younger than David, David's life might after all have gone out under a Philistine. His body-guard saw the danger and said : "You must go no more to battle : you will quench the light of Israel." Three other giants were slain afterwards by his brave men : the giant Siph, by Sibbechai, the eighth captain over David's army divisions of twenty-four

---

* It is possible that these events occurred during previous wars as some suppose.

thousand; the brother of Goliath of Gath, who had a spear-staff like his brother Goliath's, if not Goliath's own, by Elhanan of Bethlehem; and the six-fingered, six-toed monster,* who defied Israel, like old Goliath, by David's nephew, Jonathan, who rivaled his great uncle's great exploit. These four giants were brothers. It was a comparatively easy thing now to fight and kill them when David had led the way, when the power of his name was felt, and the prestige of the kingdom was established, and when the Philistines were a mere remnant cowed under more than forty years' reverses.

Quite likely these parallel challenges and fights belonged to one short campaign — the end of the great warrior's military career. At length, all the lying nations were subdued,—Philistia, Edom, Ammon, Syria of the two rivers. The internal dissensions had been put down, more grievous and more painful than all foreign wars. The famine was over. The land was now in broad possession of peace. The orderly observance of government and of religion was universally renewed. As old age was now coming on, the king looked out over a tranquil land, from north to south, marked with personal conflicts with enemies from east to west, filled with scenes of his personal mistakes and sins. As he retires from his life of military warfare, he takes in the broad survey. A tide of emotion fills his soul. Devout thanksgivings and ascriptions of glory to God well up. Always in every instinct a poet, his genius ripens with a culture which is spiritual — the culture of the soul rather than the culture of the intellect or of the heart. In lofty imagery and sublime descriptions of God,

---

* "Men with six fingers and six toes have been met with elsewhere. Pliny speaks of certain six-fingered Romans. This peculiarity is even hereditary in some families."—*Keil and Delitzsch.* Six-fingered families are not unknown in this country.

he reviews his marvellous career. Revising a psalm of thanksgiving originally written after deliverance from Saul, he gives it a noble enlargement and sends it to the heavenly tabernacle as the song which he "spake unto the Lord, in the day that the Lord delivered him out of the hands of all his enemies, and out of the hand of Saul," and which afterwards, with slight alterations, took its place in the Book of Psalms.

DAVID'S SONG.

The Lord is my rock, and my fortress, and my deliverer,
The God of my rock ; in him will I trust ;
My shield and the horn of my salvation,
My high tower and my refuge, my Saviour,
Thou savest me from violence.
I will call upon the Lord, who is worthy to be praised,
So shall I be saved from my enemies.
When the waves of death compassed me,
The floods of ungodly men made me afraid,
The sorrows of hell compassed me about,
The snares of death prevented me,
In my distress, I called upon the Lord, and cried to my God ;
And he did hear my voice out of his temple,
And my cry did enter into his ears.   —*Psalm* xviii.

Then follows one of the sublimest descriptions of the progress and power and overwhelming prowess of God as a warrior, beside the simplicity of which Milton's descriptions are dim indeed. Such expressions afterwards, as

The Lord rewarded me according to my righteousness,
According to the cleanness of my hands, hath he recompensed me,
For I have kept the ways of the Lord,
And have not wickedly departed from my God.
. . . .
Therefore the Lord hath recompensed me according to my righteousness,
According to thy cleanness in his eyesight,

cannot, of course, for a moment refer to the purity and innocence of his whole personal life, but must refer either to his official integrity in administering the kingdom, or to his honorable and righteous treatment of the Anointed Saul.*

All the acts of his own prowess — so great in the eyes of the nation — he attributes to God.

> For by thee I broke through a troop,
> And by my God I leaped over a wall (the walls of towns).
> . . . .
> He made my feet like hinds' feet,
> And set me upon my high places.
> He taught my hands to war,
> So that a bow of steel was broken by my hands.
> Thou didst also give me the shield of thy safety,
> And thy gentleness made me great.

The first part of this song naturally refers to early and later troubles, and the last part to the later part of his life, and to his confidence in his future maintenance of his house :

> It is God that avengeth me,
> And that bringeth down the people under me,
> And that bringeth me forth from my enemies,
> Thou hast also lifted me up on high,
> Above them that rose up against me,
> Thou hast delivered me from the violent man ;
> Therefore I will give thanks unto thee, O Lord, among the heathen,
> And I will sing praises unto thy name.
> He is the tower of safety for his king,
> And showeth mercy to his anointed.
> Unto David and to his seed forevermore.

During this period of his life were written certainly two other psalms, the Seventy-first and the Thirty-seventh, both of which contain allusions to his old age. One of them, the Seventy-first, expresses the trembling trust with which earlier psalms begin, pleads against his enemies and warms into strong confidence at the end.

> In thee, O Lord, do I put my trust,
> Let me never be put to confusion,
> Deliver me in thy righteousness, and cause me to escape.
> Incline thine ear unto me and save me.

---

* See 1 Samuel xxvi. 23, for parallel language.

Be thou my strong habitation, whereunto I may con..nually resort.
Thou hast given commandment to love me,
For thou art my rock and my fortress.
Deliver me, O my God, out of the hands of the wicked ;
Out of the hand of the unrighteous and cruel man,
For thou art my hope, O Lord God,
Thou art my trust from my youth.
By thee have I been holden up from the womb,
Thou art he that took me out of my mother's bowels.
My praise shall be continually of thee.
I am as a wonder unto many,
But thou art my strong refuge,
Let my mouth be filled with thy praise
And with thy honor all the day,
Cast me not off in the time of old age,
Forsake me not when my strength faileth,
For mine enemies speak against me,
And they that lay wait for my soul take counsel together,
Saying : " God hath forsaken him,
Persecute and take him : for there is none to deliver him."
. . . .
O God, thou hast taught me from my youth,
And hitherto have I declared thy wondrous works ;
Now, also, when I am old and grey-headed, O God, forsake me not!
Until I have showed thy strength unto this generation,
And thy power to every one that is to come.
. . . .
Thou who hast showed me great and sore troubles,
Shall quicken me again,
And shalt bring me up again from the depths of the earth.
. . . .
My tongue also shall talk of thy righteousness all the day long.
For they are confounded, for they are brought to shame
That seek my hurt.

The other psalm, the Thirty-seventh, is a psalm of instruction and exhortation against evil-doers, and against the irritation which arises from their apparent success—such a didactic psalm as a wise old man might properly give to a younger generation, and put into their lips as a familiar chant.

   Fret not thyself because of evil-doers,
   Neither be thou envious against the workers of iniquity,
   For they shall soon be cut down like the grass,
   And wither as the green herb.
   Trust in the Lord, and do good ;
   So shalt thou dwell in the land, and verily thou shalt be fed.
   Delight thyself also in the Lord,
   And he shall give thee the desires of thy heart.

Commit thy way unto the Lord ;
Trust also in him, and he shall bring it to pass,
And he shall bring forth thy righteousness as the light,
And thy judgment as the noon-day.
. . . .
For evil-doers shall be cut off,
But those that wait on the Lord,
They shall inherit the earth.
. . . .
The steps of a good man are ordered by the Lord,
And He delighteth in his way.
Though he fall, he shall not be utterly cast down.
For the Lord upholdeth him with his hand.
I have been young, and now am old ;
Yet have I not seen the righteous forsaken,
Nor his seed begging bread.
. . . .
I have seen the wicked in great power,
And spreading himself like a green bay-tree.
Yet he passed away and lo, he was not ;
Yea, I sought him, but he could not be found.
Mark the perfect man, and behold the upright,
For the end of that man is peace, etc.

Fifty-fourth Sunday.

THE CENSUS AND THE PESTILENCE.

LESSON.

2 Samuel xxiv. ; 1 Chronicles xxi. ; xxvii. 23, 24 ; 2 Chronicles iii. 1.

THE whole wide dominion was at length in the benignant dawn of a long and peaceful day. But even in the very dawn, luxury began its natural influence. Vanity, pride, formalism, and a sensuous life were dissipating and degrading the spiritual life of the people. The king himself after all, in his survey of the mighty results in the power, populousness, and wealth of his kingdom, was elated with a personal pride. It was necessary, therefore, that both ruler and people should be chastened, were they to enter healthfully into the greater grandeur of Solomon. God determined to humble, therefore, king and people. This he did by permitting their sin of heart to have its natural growth into outward transgression and outward punishment. Without any due respect to the glory of God, the king entered on a vain-glorious reckoning of his power, and involved his people in it. So that a national census became the open index of a great sin and of its punishment.

According to the stand-point of the writer, the instigation to this sin arose from God or from Satan. In the records of Samuel, it is " the anger of the *Lord* was kindled against *Israel*, and *he moved* David against them," that is, he permitted David to do so.* In the record of Chronicles it is, "And *Satan* stood up against Israel," that is, he was permitted to be the exciting cause, "and provoked David," by operating through his luxury and power to excite his pride.

The census had in itself nothing wrong. Such an enumeration had been more than once made—indeed, ordered by God himself under Moses. There was then, however, a high religious use for it.† David evidently had no religious purpose in his order; no plan for the support of the Sanctuary by collection of atonement-money. There was in some form a willful and worldly scheme at the foundation of it.‡ Joab saw this spirit of the king's order. Whether he looked at it from the worldly side or the spiritual side, he saw no good in it. He esteemed it either impolitic or absolutely bad. And when he said, "No matter how many the people be: the Lord multiply them a hundredfold: why take delight in this thing?" He implies that it was for personal gratification that David was doing it. It was a virtual contempt of the Lord's declaration that he would make his people innumerable.

The king was in no mood to be overruled by Joab. He was too conscious of affluence of power or too set on

---

* "In 1 Chronicles xxi. 1, the statement is, And an adversary (not Satan as in the authorized version, since there is no article prefixed as in Job i. 6, 7, 8, etc.) stood up, etc., just as first Hadad and then Rezan is said to have been an adversary (Satan) to Solomon and to Israel. Hence the text, 2 Samuel xxiv. 1, should be rendered, 'For one moved David against them.'"—*Speaker's Commentary*.

† Read the law in Exodus xxx. 11-16.

‡ "The history of the numbering of the people implies the purpose of some act of despotism, a poll-tax or conscription, such as startled all his older and more experienced counsellors."—*Plumtre*.

the self-exaltation of his mighty power among the nations. Joab was compelled to take his officers and go. The captains of the host went with him through the land; the rulers of the people, in their tribes and cities, no doubt, making up their reports—not half-shekels in the columns, but a mere enumeration of warriors from twenty years old.

Joab and the captains began their circuit straight across the Jordan, mounting to the high lands south of Heshbon, and passing up to Jezer, in which two places they received returns, no doubt, through rulers of hundreds and of thousands, from Reuben and the southern part of Gad. After they had remained there some month or so—for they took about ten months for ten tribes, and the outlying large tribes would, of course, require more time than the small tribes—they went on to Gilead. There they received the statistics from the northern part of Gad.

Where the land of Tahtim-Hōdshi was, no one knows.* As, however, they were on their way to Dan-jaan, we may assume that the region was in the lower part of Manasseh. Joab and his officers cross, therefore, the head-waters of the Yarmuk, taking a wide circuit through Manasseh— visiting probably the outlying garrisons at Tibhath and Damascus. We may suppose that some four months were consumed in this outlying, wide-spread east country. The attention of all the people was directed to the scheme and its progress. From Tahtim-Hōdshi—wherever it was— to Dan-jaan and to Zidon, the census-takers crossed the extreme north limit of the land, and thence took their orderly way southward, passing down the sea-coast to Tyre, estimating the strength of the *northern* Hivites, or of the four Gibeonite cities perhaps as Hivites, gathering the military valuation of the midland tribes, of the old

---

* " This name is a puzzle to all interpreters."

Canaanite lands, and cities now subjugated, and ending in Simeon at Beersheba and Ziklag. The Levites Joab would not number; they were not warriors; they had not been required to pay the half-shekel; they should not be reckoned for vain-glory. The Benjamites, too, he would not reckon; "it was small enough, the proud, little tribe; why count it and compare it?" For, before he had finished—perhaps before he returned on his round to Benjamin—"there fell wrath" on the nation, and the census was really never ended. The sums-total were probably never made up for preservation, except in a rough way; they were never put into the official chronicles. In the rough, round numbers of the two books of Samuel and of Chronicles, there is a difference of many thousands in the enumeration. A rough enumeration—not counting Benjamin—made the warriors of Israel eight hundred thousand, and of Judah five hundred thousand, or one million three hundred thousand in all. Or, taking the other estimate, there were one million one hundred thousand warriors of Israel, and four hundred and seventy thousand warriors of Judah, or one million five hundred and seventy thousand in all.* This showed a population of from five to seven millions for the whole land. Considering all the wars, servitudes, and internal conflicts during the generations, this was a great increase from the six hundred and one thousand warriors and three millions of people under Moses on the plains of Moab. Perhaps it was just this comparison which David wished to make, which constituted his sin. As Moses just before his death made such an enumeration, so he would make an enumeration before his death. There was a reason for *commanding* Moses to do it, for the people under

---

* The standing army of 288,000 (12 courses of 24,000 each) may account in round numbers for this difference; or the tribes of Levi and of Benjamin may have been *estimated* by one writer and excluded by the other.

Joshua would need for their conquest the consciousness of numbers and the demonstration of God's increase since they came from Egypt. There was a reason for *forbidding* David to do it, for the people under his successor would have no conquest to make, and needed protection from the vanity of glory. Moses' enumeration under the command of God, set the nation on a true career. David's enumeration, without consultation with God, was in danger of setting the nation on a false career—of turning their attention from the spiritualities of a future temple, to the low temporalities of common national emulation and display.

Probably it was while the census was in progress that David's conscience smote him. He began to see his real motive. He saw the real tendency. He was transgressing the letter and spirit of the Mosaic law. He was not seeking the real good of his people, nor good for himself, nor the ends which God's goodness seeks, but a trivial gratification indifferent to the good of the people, obtained at great outlay before the people, and regardless of an example which would corrupt all public and private virtue. Enticed by this blandishment of a subtle pride, he might be leading his people upon the hard, high, cruel road of foreign conquest for vain-glory. Some such thoughts as these, we may suppose, began to stir in him, before Joab came to the last tribes. With some superficial consciousness of his sin, David confessed his guilt unto God, praying for forgiveness—a private confession for a sin now public and already publicly corrupting the people—a consciousness which needed to be deepened into a profound contrition for .his Absalom-like sin of his old age. The people, too, have so eagerly committed themselves to these trivial and vain motives—the origin of horrid, ambitious, and cruel wars the world over—that the tendency in them must be thoroughly corrected.

His chosen personal prophet came to the king, therefore. Again on his divan or on his housetop, early in the morning, he received him, ready for his solemn message. There is no need of a parable as when Nathan came. "Three things," said Gad,—himself solemnly impressed with his fearful message—"God instructs me to offer thee : seven years of famine in the land; flight three months before your enemies; three days pestilence; choose thee. I will carry back thy answer." Reduction of numbers, this was involved in either choice. Humiliation of pride, this was involved. The punishment meets exactly the motive and the form of the sin. Reduction by his own choice, by famine, or war, or pestilence—a terrible and humiliating choice !

Probably the pestilence was the best choice for the people, as well as for himself. Better for the nation three days pestilence than seven years of Egyptian famine. Better too, no doubt, for the people, three days pestilence, than the whole land harried by domestic revolution, the foundations of the kingdom moved under the spectacle of the aged king chased by Benjamites, or Ephraimites, or Syrians. How easily the terrors under Absalom might be repeated, the attempt of his son Adonijah would shortly show. David too might hope that mercy would be divinely exercised before the pestilence should spend its force. He knew, too, the mellowing influence of affliction.

At the choice, on the morning, the pestilence began. Seventy thousand died within the three days, throughout all the tribes : that is, from one-seventieth to one-hundredth part of the whole population.* Jerusalem was about to

---

* "It is the most destructive plague recorded as having fallen on the Israelites. In the plague that followed the rebellion of Korab, there died 14,700 persons ; in the one that followed the idolatry of Baalpear, 24,000 persons. The angel, however, that

be destroyed, so great was the anger of God against the people's self-complacent forgetfulness of him. The angel charged with execution stopped outside the eastern wall.

Meanwhile inside the city there was humiliation and grief. King and elders had clothed themselves in sackcloth, and were no doubt offering sacrifices in the tabernacle. David's eyes were opened to see the angel's sword uplifted over the city, and he was greatly afraid.

And now, in the infliction of justice, comes out the merciful far-reaching purposes of God. Out of the depth of his grief, the king cried to Him, " It is I who am guilty. I commanded the enumeration ; why let thy wrath fall on these sheep ? On me, on my house, let the blow fall, not on the people." That day came Gad the prophet, with a message, " Go set up an altar on the threshing-floor of Araunah the Jebusite. There will Jehovah meet thee."

Araunah or Ornan was, it may be, king of Jebus, or some subordinate sheikh of the old Jebusites, who still held his possession outside the city wall. It may be that he had long lived with the people of Judah and Benjamin, who had dwelt for many years with the Jebusites in that part of the city. He, too, had had his eyes opened to the presence and attitude of the angel. His four sons as well as himself, awed at the sight, hid themselves. Perhaps they all had hitherto refused to yield this piece of land.

Soon as they looked out from behind the sheaves, they saw coming king David in person, and his servants, with the form and dignity of an important errand. Araunah goes to meet them with oriental prostration. " Wherefore is my lord the king come to his servant ? " " To stay the

---

smote Sennacherib's army, destroyed 185,000 persons in one night. Diodorus Siculus (quoted by Thenius) relates a plague in the Carthagenian army before Syracuse, which carried off 100,000 men."

plague by the Lord's direction. The Lord directs an altar on this threshing-floor. I will give thee a full price. Sell it to me, and the plague shall be stayed." The purchase

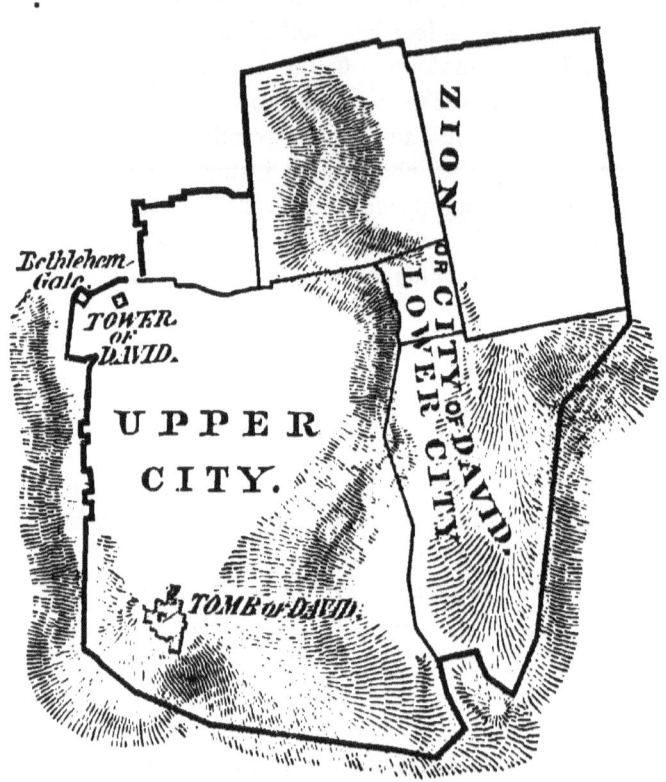

The outside wall of this outline represents the location of the oldest walls, according to opinions based on the recent explorations at Jerusalem. The diagram may be taken as a conjecture in respect to the appearance of the city in David's later life. Compare it with the outline of Jebus on page 208. It will be seen that the two diagrams give different theories in respect to the location of the Upper City, the Lower City, Zion and the City of David.

and sale are conducted in truly oriental form, but with a royal bearing on each side — Araunah offering oxen and threshing instruments, and wheat as they stand, for sacrifice and offering. As the gift of a king to a king, did he nobly offer them, saying: "Jehovah thy God accept thee.". More noble is the lofty reply of the aged king, "Burnt-offerings at such a time as this, should be with cost. Neither land nor oxen will I accept but with a price." Fifty shekels of gold, or six hundred shekels of silver, was his royal price,* freely given. Whether this place be the true Mount Moriah or not, there David, like Abraham of old, built an altar and laid the wood in order, and laid the oxen on the wood, and called upon the Lord for pardon and salvation. There the Lord answered by fire from heaven, and there the angel put up his sword into his sheath.

---

* "The explanation by Bochart may possibly be true, that the fifty shekels here mentioned (2 Samuel xxiv. 24) were gold shekels, each worth twelve silver shekels, so that the fifty gold shekels are equal to the six hundred silver, and that our text should be rendered, 'David bought the threshing-floor and the oxen for money, viz.: fifty shekels,' and that the passage in Chronicles should be rendered, 'David gave to Ornan gold shekels of the value (or weight) of six hundred shekels.'"— *Speaker's Commentary.*

Fifty-fifth Sunday.

PREPARATIONS FOR THE FUTURE TEMPLE.

LESSON.

1 Chronicles xxii., xxiii., xxiv., xxv., xxvi. 1–28, xxviii. 11–21, xxix. 2–5, vi. 31–48;
2 Samuel viii. 8–12.

BROUGHT back now into a healthy state of mind, the king turned his attention from personal glory to the material glory of the Lord. For long years he had been accumulating materials for the temple. From that day—about the fourteenth year of his reign—when he knew that his son would build a temple, he had kept the future building in mind. Many a time, on his distant marches, had his thoughts revolved around its proportions. Many a night, in tent and palace, had his poetic fancy pictured its glories. From Zobah and Syria and Ammon and Moab, from Philistines and Amalekites, had he selected precious stones out of gathered spoils. What Saul himself had dedicated to the throne and kingdom, David had rededicated to the future house. And now, in a vigorous old age, he takes up these accumulations, and the whole order of the service also, to put them into a worthy form for the temple and for future ages. We conceive of him, therefore, as passing in review, one by one, the different parts of the preparation, completing defects, and correcting errors so far that Solomon could enter on the plans early in his reign. Let us take up the different things prepared:

1. Materials. There was an ample preparation and of different kinds.

Stone.—Both the foundation of the building and of the building itself, was to be built of stone. From the two kinds of limestone on which Jerusalem is situated, the blocks were undoubtedly quarried, of all sizes, from the large block measuring nearly a score of cubic yards, to the short-dressed ashlar ; some from the upper bed of the very hard, compact stone—in color from white to reddish brown—which the Arabs now call "mezzeh," and some from the lower bed of soft, white stone — a smoky and dark grey — which they now call "melekah." Special stones of smaller size may have been brought on the backs of camels from the bed at the south-east corner of the Salt Sea, or by float and camel from the mouth of the Arnon opposite Engedi. Sandstone in quite a variety of colors is found in those places.

Marble stones in abundance were procured from Lebanon,[*] or from Arabia, or even from Persia.

We do not read that any *stone* was brought at this time from the ranges back of Tyre. Under the directions of Tyrians, skilled in hewing stone, many of the old Amorites, Hittites, Perizzites, Hivites, and Jebusites[†] were occupied no doubt about Jerusalem during the later days of David, in quarrying the beds, sawing[‡] the blocks, and dressing the courses.

Timber.—The cedars of Lebanon were then, as now,

---

[*] The Hebrew word translated "marble," may mean only "shining stone ;" such as the "Jura limestone" of Lebanon—the same as that out of which the Temple of the Sun at Baalbec is made.

[†] See 1 Kings ix. 20, 21.   [‡] 1 Kings vii. 9.

the noblest trees for grandeur or for timber. "Beams of cedar and rafters of fir"* were the highest style of luxury. The people of Sidon and of Tyre had already found a ready market for this timber at Jerusalem, occasioned probably by David's employment of Hiram on his house. We do not suppose that David ordered the timber hewed, or sawed, or dressed into plates and sills and boards, but that he simply began to make ready the trees themselves in the mountains—to select and mark them and cut some of them, so that there might be no delay when the reign of his successor should begin.

Iron and Brass.—Whence came the iron and the brass which David purposed without weight? The iron was probably either smelted out of the basalt, or was brought out of Assyria, or was the accumulations from long-continued and widely-extended traffic and conquest. The "brass" was not our compound of copper and zinc, but more properly copper or bronze (copper and tin). The ores from which it was smelted were probably found in the tribe of Asher,† or the metals themselves gathered from subjugated cities like Tibhath and Berothai. For sixty years or more confiscated idols, vessels, utensils, weapons, shields, cymbals, curiosities, had been preserved by Samuel, Saul, Abner, Joab, and David, and now made a great store of metal.‡

Silver and Gold.—The growing wealth of the nation could furnish now the generous abundance of silver and gold which David supplied. The Hebrews have always been a money-getting people, fond of ornaments made of

---

* Song of Solomon i. 17.

† Compare Deuteronomy viii. 9, with xxxiii. 25, *margin.*

‡ See xxvi. 27, 28. It was evidently a practice more or less in use to consecrate spoils to religious use. See Numbers xxxi. 50–54.

PREPARATIONS FOR FUTURE TEMPLE. 423

these metals, and able to procure them. A hundred thousand talents of gold, after making every reduction made necessary by changes in the value of the talent or by mistakes in transcribing the Hebrew text, must have amounted to some eighteen millions of dollars; and a million talents of silver must have been equal to about the same amount.*

We shall see also that King David gave also special gold for special use out of his own private treasure. These metals were for temple vessels and utensils. He had had it weighed for each class of articles—gold for candlesticks, lamps, flesh-hooks, bowls, cups, tables of shew-bread, and altars of incense; silver for tables, basins, candlesticks, etc.

Precious Stones.—These were for ornamentation or for symbolization in the priests' dress: onyx-stones and sparkling-stones of various kinds and colors—for example, the onyx and the sard-onyx (cornelian), the amethyst (rose quartz), the agate, the topaz, the carbuncle, the emerald,† and the coral—procured from merchants or dealers from

---

* "It is no doubt true that we do not know the value of the Hebrew talent at this period; and it is therefore just possible that these numbers (xxii. 14) may be sound. But in that case we must suppose an enormous difference between the pre-Babylonian and the post-Babylonian talents—such a difference as is most improbable. Estimated according to the value of the post-Babylonian Hebrew talent, the gold here spoken of would be worth more than one thousand millions of our pounds sterling, while the silver would be worth about four hundred millions. Accumulations to any amount like this are, of course, quite inconceivable under the circumstances, and we must therefore either suppose the talent of David's time to have been little more than one-hundredth part of the later talent, or regard the verse as augmented at least one hundred fold by corruption of the text. Of the two, the latter is certainly the more probable supposition."— *Speaker's Commentary.*

† See xxvi. 20–28. These stones, and others, Josephus describes as belonging to the high-priests' breast-plate. See Ezekiel xxvii. 16.

the East, or handed down as souvenirs and heir-looms for generations. The robes of the kings themselves, like the breast-plate of the priest, were no doubt covered with brilliant gems. Over all these dedicated things, Shelomith had been appointed as keeper and superintendent, with fellow-Levites as assistants.

2. A plan for the temple. Although David was not to build the temple, he was to have the satisfaction of preparing the plan as well as the material for it. Some parts of this plan—the improvements or the amplification of the original form of the tabernacle—were communicated unto him by the spirit of God. The general plan, as an examination of the temple under Solomon shows, was the ground-plan of the tabernacle. Around a holy and most holy place, was a court, or courts. The ancient pattern given in the wilderness furnished the essential general ideas, but, with adornment and enrichment, the new was to surpass the old, as a house surpasses a tent. The building was to take its place as a permanent and mighty educator. It was to stand during the changes of generations and the shock of armies, as the powerful conserver of the people's attachment to holy things.

Observe the things of which David had a pattern revealed to him : a porch, with houses for priests and Levites, no doubt ; treasuries and upper chambers and inner parlors in the porch : the courts outside, with chambers and treasuries, and " treasuries or store-houses for the dedicated things." These court-chambers were, we suppose, the places for the priests in their twenty-four courses, and others were proper rooms for keeping the sacred vessels, or rooms for cleaning the hooks, bowls, cups, basins, etc., not in use in ordinary times. Gold, specially refined, was prepared also for the incense-altar and for the cherubim of the holiest place.

The declaration that " the Lord made me understand

in writing all this by his hand upon me," may mean either that he was divinely guided in studying the Mosaic model, or that he was specially inspired to write out the details of the enlargement.

David's preparation, however, did not stop with the outward material. His plan took in, also, the conception of worship in the temple. The fundamental ideas of the sacrifices were not, of course, to be changed, but the praises and smaller arrangements which surrounded these sacrifices might be set into such proportions as to exalt the sacrificial system itself.

3. The Levites. The Levites over thirty years of age were twenty-four thousand, separated to the sacrificial service, four thousand more for porters and four thousand more for musicians, making thirty-two thousand. Beside these there were six thousand appointed to the judicial and legal offices in the Levitical cities of the land; to give instruction in the law, the service, etc.—a careful and beautiful provision where the printing-press had not yet come. The twenty-four thousand had their regular months of residence at home and their regular time at Jerusalem.* Some of the Levites were between twenty and thirty years of age.† They also were attendants on the priests in the preparation of the chambers and courts, in preparing the bread, flour, cakes, etc., in praising and sacrificing, in keeping the appointments for Sabbaths, moons and feasts, and in general charge of the holy house. David had now had twenty-five years experience of the wants of an orderly and elaborate service, and could enter into the spirit of perfecting every arrangement; and as many of the Levites no longer had the work of "carrying," new duties were devised.

The Levites were divided, as from the beginning, ac-

---

* See Luke i, 5, 8, 9, 39, 40, 65. † xxiii. 27-32.

cording to the patriarch Levi's sons, into Geshonites, Kohathites and Merarites. Aaron and his descendants, who only were priests, were in the Kohathite line. In other departments of Levitical service, such as singing, instrumental music and the work of the porters, the Kohathites were eminent. They took their places, Kohathites and all—fathers and younger brethren, in their orderly turn of the extensive service, by lot. A few of them were the king's scribes—copyists, recorders, historians, private secretary, registrar of the courses and lots, etc. In their home cities, they had no doubt charge of manuscript copies of the law—they copied the rolls—they stood to the people in the place of numerous books and unfolded the meaning of the sacred writings.

Porters.—The four thousand porters must also have been divided into their regular courses. Twenty-four courses would give about one hundred and sixty-six to each course. Probably the distribution was such that many more than a single course would be in attendance at the great feasts. The gates were assigned to keepers by lot, six each day to the east gates, four to the north, four to the south, "towards Asuppim two and two," and at Parbar westward, four at the causeway and two at Parbar. Other porters brought the wood, carried out the skins and offal, the ashes, etc., transported the utensils, brought in the water, received first-fruits, stored the provisions which were the perquisites of the sacred office—all in order.

Musicians.—From the four thousand musicians, were no doubt taken freely as many as were desired for grand occasions. But there were two hundred and eighty-eight who were select, skilful and specially instructed. Over these were Asaph of the Gershonite line, Ethan or Jeduthun of the Merarites and Heman of the Kohathites. This select choir, composed of teachers and scholars, was divided into twenty-four companies or sub-choirs of twelve each, who also took their turns by lot and who probably had some flexible mode by which they assisted each other in their important service. Heman is called the King's Seer "in the matters of God to lift up the horn." He was probably the king's counsellor in musical matters, for he was first of the three leaders, with Asaph on the right hand and Ethan on his left. (vi. 33, 39, 44.) He is called pre-eminently "the singer" or "the musician." An inspiration to the choirs and choruses, he must have been, with his fourteen sons and three daughters around him, with their mature and young voices, trained by their father, and accompanied by cymbals, psalteries, harps and the grand chorus!

4. The Priests. Moses' position was special. He was a lawgiver, who was a priest in an exalted sense, but not a formal and ceremonial high-priest. Aaron and his descendants only were priests. Of Aaron's four sons, two were stricken with death. The whole priesthood therefore descended from Eleazar and Ithamar. The *high* priesthood continued in the house of Eleazar—through Phinehas—until Eli, who belonged to Ithamar's line. The high-priesthood continued then in Ithamar's line through David's life, until it was restored to the Eleazar line by the execution of the sentence on Eli's house, when the office was restored to Eleazar's house in the person of Zadok. Abiathar and Zadok were the chief of the priests. Abiathar, who fled from Nob when his father was slain, and who came bringing the ephod to David, continued the fast friend of David, throughout all his wanderings. Zadok, of the Eleazar line, who had adhered to Saul during David's wandering, but who came over to David at Hebron with twenty-two captains of his princely house, had been faithful to David even at Jerusalem under Absalom, was the first to bring the king back, and was the highest in the Eleazar line and ruler over all the "Aaronites."

Under these two leaders, the priests were divided into

twenty-four courses, but the Eleazar side had sixteen and the Ithamar side only eight. The twenty-four courses of Levites were no doubt intended to match these twenty-four courses of priests, as the twenty-four courses of singers and musicians were intended to match both. But while the courses of the Levites were distributed for residence and for instruction into all the tribes, the courses of the priests for residence were distributed only in three tribes. They had thirteen cities, eight of which were in the hill-country of Judah, and four in Benjamin. They were therefore all near at hand to the sanctuary for their labors for any occasion of consequence. The period of their service too was probably shorter than that of the Levites. Probably each course served only for one week "coming in on the Sabbath and going out on the Sabbath." (2 Chronicles xxiii. 8.) Their work was more difficult and more laborious than that of the Levites. "Assisting the high-priest, they were to watch over the fire on the altar of burnt-offering and to keep it burning evermore both by day and night, to feed the golden lamps outside the vail with oil, to offer the morning and evening sacrifices, each accompanied with a meat-offering and drink-offering at the door of the tabernacle. These were the fixed, invariable duties, but their chief function was that of being always at hand to do the priest's office for any guilty or penitent or rejoicing Israelite. The worshiper might come at any time, "a rich man with a bullock, a poor man with a pigeon, a mother, a husband, a leper, a nazarite." Any priest might be present at any time to offer assistance, if he did not interfere with those serving in the regular place. During the twenty-three weeks (nearly six months) during which they were absent, or during the shorter interval of absence when they were called up to the great feasts, they were occupied, we suppose, in teaching the law, in prophetic labors, at schools of the prophets, as judicial advisers, as judges of appeal, as special referees in special cases.

All these arrangements had been growing, no doubt, into an order, during David's life, but now he sought to make the system complete, and adjusted them to the proprieties and the grandeur of that coming reign which was to be "rest" and "peace and quietness."

Fifty-sixth Sunday.

ADONIJAH'S CONSPIRACY.

LESSON.

1 Kings i.; 1 Chronicles xxix. 27.

KING DAVID was now on the eve of his seventieth year. It may be that he had already entered it. It was not a very advanced age. Moses died at one hundred and twenty; Joshua at one hundred and ten; Samuel probably at upwards of eighty; Joab, hardly younger than David, outlived him. But the rough wear of military life, the marvellous energy and strain of his body, the family cares and afflictions, the public cares and civil commotions, had at length exhausted his extraordinary vigor. The ruddy boy was now an old man, his mind clear, but not strong, yet capable of resolute action, and his body wrinkled and withered and cold. Quite in accordance with the usages of polygamy, and the modern treatment of physicians in the East, David's physicians recommended that a young concubine be added to the royal harem, who should nurse the king, and prolong his valuable life by imparting her health and warmth to his enfeebled system.*
After the Oriental manner, as Esther was sought for King

---

* The expedient recommended by David's physicians is the regimen prescribed in similar cases still in the East, particularly among the Arab population, not simply to give heat, but " to cherish," as they are aware that the inhalation of young breath will give new life and vigor to the worn-out frame. The fact of

Ahasuerus, the country was explored for the fairest damsel. She was found at Shunem, where the Philistines encamped before Saul's last battle, and was probably already known for her beauty as Abishag the Shunamite.

Taking advantage of the king's feeble and bed-ridden condition, Adonijah began to plan for himself. He was the oldest surviving son—Amnon having been slain by Absalom, Chileab, Abigail's son, having died, as we suppose, and Absalom having met his miserable fate. No law of succession has as yet been established in the Hebrew kingdom. It was well understood that Jehovah nominated the successor, and whether the law of the first-born would be adopted had not been made known. Neither the pious Jonathan nor his surviving brother Ish-bosheth was permitted to succeed Saul. Still, as the succession in David's family had been divinely approved, Adonijah and his abettors might reason that unless there is direction to the contrary, the ordinary family law of birthright is to be assumed.*

---

the health of the young and healthier person being, as it were, stolen to support that of the more aged and sickly, is well established among the medical faculty. And hence the prescription for the aged king was made in a hygeian point of view for the prolongation of his valuable life, and not merely for the comfort to be derived from the natural warmth imparted to his withered frame."—*Dr. Jamieson.*

* "Side by side with what may be called the natural right of hereditary succession, there existed, especially in the East, a right, if not of absolutely designating a successor, yet at any rate of choosing one among several sons. Aligaltes designated Croesus ; Cyrus designated Cambyses, and Darius designated Xerxes. Herodotus even calls it 'a law of the Persians' that the king should always *appoint* a successor before leading out an expedition. A still more obsolete right of nomination was exercised by some of the Roman emperors, and occasionally by the caliphs."—*Speaker's Commentary.*

The promise to David that a son should build the temple, seemed to signify a son that *was to be.* But this Adonijah might construe to mean not a son to be born, but a son to arise.

Adonijah was at least thirty-three years old, for he was one of the six sons born in Hebron; more likely he was thirty-five or thirty-six years old, while Solomon could hardly have been more than twenty years of age. Adonijah was born shortly after Absalom, was beautiful, like his beautiful brother; like him had been indulged by a busy and lenient father, and by his wilfulness and self-ambition was as little fit to reign. He was suspicious of his own title to the succession, otherwise he would have invited Solomon to his feast. Very likely he cared little for the legal and divine conditions, but determined to be king by his own wisdom and will.

Taking advantage, therefore, of the king's retirement and feebleness, he laid his plan. He gained Joab, whose spirit naturally agreed with the warlike and controllable Adonijah rather than with the calm and peaceable and resolute Solomon. Abiathar the priest, too, was ready to go with him, perhaps the more easily persuaded because Adonijah courted him, while under David's arrangement the line of Eleazar had more place as priests. With Joab and Abiathar, Adonijah gained enough of the captains and soldiers and of the priests to make a fair show. Like Absalom, he arrayed a retinue of state, composed of chariots and horsemen, and fifty men to run before him—a personal retinue which might be esteemed becoming a prince. The next thing was to plan an *occasion* at which he could bring over a considerable body of the people, and he could be proclaimed with acclamation. Adonijah no doubt hoped for the assent or at least the acquiescence of the king. His father would not deny him; and he estimated his father's disposition so well that he came quite near succeeding. As the plan was to circumvent rather than to resist the king, there was no need of placing the occasion at a distance, as Absalom did at Hebron. A feast, therefore, was contrived at En-rogel, just below the city, within a half-mile of the walls, and within a mile of the gate. Thither, like Absalom, when he invited Amnon to the sheep-shearing, he invited his brothers, the king's sons; but he managed to evade Solomon in the invitation. His object was to give the festival the royal approval in the eyes of the people, and to reduce them into an enthusiasm for a new proclamation. There at the stone of Zoheleth —a stone by some supposed to have been used as a stone on which fullers or washerwomen pressed out the water after washing, at the well En-rogel—a place of resort near the city*—the feast was spread—a splendid open-air entertainment, in the midst of verdure, water, and probably shade, the fat cattle slain on the spot, with oxen and sheep in princely munificence for the multitude. The abundant provision shows that Adonijah had in his eye a surrounding multitude of people.

Zadok and Nathan had already taken the alarm. They and the loyal captain of the king's body-guard, Benaiah, were too loyal to be invited. Shimei and Rei (perhaps the same as Raddai), who have been supposed to be David's brothers, and other mighty men, were either so near to David's person, or so well reputed for their attachment, that they were passed by.

Nathan was the first to move in counter-check. He knew that the king's purpose was that Solomon should be

---

* "E. G. Shultz supposes the stone or rock of Zoheleth to be the steep, rocky corner of the southern slope of the valley of Hinnom, which casts so deep a shade. This neighborhood is still a place of recreation for the inhabitants of Jerusalem."— *Keil.*

his successor. He understood also the divine purpose. He knew too that David had communicated this purpose to Bathsheba, and had solemnly sworn to her that her son should take the throne. He further perceived that Adonijah's adventure, though apparently so open, was conducted in entire secrecy so far as the king was concerned. He saw therefore that, if Adonijah should succeed, through the aged king's reluctance to transfer the crown, or through his seclusion from outside activities, even if David's life was spared, Solomon would be looked upon as a dangerous claimant on the throne. Oriental jealousy would put in peril his life and the life of his mother, if the very first act of his reign would not be to destroy all the seed royal. Moved, therefore, either by divine impulse, or by his own wisdom under divine guidance, he hastens to the court. He sets before Bathsheba the perils of the hour; that Adonijah is stealthily taking the throne; that her son's life and her own are in danger; that something must be done to arouse the king and compel him to declare publicly the succession. He has a plan. She shall go in and remind the king of his solemn oath, and show him that Adonijah is attempting to outwit Solomon and the king too. He will come in and confirm her representation; and thus, without too sudden excitement, they will arouse him to what is transpiring and to action. She shall first move him by affection, and then he will present the reasons of State.

And now we have a picturesque oriental scene. We must represent to our minds the king's palace, enlarged on this side and on that by branching apartments, as his family and his court have increased, until the palace and its adjacent and connected buildings spread widely over the south-western hill of Jerusalem. In the king's own edifice, in an upper room connected with the inner court and its connections, reclines the aged king upon the ample divan, the keen eye still glittering from the sunken socket, the nervous life still resolute and decisive, but the body bearing marks of age and feebleness. Supported by mattresses and cushions in his corner, and covered with robes and shawls, the beautiful Abishai attends upon his wants; wall and ceiling are rich with hangings, the floor with brilliant rugs, the divans with embroidery, the special places with rarities, taken as spoils or presented as gifts. Porters and ushers attend. Bathsheba enters, still bearing the traces of her early beauty, and prostrates herself before her lord. At his word, she rises, and at his demand for her wish, speaks as a woman confident of her royal lord's constancy to his purpose. She tells him of his oath; she carries his mind by a single touch back to the days of God's promise to him. She declares to him that Adonijah, at En-rogel, where he may be seen almost from the palace top, is declaring himself king. He has a great feast; the people are there; the king's sons have been invited; Joab and Abiathar are there; Solomon is *not* invited, and all the people are in expectation of an announcement of the succession from the king. She points out to him, that if Adonijah succeeds by this occasion, without protest from the king, when he sleeps with his fathers, she, herself and her son, if they put forth the king's purpose, will be reckoned traitors to the crown.

During her speech, the attendant announces: "*Nathan the Prophet.*" And as she finishes and withdraws with queenly obeisance, the prophet enters. Powerful memories enter with him; for with this wise and godly man on the house-top, David conferred, when he thought of building Jehovah's house, and from him heard the response, "The Lord will build *thee* a house!" "Not thou, but thy son *to be*, shall build the Lord's palace." As that grave man in his plain robes bowed before him, the king saw one who best knew the purposes of God with respect to

Bathsheba and the king's pledges to her. With what power of godliness and of sincere affection, then, did this younger man — still hardly beyond his prime — say to him: " My Lord, O king, *hast* thou declared *Adonijah* king ?" The lips which once uttered the parable of the ewe-lamb, then set before the king, Adonijah's feast, the increasing multitude, the guests invited, that the army and the priesthood are powerfully represented, and that in the midst of the festivity, the people are already beginning to hail Adonijah, king. *But*, he says, the Lord's prophet, the priest of the older line, the captain of the body-guard, the prince-royal, they have not invited. Has the king *changed his purpose* and kept it from his counsellors?

King David was not only quick to see, but to know what to do. " Call me Bathsheba," he directs. Nathan retires and she enters. With a royal gesture, he forbids her obeisance and she *stands*. What power and majesty and affection are there in his words to her who, of all others, had known the depth of his domestic and civil troubles, when he said to her: " As Jehovah liveth, who hath *redeemed my soul out of all distress*, as I swore unto thee by Jehovah, God of Israel, that thy son Solomon shall take my throne, so shall it be THIS VERY DAY." *Then* she bowed in thanks and reverence, with stately salutation of blessing, low before him.*

Even before she goes, the king gives order for Zadok and Nathan and Benaiah. They attend. His order is, " Take the royal body-guard; take the royal mule ;† take

---

* " In the Assyrian sculptures, ambassadors are represented with their faces actually touching the earth before the feet of the monarch."—*Speaker's Commentary.*

† " The Rabbins tell us that it was death to ride on the king's mule without his permission."—*Speaker's Commentary.*

the sacred oil. Go down to Gihon ; put Solomon on the mule ; anoint him ; blow the trumpet ; proclaim Solomon king ; put yourselves under his authority, and conduct him to the throne. See that it is done for *him whom I have appointed* king over Israel and over Judah." "*Amen*," said the soldier responding for the three. "Jehovah God of our king, say Amen also." "Jehovah be with Solomon as he hath been with thee, and make his throne greater than thy throne."

Gihon was the place designated. It was probably on the west side of the city near the head of the valley of Hinnom.* Adonijah was at the foot of this valley, from a mile to a mile and a half away. The two places were thoroughly concealed from each other by the bend of the valley and its high, rocky sides. Gihon was quite near the gate—the Bethlehem gate.

The departure of the Cherethites and Pelethites with the king's mule, and with Solomon the prince, with Zadok and Nathan, with priests and Levites, to this place, at a time when it was known that Adonijah was holding a feast below at En-rogel, and the news from the king, which they now took little pains to conceal, of course created commotion in the city. No sooner were they fairly at the place, than the people thronged out the gates. Then came the ceremony. Solomon was placed on the king's mule. A horn of sacred oil out of the tabernacle was produced by Zadok. A statement of the desire and the decree of David was made ; the solemn anointment, with solemn words, was performed by the priests ; the trumpets were blown ; the hills rang ; and the people, led by the counsellors, shouted, "God save King Solomon !" Immediately the royal mule and royal rider were turned towards the city, the Levites struck up their flutes and

---

* See map on p. 208.

pipes, and the increasing multitude entered the Bethlehem gate with a chorus of acclamation which drew forth the whole population, and swelled the rejoicing as they went home to the palace.

A blast of the trumpet down the valley struck Joab's ear, alert to hear what would happen when Adonijah's attempt became known. "What is the noise in the city!" is his startled exclamation. Abiathar's son from the city soon tells the story, and adds that King David was not content till Solomon was publicly honored on his throne, and from his divan had given his solemn, patriarchal blessing of the whole transaction, as Solomon returned to him.

Consternation struck the stoutest man at En-rogel. Every one was a traitor caught at that assembly; if Solomon prove like many eastern monarchs, his end was come. Joab and Abiathar fled, perhaps to their homes in the city, perhaps to their homes in the tribes. Adonijah fled to the altar on the threshing-floor of Araunah. Solomon did not pursue him, but a guilty conscience. Word came to Solomon that Adonijah did not defy him, but feared him; he asked his oath that he should not be slain. Solomon's answer is the first sign of his wise mind, revealing neither a weak magnanimity in time of elation, nor a rigid exaction of justice. "If he will show himself a loyal man, not a hair shall fall; but if he attempt treason, let him know that he shall die." A pledge which the wise Solomon executed to the letter, in the death of Adonijah afterwards. With this message, Solomon's officers brought him to the king, and when he had made proper ceremonious acknowledgment of his royalty, the young king said, "Go now to thine house."

Fifty-seventh Sunday.

JEHOVAH'S CHOICE.

LESSON.
1 Chronicles xxiii. 1-2, xxviii. 1-2, xxix. 22 ; Psalm cxlv.

THE sudden inauguration of Solomon little comported with the aged king's conception of the dignity due such an occasion. Solomon had only been made king in Jerusalem, and it was not only fitting, but essential, that the nation should participate and consent in the compact. There were grave matters, also, entrusted to the future reign, which should be well advanced by public solemnities before the nation. Solomon was a young man to be king over such a people—ten years younger than David when he began at Hebron. The kingdom needed to be compacted about him before the aged monarch should sleep.

The king therefore determined on a grand national occasion in which God and his house should be honored, and in which Solomon should be crowned in solemnities more noble than the kingdom itself. The two things should be joined; and Jehovah's chosen ruler should be inferior to the loftier glory of Jehovah's holy worship in all the earth.

The royal decree was sent. The posts carried it in sealed letters, or special messengers announced the orders east and west and south and north to Eleazar in Reuben, to Iddo in Manasseh east, and Joel in Manasseh west, to Ishmaiah and Jerimōth in Zebulun and Naphtali, to

Omri and Hoshea in Issachar and Ephraim, to Shephatiah in Simeon, and to David's venerable mother, Elihu, in Judah. Hashabiah on the west side, and Jerijah on the east side, received orders for the special attendance of Levites. The news of the counter-plot against Adonijah at Jerusalem, and of the great assembly to inaugurate the new reign, would everywhere create excitement and interest. The twelve princes and the elders of their cities, the twelve captains and their regiments, or chosen companies out of their regiments, the treasurers and stewards over storehouses and tillage and orchards and flocks, the officers of special note, the military heroes and celebrities, were all invited. The people flocked in throngs. Caravans and irregular droves of oxen, sheep and lambs, with shouting drivers and calling shepherds blocked here and there the narrow paths. Every road of mountain and valley, every greeting of friends, every company and cavalcade were filled with talk of the old king's grand preparations for the future house, of the accumulations to be seen at Jerusalem, of the wisdom and the appearance of the young king, of Adonijah's defeat, of Joab and Abiathar's degradation, and their absence from the grand occasion, and of the wealth and power of the marvellous old king. King David had desired, too, that they come with gifts to offer, as in the days of building the tabernacle in the wilderness, for this more glorious house. Treasures of gold and of precious stones were in trusty hands in all tribal companies, for the golden dawn not only filled the eyes but commanded the possessions of the nation. Every room of every house in Jerusalem was full; every house-top spread with booths and tents; every available space in every street filled with temporary lodges; every mountain round about Jerusalem spread with camps, especially over against Araunah's threshing-floor, where stood the new altar and the smoking, perpetual fire.

Somewhere near the palace on Zion was the first place of assembly when the day arrived. But as the grand convocation had even more respect to the Holy House than to the new Ruler, it would be properly appointed outside the walls on the threshing-floor purchased from Araunah. Held there, with materials lying on the hill and in the valleys below, the words of David have great power.

We can imagine the scene, as the hour arrives. Let us locate it at the threshing-floor. The priests have offered the customary sacrifices at the tabernacle on Zion, multiplied in number from early dawn, presented by those who embrace the opportunity for themselves and to hallow the day. They sanctify also the day and the place, by unusual sacrifice on the altar of the threshing-floor, for we must suppose that the daily burnt-offering had been observed at that place since the time when David said: "This is the house of Jehovah, God of Israel; and *this* is the *altar* of the *burnt-offering* for Israel." * The people are early at the place. The Levites increase in number as their special duties at the tabernacle successively end. The brilliant turbans and flashing robes of princes and elders of Ephraim and Judah outnumber the rulers of less powerful tribes. Grey-beards mingle with flowing black, and grave old faces with the ruddy and robust. Spears flash in the sun, and swords and scabbards clink against mail of armor, or stand stifly out, stuck through the broad, sash-like girdle. Singers and musicians, with scrolls of parchment—some well-worn copies of familiar psalms, and one at least a clean and new " Psalm for Solomon "—and harps and cymbals in singers' robes take their appointed places among the Levites; and adventurous women not a few stand on the margin of the multitude. The cavalcade from the palace and tabernacle approaches. The Cherethites

---

* 1 Chronicles xxii. 1.

and Pelethites clear the way through the streets, and outward beyond the entrance to the main city.* The porters of the Levites keep clear a wider space from Araunah's hill westward to the intervening valley. As the head of the column dips into the little valley, the famous captains and mighty men appear: Adina, the Eznite; Shimmah, the Harodite; Abishai, Joab's brother; Adina, the Reubenite, with the remnant of his thirty; Ira, from Tekoa below Bethlehem; Hesrai, from Carmel below Hebron; one or two survivors of the eleven lion-like, roe-like Gadites, who joined David forty years before; and Elhanan of Bethlehem, all veterans of the companies,† and chosen captains with them. The full company of musicians appears next, their voices swelling into a fuller chant, as their harps and cymbals issue from the wall—it may be "damsels playing with timbrels"‡ among them— the full chorus of two hundred and eighty-eight led by Heman, Asaph, and Jeduthun. sending upwards as the powerful volume of their song:

> For who is God save Jehovah,
> And who is a rock save our God?
> It is God that girded me with strength,
> And made my way perfect.
> . . . .
> Thou gavest me the shield of thy salvation,
> And thy right hand held me up,
> And thy gentleness made me great.
> Thou didst make large my steps under me
> So that my feet did not slip.
> I pursued my enemies and overtook them,
> Nor did I turn back till I consumed them.

---

* See maps on pages 208 and 418.

† General lists of David's valiant men are given in 2 Samuel xxiii., 1 Chronicles xi. and xxvii. Some of these valiants, like Abishai and Benaiah, we know were living at this time, and it is fair to suppose that some such number survived as those above described.

‡ Psalm lxviii. 25.

JEHOVAH'S CHOICE. 443

For thou didst gird me with strength for the battle,
Thou didst cause to bow, those that rose up against me.
. . . .
He is a tower of salvation for his king,
And showeth mercy to his anointed,
To David and to his seed for evermore.
—*From Psalm* xviii. *and* 2 *Samuel* xxii.

Next comes the royal mule, covered with brilliant mats and on him the Prince Royal already anointed, as David and Saul were first anointed by private direction, who is to be more solemnly anointed to-day, his splendid turban and broad girdle embroidered in colors by royal fingers, his robes dignifying his youthful person, his face a picture of beauty sobered by wisdom, or of wisdom enriched by the parental graces of David and Bathsheba. The Royal King keeps company next behind, his eye kindling anew, his face filled with majesty and spiritual thought, his lordly will bearing erect his feeble body amid its adornments, as his faithful mule bears him gently on. On the one side the army is represented by Benaiah in spear and corselet: on the other side, the priesthood by Nathan, whose prophecy first revealed the house royal and the house spiritual. The royal princes come next. Out of David's fifteen sons, eight or ten we may suppose alive and present. Shephatiah and Ithream born in Hebron thirty-three years ago; Shimea, Shobal and Nathan, own brothers to Solomon, and the younger princes equal or inferior in age to their brother the king. Next come the officers of the court—Adoram the Chief Treasurer, Jehoshaphat the Recorder, Sheva the Scribe, and Ira the Jairite, a chief ruler, Jonathan, David's uncle, the counsellor, and Jehiel, instructor of the king's sons. Following all, were honorable citizens, and on every side, the multitude shouting at times, and waving their hands and greeting each other and the procession with every sign of joy.

The head of the procession has already mounted the little hill and passed along its side within the multitude, outside the altar and the priests. The youthful king dismounts at the bounds set by the Levites; his aged father, supported by Nathan and Hushai or Benaiah, advances with the son towards the altar. The body-guard at the head of the procession have returned on the opposite of the grounds, and the singers are at their place over against the altar. Sacrifices have already been offered we must believe in the tabernacle, by direction of the king, for himself and family, but here they are renewed. Attendants bring in the oxen and rams and lambs—some for burnt-offerings and some for peace-offerings—the distinctive sin-offering being offered before the vail of the tabernacle as a peculiarly holy sacrifice of atonement—as expressions of expiation, of self-dedication unto God, and of thanksgiving to Him. The aged monarch and the young lay their hands on the heads of the victims as they are delivered to the Levites, and for themselves and the royal house, signify their consecration to Jehovah, God of their fathers and of the nation. The Levites slaughter the animals and deliver them to the priests. The meat-offerings, or rather *meal*-offerings, of flour, oil and wine, accompany them, as they are variously offered on the great altar and on the subordinate altars erected for the occasion. As the flames and smoke ascend, the great choruses of the singers strike in with solemn chants, such as these:

> The earth is the Lord's, and the fulness thereof;
> The world and they that dwell therein.
> For he hath founded it on the seas,
> And established it on the floods.
> Who shall ascend into the hill of the Lórd?
> Or who shall stand in this holy place? etc. —*Psalm* xxiv.

> Make a joyful noise unto God, all ye lands:
> Sing forth the honor of his name;
> Make his praise glorious.
> Say unto God, How terrible art thou in thy works!
> Through the greatness of thy power.

JEHOVAH'S CHOICE.

Shall thine enemies submit themselves unto thee.
All the earth shall worship thee ; and shall sing unto thee ;
They shall sing unto thy name, etc.   —*Psalm* lxvi.

I will extol thee, my God, O king ;
And I will bless thy name for ever and ever.
Every day will I bless thee ;
And I will praise thy name for ever and ever.
Great is the Lord, and greatly to be praised ;
And his greatness is unsearchable.
One generation shall praise thy works to another,
And shall declare thy mighty acts.
I will speak of the glorious honor of thy majesty,
And of thy wondrous works.
And men shall speak of the might of thy terrible acts ;
And I will declare thy greatness.
. . . .
All thy works shall praise thee, O Lord ;
And thy saints shall bless thee.
They shall speak of the glory of thy kingdom,
And talk of thy power ;
To make known to the sons of men his mighty deeds,
And the glorious majesty of his kingdom.
Thy kingdom is an everlasting kingdom,
And thy dominion endureth throughout all generations, etc.
   —*Psalm* cxlv.

When the sacrifice was ended, during the latter part or the principal part of which, the enfeebled king has been seated on a divan of state, the king stood up upon his feet and made his address, every word and gesture in which must have made a profound impression upon the listening thousands as the wise, old warrior, king and psalmist, with the simplicity of a little child graciously says, "*Hear me, my brethren and my people.*"

Fifty-eighth Sunday.

JEHOVAH'S HOUSE AND JEHOVAH'S BUILDER.

LESSON.

1 Chronicles xxviii. 2-21 ; xxix. ; Psalm lxxii.

OBSERVE now the principal parts of his address, doubly impressive, if uttered on the hill of Araunah, with the temple-materials collected around him.

THE HOUSE OF GOD AND ITS BUILDER.

I. The first thing is not his successor; but the house of God. He rehearses the purpose of his early reign, to transfer the ark from curtains to a permanent house: the divine approval of the plan, but the divine refusal that himself shall do the work. (Verses 2 and 3.)

II. God's sovereign choice in the kingship is to be honored. Judah he has made chief tribe; Jesse's house first of Judah; and David before all the sons of Jesse. Such, says the king, was God's wish in respect to myself. So also out of my many sons, *Jehovah* hath chosen Solomon, and his wish is also my sovereign decree. He chose me for a man of war to subdue the nations: so his purpose in him whose name is Peace, is that he should build His Temple of Worship. (Verses 4-6.)

III. His pledges and covenant of good, however, are

dependent on your loyalty to God and to each other. Before the congregation of the kingdom and in the presence of our God, I charge upon you the people, the commands of Jehovah, with respect to Him and His kingdom; and you, my son, with a perfect heart and willing mind, serve the God of thy fathers. Thou canst not deceive him in the thoughts of thy mind—if you seek him, he will be found; but though thou art the chosen seed, if thou forsakest him, he will cast thee off for ever. Abide both of you in this covenant with Jehovah; and this good land shall be your children's for ever, and the throne will be for thy sons to all generations. (Verses 7–10.)

IV. This house of God is to be thy great work, the house which shall be Jehovah's sanctuary, the construction of which is now delivered to thy wisdom and thy care. Then came the delivery to young Solomon as he stood forth, the plans of the future temple—in all its apartments within and without—the carefully prepared orders too for the courses of the Levites and priests, including the porters and singers, carefully engrossed by his private scribes, one or more of whom were ready with them at hand. Also at the king's bidding they produced also the schedule of the gold, with the things designated to which the gold was to be applied, and of silver, with the things to which the silver was to be applied, with the amount by weight in tables. These things, said the king, which are for the house of God, in written descriptions also, Jehovah hath made fully known to me, and the construction he hath delivered to you. Jehovah will not fail thee nor forsake thee, until thou dost finish the house of Jehovah. Have courage and be undaunted, for it is the God who has been with my eventful life, who will be with thee in the time of peace. He will supply thee wisdom. The courses of the priests and Levites will assist thee to complete the service. Willing men, skilled for their work, will be ready for workmanship.

Princes and people will be ready at thy command. (Verses 10–21.)

V. He appeals to the people for their assistance. The work to be done is very great, a palace for Jehovah, not for Solomon. And he, whom only of my sons, God hath called younger than myself to the throne, and on whom God has put this burden, is tender. Therefore, have I, as your king, made all this preparation. But besides the public preparation, for the love which I bear, as a person, to the house of God, from my private substance do I contribute of the pure gold of Ophir, three thousand talents and seven thousand talents of silver to overlay the walls and for the refined work of the artificers. And you have not appeared from your tribes empty before the Lord! Who then of you is willing to consecrate his substance and service unto the Lord? (xxix. 1–5.)

Forthwith, amid the silence, the fathers and princes of the tribes came forward, one by one, as they signified their gifts, placing the mat once under Jehiel, the special treasurer's hand, or pledging their presentation before the needed time.—Zebadiah, the son of Asahel, or Ira from Tekoa, or the aged Eliab, whom Samuel first thought to be the king, for the tribe of Judah among the first, and Jaasiel, Abner's son, for the tribe of Benjamin not the last. The substance of the pledges and of the contributions according to the present Hebrew and English text, amounted to:

	Talents.	Drams.	Equal to.
Gold...	5,000	10,000	$90,053,000
Silver..	10,000	00,000	18,000,000
Brass...	18,000	00,000	
Iron...	100,000	00,000	

a sum total too magnificent!*

---

* The talent of gold is reckoned by Keil as equal to $18,000, and the talent of silver at $1,800. The "Speaker's Commen-

JEHOVAH'S HOUSE AND ITS BUILDER.

Precious stones, too, were offered from those whose traffic with the east and south had procured them or who inherited them as legacies in the family. Then burst forth new expressions of joy, which could only be expressed by songs of praise—psalms—at a signal from the chief musician, and in which even David joined :

> O sing unto the Lord a new song,
> Sing unto the Lord, all the earth, etc.
> —*From Psalm* xcvi.
>
> Arise, O Jehovah, into thy rest,
> Thou and the Ark of thy Strength.
> Let thy priests be clothed with righteousness,
> And thy saints with joy.
> For thy servant David's sake,
> Turn not away the face of thine Anointed.
>
> Jehovah hath sworn in truth unto David,
> He will not turn from it.
> Of the fruit of thy body will I set upon thy throne,
> If *thy* children will keep my covenant
> And my testimony that I shall teach them,
> *Their* children shall also sit upon thy throne for evermore.
>
> For Jehovah hath chosen Zion,
> He hath desired it for his habitation.
> This is my rest for ever : here will I dwell ; for I have desired it.
> I will abundantly bless her provision,
> I will satisfy her poor with bread ;
> I will also clothe her priests with salvation,
> And her saints shall shout aloud for joy.

---

tary" says : " The word here translated dram is regarded by most critics as the Hebrew equivalent of the Persian daric or ordinary gold coin worth twenty-two shillings of our (English) money." This would make a total of over $108,000,000 for the silver and gold for 7,000,000 of people, or over $15 for each person, which is possible. The cost of our late war in the United States was over $2,300,000,000, and during the past ten years, over $700,000,000 of it had been actually paid by 40,000,000 of people. The receipts reported in 1873 and 1874 from internal revenue in the United States were $116,100,000, or $108,000,000 each year. This was the smaller part of the United States' tax, the whole of which is still much smaller than the additional State and county and town taxes.

> There will I make the horn of David to bud,
> I have ordained a lamp for mine Anointed,
> His enemies will I clothe with shame;
> But upon himself shall his crown flourish.
> —*From Psalm* cxxxii.

At the end of the psalm or psalms, or other expressions of joy, the king in all his venerable dignity and simple piety, stands forth in the attitude of prayer—in a sublime and simple prayer of blessing and praise to God — in which the principal thoughts are :

Ascriptions of Royal Attributes unto God, as King of Israel, and as universal and eternal King. (Verses 10, 11.)

Recognition of God as the source of all individual riches and honor and exaltation. (Verse 12.)

Thanksgiving and praise. (Verse 13.)

Expression of the humble dependence and insignificance of both earthly king and people. (Verses 14, 15.)

Consecration of substance to God's house only as God's own possession. (Verse 16.)

Declaration of the purity of the king's motive in the preparations and offerings, and of the king's joy at the people's willingness. (Verse 17.)

Supplication that God would ever keep his honor and this purity of motive in the people's thoughts. (Verse 18.)

Supplication for Solomon, that he may honor God, obey him and build the palace for which the provision has been made. (Verse 19.)

Then the old king having performed his last public acts, the high-priest Zadok, who since Adonijah's attempt has occupied the highest place, and who that day had been formally anointed in the tabernacle—comes forth with the horn of sacred oil. Advancing to the young Solomon, he lifts the horn, and as he pours the fragrant ointment on his head, repeats some such solemn words as these : "Jehovah, God of Israel, anointeth thee his king over his people, to keep and to defend his commandments, to build his house and to exalt his name before his chosen and in the eyes of all the heathen world. Jehovah bless thee and keep thee. Jehovah make his face shine upon thee and be gracious unto thee. Jehovah lift up his countenance upon thee and give thee peace."

As sacrifices were connected with the anointed of high-priests, we must suppose that Solomon's personal sacrifices had already been made at the tabernacle, or that he so participated in the sacrifices at that place, that they were considered his. Then followed, we may think, that special psalm composed by David for Solomon,* and most nobly appropriate to such a time as this—a psalm composed by David when in high spiritual meditation on God's promise to his seed, and on the inestimable excellence of that Messiah who was to appear as the Great King of his Line. With this psalm prepared for the anointment, in the hands of the choruses of singers, and all the people in expectation of its lofty use at this point of the day's service, we can imagine, a little, the effect, as the venerable king stretches forth his hands towards his son and his people, and says, "Now bless Jehovah your God," at which under the musicians a mighty psalm of praise and prayer arose.

A PSALM FOR SOLOMON.

Give the king thy judgments (or justice) O God,
And thy righteousness unto the king's son.
He shall judge thy people with righteousness,
And thy poor with judgment (justice.)
The mountains shall bring forth peace to the people
And the little hills ; by righteousness
He shall judge the poor of the people ;
He shall save the children of the needy,
And shall break in pieces the oppressor.

---

* The title may read either "A Psalm *for* Solomon" or "A Psalm *of* Solomon." Nothing could be more apposite to the coronation of a son in the line of descent towards Messiah than this psalm, as David's Psalm *for* Solomon.

They shall fear thee as long as the sun and the moon endureth.
Throughout all generations
He shall come down like rain on the mown grass;
As showers that water the earth.
In his days shall the righteous flourish,
And abundance of peace so long as the moon endureth.
He shall have dominion from sea to sea
And from the river to the ends of the earth.
They that dwell in the wilderness shall bow before him,
And his enemies shall lick the dust.
The king of Tarshish and of the isles shall bring presents;
The kings of Sheba and Seba shall offer gifts.
Yea, all kings shall fall down before him,
All nations shall serve him.
For he shall deliver the needy when he crieth.
The poor also, and him that hath no helper.
He shall spare the poor and the needy,
And shall save the souls of the needy.
He shall redeem their soul from deceit and violence,
And precious shall their blood be in his sight.

And he shall live, and to him shall be given of the gold of Sheba.
Prayer also shall be made for him continually,
And daily shall he be praised.
There shall be a handful of corn in the earth
On top of the mountains.
The fruit shall shake like Lebanon,
And they of the city shall flourish as the grass of the earth.

His name shall endure forever.
His name shall be continued as long as the sun;
And men shall be blessed in him.
All nations shall call him blessed.

Blessed be Jehovah God, the God of Israel,
Who only doeth wondrous things;
And blessed be his glorious name forever;
And let the whole earth be filled with his glory! AMEN AND AMEN!!

The prayers of David the son of Jesse are ended.

As the voices ceased, Solomon received the submission of the tribes. The representative princes and elders of the States of Israel, the sons of David, from Ahithophel to the youngest prince, the captains and mighty men of the army gave the hand* of loyal submission to Solomon.

---

* xxix. 24. "Submitted themselves to Solomon." See Hebrew in margin, "gave the hand under Solomon." This "submission" may have followed after the return to the city of David.

His grace and dignity and wisdom made a wonderful impression upon them, and exalted him in glory and honor far beyond the great inauguration of his father at Hebron thirty-three years before.

Now followed sacrifices of peace and thanksgiving, meat-offerings and drink-offerings, after which the portions of the offerings reserved for feasting and belonging to the priests, the joints and ribs, and shoulders, and breasts, quickly boiled or roasted after the oriental manner, were distributed for the open-air feast and eaten in the presence of the Lord. Thenceforward throughout the day, the flocks and herds were slaughtered in sacrifice and for feasting, and the sacred festivities passed into social and domestic enjoyment.

For the two full days sacrifices were kept up in sanctuary and outer altar, in uncounted numbers, the people bearing their meats from the sacrifices to their houses, tents and booths, the rulers and princes completing the arrangements for their gifts to the temple, and caravan after caravan at length departing to the tribes and distant cities, with chants and songs, and joyful conversation over the mountains and along the valleys of Israel. The dawn of peace had fully risen. The glory of the temple's magnificence was even already shining.

Fifty-ninth Sunday.

THE LAST DAYS.

LESSON.

1 Kings ii. 1-10; 2 Samuel xxiii. 1-7; 1 Chronicles xxix. 28-30.

THE crowning solemnity of David's eventful life—a solemnity in which he had tried to make the glory God's and not man's—was now completed. All the preparations for God's Great House, so long the subject of careful and profound thought, had now been transmitted to a worthy son, approved in a lofty sense by God, accepted, admired, and revered by the people. One thing remained—to remove all serious danger which threatened the security of the new throne. Anxious thoughts filled the father's sagacious mind in respect to opposition which might arise while the reign was yet tender. Joab and Abiathar were guilty of treason. As for Adonijah, he alone was harmless, and might be left to Solomon in his youth. Only when supported by designing and wily men, would he be strong. Abiathar was already removed from his position of power. Joab only was strong—a bold man, confirmed through a long life in a vindictive habit of mind, whose very defeat now would provoke resentment against the new king. He that slew Abner in treachery, he that slew Absalom in defiance of the king's command, he that slew Amasa in malicious jealousy, deserved before to die for his crimes, but he had now added to all these the direct treason of stimulating and supporting Adonijah. If he had done this in revenge upon David for displacing him from the army, he certainly would attempt some traitorous counter-check to Solomon's succession. Had not his impious will driven often headlong over his kind-hearted king, at times when Joab could plausibly justify his deeds by political necessity, long since would he have been brought to justice. It was right that he should die. It was not only right, it was necessary. Holiness and truth demanded it. Such riot over right government, such examples of rash and murderous impatience, by a bold will, set the example of lawlessness everywhere, to bold, unscrupulous men, on the accession of a new king. Both the old and new king before the old king's death should demonstrate the power of their justice as well as the glory of their grace. When, therefore, David saw that his end was near, he summoned Solomon to him and counseled him. He appealed to him by his manly qualities. He appealed to his loyalty to God's law in which he had been carefully instructed, the foundation of his future prosperity. He appealed to him by the perpetuity of his throne to keep and exact Jehovah's law, and bring to its fulfilment Jehovah's promise in respect to the chosen line, and therefore to take heed to his children. In immediate connection with these solemn appeals to his observance of God's holy law, he pointed out Joab and his ill-deserts. He showed his unscrupulous and self-willed character, and painted his descriptions by his crowning crimes of a horrible, bloody, treacherous assassination of the rival captains of the host. As to Absalom's death, that might be overlooked, in view of his zeal for the throne. Barzillai of blessed memory, let him be cared for with all personal attentions. But Joab, now traitor as well as criminal, who has now filled up the measure of his crimes, bring on him the just punishment of his crimes.

Justice requires—the stable and true government of your own people requires his execution. He imposed horribly on my kind nature, and defied the laws of God and man. If he come to his grave full of honor and peace, it will commend his life and his crimes to the people. His grey head, grey though it may be, ought to come down to the grave with blood, for he was the real conspirator against your throne. But be wise in the manner of executing this punishment, for he is a man of power.

As to Shimei of Bahurim, who blasphemed the Lord's anointed in the time of his weakness, his horrible crime deserves death; but as he hastened to undo his wickedness on the day of my return over Jordan, I swore that *I* would lay no hand upon him. But he is verily guilty, and fully understands that he has no security beyond the end of my life. Thou knowest the law, the demands for its honor and purity before men, and his great guilt. Use thy wisdom, and enforce thy sense of right, and see that his grey head receives the stroke which it deserves.

Besides, what is here revealed of Shimei, it may be that he had been a pest and scoffer all the days of David's restoration; and although keeping beyond the reach of authority and relying on the king's oath, had been beyond David's hearing, a well-known reviler of the Lord's Anointed. With a pretended, subservient repentance, he had been a hypocrite and blasphemer all his days. As much as in him lay, he had brought the worship and work of God into contempt.*

* "Shimei remains rather a proof of David's magnanimity than of vengeance. It was not a little thing to tolerate the miscreant in his immediate neighborhood for his whole life long (not even banishment being thought of.) And if under the following reign also he had been allowed to end his days in peace (which had never been promised him) this would have been a kindness which would have furnished an example of unpunished hypocrisy that might easily have been abused."—*Hess, quoted by Keil.*

THE LAST DAYS.

It is unlike the life-long career of David to suppose that he was actuated by malignity or mere resentment. There may have been something of oriental vindictive indignation, but a sense of justice and the imperative security of God's anointed, tided on the indignation to a righteous conclusion. The narrative puts the execution of Joab distinctly on the ground of the murder of Abner and Amasa. At any rate, Solomon, trained under all the kindly amenities and indulgence of David's family, treated his father's wishes with religious scrupulosity.

There seems to be some reference to this charge to Solomon, in the last words of David. During the last failing months, and perhaps even just before his death, the poet and the saint, from his divan, syllables forth once more his rythmic descriptions of the just ruler. And, as if to fix it forever in the memory of his son and his court, and conscious of noble endowments from God himself, he sets the picture in a framework both of his own divinely illustrious title, and of his own claim to inspiration.

THE LAST WORDS OF DAVID.

David, the son of Jesse, said:
And the Man who was raised up on high (as if from a lowly origin)
The Anointed of the God of Jacob,
And the Sweet Psalmist of Israel, said:
 " The spirit of the Lord spake by me,
  And his word was in my tongue.
 The God of Israel said
 The rock of Israel spake to me:
  ' He that ruleth over men must be just,
   Ruling in the fear of God;
   And he shall be as the light, (of the morning when the sun riseth)
   Even a morning without clouds;
   As the tender grass springing out of the earth
   By clear shining after rain.'

    Although my house be not so with God, (as if conscious of his imperfec-
    Yet he hath made with me an everlasting covenant,   [tions,)
    Ordered in all things and sure,
    For this is all my salvation and all my desire,
    Although he make it not to grow.

> But the sons of Belial
> Shall be, all of them, as thorns thrust away,
> Because they cannot be taken with hands.
> But the man that shall touch them
> Must be fenced with iron and the staff of a spear,
> And they shall be utterly burned with fire in the same place."

At no distant day the king fell asleep, his eyes closed by his faithful attendants, his last days nourished and comforted by Bathsheba and his courtiers.

What a mourning must that have been which followed! for no sooner has the feeble life departed, than the memories of the extraordinary character of this truly great monarch rush upon every mind! his mighty prowess and his tender affection! his valiant youth and his sagacious old age! his music and his tears, his firmness and his leniency! his devotions and his penitence, his magnanimity and his justice, his lofty truth and his gentle humility, his great warfare in the kingdom in the name of God, his greater warfare in his tempest-tossed soul! In all the studied publicity of oriental mourning, they bore him to his burial. Shrill cries of women resounded through the palace. Grave men rent their garments and remained silent. The household and friends and court put on sackcloth, covered their faces and fasted.* Servants and attendants and hired mourners cast earth and ashes on their heads. And amid singing men and singing women† who chanted after him one of his own psalms or the great psalm of Moses, they bore out on a bier the precious body swathed in spices to the excavated sepulchre prepared in the city of David. There, on the southern point of the hill of Zion,‡ no doubt amid some of his own household who had preceded him, they placed him; closing upon him the massive sliding doors

---

* See the mourning for Saul and Jonathan and for Abner, 1 Samuel xxxi. 13; 2 Samuel i. 11, 12; 2 Samuel iii. 31–33.

† 2 Chronicles xxxv. 24, 25.   ‡ See map on page 418.

of stone, while the great multitude from all Judah and Jerusalem, and all Israel returned to continue for thirty days* their manifestation of grief and of respect. Every generation from Solomon to Nehemiah and from Nehemiah to St. Peter, could say as St. Peter did at Pentecost, "His sepulchre is with us unto this day."†

In many respects David is the greatest character in the Old Testament history. He combined with consummate ability, a wide sweep of action, the warmest and deepest heart and the loftiest purposes of human life ; and a large use of faculties belonged to every department of his character. His productive mind, energetic body and ready address triumphed the same, in the most unlike emergencies. His powerful will, sagacious judgment and quick decision, rushed to the insolent challenge of enemies, commanded the universal respect of his subjects and held his personal friends in strong admiration. His personal speech and quick wit moulded hostile persons and occasions. His tender sympathy swayed his friends as with a woman's affection and forgave personal injuries with a magnanimity truly divine. His musical genius enriched his nation and his age, while his poetic instincts have seized and swayed the deepest thoughts of all ages and races. His moral courage faced not only foes at home and abroad with fearless heroism, but his own terrible sins, with more heroic, public confessions of his shame. His sense of truth and sympathy with holiness, divinely inwrought by the acknowledged Spirit of God, ruled his ideas of ruling and mightily "restored his soul" to the paths of righteousness.

---

* For Jacob, seventy days (Genesis l. 3); for Aaron and for Moses thirty days (Numbers xx. 29 ; Deuteronomy xxxiv. 8); for Saul, seven days (1 Samuel xxxi. 13).

† See Nehemiah iii. 16, and Acts ii. 29.

Like Noah, he was called to maintain justice against incorrigible wickedness ; but while Noah was called only to witness God's punishment of the world, David was required himself to punish races with his own strong sword. He was not like Abraham called to test his faith by leaving home and kindred, but he was called to rule over a union of patriarchal tribes, to lead them up the growth of an ascending civilization, and to turn from the death of his beloved children to God's more important work. He was not like Moses an original lawgiver, but he addressed himself to the more difficult task of executing the great Lawgiver's code among that passionate, headstrong people when they had grown free and powerful in the promised land itself, and when Egyptian tyrants and the terrible wilderness no longer constrained them to respect their leader. He was not simply a priest and judge like Samuel, but king indeed over priests and judges, himself king and priest pre-eminent through the rounded period of his life. Under him that nation of great moral forces, attained to the culminating level of its grand history. Like Noah, he was "a preacher of righteousness." Like Abraham, he was "a friend of God." Like Moses, he was a promulgator of law and the lofty psalmist. Like Samuel, he was a grand reformer and inspirer. He amplified and combined the grand qualities of them all, each quality moulded and shaded by its blended union with the others. No one of them all was so bruised and broken by the long, fierce, recurring assaults of affliction. No one of them all, for drunkenness or falsehood or ignoble impatience, so humbled himself in a sublime humility and grief for the divine honor's sake. No one of them made the language of feeling bear on its free flow the grandeur and variety of God's holy law—in wealth of song and prayer and praise. None of them swept again and again from youth to old age the thrilling hearts of a whole nation by valiant, high-toned deeds both in material and in spiritual life. Moses, the greatest of all before him, gave the law. David, like his Great Son, gave grace and truth to the law, by making patriotic occasions and personal attractions, and wealth of sensibility and royal affluence and every event great and small, exalt the worship and character of Jehovah, God of Israel. Abraham rejoiced to see the Messiah's day and was glad, but David seized upon God's gift to his own house of his Great Son, and looking down the coming line, bade himself and his successors call the Messiah, LORD. His great faults and great crimes were accompanied with such a great penitence and sublime submission to punishment, that God was not ashamed to select Bathsheba's son as the ancestor of Christ. Even with all his faults, David was a type of Christ. And therefore Christ, when he came in Bethlehem of Judah, was not called the Son of Noah, the Son of Abraham, the Son of Moses, or the Son of Samuel, but THE SON OF DAVID.

INDEX TO THE PSALMS.

PSALMS OF DAVID.

PSALM	PAGE
II.	276, 277
III.	363
IV.	364, 365
V.	247, 248
VI.	336, 337
VII.	362
VIII.	249, 250
IX.	275
X.	
XI.	90, 92
XII.	
XIII.	129, 197
XIV.	393
XV.	245
XVI.	256, 257
XVII.	372
XVIII.	407, 408, 442, 443
XIX.	267, 268
XX.	265
XXI.	274
XXII.	393, 394
XXIII.	89, 90, 308
XXIV.	230, 444
XXV.	141, 197
XXVI.	196
XXVII.	194, 195
XXVIII.	345, 394
XXIX.	311, 312
XXX.	121
XXXI.	147
XXXII.	335, 336
XXXIII.	268
XXXIV.	99, 100
XXXV.	162, 163
XXXVI.	244
XXXVII.	409, 410
XXXVIII.	344
XXXIX.	346, 347
XL.	354, 390-392
XLI.	372

INDEX TO THE PSALMS.

PSALM	PAGE
XLII.	370
XLIII.	371
XLVII.	322, 323
LI.	333, 334
LII.	111
LIII.	393
LIV.	118, 119
LV.	372, 373
LVI.	102
LVII.	123, 124
LVIII.	194
LIX.	92–94
LX.	271, 272
LXI.	395
LXII.	134, 135
LXIII.	363, 364
LXIV.	371
LXV.	246, 247
LXVI.	324
LXVII.	247
LXVIII.	403, 404
LXIX.	345
LXX.	392
LXXI.	408, 409
LXXII.	451, 452
LXXXI.	324, 325
LXXXVI.	197, 198
XCII.	310
XCIII.	326
XCV.	243
XCVI.	231, 449
XCVII.	326
XCVIII.	242, 243
XCIX.	244, 326
C.	325
CI.	222
CIII.	301
CIV.	296
CV.	198, 199, 231
CVI.	232
CVIII.	271, 272
CIX.	395–397
CX.	257, 258
CXX.	318
CXXI.	314, 315
CXXII.	292, 293
CXXIV.	315
CXXVII.	
CXXVIII.	286

PSALM									PAGE
CXXXI.	.	.	.	.	.	.	.	.	258
CXXXII.	.	.	.	.	.	.	.	255, 256,	449, 450
CXXXIII.	.	.	.	.	.	.	.	.	285
CXXXIV.	.	.	.	.	.	.	.	.	313
CXXXVI.	.	.	.	.	.	.	.	.	239, 240
CXXXVIII.	.	.	.	.	.	.	.	.	248
CXXXIX.	.	.	.	.	.	.	.	.	353, 354
CXL.	.	.	.	.	.	.	.	.	
CXLI.	.	.	.	.	.	.	.	.	
CXLII.	.	.	.	.	.	.	.	.	123
CXLIII.	.	.	.	.	.	.	.	.	381
CXLIV.	.	.	.	.	.	.	.	.	213, 214
CXLV.	.	.	.	.	.	.	.	.	309, 444, 445
"The Bow."	.	.	.	.	.	.	.	.	165, 166
Over Abner.	.	.	.	.	.	.	.	,	193
The Last Song.	.	.	.	.	.	.	.		457, 458

PSALMS OF ASAPH.

L.	.	.	.	.	.	.	.	.	277
LXXIII.	.	.	.	.	.	.	.	.	277
LXXV.	.	.	.	.	.	.	.	.	
LXXVI.	.	.	.	.	.	.	.	.	277, 323
LXXXI.	.	.	.	.	.	.	.	.	324, 325

PSALM OF MOSES.

XC.	.	.	.	.	.	.	.	.	312, 313

www.ingramcontent.com/pod-product-compliance
Lightning Source LLC
Chambersburg PA
CBHW051859300426
44117CB00006B/465